From Classical
to Contemporary
Psychoanalysis

Psychological Issues Book Series

Volume 70

PSYCHOLOGICAL ISSUES BOOK SERIES

DAVID WOLITZKY
Series Editor

The basic mission of *Psychological Issues* is to contribute to the further development of psychoanalysis as a science, as a respected scholarly enterprise, as a theory of human behavior, and as a therapeutic method.

Over the past 50 years, the series has focused on fundamental aspects and foundations of psychoanalytic theory and clinical practice as well as on work in related disciplines relevant to psychoanalysis. *Psychological Issues* does not aim to represent or promote a particular point of view. The contributions cover broad and integrative topics of vital interest to all psychoanalysts as well as to colleagues in related disciplines. They cut across particular schools of thought and tackle key issues such as the philosophical underpinnings of psychoanalysis, psychoanalytic theories of motivation, conceptions of therapeutic action, the nature of unconscious mental functioning, psychoanalysis and social issues, and reports of original empirical research relevant to psychoanalysis. The authors often take a critical stance toward theories and offer a careful theoretical analysis and conceptual clarification of the complexities of theories and their clinical implications, drawing upon relevant empirical findings from psychoanalytic research as well as from research in related fields.

The Editorial Board continues to invite contributions from social/behavioral sciences such as anthropology and sociology, from biological sciences such as physiology and the various brain sciences, and from scholarly humanistic disciplines such as philosophy, law, and esthetics.

PSYCHOLOGICAL ISSUES BOOK SERIES

DAVID WOLITZKY
Series Editor

Published by Routledge

71. *Memory, Myth, and Seduction: Unconscious Fantasy and the Interpretive Process*, Jean-Georges Schimek & Deborah L. Browning
70. *From Classical to Contemporary Psychoanalysis: A Critique and Integration*, Morris N. Eagle

Published by Jason Aronson

69. *Primary Process Thinking: Theory, Measurement, and Research*, Robert R. Holt
68. *The Embodied Subject: Minding the Body in Psychoanalysis*, John P. Muller & Jane G. Tillman
67. *Self-Organizing Complexity in Psychological Systems*, Craig Piers, John P. Muller, & Joseph Brent
66. *Help Him Make You Smile: The Development of Intersubjectivity in the Atypical Child*, Rita S. Eagle
65. *Erik Erikson and the American Psyche: Ego, Ethics, and Evolution*, Daniel Burston

Published by International Universities Press

64. *Subliminal Explorations of Perception, Dreams, and Fantasies: The Pioneering Contributions of Charles Fisher*, Howard Shevrin
62/63. *Psychoanalysis and the Philosophy of Science: Collected Papers of Benjamin B. Rubinstein, MD*, Robert R. Holt
61. *Validation in the Clinical Theory of Psychoanalysis: A Study in the Philosophy of Psychoanalysis*, Adolf Grunbaum
60. *Freud's Concept of Passivity*, Russell H. Davis
59. *Between Hermeneutics and Science: An Essay on the Epistemology of Psychoanalysis*, Carlo Strenger
58. *Conscious and Unconscious: Freud's Dynamic Distinction Reconsidered*, Patricia S. Herzog
57. *The Creative Process: A Functional Model Based on Empirical Studies from Early Childhood to Middle Age*, Gudmund J. W. Smith & Ingegerd M. Carlsson
56. *Motivation and Explanation*, Nigel Mackay
55. *Freud and Anthropology*, Edwin R. Wallace IV
54. *Analysis of Transference, Vol. II: Studies of Nine Audio-Recorded Psychoanalytic Sessions*, Merton M. Gill
53. *Analysis of Transference, Vol. I: Theory and Technique*, Merton M. Gill & Irwin Z. Hoffman
52. *Anxiety and Defense Strategies in Childhood and Adolescence*, Gudmund J. W. Smith & Anna Danielsson Smith
51. *Cognitive Styles, Essays and Origins: Field Dependence and Field Independence*, Herman A. Witkin & Donald R. Goodenough

PSYCHOLOGICAL ISSUES BOOK SERIES

DAVID WOLITZKY
Series Editor

PSYCHOLOGICAL ISSUES BOOK SERIES

DAVID WOLITZKY
Series Editor

From Classical to Contemporary Psychoanalysis

A Critique and Integration

MORRIS N. EAGLE

Routledge
Taylor & Francis Group
New York   London

Routledge
Taylor & Francis Group
711 Third Avenue
New York, NY 10017

Routledge
Taylor & Francis Group
2 Park Square, Milton Park
Abingdon, Oxon OX14 4RN

Printed and bound in the United States by Edwards Brothers, Inc, Lillington, NC
10 9 8 7 6 5 4 3 2

International Standard Book Number: 978-0-415-87161-7 (Hardback) 978-0-415-87162-4 (Paperback)

Library of Congress Cataloging-in-Publication Data

Eagle, Morris N.
   From classical to contemprorary psychoanalysis : a critique and integration /
Morris N. Eagle.
      p. cm. -- (Psychological issues)
   Includes bibliographical references and index.
   ISBN 978-0-415-87161-7 (hbk. : alk. paper) -- ISBN 978-0-415-87162-4 (pbk. :
alk. paper) -- ISBN 978-0-203-86855-3 (e-book)
   1. Psychoanalysis. I. Title.

BF173.E156 2011
150.19'5--dc22   2010028742

Visit the Taylor & Francis Web site at
http://www.taylorandfrancis.com

and the Routledge Web site at
http://www.routledgementalhealth.com

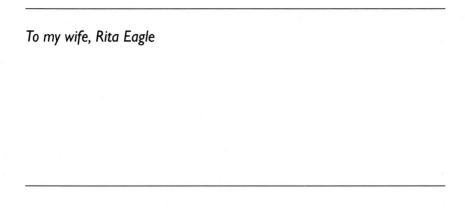

To my wife, Rita Eagle

Contents

Preface

The last 40 or so years have witnessed a period of great ferment in psychoanalysis. New theories have appeared that seem to constitute radical departures from traditional theory. What is the nature of the major developments that have taken place during this time, and how does one understand them? What alternative formulations and perspectives are being proposed in these contemporary theories? Are there grounds for at least a partial integration between traditional and contemporary theories, as well as among different contemporary theories? These are some of the questions that will be addressed and clarified in this book.

There is little doubt that reactions to various aspects of Freudian theory constitute the major point of departure for contemporary psychoanalytic theories. Therefore, an adequate contextual understanding of these newer formulations and ideas will be facilitated by a full grasp of the fundamentals of Freudian ideas. Accordingly, I begin this book, in Part I, with a lengthy introductory chapter in which I elucidate the basic tenets of Freudian theory as a foundation for understanding contemporary developments. Thereafter, the book is organized around four fundamental topics of psychoanalytic theory and practice:

1. Conceptions of mind
2. Conceptions of object relations
3. Conceptions of psychopathology
4. Conceptions of treatment

Part I of the book, consisting of five chapters, spells out how Freudian theory addresses each of these topics.

In an attempt to understand the trajectory from classical to contemporary views, in Part II of the book, I identify, attempt to clarify, and critically examine how contemporary psychoanalytic theories address each of these fundamental topics. I try to make sense of the trajectory from the classical to the contemporary views. Part II consists of five chapters devoted to the same topics covered in Part I (an otherwise overly long section on conceptions of treatment is divided into two chapters).

Part III of the book consists of a single long chapter devoted to an attempt to delineate some areas of divergence and convergence among different psychoanalytic theories and to point to the possibility of at least partial integration among different psychoanalytic perspectives.

Although I refer to other approaches, my focus is on the object relations theory of Ronald Fairbairn, the relational theory of Stephen A. Mitchell, the self psychology theory of Heinz Kohut, and the intersubjective theory of Robert Stolorow and his colleagues. My friend and colleague Stephen Portugues has pointed out to me that I have omitted what one might refer to as *contemporary* ego psychology (e.g., represented by Paul Gray, 1994, and his followers), the "modern Freudians" (see Ellman, Grand, Silvan, & Ellman, 1998), and the contemporary Kleinians (see Schafer, 1997) and therefore leave the impression that what is "contemporary" in psychoanalysis is entirely constituted by the theories I cover in the book. Although I think Portugues has a valid point, I focus on these theories because in contrast to the other theoretical perspectives that he has identified, they represent the most radical departures from and challenges to classical psychoanalytic theory. I also think it is fair to say that these theories are more representative of the current zeitgeist. Finally, if psychoanalysis is to achieve any degree of unity, it is these theories that constitute the greatest challenge to integration and therefore need to be more fully confronted.

Although there are differences in how these contemporary psychoanalytic theories address the fundamental topics listed above, there are a number of themes that recur: a rejection of drive theory, a relative de-emphasis of insight and self-knowledge, reconceptualization of unconscious processes and defense, de-emphasis of inner conflict, a reconceptualization of transference and countertransference, alteration of the analytic stance, and an emphasis on environmental failure. You will see these themes emerge again and again as I explore how each theory addresses the four fundamental topics listed above.

WHAT THIS BOOK IS AND WHAT IT IS NOT

Let me say a word or two regarding what this book is not about. There are relatively few clinical vignettes included and even fewer accounts of my clinical experiences—for example, my personal reveries during clinical sessions. I know from my experience with graduate students and analytic candidates that these accounts can be very stimulating and evocative, particularly when they also possess a modicum of literary quality and a dose of what one might call aesthetic ambiguity. However, I do not believe that these sorts of accounts—evocative though they may be—will advance our field. I think this is so for a number of reasons. One reason is that for the most part, I do not believe that published accounts of clinical material, based on recollection and notes, necessarily constitute reliable indications of many of the critical phenomena that take place in sessions, including subtle expressions of tone, phrasing, gestures, timing, and so on. Instead, as Spence (1987) has pointed out, readers get smoothed out, "normalized," and highly selected versions of analysts' and patients' productions and interactions. The discrepancy between what is reported in good faith and what actually takes place in psychotherapy sessions has become especially clear to me in recent supervision I have carried out that includes the availability of videotaped sessions. There is a great deal going on in the sessions of which the therapist is not and perhaps cannot be aware.

In any case, this is not a "how to" book. I do not describe how I do therapy, the kinds of interventions I make, the things I say, the reveries and thoughts I have, and so on—beyond using clinical material as illustrative of a general theoretical point. For one thing, as noted above, I doubt that any such description would reliably and fully reveal the things I actually say or how and when I actually say them. In contrast to clinical vignettes, an account of how I understand certain concepts, my critiques of them, and what I think and believe, stands on its own. That is, in contrast to the situation in which I need to be concerned with whether or not my description of what I say to patients accurately reflects what I actually do say, I have no such concern about what I think and believe about certain psychoanalytic concepts and formulations.

This book also does not propose yet another, new psychoanalytic theory or school. Rather, as is the case in my 1984 book, *Recent Developments in Psychoanalysis: A Critical Evaluation*, I aim to describe and critically evaluate the major psychoanalytic developments that have already taken place, in an understandable and clear manner. However, this does not mean that I am neutral or impartial regarding the theoretical developments that I describe and evaluate. My own views and biases will be evident. It will be very clear that I believe that some ideas are unwarranted, wrong-headed, or untenable and that other ideas are more warranted, likely to be correct, and tenable.

I hope that after reading this book, the reader will be better able to make sense of the ferment that has characterized our discipline during the last 25 to 35 years. I also hope that the reader will have a better and deeper understanding of the fundamentals of both classical and contemporary psychoanalytic conceptions of mind, of object relations, of psychopathology, and of treatment. Whether this will make someone a better therapist, at least in a direct sense, I cannot say, although it does seem reasonable to expect that confronting vital issues and clarifying one's thinking about them would sharpen one's clinical acumen. However, it must be remembered that classical psychoanalysis was never simply or only a form of treatment. Rather, it is an elegant and complex theory that attempts to identify the fundamental laws underlying personality functioning, the development of psychopathology, and indeed human nature itself. Therein lies its main claim on posterity. If I have any greater ambition in this book beyond clear description and evaluation, it is the hope that, through critical analysis and sifting of ideas, I can point the way to the possibility of a partial integration of classical and contemporary theory, one that retains or approaches the clinical and conceptual breadth and depth of classical theory in attempting to identify and understand the fundamental laws governing how and why we think, feel, and relate to others and ourselves the way we do.

Acknowledgments

I want to thank my editor, Kristopher Spring, for his support and help throughout the entire process. I also want to thank Cathi Scott who heroically deciphered my handwritten pages. Above all, I want to express my deep appreciation to my wife, Rita Eagle, who carefully read and critiqued every chapter. If the chapters have a coherent organization, it is mainly due to her.

Part I

Freudian theory

Chapter 1

Basic paradigm of Freudian theory

This chapter is intended to highlight what I believe to be the fundamental ideas of Freudian theory and serve as a foundation for the later discussion of the ways in which contemporary developments in psychoanalysis represent a departure from the essential and core ideas of classical theory. Virtually every major theoretical difference from Freudian theory since Alfred Adler and Carl Jung, and including Fairbairn, Kohut, and relational psychoanalysis takes as its major point of departure the modification or rejection of one or another of these fundamental Freudian ideas.

The following ideas I take to be fundamental in the sense that they constitute the foundation for Freudian conceptions of mind, of psychopathology, and of treatment:

1. The constancy principle
2. The pathogenic effects of the isolation of mental contents
3. Repression, inner conflict, and the "dynamic unconscious"
4. Drive theory

THE CONSTANCY PRINCIPLE

I begin with the constancy principle because, as I will try to show, undergirding drive theory as well as other central Freudian concepts and formulations, such as the pleasure principle and the pathogenic consequences of repression, are a set of fundamental assumptions regarding the nature of the "mental apparatus." These assumptions, referred to as the *principle of constancy* or the *constancy principle,* which Freud never relinquished, were first stated as early as 1893 in the following way: "If a person experiences a psychical impression, something in his nervous system which we will for the moment call the sum of excitation is increased. Now in every individual there exists a tendency to diminish this sum of excitation once more in order to preserve his health" (1893b, p. 36).

As late as 1920, 27 years after the constancy problem was first stated, Freud writes: "The facts which have caused us to believe in the dominance of the pleasure principle in mental life also finds expression in the hypothesis that the mental apparatus endeavors to keep the quantity of excitation present in it as low as possible or at least to keep it constant" (p. 62). According to the constancy principle, a primary function of the nervous system or mental apparatus is to rid the organism of excessive stimulation. The failure to do so has pathogenic consequences, including the development of symptomatology.

Quota of affect

The influence of the basic metapsychological assumption of the constancy principle on Freud's thinking is seen in a number of ways. Early in his writings, in effect, articulating an implication of the constancy principle, Freud (Breuer & Freud, 1893–1895, p. 166) proposed that every experience is accompanied by a "quota of affect" (p. 9), which normally is discharged through conscious experience, including labeling it and talking about it. The quota of affect accompanying an experience is also worn away through connecting ideas linking the experience with other mental contents. In other words, every experience has an affective component—or, one can say, triggers excitation—that is normally discharged through ordinary means. However, when an experience is accompanied by a large quota of affect, and particularly when, for whatever reasons, the expression of affect is inhibited, the tasks of discharge and of associative connection to other mental contents becomes more difficult. That is to say, the more affectively intense the experience, the more difficult it is for the normal and required processes of discharge of affect and associative connection of ideas to occur. When neither of these tasks is carried out effectively, as is the case in hysteria, the affect remains in a *strangulated* state, and the memory of the experience is cut off from association connection to other mental contents, that is to the individual's "great complex of associations" (p. 9). The failure to carry out these tasks contributes to hysterical symptoms, the former through the *conversion* of strangulated affect to somatic symptoms through a process that Freud acknowledges he did not understand, and the latter through the pathogenic consequence of the isolation of mental contents from the rest of the personality.

One can understand Freud's formulation as a two-factor theory of hysteria characterized by the interrelated factors of an inability to discharge affect and the failure to connect mental contents to the individual's dominant mass of ideas, with the result that these mental contents remain isolated from the individual's personality. As we will see, differences in how this failure is understood—the reasons for it—mark the dividing line between Pierre Janet and Freud and usher in the birth of psychoanalysis. Before turning to that issue, however, I want to devote some discussion to this question of the consequences of the isolation of mental contents.

PATHOGENIC EFFECT OF ISOLATION
OF MENTAL CONTENTS

The single most continuous and central idea running from the prepsychoan-alytic formulations of Jean-Martin Charcot, Pierre Janet, and Alfred Binet through the psychoanalytic theorizing of Freud to contemporary psychoanal-ysis is that mental contents that are isolated and unintegrated into one's per-sonality or self-organization constitute pathogens that bring about various forms of pathological symptoms. It is clear that when Freud first confronted the phenomena of hysteria, the predominant view of what Ellenberger (1970) refers to as "dynamic psychiatry" was that mental contents isolated from the central personality or the ego functioned as pathogens that produced hysteri-cal symptoms. Charcot refers to "a coherent group of associated ideas, which become lodged in the mind in the manner of a parasite, remaining isolated from all the rest"; he goes on to note that these isolated ideas are "screened from the control of that large collection of personal ideas long accumulated and organized which constitute the conscience properly" so-called, the *ego* (Macmillan, 1991, pp. 64–65). Janet writes rather dramatically:

> One would have to go through all the mental pathology and part of the physical pathology to show the disturbances produced by an idea excluded from personal consciousness.... The idea, like a virus, devel-ops in a corner of the personality inaccessible to the subject, works subconsciously, and brings about all disorders of hysteria and of mental disease. (Ellenberger, 1970, p. 149)

In his early writings on hysteria, Freud's views were not essentially dif-ferent from those of Charcot and Janet. In agreement with them, he consid-ered the associative isolation of ideas as the critical element in hysteria. For example, in one of his earliest papers, "Some Points in a Comparative Study of Organic and Hysterical Paralysis," Freud (1893 [1888–1893]) writes: "Considered psychologically, the [hysterical] paralysis of the arm consists in the fact that the conception of the arm cannot enter into association with the other ideas constituting the ego of which the subject's body forms an important part" (p. 170). Freud is suggesting here that hysterical paralysis of the arm is attributable to the fact that representations of the arm are cut off from associative connection with ideas that also include psychic representations of the rest of the body. Note that at this point, nothing is said about wishes and motives or even about one set of ideas being at odds or in conflict with another set of ideas. Completely in accord with Janet, he accepts the proposition that mere associative isolation, however it is brought about, is an adequate explanation for hysterical paralysis.

In other respects too, Freud shows that he has no real quarrel with Janet. Along with Janet, Freud believes that trauma is the precipitating cause of hysteria. He refers to the memory of the trauma acting like a "foreign body" or "parasite"; appeals to such concepts as "splitting of consciousness," "hypnoid states" (undoubtedly reflecting Breuer's influences), and the "formation of second psychical groups"; and specifically comments that he concurs with Janet's account of hysteria.

However, as we have seen, even at this point, prior to the introduction of the concept of repression, Freud introduces the new concepts of quota of affect—which is applicable to general mental functioning—and strangulated affect, which, according to him, is central to the development of hysterical somatic symptoms.[1] Indeed, it is recognition of the role of strangulated affect and isolation of mental contents that leads Freud to propose that hysterical symptoms can be therapeutically removed through abreacting the affect by an adequate response, including a verbal response, and by bringing the memory of the trauma into associative connection with other ideas. As Freud (Breuer & Freud, 1893–1895) puts it, psychotherapy allows "strangulated affect [of the idea] to find a way out through speech," and also subjects the idea to "associative correction by introducing it into normal consciousness" (p. 17). Note that both are accomplished by bringing the memory and its accompanying affect to conscious experience. The use of hypnosis fits neatly into this formulation. Freud writes that certain memories plus the intense affect that accompanies them emerge only under hypnosis. Thus, we see here that prior to the introduction of the concept of repression and the formulation of his topographic model, Freud is already emphasizing the therapeutic value of bringing isolated neutral contents into conscious experience—a precursor to the later psychoanalytic goal of making the unconscious conscious.

REPRESSION AND THE ISOLATION OF MENTAL CONTENTS

We have seen that Freud adopted the basic idea, then prevalent, that mental contents "excluded from personal consciousness" have pathogenic potential and put his own personal stamp on it with such concepts as quota of affect and strangulated affect. However, the distinctive *psychoanalytic* stamp of this basic idea comes with the introduction of the concept of *repression*, which Freud (1914a, p. 16) understandably referred to as the "cornerstone" of psychoanalysis. In *Studies on Hysteria*, Breuer and Freud (1893–1895)

---

[1] Macmillan (1991) observes that Freud's introduction of the role of affect hysteria represents an original contribution over and above Janet's account of hysteria. He also notes a precursor of Freud's idea in Maudsley's (1876, as cited in Macmillan, 1991, pp. 307–308) observation that strong emotion prevented "the free course of varied associations" and in his general view that "in proportion to the degree of persistent tension must be the retardation of, or hindrance to, the process of association." Further, Macmillan suggests that Freud knew of Maudsley's work because it had been cited by Charcot.

make clear their disagreement with Janet on one point. They state that "Janet, to whom the theory of hysteria owes so very much and with whom we are in agreement in most respects, has expressed a view on this point which we are unable to accept" (p. 230). The idea they are unable to accept is that "the 'splitting of a personality' rests on an innate psychological weakness (*'insuffisance psychologique'*)" (p. 230). They also write:

> It is not the case that the splitting of consciousness occurs because the patients are weak-minded; they appear to be weak-minded because their mental activity is divided and only a part of its capacities at the disposal of the conscious thought. We cannot regard mental weakness as the *typus hystericus*, as the essence of the disposition to hysteria. (p. 231)

Rather than attributing hysteria to psychological weakness, in the *Neuropsychoses of Defense*, Freud (1894) writes that "the splitting of the content of consciousness is the result of an act of will on the part of the patient; that is to say, it is initiated by an effort of will whose motive can be specified" (p. 46). This form of hysteria, which Freud refers to as "defense hysteria," is triggered

> when *an occurrence of incompatibility took place in their ideational life* ... which aroused such a distressing affect that the subject decided to forget about it because he had no confidence in his power to resolve the contradiction between that incompatible idea and his ego by means of thought-activity. (p. 47)

Freud also registers his disagreement with Janet in his case studies. With regard to Frau Emmy von N., he notes that she shows no evidence of "psychical insufficiency." In the case of Miss Lucy R., Freud (Breuer & Freud, 1893–1895) declares: "Now I already know from the analysis of similar cases that before hysteria can be acquired for the first time an essential condition must be fulfilled: An idea must be intentionally *repressed from consciousness* and excluded from associative modification" (p. 116). Later, in discussing the same case, he boldly claims, "It turns out to be a *sine qua non* for the acquisition of hysteria that an incompatibility should develop between the ego and some idea presented to it" (p. 122). He goes on to refer to the "advantage" of conversion symptoms consisting in the fact that "the incompatible idea is repressed from the ego's consciousness" (p. 122). In the case of Elisabeth von R., after referring to her conflict between her guilt at leaving her sick father for an evening in order to meet a young man and the "blissful feelings she had allowed herself to enjoy" that evening, Freud writes, "The outcome of the conflict was that the erotic idea was repressed ..." (p. 146).

In the theoretical section of *Studies on Hysteria* (Breuer & Freud, 1893–1895) entitled "Psychotherapy of Hysteria," Freud states, "I have shown how, in the course of our therapeutic work, we have been led to the view that hysteria originates through the repression of an incompatible idea from a motive of defense" (p. 285). Although he seems to refer to all cases of hysteria in the above assertion, Freud goes on to note "Breuer and I have repeatedly spoken of two other kinds of hysteria, for which we have introduced the terms 'hypnoid hysteria' and 'retention hysteria'" (p. 285). With regard to hypnoid hysteria, Freud noted Breuer's view that "no psychical force ... has been required in order to keep an idea apart from the ego and no resistance need be aroused if we introduce it into the ego ..." (p. 286). However, despite Freud's apparent acceptance of the category of hypnoid hysteria (he stated, "I willing adhere to this hypothesis on there being a hypnoid hysteria"), he writes, "any [case of hypnoid hysteria] that I took in hand has turned into a defense hysteria" and finally concludes, "I am unable to suppress a suspicion that somewhere or other the roots of hypnoid and defense hysteria come together and that the primary factor is defense." Freud then adds the somewhat disingenuous last sentence of the paragraph: "But I can say nothing about this" (p. 286).

As for retention hysteria, here too Freud writes

> I ... suspect though once again subject to all the reserve which is proper to ignorance, that at the basis of retention hysteria, too, an element of defense is to be found which has forced the whole process in the direction of hysteria. (Breuer & Freud, 1893–1895, p. 286)[2]

His final comment on this topic is a seemingly open-minded hope "that fresh observations will soon decide whether I am running the risk of falling into one-sidedness and error in thus favoring an extension of the concept of defense to the whole of hysteria" (p. 286).

At this point in his writings, Freud thinks of repression as voluntary and conscious. For example, he refers to patients' ability to recall their intention of "pushing things away" (p. 47). Although pushing the thing away succeeds in freeing the ego from a contradiction, "it has burdened itself with a mnemic symbol, 'lodged in consciousness' like a sort of parasite, either in the form of an unresolvable motor innervation or a constantly recurring hallucinatory sensation." The consequence is that "the memory trace of the repressed idea ... forms the nucleus of a second psychical group" (p. 49). Freud's description of the consequences of repression, even the language he uses, is very similar to Janet's language and conception of the pathogenic effects of mental contents isolated from consciousness and the rest of the

---

[2] The term retention hysteria appears to originate with Breuer and refers to the conversion somatic phenomena that presumably occur when one cannot discharge excitation by communicating one's experience to another; retention hysteria played no role in Freud's further theorizing.

personality. Freud's reference to "a sort of parasite" is paralleled by Janet's (1889) description of a virus that is "inaccessible to the subject, works subconsciously, and brings about all disorders of hysteria ..." (Ellenberger, 1970, p. 149), and Freud's reference to a "second psychical group" suggests the kind of dissociative process emphasized by Janet.[3]

Thus, although Freud and Janet agree regarding the pathogenic potential of isolated mental contents, they disagree regarding the means by which isolation comes about. Moreover, with the introduction of the concept of repression, the emphasis shifts with regard to the kind of mental contents that are isolated from "personal consciousness." For Janet and for prerepression Freud, the mental contents that are unintegrated into the personality are memories of *external traumas*. Once repression and the concept of defense hysteria are introduced, the emphasis shifts to "an incompatibility ... between the ego and some idea presented to it" (Breuer & Freud, 1893–1895, p. 122)—and the incompatible idea invariably turns out to be linked to erotic desires and fantasies. For Lucy R., it is her desire for her employer's love; for Elisabeth von R, it is the young man with whom she wants to spend the evening; and so on with the others. In short, the emphasis shifts from an external event to an inner wish, from external trauma to inner conflict.

Why should the isolation of mental contents—in relation to either an external event or an inner wish—from personal consciousness have such pathogenic potential? Janet's answer seems to be that although the failure to integrate mental contents (e.g., a memory of a trauma) bespeaks constitutional weakness or "psychical insufficiency," it contributes to further weakness and pathology. Why, though, should failure to integrate mental contents weaken the personality? Why should "an idea excluded from personal consciousness" function like "a virus" that can bring about "all disorders of hysteria" as well as other forms of mental and physical disease?

REPRESSION, STRANGULATED AFFECT, AND THE CONSTANCY PRINCIPLE

As we have seen, Freud's early answer to this question is that the undischarged quota of affect that accompanies a trauma[4] remains in a strangulated state and, through a process that Freud acknowledged that he did not understand, becomes converted into somatic hysterical symptoms. However,

---

[3] As noted, I think it is fair to say that the assumption that mental contents isolated from the rest of the personality have pathogenic consequences is the single most continuous idea running uninterruptedly from prepsychoanalytic to classical to contemporary psychoanalytic and psychiatric theorizing. This basic idea continues to influence therapeutic approaches, for example, to grief and trauma.

[4] Indeed, implicit in Freud's view is a conception of trauma as an experience in which the quantity of affect that is generated is too great to be discharged.

as Strachey asks, in the editor's introduction to *Studies on Hysteria*, "why should affect need to be 'discharged'? And why are the consequences of its not being discharged so formidable?" (Breuer & Freud, 1893–1895, p. xix). The answer to these questions, Strachey notes, is found in Freud's "principle of constancy." Freud (1893b) writes: "If, however, there is no reaction whatsoever to a psychical trauma, the memory of it retains the affect which it originally had" (pp. 36–37). In other words, when an adequate reaction does not occur, as is the case when the memory of the trauma is repressed, the sum of excitation fails to be diminished and will find expression in a variety of pathological ways (e.g., conversion symptoms).

Later in Freud's writings, when his drive theory had been formulated, it is instinctual wishes and impulses rather than external trauma that constitute the main sources of potentially excessive increases in the sum of excitation and therefore the main threat to the integrity of the nervous system (or the mental apparatus). One can see a direct link between the early 1893 formulation of the principle of constancy and the later central role given to instinctual wishes and impulses. What remains unchanged is the idea that increases in the "sum of excitation"—whatever their source—and the need to reduce excitation in some fashion play a central role in the formation of neurotic symptoms. Thus, insofar as it prevents an adequate discharge and reduction of the sum of excitation, repression possesses pathogenic potential.

Repression prevents associative rectification

A barrier to the adequate discharge of affect and excitation is only one aspect of the pathogenic significance of repression. Still another reason for the pathogenic potential of repression—one that has not received adequate attention in discussions of repression—is that it prevents mental contents from entering "the great complex of associations" (Breuer & Freud, 1893–1895, p. 9) and thereby being worked over and being subjected to the normal "wearing away" process (Freud, 1893b, p. 37). Normally, when an idea does enter "the great complex of associations," it comes alongside other experiences, which may contradict it, and ... subject [it] to rectification by other ideas" (Breuer & Freud, 1893–1895, p. 9). Because repression prevents this wearing-away and rectification process, a repressed idea (e.g., a memory of a trauma) retains its "freshness and affective strength" (p. 11), with the result that the "psychical traumas which have not been disposed of by reaction [Freud is referring here to an adequate reaction or abreaction] cannot be disposed of either by being worked over by means of association" (p. 11).[5] In most accounts of early Freudian theoretical formulations,

---

[5] Although affective abreaction and the associative wearing-away process are related to each other (e.g., the associative wearing-away process also reduces an idea's affective strength)

primary attention is usually paid to his concepts of strangulated affect and abreaction. However, as I have tried to show, Freud gives equal importance to the normal corrective and wearing-away function of a mental content being associatively linked to other mental contents, and to the pathological consequences of the failure of an idea to come into "extensive associative connection" (p. 11) with other ideas—in short, to the pathological consequences of the isolation of a mental content from what one may refer to as personal consciousness.

Although Freud does not make it entirely explicit, he identifies two adaptive components of the associative wearing-away process. One, as noted, is its capacity to reduce the affective strength of an idea—even when, or particularly when, abreaction does not occur. The other adaptive component is what one might call its cognitive rectification function. Freud clearly has in mind this latter function when he talks about the memory of a trauma coming "alongside other experiences, which may contradict it, and [subjecting it to] rectification by the other ideas" (Breuer & Freud, 1893–1895, p. 9). In effect, Freud is referring to what we would normally call putting an experience or mental content into perspective. One might say that whereas abreaction of affect directly addresses the quantitative factor, that is, it reduces the sum of excitation of the quota of affect through direct discharge of affect, the wearing-away and rectification process focuses on the cognitive and meaning aspects of mental contents and modifies the "affective charge" of an experience through cognitive means.

It is surprising that near-exclusive attention has been given to concepts such as strangulated affect and abreaction and so little to the process of associative correction and wearing-away in the usual histories of early psychoanalysis. The fact is that whereas the concept of abreaction was soon discarded (largely because of the failure of abreaction to bring about lasting therapeutic change), the concept of associative correction contained the seeds of, and was assimilated into, later formulations regarding the therapeutic value of insight and making the unconscious conscious; in that sense, it has had a more important and lasting influence on psychoanalysis.

Repression divides and weakens the personality

There are additional ways in which repression contributes to pathology. Insofar as repression entails the splitting of consciousness and the formation of second psychical groups, it weakens the personality to the extent that it

and have similar consequences, Freud clearly views them as somewhat separate processes and repeatedly distinguishes between abreaction and the associative wearing-away process. For example, at one point he writes that "even if [a psychical trauma] has not been abreacted," other methods of "dealing with the situation ... [are] open to a normal person" (Breuer & Freud, 1893–1895, p. 9), and the method that he identifies is the associative wearing-away and rectification process.

leads to the presence in the personality of a set of mental contents, including aims and motives, that are at best irrelevant to one's central conscious aims and at worst contrary to and undermining of these aims. In the latter case, the personality structure is weakened by internal divisions and rifts. Surely this is the sort of thing Freud has in mind when he uses such terms as "separate psychical groups" and a "parasite" that is "lodged in consciousness" to describe mental contents isolated by repression. Although Janet does not, of course, invoke the concept of repression when he compares an idea excluded from personal consciousness "to a virus ... that brings about all disorders of hysteria" (Ellenberger, 1970, p. 149), he also suggests that isolated mental contents weaken the personality.[6]

As noted, one can think of this aspect of repression as the qualitative counterpart to the quantitative idea that the failure of drive gratification due to repression results in the buildup of excitation. That is, the motive and the mental content (i.e., an idea, wish, or desire) associated with the drive impulse continues to be active in the mind *but unintegrated* into the individual's personality. Thus, a set of ideas and intentions isolated from and often inimical to the rest of the personality and unavailable to the individual's conscious awareness remains active in the mind. The result is a structure divided and therefore weakened. Note that this aspect of repression is essentially a description of the pathogenic consequences of unresolved *inner conflict* independently of its presumed consequence of preventing the discharge or reduction of the sum of excitation. That is, even if repression did not (presumably) interfere with the normal discharge of the sum of excitation, the isolation and sequestering of mental contents would nevertheless possess pathogenic potential. This is so not only because pursuing conflictual and contradictory aims weakens the personality[7]—one is a house divided—but also because the use of repression presents the inner conflict from being confronted and resolved.

The linking of repression to inner conflict results in a shift from an emphasis on warded-off memories (i.e., of traumatic experiences) to an emphasis on wishes, desires, intentions, and aims that are currently active. To put it simply, repression weakens the personality not because it blocks access to memories but because, as noted, it means that the same individual is, at one and the same time, pursuing contradictory aims or, at the very least, that

---

[6] One also finds a version of this basic idea in Fairbairn's (1952) comment that although repression of the bad object protects the individual from experiencing the original bad object situation (i.e., from experiencing the original trauma) it results in "splits in the ego," characterized by an "internal saboteur" being lodged in the mind and becoming part of one's personality structure. Here, too, one sees the basic idea of an unintegrated "foreign body" weakening and undermining the personality.

[7] As Freud (1918/1919) puts it, "In actual fact, indeed, the neurotic patient presents us with a torn mind divided by resistances" (p. 161).

one set of potent aims and motives are not adequately represented in the individual's conscious experience and consciously avowed intentions.

The shift from the external to the inner, from trauma to conflict, which is at the core of traditional psychoanalytic thinking, is also, of course, reflected in Freud's (1914a) substitution of an actual seduction etiological theory with the notion of seduction fantasy, which is embedded in conflictual wishes and desires. As we will see, it is consideration of conflicted wishes and desires, the anxiety they elicit, and the defenses against their conscious experience—not external trauma—that is at the core of Freud's development of the theory of psychoanalysis.[8]

Repression increases the strength of fantasy

In his later work, following the development of drive theory, Freud (1915c) gives still another reason for the pathogenic potential of repression that is different in kind from the other stated reasons. He writes that the "repressed instinct-presentation ... develops in a more unchecked and luxuriant fashion. It ramifies, like a fungus, so to speak, in the dark and takes on extreme forms of expression" that are alien to and terrify the individual because of "the way in which they reflect an extraordinary strength of instinct. This illusory strength of instinct is the result of an uninhibited development of it in phantasy and of the damming-up consequent on lack of real satisfaction" (p. 149). This passage is especially interesting because it is one of the few occasions in which Freud suggests that the experienced "strength of instinct" may be partly illusory, the result of a fantasy that is unchecked and not exposed to the light of reality because it has been subject to repression. In most of his other writings, Freud clearly suggests that the strength of instinct, rather than being illusory, is entirely real because of its carrying the danger of excessive excitation. It is this presumed "dangerous" property of instinct that also leads Anna Freud (1966) to posit "the id's primary antagonism to the ego" (p. 157) and to write about the ego being overwhelmed by the strength of instinct in psychosis.

Repression depletes the ego

As Freud notes, repressed wishes continue to press for discharge and for expression in consciousness and in action. Therefore, in order to keep anxiety-laden thoughts and feelings from consciousness, repression must be ongoing. As Freud (1915c) puts it, repression entails a "constant

---

[8] As we will also see, the shift from external trauma to inner conflict is, at least in large part, reversed in much of contemporary psychoanalytic theorizing. That is, in an ironic historical turn, the etiological role of inner conflict is minimized and the role of external trauma is prominent once again in much of contemporary psychoanalytic theorizing.

expenditure of energy" (p. 151). The result is a degree of ego constriction and depletion—depletion because energy that could go to other activities and pursuits is expended to maintain repression, and constriction because a range of contents and feelings associated with the repressed wishes cannot be consciously thought about or experienced without the risk of triggering anxiety.

RETURN OF THE REPRESSED

Up to this point, the reasons for the pathogenic potential of repression that I have identified have to do with the process of repression itself, or at least the consequences of repression itself. However, later in his writings, the role of repression (and other defenses) becomes more complex. Repression comes to be understood as having an adaptive function—necessary for adaptive living in a society—as well as pathogenic significance. When it functions adequately, repression keeps certain wishes and impulses that, if acted upon, could be inimical to the welfare of the individual (as well as to the society in which the individual lives) from gaining access to motility, that is, from finding expression in action. This is one of the adaptive aspects of repression. Repression also bans from consciousness certain ideas and feelings that, if consciously experienced, would trigger much anxiety. This anxiety-avoiding function is another adaptive aspect of repression (as well as all other defenses) that, paradoxically, can be understood as preventing the buildup of excessive excitation. That is, insofar as the quantitative nature of anxiety itself is characterized by excessive excitation, a defense (e.g., repression) that succeeds in preventing or minimizing anxiety (i.e., keeping it at the level of signal anxiety) is, in an important sense, preventing the buildup of excessive excitation. From this latter perspective, it is the *failure* of repression and the consequent return of the repressed that is implicated in the outbreak of neurosis. In short, repression has both adaptive and maladaptive consequences for mental functioning.

RECAPITULATION

Let me stop for a moment and recapitulate the discussion thus far. The constancy principle, undischarged or strangulated affect, isolation of mental contents, and repression, all combined in a logical structure, come into play in accounting for hysteria. As noted, the most fundamental assumptions are that a basic function of mind is to discharge excitation and that the failure to do so, that is, the buildup of excessive excitation, has pathogenic consequences. One form in which these basic assumptions are stated is that every experience is accompanied by a quota of affect and that the failure to discharge this quota of affect has pathological consequences. Freud then links these basic assumptions to Janet's and Charcot's formulations regarding the pathogenic significance of the associative isolation of mental contents from the rest of the personality in the following way: In accord with the constancy principle, because, among other effects, associative isolation prevents the discharge of affect (excitation), it contributes to the development of pathology. One primary means—and this formulation marks the birth of psychoanalysis—through which associative isolation and the failure to discharge affect (excitation) occurs is repression, that is, the purposeful banishment—an act of will—of unacceptable mental contents from consciousness. Hence, repression is a critical factor in the development of hysteria and other forms of pathology. Given the role of associative isolation and failure to discharge affect in the development of pathology, it follows that treatment should address both factors, the former through bringing isolated or repressed thoughts to consciousness (via hypnosis) and the latter through abreaction of undischarged or strangulated affect. This is the model or logical structure that Freud formulates to account for pathology and to guide treatment. Further, it is essentially this model that is adapted to later developments, including the formulation of drive theory and the structural model.

DRIVE THEORY

Let me turn next to drive theory, another set of Freudian fundamental ideas.[9,10] My intention is to locate Freudian drive theory in the framework of summarizing those fundamental Freudian ideas the reaction to which

---

[9] As a number of theorists have pointed out, *drive* and *instinct* need to be distinguished. Freud used both the German terms *Trieb* and *Instinkt*. However, as Schmidt-Hellerau (2005) has noted, although Strachey translated Freud's term *Trieb* as *instinct*, it is more accurately translated as *drive* and is to be distinguished from *instinct*, for which the German word is *Instinkt*. Although Freud referred to *Trieb* repeatedly, he used the term *Instinkt* only six times in all his writings (Schmidt-Hellerau, 2005). For Freud, instinct referred to "an inherited mental formation" (1915c, p. 155) and is best understood in terms of Lorenz's (1981) and Tinbergen's (1951) "fixed action patterns." Drive is best understood as a relatively indeterminate (Laplanche & Pontalis, 2003) pressure "originating in a bodily source and aiming toward an object through which the drive is able to achieve its aim" (Freud, 1915a, p. 122). However, unlike instincts and their fixed action patterns, drives can be expressed in different ways, and their satisfaction can be achieved through many different actions. It is this "relatively indeterminate" nature of drive pressure that partly accounts for the variegated ways in which drives, in particular, the sexual drive, can influence mental life.

[10] In Freud's earlier writings, his dual drive theory comprised sexual drives and self-preservative or ego drives. As Freud (1910a) wrote: "[There are] ... drives which subserve sexuality, the attainment of sexual pleasures, and those other drives, which have as their aim the self-preservation of the individual—the ego drives. As the poet said, all the organic drives that operate in the mind can be classified as 'hunger' or 'love'" (pp. 214–215). He also distinguished between object-libido and ego-libido (1914b). However, following

comprises a good part of contemporary psychoanalytic theory. Note first that the entire structure of Freudian ideas discussed thus far required no reference to drive theory. The key ideas and concepts of the constancy principle, the quota of affect, strangulated affect, repression, and the pathogenic significance of isolation of mental contents were articulated by Freud long before he formulated his drive theory and do not rest on the logic of drive theory. However, the above ideas fit neatly into drive theory once it is formulated. Thus, it is now instinctual wishes and impulses that constitute the main sources of potentially excessive increases in the sum of excitation and therefore the main threat to the integrity of the nervous system (or the mental apparatus).

One can see a direct link between the early 1893 formulation of the principle of constancy and the later central role given to instinctual wishes and impulses in drive theory. What remains unchanged is the basic idea that the failure to reduce the sum of excitation through normal means plays a central role in the formation of pathological symptoms. The constancy principle can be restated in the language of drive theory. That is, if, as Freud's conception indicates, drives constitute the most significant and unrelenting source of internally generated excitation—a demand made upon the mind (Freud, 1915a)—and if the function of mind is to discharge excitation, it then follows that a primary function of mind is to seek drive gratification or discharge. Or, to put it another way, given Freud's assumptions regarding the nature of drives, to say that a primary function of mind is to seek drive discharge is essentially to describe the operation of the constancy principle. In short, Freud's very conception of drives and of their role in mental functioning is shaped by the assumption of the constancy principle. It is also essentially a description of the operation of the pleasure principle. There is a strong family resemblance among the concepts of the constancy principle, drive gratification, and the pleasure principle. The common element to which all these concepts point to is the primary tendency of mind to seek discharge of excitation.[11]

Freud's (1923) metapsychological revisions, and continuing to the present day, we all tend to think of sex and aggression as the basic drives posited by Freudian theory.

[11]It will be noted that Freud essentially equates gratification and pleasure with discharge of excitation. Thus, in the context of the pleasure principle, the term *pleasure*, as used by Freud, although related to the ordinary sense of pleasure, is somewhat of a technical term, defined as equivalent to reduction or discharge of excitation. For Freud, behaving in accord with the pleasure principle means seeking immediate gratification or discharge. This equation of pleasure with discharge of excitation created certain problems for Freud. For one thing, he was aware that in its ordinary usage, the experience of pleasure is related not only to quantity of excitation, but also to qualitative factors (Freud, 1924). Second, Freud was also aware that, in certain circumstances, increases in excitation can be pleasurable. If Freud's understanding of the term was to retain meaningful links to the ordinary concept of pleasure, these problems needed to be addressed. However, although he was aware of these issues, Freud never really successfully reconciled his conception of pleasure (and

Grounding this tendency in our psychobiological nature—the drives— has important implications for the other formulations I have discussed. Thus, the rootedness of our wishes, desires, and impulses in our psychobiological nature gives added force to the claim that despite their banishment from consciousness and the associative isolation of ideas related to them, they remain active in some form and continue to press for discharge. Therefore, to repress them is not to remove them from psychic life, nor is it a one-time affair. Rather, insofar as the repressed remains active, repression requires a "constant expenditure of energy" (Freud, 1915c, p. 151). In short, it is the rootedness of our desires and wishes in our psychobiological nature that lends plausibility to formulations regarding the pathogenic consequences of repression and isolation of mental contents. Were our desires and wishes not a fundamental aspect of our human nature and were they, therefore, not pressing for gratification and discharge, repressing and isolating them would not require a constant expenditure of energy, nor would they divide the personality.

It should be noted that insofar as they constantly press for discharge, desires and wishes function differently from memories of external events, including traumatic events. Although memories of traumatic events can and do intrude into consciousness, the processes through which this occurs is different from the processes involved in the influence of biologically rooted desires and wishes on consciousness. Recall that for Freud the pathogenic potential of repressed traumatic memories lies in the fact that the quota of affect connected with the original experience has not been adequately discharged, with the consequence that the affect remains in a strangulated state. That is, it is not so much that the memory itself remains active but rather that the affect linked to it has not been discharged. Hence there is the presumed therapeutic value of catharsis and abreaction.

In contrast to memories of external traumas, instinctual desires and wishes are internally generated, have an aim, and require an object for gratification and discharge. Imagine that despite being thirsty or hungry, one banished all thoughts of water or food from one's consciousness. Despite such banishment, the desire and need for water or food would not disappear but would continue to make demands on the mind. That is, one would continue to be thirsty or hungry. In contrast, imagine that one has banished from consciousness the memories of a trauma in which one was deprived of water or food for along period of time. In the latter case, on the logic of Freud's early theorizing, once the affect associated with the trauma was discharged, the memory would no longer make demands on the mind.

The contrast between isolated and unintegrated memories of traumatic external events and isolated and unintegrated desires and wishes is also

---

unpleasure) in terms of quantity of excitation with either its qualitative nature or with the fact that increases in excitation could be experienced as pleasurable.

made evident when one considers Janet's (Ellenberger, 1970) therapeutic approach of substituting, through hypnotic suggestion, memory of a benevolent event to replace the sequestered memory of the traumatic event. Whereas it may be relatively easy to implant memory A to replace memory B, it is likely to be more difficult to implant desire A to replace desire B. This is so because if, indeed, our desires reflect our psychobiological nature, desire A will persist despite the attempt to replace it with desire B. Going back to the example of being thirsty, one can say that despite the desire for water being replaced by hypnotic suggestion by, say, the desire for food, the desire (as well as need) for water will persist in some form and remain active in the mind.

It is important to note that even early in his work when Freud wrote about strangulated affect and repressed memories of external trauma, his emphasis in his case histories was on conflictual desires, wishes, and fantasies. For example, in the case of Lucy R., it is her repressed fantasy of marrying her employer that plays a central role in her symptomatology. As another example, in the case of Elisabeth von R., it is the conflict between her desire to be with a young man and her duty to be with her ailing father—"a situation of incompatibility" (Breuer & Freud, 1893–1895, p. 146)—that plays a central role in her symptomatology.

UNCONSCIOUS MENTAL PROCESSES

To claim that desires remain active despite repression and associative isolation is nothing less than to posit the existence of dynamic unconscious mental processes. To say that desires remain active despite repression, that is, despite not being directly consciously experienced, means that a set of mental contents associatively or symbolically linked to these desires are likely to be activated by the persistence of these desires and are likely to be expressed in some fashion in our experience and behavior, including dreams, the compromise formation of associations, slips, and neurotic symptoms.

Let me refer to the example of thirst again, which I use for its simplicity and precisely because it is *not* one that would likely appear in a psychoanalytic context. Imagine, again, that one repressed one's desire for water with the result that feelings and thoughts about water are not directly represented in consciousness. Given the role that the need for water plays in our functioning, one would expect that despite the desire for water being repressed, mental contents linked to water will appear in one's psychic life in one form or another. The result will be that indirect and disguised expressions of water and the desire for water—compromise formations— will likely appear in one's associations, dreams, slips, and, in certain circumstances, neurotic symptoms. Now substitute sexual and aggressive wishes and desires for the desire for water and one will get a clear picture of the role of drives in Freud's theory of psychic functioning. One will also get a clear picture of the nature of the dynamic unconscious as "a seething cauldron of excitations" (Freud, 1932/1933, p. 73) pressing for discharge, being prevented from discharge by counter-forces, and finally partially discharged through indirect and disguised compromise formations.

It is generally accepted that one of Freud's major contributions to our understanding of mind lay in his claim that the major part of mental life goes on outside awareness. Although perhaps widely accepted today, Freud's argument that mental states can be unconscious, indeed, that they are most often unconscious, challenged the dominant Cartesian view equating the mental and the conscious. From that point of view, to posit unconscious mental stated constituted an oxymoron (see Eagle, 1982; Wakefield, 1992). However, the existence and ubiquitousness of unconscious mental states are widely accepted in contemporary cognitive science, and in that sense, Freud's claims regarding at least the descriptive unconscious have been assimilated by contemporary cognitive psychology and are no longer distinctively psychoanalytic—although, if Wakefield is correct, Freud's importance as a pivotal figure in contemporary philosophy of mind has not been adequately recognized.

What is and remains distinctively psychoanalytic—at least in the context of traditional psychoanalytic theory—is Freud's formulation of the so-called dynamic unconscious, that is, an unconscious of desires and wishes pressing for representation in consciousness and for discharge and prevented from achieving conscious representation and discharge by counter-forces (e.g., repression). Although, as Wakefield (1992) points out, there could be no meaningful talk of a dynamic unconscious without establishing a good case for the possibility of unconscious mental states—that is, for a descriptive unconscious—it is the former that is distinctively psychoanalytic, that is most directly linked to Freud's other fundamental ideas, and that is most disputed (often implicitly) in contemporary psychoanalytic theorizing. In contrast to the descriptive unconscious, the dynamic unconscious rests on a set of assumptions concerning unconscious drive-related wishes and desires opposed by other forces in the personality. In short, the positing of a dynamic unconscious is, in effect, a description of the nature of inner conflict. We will see in later chapters the extent to which the dynamic unconscious and inner conflict remain as central ideas in contemporary psychoanalytic theories.

Chapter 2

Conceptions of mind in Freudian theory

This chapter deals with the conception of the nature and origin of mind in Freudian theory. As in other chapters, I will focus on what I believe to be the basic tenets—as a point of comparison with contemporary psychoanalytic theories. In a sense, this chapter is a continuation of the discussion in Chapter 1 of the basic paradigm of Freudian theory.

MIND AS AN "APPARATUS" TO DISCHARGE EXCITATION

Most fundamentally, for Freud, the mind is an apparatus for the discharge of excitation. As we have seen in Chapter 1, in accord with the constancy principle, the primary function of mind or the mental apparatus is to discharge excitation or at least to keep "the quantity of excitation present ... as low as possible or at least to keep it constant" (Freud, 1920, p. 9). This fundamental idea predated drive theory by many years. When, so to speak, joined to the later drive theory, to say that the primary function of mind is to discharge excitation becomes equivalent to saying that the primary function of mind is drive gratification or drive discharge, insofar as drives constitute the major source of internally generated excitation. As Freud (1920) puts it, "the most abundant sources of ... internal excitation are what are described as the organism's instincts" (p. 34).

The conception of the mind as an apparatus for the discharge of excitation is also equivalent to saying that the mind operates according to the pleasure principle, insofar as unpleasure and pleasure in Freudian theory are defined, respectively, in terms of the buildup and discharge of excitation. Thus, putting together the constancy principle, the pleasure principle, and drive theory, one concludes that a basic tendency of mind is to seek pleasure and avoid unpleasure—that is, to discharge excitation and avoid the buildup of excessive excitation—through the gratification of basic drives.

One can think of the Freudian theory of mind as a quasi-Darwinian theory in which the functions of mind have been selected out in the course of evolution because of their adaptive value in meeting the basic needs of the individual and of the species. The quasi-Darwinian nature of the Freudian theory of mind is more evident in Freud's earlier dual ego instincts and object instincts, in which the hunger drive is the prototypic instantiation of serving the survival of the individual, and the sexual drive is the prototypic instantiation of serving the survival of the species as well through the propagation of the individual's genes.[1]

In this view, primary biological drives (e.g., hunger, sex) generate tensions that energize and propel behavior. When drive tensions are reduced, activity is reduced, and the organism is returned to a quiescent state. One implication of what came to be known as drive-reduction or tension-reduction theory is that were there no primary drives to propel the organism into activity, the organism would remain inert and inactive. Along with Freudian theory, a tension- or drive-reduction theory also characterized the dominant theory of mind in the behaviorist psychology of the United States during the 1930s to the 1950s. It is no mere happenstance that Clark L. Hull, an experimental psychologist and a dyed-in-the-wool behaviorist, was aware of and very much interested in Freudian theory. Indeed, one of Hull's (1939) earliest papers dealt with Freudian theory.

The link between American drive-reduction learning theory and Freud extends beyond Hull. *Personality and Psychotherapy*, a book by two neo-Hullians, Dollard and Miller (1950), is essentially an attempt to translate core concepts of Freudian theory into neo-Hullian stimulus-response, drive-reduction theory. It is difficult to imagine, from today's perspective, a period in the history of psychology in which there was a love affair between American behaviorism and Freudian theory, but indeed there was. A key factor that made this possible was the common assumption they shared regarding the central role of drive or tension reduction in behavior. Both American behaviorism and Freudian theory adopted a quasi-Darwinian perspective governed by the central idea that the organism's attempt to reduce internal tension generated by innate primary drives not only ensures survival but also energizes and shapes behavior. In the Freudian context, this perspective is reflected in the assumption that the basic function of the mental apparatus is to discharge excitation.

Furthermore, both also assume that a wide range of behaviors that are not themselves directly linked to primary drive or tension reduction can be accounted for and understood in terms of their *indirect* links to primary

---

[1] Parenthetically, with regard to the latter, Freud's conception of the role of the sexual drive in enabling the individual to achieve the closest possible thing to immortality is a clear anticipation of the contemporary selfish gene theory (Dawkins, 1976/2006) to the effect that, from an evolutionary point of view, we are primarily vehicles for the propagation of our genes.

drive reduction. As we will see in Chapter 2, a classic example of this assumption is the account of the infant's attachment to its caregiver in terms of the latter's role in hunger reduction. In the psychoanalytic context, more subtle expressions of the linking of a wide range of behaviors to drive reduction are seen in such concepts as displacement and sublimation. In the case of sublimation, although one is not directly pursuing drive gratifications, gratification is nevertheless indirectly achieved through the links between sublimatory behavior and sublimated drive aims. As Freud (1901/1905) puts it, sexual aims are "diverted to higher asexual aims" (p. 50).

In short, in both Hullian and Freudian drive-reduction theory, virtually all behavior can be understood as in either the direct or indirect service of drive reduction. Given the complexities that characterize Freudian theory (and, to a certain extent, Hullian theory), the principle is a remarkably simple one (just as the principle of constancy is). The complexities (and subtleties), however, lie in the various ways and the wide range of behaviors that can presumably indirectly serve gratification aims. Compared with Hullian theory, psychoanalysis is much richer in the complexities it identifies and the processes underlying these complexities. For example, indirect gratification can be disguised and can reflect the operation of defense and compromise formation. Through positing these processes, behaviors that on the surface appear entirely remote from drive gratification (e.g., sublimated behaviors) are, nevertheless, understood as providing indirect drive gratification.

The point to be made here is that if one assumes that all behavior is in the service of direct or indirect drive gratification—an assumption shared by Hullian and Freudian theory—one looks for and finds ways of linking behaviors that appear unrelated to direct drive gratification with indirect drive gratification. Hull finds these links primarily through invoking the concepts of conditioning and secondary reinforcement and secondary drive, and Freud does so through appeal to a variety of complex concepts and processes, including displacement, compromise formation, defense, censorship, symbolic themes, association of ideas, disguise, manifest and latent meanings, and so on. However, both share the central quasi-Darwinian vision that virtually all behavior is energized and directly or indirectly shaped by the organism's selected-out imperative to seek reduction of tensions generated by primary drives.

THE ORIGINS OF THINKING

According to Freudian theory, the basic tendency of mind to gratify drives and thereby discharge excitation (i.e., to seek pleasure) initially exists independently of reality considerations. One way to put this is to say that *wishes* dominate thinking, when the wish is defined in terms of reinstituting

previously experienced conditions of pleasure (Freud, 1900).[2] Wishes operate according to primary process thinking, which is characterized by, among
other things, immediate gratification without regard for consequences, for
real objects and for means-ends relationships that are necessary for gratification in reality. Primary process thinking is also characterized by the
formal properties of condensation, symbolization, and displacement, all of
which, according to Freudian theory, one can see operating in dreams.

An early and primitive expression of an attempt to gratify a wish directly
and immediately without recourse to reality, according to Freud (1900), is
the infant's attempt to reinstitute an earlier condition of pleasure through a
process "in which wishing ended in hallucinating" (p. 566). However, obviously, "hallucination of the breast" does not succeed in removing hunger
tensions (i.e., excitations), and the infant is forced to turn to real objects in
the world. According to Freud, this marks the beginning of the emergence
of the reality principle in the development of cognition and its modification
of the pleasure principle. Furthermore, although reality-oriented thinking
does eventually develop, it is, Freud writes, "only a roundabout or detour
method of achieving drive satisfaction" (1900, pp. 605–606). The clear
implication here is that if wishing could make it so, that is, if hallucination
of the breast could somehow automatically and directly reduce hunger tensions and produce satisfaction, "roundabout" or "detour" reality-oriented
thinking would never develop.

Although in the course of normal development, the reality principle gradually replaces the pleasure principle, wishful thinking continues to operate
in psychic life and continues to influence cognition in various ways. The
influences of wishful thinking on the formation of dreams and of fantasies
serve as good examples of the operation of primary process thinking.

DRIVE ORGANIZATION OF COGNITION

In Freudian theory, the influence of drives on cognition can range from
blatant intrusions into thinking and distortions of reality, as seen in psychosis (or, say, in a severely water-deprived person hallucinating water) to

---

[2] See Holt (1915) for an interesting discussion of the Freudian concept of the wish. Holt
viewed the wish as the basic unit of psychology, replacing the older structural unit of sensation, as a *content* of consciousness. For Holt, psychology was the study of an active organism in interaction with its environment. Holt, a psychologist and philosopher who, among
his other activities, carried our empirical work on vision, believed that "Freudianism" quite
naturally belonged to functionalist and behaviorist camps of philosophy. He wrote:

   The Freudian psychology is based on the doctrine of the "wish," just as physical science
   is based, today, on the concept of function. Both of these are what may be called dynamic
   conceptions rather than static; they envisage natural phenomena not as things but as
   processes, and largely to this fact is due their preeminent explanatory value. (p. 3)

more subtle influences, such as increasing the perceptual salience and value of drive-related stimuli or determining the dimension along which objects are categorized. With regard to the former, comparing one's food shopping behavior when hungry versus when satiated should be sufficient to convince one of the influence of drive on perceptual salience. Similarly for relative differences in perceptual salience of certain stimuli as a function of degree of sexual arousal.[3]

The vicissitudes of drive also result in multiple organizations of affect, cognition, and attitudes. Thus, picture one's psychic state, including the organization of affect and cognition, during and after states of intense hunger or sexual arousal. During the state of arousal, the world, particularly drive objects, is experienced in a very different way than it is experienced after satisfaction of hunger or sexual gratification. The actions and plans one would make, the attitudes one has, the affects that one experiences, the hierarchy of salience of stimuli, the thoughts and memories that one would have—all of these vary as a function of drive arousal versus drive gratification. In a certain sense, personality organization during drive arousal and personality organization following drive gratification differ from each other in significant ways. To be noted here is that the influence of drives upon cognition need not take the form of distorting reality or violating the reality principle. Thus, the increased perceptual salience and value of food when hungry reflects an adaptive and selective rather than a distorting influence of drives on cognition. The situation is similar for the influence of, say, sexual arousal on the perceptual salience and interest value of certain stimuli.[4]

The influence of drive organization on cognition is also reflected in how external stimuli are categorized. In a blatant expression of drive organization, one could categorize, say, a baseball bat and a golf club as ways to hurt or kill someone rather than as objects used in athletic games. However, it would involve no obvious or blatant perceptual distortion of reality or the reality principle so long as the bat is accurately perceived as a baseball bat and the golf club as a golf club. The intrusion of drive in cognition is seen here in the functional organization of objects rather than in the formation of the percept.

The influence of drive or cognition organization can be subtle and complex. Say, for example, that the individual has no difficulty in categorizing

---

[3] It should be noted that it also works the other way around. That is, the perception of external stimuli can also influence level of drive arousal. For example, looking at or smelling food can stimulate feelings of hunger and looking at sexual stimuli can increase sexual arousal. In short, there is a circular causal relation in which drive state can influence perceptual salience and in which perceptual experience can influence drive state.

[4] It is obvious that advertisers rely on and exploit this property of mental functioning. Also, the overwhelming frequency of sexual and aggressive themes in movie previews attests to their role in enhancing perceptual interest and salience.

the baseball bat and golf club as objects in athletic games. It may be the case, however, that paralleling this normative categorization are forms of unconscious organization in which the unifying principle is "sexual phallic objects" or "tools of aggression." The evidence for these parallel forms of organization might emerge only in special circumstances, such as dreams, free association, otherwise weakened ego control, or heightened drive.

I recall George Klein's intriguing theoretical suggestion that the cognitive response to every stimulus entails the processing or encoding not only of a predominant denotative meaning but also of a hierarchy of connotative meanings (see Bucci, 1997, for a formulation of a dual coding theory). Applying that idea in the present context, one could say that along with the usual predominant denotative meaning of the baseball bat as an object to hit the ball in a baseball game is a complex of connotative meanings hierarchically ordered. That is, these different connotative meanings will have different thresholds of activation, depending upon a number of factors, including context. Furthermore, because some of these connotative meanings will be drive related and drive organized, their threshold for activation will particularly vary with the drive state of the individual. An example of this is the demonstration that compared with a control condition, in a sexually arousing situation, slips of the tongue were more likely to be sexual in content (Motley, 1980). Also supporting Klein's "connotative hierarchy" hypothesis is the finding that even when one makes an error in recognizing a stimulus word that has been previously presented, the error is not likely to be random. Rather, one is likely to "recognize" a word that is related to the stimulus word in some way (e.g., a synonym or an associate). This suggests that when a stimulus word is presented, a network of words linked to the stimulus word (probably hierarchically organized) is also activated.

What Klein refers to as a connotative hierarchy seems quite similar to the concept of associative network in the linguistic context. When perceiving and encoding a word, what is activated is not only a specific denotative meaning of the word but an associative network in which that word is embedded. Given the richness of language and the complexity of linguistic associative networks, language is an especially fertile ground for the drive organization of cognition.

The concept of drive organization of cognition can be understood as a subcategory of the general phenomenon of state-dependent cognition. That is, there is much evidence that different aspects of cognition are influenced by the state in which the cognition takes place. For example, if, through hypnosis, a negative mood is induced in the individual, memories marked by negative affect are more likely to be accessible to consciousness (Bower, 1981). This finding parallels the common observation that depressed individuals have ready access to negative memories, a phenomenon suggesting the organization of memory along the dimension of the individual's dominant affect. When one is in a depressed state, it is more difficult to gain access to happy memories and thoughts (that is part of what it means to be depressed); conversely, when one is in a happy state, it is more difficult to gain access to depressing memories and thoughts. This suggests not only that memories are organized along affective dimensions but also that affect or mood influences the threshold of activation of different memories. In this regard, the influence of affect or mood on memories parallels the earlier noted influence of drive state on perceptual salience.

As another example of state-dependent cognition, there is a good deal of evidence that what is learned in a particular psychological state is more retrievable when one is in that same state as compared with being in a different psychological state. For example, if a rat has learned to run a maze in a particular drug-induced state, it will show superior performance when returned to that same drug-induced state. The fact of state-dependent cognition (that is, the influence of affect, mood, drive state, and other dimensions of one's psychological state on various aspects of perception and cognition) suggests an ordinary mechanism for subtle forms of dissociation, what one might think of as the dissociations of everyday life. That is, as a function of normal variations of attitudes, affects, moods, drive states, level of energy, and so on, one's behavior varies and one's inner and outer world is experienced in subtly different ways. Under normal circumstances, these variations do not threaten the integrity or unity of mind and personality. However, when, because of either trauma or other factors, "pockets" of affects, moods, drive states, and so on are too discrepant to be integrated into one's normal level of adaptation, the result is pathological dissociation. This is discussed further in Chapter 4.

An interesting question that has occupied some psychoanalytic theorists is the relationship between drive organization of cognition and creativity. The concept "regression in the service of the ego" (Kris, 1952) captures the hypothesis that creativity entails the individual's flexible ability to relinquish reality-oriented, secondary-process thinking in favor of more primitive, primary process modes of organization. Insofar as primary process organization reflects the influence of drive upon cognition, one can understand the hypothesis that drive organization and creativity might be related. However, the issue is a complex one, for if one's cognition were rigidly characterized by drive organization, it would hardly be likely to be creative. Thus, to return to the earlier example, to perceive a golf club only as an object to hurt or maim someone is more likely an indication of psychopathology and hardly an example of creative thinking. On the other hand, to be able to imagine different uses for an object, such as a golf club, beyond its ordinary use or sole use *is* seen as an expression of creativity (e.g., Christensen, Guilford, Merrifield, & Wilson, 1960; Sternberg & Lubart, 1996). A key factor, then, in distinguishing between pathology and creativity is flexibility versus rigidity of thinking. Flexibility in being able to "regress in the service of the ego" has been referred to as "adaptive regression." In a series of studies, it was found that individuals who were assessed as showing a high level of adaptive regression showed both greater intactness of cognition under conditions of sensory deprivation and higher scores on tests of creativity (Goldberger & Holt, 1961). (See Knafo, 2002, for a further discussion of the concept of repression in the service of the ego.)

PRIMARY PROCESS COGNITION

Another expression of the continued importance of the topographical model in Freudian theory is reflected in the concepts of primary process and secondary process thinking, which are viewed by some (and perhaps by Freud himself) as among Freud's most creative contributions to an understanding of the nature of mind. According to Freudian theory, unconscious mentation is governed by primary process modes of thinking. As emphasized by Lacan (2002), one can say that unconscious mentation has its own language. That language, most clearly seen in dream work, is characterized by wishful thinking and the formal properties of condensation, displacement, and, less centrally, symbolization. Freud (1938/1940) defines condensation "as an inclination to form fresh unities out of elements which in our waking thought we should certainly have kept separate" (p. 167). Displacement refers to a transfer of affect, interest, and emotional investment from one mental content to another. Finally, symbolization refers to the representation of something (e.g., a wish) by something else. In the psychoanalytic context, a symbol can simultaneously express and conceal unconscious thoughts and wishes.

In contrast to primary process, secondary process thinking is characterized by delay, consideration of consequences, generally logical structure, and taking due account of reality, as reflected in planning and awareness of means-ends relationships. Reality-oriented thinking can also be understood as a kind of "experimental action" that permits imaginative anticipation of the consequences of an action with the expenditure of small quantities of energy and without incurring the cost of the possibly harmful consequences of the action (Freud, 1900). As Schimek and Goldberger (1995) note:

> Primary process operates not on rational or realistic principles but on the basis of quite insignificant similarities between elements and what Freud (1900) calls "external and superficial" links, which are often based on "assonance, verbal ambiguity, temporal coincidence association of the kind that we allow in jokes or in play upon words" (p. 530). (pp. 210–211)

Although primary process makes use of words (e.g., puns, verbal ambiguity), from a developmental point of view, its natural currency is concrete pictures and images. Thus, a central aspect of the development of an increasing capacity for secondary process thinking is the development of language and speech. The shift from the "thing-presentation" to the capacity for "word-presentation" (Freud, 1915b, p. 203)—that is, the availability of words—makes it possible for thinking to encompass and manipulate relationships among elements of experience and to allow reflection on one's experiences. As Schimek and Goldberger (1995) point out, from this perspective, "making the unconscious conscious is more than retrieval from specific memories from repression [and, I would add, specific thoughts and desires]—but involves 'a higher stage of psychical organization' (Freud, 1915b, p. 192)" (see Bucci, 1997, and Loewald, 1960, for a further discussion of this idea). If unconscious mentation has its own language, it follows that in order to render the product of primary process thinking intelligible, one must engage in the work of *translation* from one language to another, from the language of primary process to the language of consensually shared secondary process thinking. In short, one must *interpret*. It seems to me that perhaps Freud viewed *Interpretation of Dreams* as his greatest work, at least partly because it constitutes his most extended exposition of the value of interpretation, the mainstay of analytic work, in understanding mental life.[5]

The idea that unconscious mentation has its own language places interpretation (translation) at the center of psychoanalysis in a number of different contexts. In the clinical context, interpretation (based on knowledge of the "rules" of primary process thinking), permits translation from the latent content to the manifest content (i.e., the unconscious wish) of the dream, a model for the more general process making the unconscious conscious. In a broader cultural context, the idea of a special language of the unconscious has provided an enormously fertile ground for literary criticism and interpretations of latent meanings in literary work.

One should also note the considerable body of empirical research and theory that has been generated by or is in some way linked to the concept of primary process (see Holt, 2009, for a summary of decades of research on primary process). For example, a number of early studies have demonstrated that compared with stimuli at the center of attention, when stimulus

---

[5] Freud draws an analogy between interpretation and translation from one language into another. For example, in commenting on the interpretation of dreams, he writes about translating from a language "whose characters and syntactic laws it is our business to discover by comparing the original and the translation" (1900, p. 277). However, it has always seemed to me that there is a fatal flaw in this project. In inferring the latent meaning of a dream, all we have is the manifest content. We cannot compare the interpretation of the manifest content to the original "text" when the only means of getting to that presumed original text is through interpretation of the manifest content of the dream. How does one compare the original and the translation when there is no independent original, only a presumed translation?

inputs are not fully attended to, they are more likely to be processed along primary process dimensions (Bach, 1961; Pine, 1960, 1961).

In one study (Eagle & Ortof, 1967), evidence was found that preventing subjects from devoting full attention to incoming stimulus words resulted in a greater tendency to encode the words along a "clang dimension" (i.e., physical sound) rather than a meaning dimension. In other words, reduction of attention resulted in a more primitive level of encoding or processing (see Craik & Lockhart, 1972, for an influential paper on levels of processing; also, see Jung's (1920) hypothesis that reduction of attention would result in more primitive word associations).

A number of interesting issues are raised by these studies. The findings suggest the possibility that quite apart from questions of defense, censorship, and motivated disguise, the sheer fact of not attending to inner and outer stimuli facilitates a more primary process mode of organization. Thus, it may be that repressed material is associated with primary process organization not only because of a defensive motivation to disguise the repressed material but also because failure to attend or deployment of attention away from a stimulus results in its greater susceptibility to organization along primary process dimensions. The motivational factor may lie as much in the decision to deploy attention away from a given stimulus as in the distortion or transformation of the stimulus.

One is reminded here of Freud's (1915c) comment that the act of repression itself has an impact on the organization of the repressed. He writes: The "repressed instinct-presentation develops in a more unchecked and luxuriant fashion. It ramifies, like a fungus, so to speak, in the dark and takes on extreme forms of expression ..." (p. 149) In other words, what Freud suggests here is that quite apart from issues of willful distortion and disguise, the mere fact that repressed material develops "in the dark"—that is, without being subjected to the "light" of attention-cathexis—is sufficient for it to take on extreme forms of expression and to lend itself to being organized along the primary process discussion of fantasy.

Linking the above discussion to Klein's concept of "connotative hierarchy," noted above (as well as to Bucci's [1997] dual coding theory), one can speculate not only that any given mental content is simultaneously organized, hierarchically, along a number of different dimensions but that various factors, such as heightened drive or deployment of attention, influence the particular dimension in the hierarchy that is dominant in organizing the mental content.

EGO FUNCTIONS

The structure that keeps in check the tendency to seek immediate discharge without regard for reality or consequences is the ego. The infant's first recognition, however inchoate, that hallucination of the breast does not work and that he or she must wait for the actual breast marks the beginning of the inextricably related ego functions of reality testing and delay of gratification. From the *Project* on, Freud (1895) posited a psychic structure that functions to inhibit and modulate the mind's tendency toward immediate gratification *in order to permit actual gratification in the real world.* Thus—and this is often overlooked in an emphasis on the ego's inhibitory and delaying functions—the ultimate function of the ego structure, as is the ultimate function of every aspect of the mental apparatus, is to prevent the buildup of excessive excitation through facilitating drive gratification in a way that accords with reality. Hence, although ego functions include delay of immediate gratification, the ultimate function of the ego is to facilitate drive gratification in a realistic way and with regard to consequences of actions taken to achieve gratification. In short, reality testing is ultimately in the service of drive gratification (see Schimek & Goldberger, 1995, for a further discussion of thinking in Freudian theory).

Ego defenses and anxiety

The ego's primary role in preventing the buildup of excessive excitation is also seen in the operation of ego defenses, which can be partly understood as cognitive functions insofar as they influence the thoughts and ideas that are permitted to enter consciousness. This may seem an odd formulation insofar as the function of defenses, such as repression, is to keep forbidden drive-related mental contents from reaching conscious awareness and from being acted on. Does not the operation of such defenses inhibit drive gratification and thereby contribute to the buildup of excitation rather than to its prevention? Defenses such as repression do, indeed, serve to inhibit gratification of drive-related forbidden wishes. However, insofar as conscious awareness of these wishes and suffering the feared consequences of acting upon them are associated with *anxiety*, and insofar as anxiety itself is a major source of excitation, ego defenses ultimately contribute to the prevention of excessive excitation. One can say that the ego makes the judgment that the quantity of excitation accumulated by the defensive prevention of gratification of forbidden drive wishes is less than the quantity of excitation that would be generated by the anxiety attendant upon the conscious awareness and the attempt to gratify forbidden wishes. In short, given the cost of anxiety, repression is the more prudent course.

It will be recalled that in Freud's first early theory of anxiety (e.g., 1900), repression causes anxiety. That is, because repression prevents drive gratification, it leads to the buildup of excitation, which is converted into and experienced as anxiety. In his later second theory of anxiety (Freud, 1925/1926), repression does not cause anxiety but is instituted by a small dose of "signal anxiety," which serves as a warning that steps must be taken to prevent certain ideas from reaching consciousness lest traumatic anxiety occur. In other words, when functioning properly, the effect of repression (as well as of other ego defenses) is to *prevent* intense anxiety and the buildup of excessive excitation that would be constituted by this degree of anxiety.

Perception and reality

There is a seeming paradox in Freud's view of cognition. On the one hand, as noted, cognition, including perception, is ultimately in the service of drive gratification. That is, the wish is always a motivational force in cognition, and on the other hand, Freud held what can be called a replica theory of perception. That is, he appeared to believe that perception, when functioning adequately, pretty much directly reflects reality. The seeming paradox is the following one: If the wish and its potential distorting influences are ever present in cognition, how can one, at the same time, maintain that perception mirrors reality? I say "seeming paradox" because it is only an apparent one. The paradox is resolved when one recognizes that for Freud, only when cognition reflects reality with reasonable accuracy can it adequately serve to achieve actual drive gratification. That is, although there is always the risk that the wish and the impulse toward immediate gratification may exert a distorting influence on perception, in adaptive functioning, perception generally accurately reflects reality, and only when it does so with reasonable accuracy can optimal drive gratification be achieved.

Freud (1895) writes:

> The removal of the stimulus (tension reduction) is only made possible ... by an intervention which ... calls for an alteration in the external world (supply of nourishment, proximity of the sexual object) which, as a *specific action*, can only be brought about in specific ways. (p. 317)

One cannot remove the stimulus or succeed in reducing tension through "an alteration in the external world" unless one's perception of the external world is reasonably accurate. Freud (1900) also writes that the perceptual system "receives the perceptual stimuli but retains no trace of them and thus has no memory ..." (p. 538). In other words, Freud is suggesting that the perceptual system receives each new perceptual stimulus afresh— "perpetually open" (p. 538), as he puts it—uninfluenced by memory. "Perceptual elements," Freud writes, "would be intolerably obstructed in performing their function if the remnant of an earlier connection were to exercise an influence on a fresh perception" (p. 539).

I believe that Freud's insistence that in normal functioning perception and cognition accurately reflect reality has tended to be overlooked. During the

New Look period in American psychology in the 1950s and 1960s, many studies were carried out that were inspired by the presumably Freudian idea that ordinary perception is influenced by personal needs and motives, including defensive motives. The experiments on "perceptual defense" were typical of the New Look work during that period. They were designed to show, for example, that the recognition threshold for words was influenced by their emotional value. Thus, the reasoning went, a taboo word was associated with a higher or delayed recognition threshold because the subject was defending against awareness of the taboo material.

The general theme underlying much of this work was to try to demonstrate that contrary to the pre-New Look assumptions (which did not reflect the influence of psychodynamic theory), perception is not an autochthonous process that simply mirrors reality but rather is strongly influenced by personal needs and motives. There were many methodological and conceptual problems with this work that need not be discussed here, but the point I want to emphasize is that, in my view, much of the rationale for this work constituted a misinterpretation or at least a radical de-emphasis of Freud's view that in accord with the development of the reality principle, in normal functioning, perception generally accurately reflects reality. In everyday life, it is only in particular defined circumstances, such as slips of the tongue, jokes, and, of course, dreams, that one can clearly see the influences of wishes on perception and cognition. In addition, of course, one can also more clearly see the influence of drive on perception and cognition in cases of failure of intact ego functioning, such as psychosis. It is only in psychosis that, according to Freudian theory, drives directly influence perception at the expense of reality testing. In considering the influence of drives or wishes on perception and cognition, one must distinguish between Freud's claim that the wish sets the mental apparatus in motion and the very different claim that under normal circumstances, the wish directly shapes the content of perception and cognition. Indeed, as I have tried to show, according to Freudian theory, in order for drives and wishes to have any chance of being actually gratified (as opposed to being gratified in fantasy or dreams), perception and cognition must be capable of adequate reality testing. Recall Freud's (1900) early formulation in which the failure of hallucinatory wish fulfillment to meet one's needs prompts the development of reality testing.

One must keep in mind that in many of the New Look experiments, special circumstances had to be contrived in order to counteract the powerful autochthonous tendency toward accuracy of perception. One such contrivance was to impoverish the stimulus in one way or another so that there would be room for the influence of personal motives and needs. Another contrivance was to present stimuli that were sufficiently ambiguous in order to maximize the influence of personal interpretation. For example, stimuli were tachistoscopically exposed for brief durations or, as in the case of the

Rorschach test, the stimuli are sufficiently ambiguous to lend themselves to different interpretations.

In elucidating Freud's view of perception, one needs to distinguish between perception of outer and inner stimuli, that is, of external and internal reality. As far as external reality is concerned, the job of the perceptual system is to reflect it as accurately as possible. Barring gross ego defects, such as one finds in psychosis, or extreme circumstances,[6] perception carries out its job pretty adequately. The distortions and elisions in perception with which psychoanalysis is mainly concerned, particularly in its theory of psychoneurosis, are those having mainly to do with *inner reality*. That is, insofar as certain thoughts and feelings linked to, say, forbidden sexual desires and wishes are removed from consciousness or distorted in some way, the inner reality of these sexual desires and wishes will not be adequately perceived.

Memory and cognition

My main point in the above discussion is that, notwithstanding the New Look work, according to an accurate rendering of Freudian theory, under normal circumstances, perception of external stimuli is likely to be highly veridical and to reflect individual wishes, motives, and needs primarily in subtle ways. This position reflects the common observation that under normal circumstances, when presented with the same external stimuli, different people, whatever their different personal wishes, motives, and needs, will generally perceive the same object. That is, as far as perception of external objects is concerned, we generally live in a consensually validated world. From a broad evolutionary perspective, one that Freud was likely to take, the primary function of perception of external stimuli is not to reflect one's motives, wishes, and needs but rather to represent physical reality with reasonable accuracy. As noted earlier, when that is the case, it will be more likely that one's needs can be met in reality.

As I understand the Freudian conception of mind, one should look beyond perception to the other aspects of cognition to find clearer evidence of the influence of motives, wishes, and needs. For example, although the function of the memory system is to keep a record of events transmitted by the perceptual system, there is a good deal of flexibility and "looseness" in regard to the mnemic records kept (see Freud, 1900). Virtually anticipating the contemporary idea that the memory of a stimulus entails constructing its different features, Freud (1900) writes that memory consists of general "*Mnem.* elements, in which one and the same excitation, transmitted by the *Pcpt.* [perceptual] elements, leaves a variety of different permanent records" (p. 539). For example:

---

[6] One is reminded of the Charlie Chaplin movie in which the character in the movie is so severely deprived of food that his boots are perceived as a gourmet meal.

The first of the *Mnem*. systems will naturally contain the record of association in respect to *simultaneity in time*; which the same perceptual material will be arranged in the later systems in respect to other kinds of coincidence, so that one of these later systems, for instance, will record relations of similarity, and so on with others. (p. 539)

Freud's implicit assumption appears to be that insofar as they are not directly linked to external stimuli, memories are more susceptible to influence by a variety of factors, including motives, wishes, and needs, as well as current perspectives. Indeed, with regard to the latter, Freud (1896, pp. 166–167) writes about the reworkings of early memories in the light of the individual's later development and perspective. The greater susceptibility to influence by inner factors would also be the case with regard to other aspects of cognition, such as, for example, judgments about what one has perceived and perceptual selectivity, including deployment of attention and perceptual salience. Also, more generally, according to Freudian theory, a central factor in the influence of drive factors, such as wishes and motives, on cognition is their *energizing* function. That is, for Freud, drives are what energize and set cognition going.

Relative autonomy of ego functions

I noted earlier in this chapter the parallels between Freudian and Hullian drive-reduction theory. The parallel between theoretical developments in psychoanalysis and American experimental psychology continues with, respectively, the emergence of psychoanalytic ego psychology and of the cognitive program in American cognitive psychology, both reactions against thoroughgoing drive-reduction theories. In both contexts, a theoretical position emerging from the reactions to drive-reduction theory asserted the autonomy of cognitive functions. The essence of this position lay in the rejection of a view in which a wide range of cognitive behaviors and functions were seen as the direct and indirect product of drive reduction. Both the psychoanalytic ego psychologists and the early cognitive theorists maintained instead that these behaviors are the product of motives and processes that are independent of primary drive reduction.

In the context of psychoanalytic ego psychology, this claim is reflected mainly in Hartmann's (1958) concepts of primary autonomy, secondary autonomy, and conflict-free sphere of ego functioning. What Hartmann means by primary autonomy is the relatively simple idea that the development of basic cognitive ego functions, such as thinking, memory, and so on, is not dependent on their association with drive gratification but rather has an inborn autonomous basis.

It will be recognized that the concept of primary autonomy essentially reflects a recognition of the reality of *maturation* with regard to ego functions (Eagle, 1984c). That is, it essentially states that given an "average expectable environment," certain ego functions will develop and unfold (according to a genetic program) independently of their role in drive gratification. Thus, implicit in Hartmann's ego psychology is a rejection of Freud's (1900) claims that thinking (a fundamental ego function) develops only because hallucinatory wish fulfillment does not succeed in reducing tensions generated by the hunger drive. In Hartmann's (1958) ego psychological view, the unfolding of thinking in an average expectable environment is genetically programmed and does not depend on its relationship to drive gratification.

Paralleling these theoretical developments in psychoanalytic ego psychology were similar developments in experimental psychology. A good deal of the work of early cognitive experimental psychology was designed to demonstrate that cognitive behaviors such as learning, problem solving, curiosity, response to novelty, manipulation of objects, and so on are not the product of secondary drive or secondary reinforcement but rather have an autonomous and independent basis. For example, in an early study, predating his famous experiment with wire and terry cloth surrogate mothers, Harlow (1950) and his colleagues (Harlow, Harlow, & Meyer, 1950) demonstrated that merely being given an opportunity to observe a novel stimulus could serve as a reinforcer of a monkey's behavior. The typical experiment of the early cognitivists was designed to demonstrate that satisfying the animal's curiosity, providing it with objects to manipulate, or giving it a puzzle to solve—all situations that have little or nothing to do with primary drive gratification—could serve as reinforcers. These results led them to assert the autonomy and independence from primary drive gratification of a wide range of cognitive motives and behaviors—similar to Hartmann's (1958) assertion of the autonomy of a wide range of ego functions.

One also needs to at least mention here E. C. Tolman (1948), the earliest and perhaps the most important of the early cognitivists. Contra the drive-reduction Hullians, Tolman and his followers repeatedly argued and presented convincing evidence that when a rat runs a maze, it learns or acquires a "cognitive map" of the maze rather than a set of motor responses reinforced by drive (most often, hunger) reduction. Furthermore, the animal's acquisition of a cognitive map of the maze may become apparent, that is, may be revealed in performance, only when it is rewarded (generally with food). To be noted here is the clear implication that the animal's acquisition of a cognitive map is independent of drive reduction. It is, rather, an expression of the animal's intrinsic cognitive abilities and functions. In this sense, it parallels the theoretical stance of the psychoanalytic ego psychologists.

One should also note other similar theoretical formulations that proposed the autonomy of certain (generally cognitive) behaviors—for example, Hunt's (1965) concept of intrinsic motivation, which points to behaviors that are learned and carried out not because they are reinforced or rewarded by drive reduction or, for that matter, by an external reward but rather for their own sake. To put it another way, the pleasures these behaviors provide are not extrinsic (e.g., leading to food) but rather intrinsic to the carrying out of the behavior itself. In the context of psychoanalytic ego psychology, Hendrick (1943) posited an "instinct to master" and White (1959) a competence motive. White also observed that certain activities such as exploration, although having survival value, are often "done for the fun of it," and "part of the fun can be described as a feeling of efficacy—or sense of mastery ..." (pp. 247–248).

At this point, I suspect, some readers will question my mixture of material on animal behavior and research together with psychoanalytic concepts and formulations, as well as the relevance of the former for the latter. What do studies on rats running a maze or monkeys manipulating puzzles have to do with developments in ego psychology? As I have tried to show, conceptual and theoretical developments in psychoanalysis have not occurred in isolation; they parallel similar developments in other contexts. As we have seen, around the same time that Hartmann was proposing the autonomy ego functions from the vicissitudes of drive gratification in humans, experimental psychologists were positing the independence from primary drive reduction of cognitive motives and functions in animals and humans. Thus, in a wide range of areas, skepticism toward drive-reduction theory and insistence on the autonomy of cognitive motives and functions seemed to be part of the zeitgeist.

THE NATURE OF UNCONSCIOUS PROCESSES IN FREUDIAN THEORY

For many, Freud's most revolutionary formulation with regard to the nature of mind is the claim that the major part of mental life goes on outside awareness. In view of the current recognition of and emphasis on unconscious processes in cognitive psychology, this does not seem especially revolutionary today, but given the commonly accepted equation between mental and conscious that dominated both common sense and philosophical thinking since Descartes, the idea of unconscious mental processes was viewed as an oxymoron by many during the time that Freud wrote. One can find articles in philosophical journals in the 1920s and 1930s questioning the meaningfulness of the concept of unconscious mental processes (e.g., Field, Averling, & Laird, 1922). As late as 1968, in a primer by a distinguished philosopher entitled "Philosophy of Mind," there is not a single reference to unconscious processes. Indeed, the author writes that "if we were asked to give a general characterization of the branch of philosophy of mind, we might say that it is the branch particularly concerned with the nature of consciousness ..." (Shaffer, 1968, p. 4). Shaffer perhaps leaves some room for unconscious mental processes when he includes under the domain of the philosophy of mind the "kinds of things ... [that] are capable of consciousness" (p. 4).

There are a number of things that can be meant by the claim that the major part of mental life goes on outside awareness. One can, for example, be referring to seemingly intelligent computational *processes* that are involved in perceptual *products*, that is, experienced percepts. What Helmholtz referred to as an "unconscious inference" in accounting for the perception of size and color constancy is a good example of such a computational process. Because the computational process seems so highly intelligent, we are tempted to think of it as mental. Helmholtz's very term *unconscious inference* strongly suggests a process that is mental but unconscious (see Rock, 1983, for a further discussion of the "intelligence of perception"). There are many perceptual and cognitive processes outside awareness that seem to partake of computational intelligence. However, what they all have in common is their impenetrability. That is, to use Shaffer's (1968) words, they are not the kinds of things that are capable of consciousness; by their very nature, they cannot be recovered in conscious awareness. If, when Freud stated that the major part of mental life goes on outside awareness, he was referring mainly to these impenetrable processes, his claim would not be distinctly psychoanalytic, and it would raise the question of whether these impenetrable processes can legitimately be viewed as mental.[7]

It is clear that Freud's claim refers, not to the impenetrable processes discussed above but to contents and processes that *are* capable of consciousness, that is, to ordinary human ideas, desires, wishes, and fantasies. From a Freudian perspective, unconscious ideas, desires, wishes, and so on are not essentially different from conscious ones, save that they lack the property of consciousness. Indeed, according to Freud, the default nature, so to speak, of mental contents is an unconscious status. In this view, the content that consciousness, which functions like a flashlight, lights up is only a very small sampling of unconscious mental processes and content.

An important distinction that Freud (1915b) makes is that between the descriptive unconscious (that is, the ordinary use of the term *unconscious* as not in awareness) and the dynamic unconscious. His interest in the descriptive unconscious is mainly to make the general case for the meaningfulness of talking about unconscious mental processes and contents. It is the dynamic unconscious that is Freud's main object of interest and that is a distinctively psychoanalytic, as well as controversial, concept. Indeed, whereas many cognitive psychologists have little hesitation in positing

---

[7] This raises a complex question that cannot be discussed here: What are the criteria for the mental For a subtle and extended argument that representationality rather than consciousness constitutes the essence of the mental, see Wakefield (1992).

ubiquitous unconscious mental processes, they have difficulty in accepting the tenability of the dynamic unconscious (e.g., Kihlstrom, 1987).[8]

What is the dynamic unconscious? Put very simply, the dynamic unconscious is conceptualized as a repository of repressed wishes and impulses, as a "cauldron full of seething excitations" (Freud, 1932/1933, p. 73). It is called dynamic because these wishes and impulses are always striving for expression in consciousness and in motor action and are prevented from doing so by counterforces of defense. There is always a dynamic tension between these two sets of forces. From this perspective, mental life, including conscious experience, is always the product of compromises between these forces.

STRUCTURAL MODEL OF THE MIND

Once Freud (1923) recognized that ego defenses are also unconscious, it became clear to him that viewing mental life mainly in terms of the topographical model, that is, the interplay between conscious and unconscious, would no longer suffice.[9] This ultimately led to, in part, supplanting the topographical model with the structural model, that is, the division of the mind with the structures of id, ego, and superego (see Arlow & Brenner, 1964, for a fully elaborated exposition of the structural model). Inner conflicts (and compromise formations) are now understood not in terms of unconscious versus conscious but in terms of conflict among the different structures of id, ego, and superego. Thus, in the conflict between drive (id) and defense (ego), both components of the conflict are unconscious. In the view of the structural model, every mental event can be viewed as a compromise among the demands of the different structures of the mind. In his very influential formulation, Waelder (1936) referred to this idea as the "principle of multiple function."[10]

---

[8] Furthermore, as discussed in Chapter 6, Freud's concept of the dynamic unconscious has essentially disappeared from contemporary psychoanalytic theories and has been replaced by what one may call a cognitive unconscious (see Burston, 1986; Eagle, 1987).

[9] A question that arises—one that will be noted but not discussed here—is what renders ego defenses unconscious. One cannot posit another defensive process without running into a problem of infinite regress. As we will see in Chapter 6, one can account for the unconscious—not the dynamic unconscious—nature of defense without being caught in an infinite regress.

[10] As will be shown in Chapters 4 and 5, the emergence of the structural model and of ego psychology in general as the dominant expression of classic psychoanalytic theory had important implications for conceptions of psychopathology and treatment, as well as treatment goals. For example, with regard to the latter, the goal of psychoanalytic treatment shifted from "making the unconscious conscious" to "where id was, there shall ego be." Implicit in this shift is an increasing emphasis on integration rather than simply bringing repressed material to awareness as the goal of treatment.

Although the topographical model was largely supplanted by the structural model, certain properties of the unconscious continued to assume great importance in the Freudian understanding of how the mind works. Among these properties is the "timelessness of the unconscious," according to which, repressed mental contents continue to be represented in a relatively unmodified way in mental life despite the passage of time. In the context of the dynamic unconscious, the timelessness of the unconscious essentially claims that unconscious infantile wishes that have been repressed do not disappear but rather persist and continue to make demands on psychic life. In other words, from a Freudian perspective, the presence in adult mental life of early experiences and of early mental contents is not simply a matter of ordinary learning—after all, much of what we learn in early in life is represented in adult mental life—but is a matter of their active persistence and active demands. To put it simply, despite being subjected to repression, early unconscious wishes and desires are timeless in the sense that they remain unchanged in their content and undiminished in their intensity. For example, for an individual who has not adequately resolved oedipal conflicts, early incestuous wishes would remain timeless, that is, unchanged and undiminished. And, as we will see in Chapter 4, it is the anxiety, conflicts, and defenses surrounding these early persistent wishes that, according to Freudian theory, provide the breeding ground for the development of psychopathology.

PRIMARY AND SECONDARY PROCESS COGNITION

The assumption of psychic determinism has consistently emerged as a central element in descriptions of the Freudian theory of mind. Indeed, as we will see, the use of free association in psychoanalytic treatment makes little or no sense without the assumption of psychic determinism. There are various ways that one can understand the concept of psychic determinism.

Psychological phenomena are determined

In its most general sense, psychic determinism can be understood as asserting that psychological phenomena are no less causally determined than other phenomena in the world. As Strachey observes in the introduction to *The Psychopathology of Everyday Life* (Freud, 1901), "the truth which [Freud] insists upon ... [is that] it should be possible in theory to discover the psychical determinants of every smallest detail of the processes of the mind" (p. xiv). What Freud insists upon, then, is that just as there are no undetermined "accidental" physical events, so, similarly, are there no undetermined psychological events. Freud (1901) devoted much of *The Psychopathology of Everyday Life* attempting to demonstrate that apparently accidental events, such as slips of the tongue, and arbitrary events, such as thinking of a number, were neither accidental nor arbitrary but strictly determined.

Freud maintained that the assumption that all psychological phenomena were causally determined was necessary if psychoanalysis (as well as psychological theories in general) was to have any legitimate claim to scientific status. Freud (1915–1917/1916–1917) writes: "If anyone makes a breach of this kind [the assumption that events are arbitrary] in the determinism of natural events at a single point, he means that he has thrown overboard the whole *Weltanschauung* of science" (p. 28). He also writes:

> Once before ... I ventured to tell you that you nourish a deeply rooted faith in undetermined psychical events and in free will, but this is quite unscientific and must yield to the demand of a determination whose rule extends over mental life. (p. 106)

Psychological determinism

If psychological phenomena are no less determined than physical phenomena, it should be possible to develop scientific laws and theories for the former as well as the latter. And here we come to a second meaning of what one might call "psychological determinism"—the assumption that it is possible and legitimate to develop scientific theoretical explanations at the molar level of psychological factors and processes without reduction to physiological or neural processes. It can be seen that this meaning of psychological determinism essentially constitutes a defense of the scientific status of all psychological theories, including psychoanalytic theory. One should also keep in mind the historical as well as the conceptual context of this meaning of psychological determinism. After Freud's (1895) dogged but inevitable unsuccessful attempt in the *Project* to develop a self sufficient protoneurological theory of the mind, he turned to the development of a scientific theory of the mind that remained at the psychological level, that is, that used only psychological terms and concepts—and remained at that level in his subsequent writings.

It is one thing to axiomatically assume that psychological phenomena, like all other phenomena, are causally determined. This is partly equivalent to insisting that one can formulate scientific theories about psychological phenomena just as one can about physical phenomena. Such theories, however, could be entirely physiological or neural and make no reference to psychological processes as explanatory factors. It is another thing to assert that one can formulate scientific theories about psychological phenomena through exclusive resource to psychological concepts and terms. It is this assertion that all theories that remain at the explanatory level of psychological terms and concepts—from behaviorism to psychoanalysis—have in common.

Motivational determinism

What is distinctive about psychoanalytic theory is the kind of terms and concepts that play a central role in explanatory accounts of psychological phenomena. When one identifies these terms and concepts, it becomes clear that psychic determinism might more accurately be relabeled *motivational* determinism. There is nothing distinctly psychoanalytic about claiming that psychological phenomena like all phenomena are subject to causal deterministic laws, including psychological laws. That assumption, as Freud (1915–1917/1916–1917) noted, is part of the "*Weltanschauung* of science" (p. 28). What is distinctly psychoanalytic is the claim that all psychological phenomena are determined by *conscious and unconscious motives, intentions, and wishes.* The psychoanalytic version of a deterministic weltanschauung is that all psychological phenomena are motivated— even when there appear to be no evident conscious motives. That Freud's determinism is, in essence, a motivational determinism is made evident by his use of motivated and determined as interchangeable. For example, he writes: "I demonstrated that a whole number of actions which were held to be *unmotivated* are on the contrary strictly *determined* ..." (Freud, 1906, pp. 104–105, emphasis added).

Psychoanalytic accounts as extensions of commonsense folk psychology: Unconscious motives

The determinants that dominate psychoanalytic theorizing are mainly intentions, motives, desires, wishes, fantasies, fears, anxiety and guilt and attempts to avoid them, conflicts and attempts to resolve them, attempts to maintain a particular image of oneself, and so on. One can see that terms such as desires, wishes, fears, and so on are essentially folk psychology commonsense terms. However, insofar as psychoanalytic theorizing is characterized by a primary emphasis on unconscious desires, wishes, fantasies, and so on, it can be understood as an extension of a commonsense folk psychology in which one understands another as well as oneself, by reference to, respectively, the other's or one's own intentions, reasons, wishes, desires, and so on (see Nagel, 1986). Furthermore, insofar as unconscious motives and so on are neither transparent nor easily accessible, one can identify and uncover them only through special means, for example, hypnosis and free association combined with interpretation. Indeed, much of the history of the psychoanalytic interventions and techniques can be seen as constituting various means to uncover and identify unconscious motives.

One can see that the extension of commonsense folk psychology to include, indeed privilege, the determinants of *unconscious* motives, intentions, and the like serves to safeguard the continuity and province of psychological determinism. That is to say, when no apparent conscious motive or intention or reason seems to account for an individual's behavior, the invoking and identification of unconscious motives, intentions, or reasons to account for that behavior preserves the axiomatic assumption that there are no psychological phenomena (beyond a certain level of complexity) that are unmotivated—the psychoanalytic equivalent of the general axiomatic assumption that there are no psychological phenomena that are undetermined.

Clinical theory and metapsychology

Although I think it is generally accurate to characterize what has been referred to as Freud's "clinical theory" (e.g., Klein, 1973) as an extension of commonsense folk psychology, this is not the case with regard to Freudian drive theory and metapsychological formulations. Thus, to explain certain behaviors, for example, in terms of unconscious beliefs and unconscious sexual desires, wishes, and fantasies remains in form at the level of commonsense folk psychology and can be understood to conform to Aristotle's practical syllogism. That is, if one has a particular desire or aim X and a belief that behavior Y will fulfill that desire or aim, then behavior Y is explained as motivated by desire or aim X. However, to explain the very existence of particular desires or aims in terms of an underlying proto-biological theory of dual instincts or to explain behavior as an expression of the tendency of the mental apparatus to discharge excitation or to account for behavior in terms of distribution of libido—all examples of Freudian metapsychology—is no longer an extension of commonsense folk psychology or a form of *psychological* determinism—although it is a form of determinism, namely, one in which psychological phenomena are ultimately accounted for by nonpsychological determinants, such as inborn instincts, the nature of the mental apparatus, and the distribution of libido (see Eagle, 1980b). Or perhaps one can soften that statement by saying that inborn instincts, the nature of the mental apparatus, and the distribution of libido, along with other factors, play an important role in determining psychological phenomena.

One of the issues that was prominently discussed in the psychoanalytic literature of the 1960s was the question of the degree to which Freudian metapsychology largely consists of thinly disguised pseudoscientific translations of ordinary discourse that have little or no explanatory power. Indeed, it has been claimed that whatever explanatory power these metapsychological accounts appear to have is parasitic upon their links to ordinary discourse and to commonsense folk psychology—so that when reading these metapsychological formulations, all one need do to cash out their meaning is to translate them into ordinary discourse. To take an example discussed in Chapter 3, the semantic meaning—the cash value, so to speak—of the metapsychological formulation in *On Narcissism* (Freud, 1914b) that it is necessary to divert libido from the ego to objects lest the ego be damaged, and the ordinary language locution that precedes it that one must love in order not to fall ill are essentially identical. The former, one can claim, is a pseudoscientific semantic equivalent of the latter and represents an attempt to presumably bestow a scientific status on the latter through pseudoscientific terms and concepts that are not linked to the empirical world.

This entire issue is a complex one and deserves fuller discussion than is appropriate for this chapter. I cannot resist, however, adding a few comments. I think one needs to distinguish between Freud's specific metapsychological concepts, which may, indeed, have little explanatory value, and what implicitly appears to be his position that a comprehensive scientific account of psychological phenomena needs to go beyond the level of the psychological phenomena themselves. As philosopher Max Black (1967) has commented, "As soon as reasons for action have been provided, an enquiring mind will want to press on to questions about the provenance and etiology of such reasons" (p. 656).

It seems to me that Freud's resort to metapsychology (as well as to drive theory) constitutes an implicit recognition that although all psychological phenomena may be determined and although one may be able to develop serviceable theories at the level of psychological terms and concepts (i.e., desires, reasons, motives, etc.), a truly comprehensive scientific theory will not be limited to these terms and concepts. Thus, whereas the ordinary discourse kind of explanation that accounts for behavior by reference to desires, motives, and beliefs (now extended to included unconscious desires, motives, and beliefs) is adequate for ordinary affairs (and may also be adequate for carrying our psychotherapy), a truly comprehensive scientific theory will go beyond the concepts of desires, motives, and beliefs. Indeed, they will account for the "provenance and etiology" of the desires, motives, and beliefs themselves (see Stich, 1983; Sellars, 1963).

One can think of Freud's metapsychology as a sort of placeholder for comprehensive explanatory accounts that await further knowledge and further theorizing. (One can think of the *Project* in the same way). As Ricoeur (1970) has recognized, Freudian theory is an odd combination of meaning and mechanism—of a clinical theory that uses the psychological language of desires and motives and a metapsychological theory that uses the nonpsychological mechanistic and energic language of forces, discharge, distribution of libido, and so on.

As far as psychic determinism is concerned, Freud clearly accepted the scientific weltanschauung in maintaining that all psychological phenomena are determined. Following the *Project*, he also appeared to endorse the legitimacy and autonomy of scientific accounts of psychological phenomena that were restricted to the psychological level of explanation (i.e., desires, wishes, motives, etc.). That is, he appeared to endorse psychological determinism. However, given his abiding preoccupation with metapsychological formulations, I believe his endorsement of psychological determinism—that is, the self-sufficiency of psychological explanatory accounts—was a pragmatic rather than a philosophical one. Indeed, one could argue, as Rubinstein (1976) does, that concepts such as unconscious desires, motives, and wishes are essentially metapsychological concepts, are only "as if" psychological concepts and are meaningful to us as psychological concepts only because we understand what conscious desires, motives, and wishes mean. However, the issue of the ontological status of unconscious desires, etc., is a complex one that cannot be adequately dealt with in this chapter.

Psychic determinism and free association

As noted earlier, the use of free association in psychoanalytic treatment to uncover unconscious derivatives would make little or no sense without the assumption of some form of psychic determinism. During the time that Freud was constructing his theory, associationism dominated German academic psychology. However, the emphasis was on "mechanical" factors, such as contiguity, that influenced the flow of association. This emphasis shifted when Ach (1905/1951) proposed that a "determining tendency"— for example, an intention—operates as an organizing principle in influencing the sequence and flow of associations in the mind. There is no great distance between Ach's "determining tendency" and Freud's idea that a wish can organize and determine the sequence of associations. Thus, as Rapaport (1967) observes, Freud

> assumed that if the patient communicated the flow of his thoughts (free associations—flight of ideas), their interconnections, their network would somehow allow insight into the patient's psychic life .... In other words, he considered free associations as the road to the unconscious. (p. 44)

Although there is much more to be said, I think that I have presented and summarized some essential elements of the Freudian conception of mind. What I find striking in reviewing and summarizing Freudian theory of mind is its complex and almost architectural structure. How do contemporary psychoanalytic theories deal with the kinds of issues regarding the nature of mind with which Freud was concerned? We will see.

Chapter 3

Conceptions of object relations in Freudian theory

In his vast writings, Freud expresses a number of different views regarding the nature of our relations to objects. However, there are two interrelated fundamental ideas that lie at the center of his overall theory regarding the origin, development, and function of objects and object relations in psychic functioning. It is the reactions to these fundamental ideas that constitute the basis for later developments in psychoanalysis.

A basic assumption of Freudian theory is that we are not inherently object relational but rather turn to objects only reluctantly, under the pressure of the need for drive gratification and discharge of excitation.[1] This speaks to the origin and development of object relations. The other related fundamental idea is that drive gratification and discharge of excitation constitute the primary *function* of objects and object relations. The latter is reflected in the very definition of the object as "the thing in regard to which or through which the instinct achieves its aim" (Freud, 1915a, p. 122). These fundamental ideas are expressed and elucidated in a number of ways and in a number of contexts. It can be seen that both ideas are ultimately derived from the constancy principle and drive theory.[2]

OBJECT RELATIONS AND DRIVE GRATIFICATION

In Freud's (1915a) view, our early relationship to objects is characterized by "repulsion" and "hate" for the object (p. 137) because objects impose unwanted excitation, that is, disturb the infant's nirvana state. We overcome repulsion and hate and are forced to develop an interest in objects because it is the nature of reality that actual objects are necessary for drive gratification. Implicit in Freudian theory, then, is the idea that neither

---

[1] As will be seen in Chapter 7, insistence on the *inherent* nature of object relations marks a fundamental disagreement between Freudian theory and object-relations theory.

[2] Although I am aware that one can distinguish between drives and instincts, for the purposes of this chapter, I use the two terms interchangeably.

object relations nor thinking (see Chapter 2) would develop if discharge of excitation and drive gratification were possible without interaction with real objects in the world. Thus, the origin and development of both object relations and thinking are fueled by the need to discharge excitations generated by drives. Just as thinking is only a roundabout or detour means of achieving drive gratification (see Chapter 2), so similarly are objects and object relations. In this view, if we lived in a science-fiction world in which wishing would automatically make things so, we would never develop either thinking or object relations.

The classic expression of Freud's early views regarding our relationship to objects is seen in his account of the infant's response to hunger discussed in Chapter 2. As we have seen in that chapter, according to Freud (1900), after experiencing satisfaction, the infant attempts to gratify its hunger through hallucinating the breast, through "the establishment of a perceptual identity along the short path of regression" (p. 605). However, when this does not succeed in removing the tensions of hunger ("satisfaction does not follow, the need persists," p. 605), the infant is forced to turn to objects in the real world. As Freud (1900) puts it, the infant is forced "to seek out other patterns which lead eventually to the desired perceptual identity being established from the direction of the external world" (p. 605).

The relationship between drive and object

The derivative nature of object relations is also seen in Freud's conception of the acquired rather than inherent relationship between the drive and the object. Freud (1915a) writes, "[the object] is what is most variable about an instinct and is not originally connected with it" (p. 122). In other words, drives are originally (and inherently) objectless and the relationship between drives and the object is a *contingent* rather than an inherent one. Drives blindly seek discharge, initially through primary process hallucinatory wish fulfillment rather than through interaction with a separate actual object. The actual object enters the picture only through the lessons of the emerging reality principle.

There appears to be an inconsistency between Freud's description of drives as originally objectless and his speculations regarding hallucination of the breast. Implicit in the latter concept is the idea that from the earliest period of life the infant already possesses a conception of an object, namely, the breast. If the primitive psychic apparatus operates by automatically attempting to reestablish earlier conditions of satisfaction, why, when hunger is aroused, doesn't the infant hallucinate the experience of fullness, of satiety? This would surely constitute reestablishing earlier conditions of satisfaction. Instead, Freud speculates that the infant wishes for and hallucinates the breast. Thus, as Laplanche (1970/1998) points out, right from the beginning the infant wishes for the object—not only for satisfaction but for the object that is associated with satisfaction. To wish for the breast (or even to hallucinate the breast) when hungry, indeed to even have the concept of the breast, is already to be capable of, even if on a primitive level, cognizing and desiring an object, of responding on the basis of some degree of means-ends relationships, and of some degree of reality testing. Hallucinating the breast requires some capacity for representation, memory, and object constancy and some primitive knowledge that an object, the breast, is necessary for satisfaction.

Object relations and secondary drive theory: The infant's attachment to the caregiver

The derived status of object relations is perhaps most clearly seen in Freud's account of the nature of the origin of the infant's attachment to the caregiver. According to Freudian theory, the infant becomes attached to its caregiver primarily because of her role in gratification of the hunger drive and the sensual pleasures associated with the different erogenous zones that the caregiver provides in ministering to the infant's needs and care. With regard to the former, quite late in his writings, Freud (1938/1940) continues to assert that "love has its origins in attachment to the satisfied need for nourishment" (p. 188).

Although also referring to other factors, both Freud and Anna Freud focused heavily on the reduction of the hunger drive as the primary basis for the infant's attachment to its caregiver. In one important respect, this is odd insofar as it is oral stimulation and pleasure rather than satisfaction of the physiological hunger drive that, one would think, would be of primary psychoanalytic interest. However, it is likely that Freud focused on hunger because unlike the sensual pleasures associated with stimulation of the erogenous zones, hunger is characterized by features that for Freud were typical of drives, namely, cyclicity, that is, buildup of excitation and tensions (when hungry) and subsequent reduction in or discharge of excitation (when sated).[3]

The claim that the infant becomes attached to the caregiver primarily because of her role in the reduction of tensions associated with primary drives (hunger) is but one expression of a *secondary drive theory*—as applied to infant–caregiver attachment. As we have seen in Chapter 2,

---

[3] The equation of unpleasure with build-up of excitation and pleasure with the discharge of excitation created certain difficulties of which Freud (1924) was aware. For one thing, Freud recognized that under certain circumstances, *increases* rather than decreases in excitation can be experienced as pleasurable. Secondly, and most important, in ordinary usage, the essence of pleasure is *qualitative* rather than quantitative. Although he was aware of these issues, Freud never really successfully reconciled his conception of pleasure and unpleasure in terms of quantity of excitation with their essential qualitative nature.

according to the quasi-Darwinist theories of both Freud and behaviorist Hull (1943, 1951), virtually all behavior is, directly or indirectly, in the service of reduction of primary drive tensions. In this view, behaviors and stimuli associated with drive or tension reduction take on reinforcing and secondary drive properties. In the present context, the application of this view leads to the claim that the caregiver takes on secondary drive properties because of her association with primary drive (hunger) reduction.[4] As we will see, within psychoanalysis, rejection of secondary drive theory played a critical role in the development of object-relations theory as well as attachment theory.

OBJECT RELATIONS AND INFANTILE SEXUALITY

As noted, an alternative or at least an addition to the assumption that the origin of object relations, manifested in the infant's attachment to the caregiver, is based on hunger reduction is the idea that it is based on infantile sexuality, that is, on sensual pleasures derived from stimulation of the infant's erogenous zones. Instead of arguing that the infant's attachment to the mother is based on drive or tension reduction (of the hunger drive), focusing on erogenous zones would place the emphasis on the sensual pleasures associated with the mother's ministrations.

In apparent accord with this view, Anna Freud (1960) states that the infant has an "inborn readiness to cathect with libido a person who provides pleasurable experiences" (p. 55). However, it is not clear which "pleasurable experiences" Anna Freud is referring to here. Is it the pleasurable experiences that result from drive (hunger) reduction, the "sensual pleasurable experiences" connected to stimulation of the erogenous zones, or both? As we have seen, from the perspective of drive theory and the constancy principle, pleasure and unpleasure are defined quantitatively, as, respectively, the discharge and buildup of excitation or tension. This

---

[4] The canonical status of the claim that object relations are subservient to drive gratification is dramatically seen in Spitz's (1960) account of the effects of maternal deprivation on the development of the infant. Because Spitz was a pioneer in demonstrating the dire effects of maternal deprivation, one tends to think of his work as belonging to and contributing to an object-relations theory perspective. However, the fact is that Spitz's account of the effects of maternal deprivation is entirely derived from drive theory. He writes: "I have to stress once again that in the emotional interchange with the love object *both* the libidinal and aggressive drives find their discharge. The loss of the love object interrupts the discharge of both drives" (p. 90). In other words, Spitz attributes marasmus and other dire effects of maternal deprivation to the fact that there is no object on which the infant is able to discharge his or her libidinal and aggressive drives. The buildup and failure to discharge these drives, then, somehow interferes with and damages the infant's development. This is as clear an instance of the constancy principle and hydraulic model at work as one can find in the psychoanalytic literature.

framework simply does not easily fit the pleasures linked to stimulation of the erogenous zones where the issue of buildup and discharge of excitation does not arise, at least not in any obvious way. Rather, the pleasures resulting from stimulation of the erogenous zones are sensual and qualitative in nature.

From a theoretical perspective, the kind of pleasure being referred to makes a great deal of difference. If, when one states that the infant has an "inborn readiness to cathect with libido a person who provides pleasurable experiences," the pleasure one has in mind is pleasure derived from drive reduction, one is essentially restating secondary drive theory. The new and theoretically important element is the acknowledgment of the infant's inborn readiness rather than reluctance to cathect objects. The emphasis on sensual pleasures associated with stimulation of the erogenous zones as the basis for infant–mother attachment is, however, compatible with a general, *nondrive reduction version* of the secondary reinforcement theory of infant–mother attachment. That is, the infant becomes attached to caregiver because she is associated with some kind of pleasures and would presumably not become attached to her were that not the case.

There are two components of Anna Freud's formulation. One, as noted, is the acknowledgment that there is an inborn readiness to become attached. This component is already a significant departure from the central claims of Freudian theory that we reluctantly cathect objects only when they are necessary for drive gratification, and reluctantly move from primary narcissism to object cathexis to avoid inundating the ego with excessive libido. These claims are expressions of the assumption of an inborn *reluctance* rather than an inborn readiness to become attached. In acknowledging an inborn readiness to become attached, Anna Freud does not seem to recognize the need to reconcile her acknowledgment of an inborn readiness to become attached with the above contradictory central assumptions of Freudian theory. The second component of Anna Freud's formulation is that the inborn tendency to become attached is directed toward the specific person who provides and is associated with pleasurable experiences linked to the erogenous zones and infantile sexuality. This raises the specific question of whether pleasures linked to the erogenous zones can serve as an adequate basis for the infant's attachment to its caregiver and the general question of the relationship between infantile sexuality and attachment to the object.

The autoerotic nature of infantile sexuality

Freud (1905) writes that infantile sexuality "has as yet no sexual object, and is thus auto-erotic" (p. 182); he also writes that it is only at the onset of puberty that "the sexual instinct [which] has hitherto been predominantly auto-erotic … now finds a sexual object" (p. 207). The assertion that infantile sexuality is autoerotic and has no sexual object appears to contradict Anna Freud's formulation that the infant cathects with libido a person who provides pleasurable experiences, for to cathect a person with libido is to have an object and an object relationship and to make a connection between the pleasurable experiences and the person who provides them. If that connection is not made, how can the pleasurable experiences of infantile sexuality serve as a basis for object relationships?

Consider Freud's examples of thumb-sucking and masturbation as expressions of the autoerotic nature of infantile sexuality. In the former, the object is a part of the infant's own body and there is no question of an object relationship. In the case of masturbation, although objects may be invoked, they are only the imaginary products of fantasy. In either case, it is difficult to understand how the pleasures derived from these activities could be connected to someone who provides them or could constitute the basis for object relations. (I will take up the issue again below in discussing the work of Widlöcher and his colleagues on the relationship between infantile sexuality and attachment.)

One should also note the contradiction between the assertion that it is only at the onset of puberty that "the sexual instinct [which] has hitherto been predominantly auto-erotic … now finds an object" (Freud, 1905, p. 207) and the Freudian emphasis on the intensity of incestuous wishes toward the object during the oedipal period—long before the onset of puberty. Surely, the child's sexual wishes during the oedipal period are assumed to be directed toward the object rather than simply autoerotic. As far as I know, this apparent contradiction between the theory of the oedipal phase and the claim that the sexual instinct remains autoerotic until the onset of puberty is not confronted in Freud's writings. By viewing infantile sexuality as autoerotic up to the point of the onset of puberty, Freud ignores the oedipal period. Let me now turn more directly to the oedipal situation.

Infant sexuality and attachment

In an essay in the book *Infantile Sexuality and Attachment*, Widlöcher (2002) tries to spell out what he believes to be the logical implications of the Freudian conception of the autoerotic nature of infantile sexuality and its relationship to attachment and the development of object relations. According to Widlöcher, "whereas the development of attachment and object love are directed toward a real person … infantile sexuality takes form as the result of an internal demand and achieves satisfaction in psychic and/or auto-erotic activity" (p. 13). Widlöcher further states that in infantile sexuality, the object is only the actor called upon to play a role in the imaginary scenario. It is interchangeable, and the same object can play different parts in the same scenario. Wish-fulfillment ... is the goal that is sought and the source of pleasure. (p. 13)

In Widlöcher's view, although the autoerotic fantasies of infantile sexuality may involve the object, it is a fantasied and interchangeable object rather than "a real person." The object's role is entirely utilitarian and instrumental, that is, entirely in the service of wish fulfillment and pleasure. The model for that kind of object is the hallucinated breast generated by wish fulfillment and the seeking of immediate pleasure. Although one can describe the hallucinated breast as an object and the infant's relation to it as some form of object relationship, it does not, Widlöcher tells us, qualify as attachment and certainly does not constitute object love. Indeed, in Widlöcher's view, the persistence of the autoerotic fantasies of infantile sexuality constitute the primary impediments to attachment and object love "directed to a real person." Widlöcher writes that psychic life is characterized by a constant "conflictual interweaving of love for the other and the quest for auto-erotic pleasure" (p. 31).

According to Widlöcher (2002) and other contributors to the same volume, certainly clinical psychoanalysis and perhaps psychoanalytic theory have little to do with and little to tell us about the origin and nature of object relations with real, actual others. That is not their bailiwick. What they do have a great deal to tell us about is the ways in which infantile sexuality uses autoerotic fantasies and primary process modes of wish fulfillment to create "imaginary scenarios" and "an imaginary relation to the object" (p. 21). In this view, psychoanalysis is concerned primarily with the identification and exploration in psychic life of these "imaginary scenarios" and "imaginary relation to the object" as well as the ways in which they invade, interfere with, and conflict with a real relation to the actual object.

According to Widlöcher (2002), the persistence and presence of infantile sexuality "in what the analysand is saying and thinking is undoubtedly of one of the fundamental aspects, if not the foundation itself, of the psychoanalytic approach" (p. 27). In agreement with Widlöcher, Scarfone (2002), another contributor to the book, writes that "infantile sexuality is not a separate object within the field of psychoanalysis. It is ... the very object resulting from the territory marked out by the Freudian method" (p. 97). He goes on to state explicitly that he "place[s] ... outside the specific domain of psychoanalysis attachment behavior, primary love, and the infantile sexuality understood here as what is continuous with adult sexuality" (p. 99).

In other words, Widlöcher (2002), Scarfone (2002), and undoubtedly others who view themselves as Freudian analysts are not simply addressing a purely theoretical perspective but are telling us that their main and perhaps exclusive focus in their clinical work is to seek to identify the derivatives of infantile sexuality—that is, primary process wish fulfillment, autoerotic fantasies, and a primarily "imaginary relation to the object" (Widlöcher, 2002, p. 21)—in the adult's psychic life. Thus, when Widlöcher or Scarfone listens to the patient's descriptions of his or her relationships with others (and undoubtedly, their patients are as preoccupied with and talk about their relationships as much as most patients in treatment), they hear these descriptions as a narrative in which the other "is only the actor called upon to play a role in the imaginary scenario." That is, clinical psychoanalysis is concerned with understanding the impediments, having mainly to do with autoerotic fantasies, that interfere with object love. It does not deal directly with the latter. Once the impediments are dealt with, object love will, so to speak, take care of itself.

In this view, clinical psychoanalysis is primarily concerned with the forces in the mind of the adult that conflict with attachment to and love for the actual object, not with the processes involved in the development of that object love and attachment. As Widlöcher (2002) and Scarfone (2002) appear to acknowledge, theoretical formulations regarding the latter are the domain of those disciplines—for example, attachment theory and research, ethology, developmental psychology and biology—that generate data based on observations of the infant, caregiver, and infant–caregiver interactions.

According to Andre (2002), another contributor to the volume, and Green (1992), theories regarding the origins of infant–mother attachment are based on observations of the real or observed child, which is contrasted with the true child of psychoanalysis. The latter, it turns out, is not the child at all, observed or true. If one ignores terms such as *real* or *observed* or *true*, what Green and Andre are saying is similar to what Widlöcher (2002) and Scarfone (2002) are saying: Psychoanalysis is not concerned with how actual object relations develop but rather with the inferred residues of infantile fantasies in the adult psyche.

They appear to be ceding that an inborn object-seeking tendency (Fairbairn), primary object love (Balint, 1937/1965), and an inborn instinctual attachment system (Bowlby, 1969/1982) constitute the basis for the establishment of infant–mother attachment and for object relations, and in doing so, they appear to relinquish Freud's and Anna Freud's claims that either hunger reduction or infantile sexuality provides the basis for the development of object relations. Indeed, they appear in effect to acknowledge that traditional psychoanalysis does not provide an adequate theory of the origins of object relations. They also appear to implicitly acknowledge the validity of criticisms of the classical theory of object relations that go as far back as Suttie (1935), are conspicuous in the work of the Balints (e.g., 1949, 1959/1965), of Klein (e.g., 1946–1963), of Fairbairn (1952), of Sandler and Sandler (e.g., 1978), of the so-called neo-Freudians (e.g., Sullivan, 1953; Horney, 1945), and of Bowlby (e.g., 1969/1982) and continue to be central in contemporary psychoanalysis.

THE TRIANGULAR NATURE OF OBJECT RELATIONS: THE OEDIPAL SITUATION

Up to this point, I have discussed the Freudian conception of object relations mainly from the dyadic perspective of the early mother–child relationship. My focus has been on what might be referred to as the preoedipal issue of the origins of object relations. However, a distinctive and central feature of Freudian theory, one that marks it off from other theories, is the emphasis on the triangular oedipal nature of object relations that arises at a particular point in the life of the child.

In contrast to contemporary theories, where the greatest emphasis is placed on the influence of preoedipal mother–child experiences on personality development, in Freudian theory, the degree of the oedipal conflict and the manner in which the child resolves it play a most powerful role in psychological development, including formation of gender identity, of the superego, later object choice, and susceptibility to neurosis. Whereas fixations at earlier psychological stages may influence character formation, it is the oedipal stage that has the most momentous and fateful influence on psychological development. Indeed, to the extent that Freud has an etiological theory of the neuroses, it is located mainly in the vicissitudes of resolution of the oedipal conflict.

Why is so much importance given to the oedipal stage? I think that one answer to this question may lie in the fact that in Freudian theory, the oedipal stage represents the clearest expression of an object relational psychosexual stage. Whereas infantile sexuality at other stages is located mainly in bodily erogenous zones, during the oedipal stage, both incestuous and hostile wishes are directed outward toward *another*. Although the infant may make a connection between the pleasures of infantile sexuality and the caregiver in a secondary reinforcement way, it is only during the emergence of the oedipal phase that the child's wishes and impulses are actively directed toward another. During the oedipal phase, the child is not simply the passive recipient of sensual pleasures at the hands of the caregiver but now experiences active wishes and fantasies directed outward. Furthermore, these wishes are embodied in an object relational drama that entails intense desires, passionate longings, conflicts, fantasies, and anxieties directed toward those with whom one has grown up and loves and to whom one is closest. It is therefore understandable that the oedipal situation would constitute for Freud a crucible in which the lessons of the heart that are learned would have a lasting impact. Although it is somewhat interesting to learn that fixation at, say, the oral and anal stage may predispose one to certain character traits, it is the sort of finding that has little drama attached to it. It tells one little about how the individual will love, whom he or she will choose to love, or how he or she will relate to others.

Although the oedipal stage marks the clear emergence of object relations, it is an object relations that emerges out of sexual and aggressive impulses and, from the start, is embedded in conflict—a conflict that is originally external in the form of opposition between one's impulses and the threat from the same-sex parent but, through identification with the aggressor, becomes internal in the form of the conflict between impulses and the superego.

It should be noted that unlike Freud's hypothesis that the infant is forced to turn to objects because of the failure of hallucinatory wish fulfillment and that the infant is forced to transfer libido from the ego to the object, the emergence of oedipal wishes is not a product of the demands of reality or the need to avoid excessive excitation forcing the turn to objects. Rather, there is a natural (genetically programmed) psychosexual unfolding of impulses directed toward the object. Of course, because the oedipal child is older than the infant who supposedly hallucinates the breast or who moves from primary narcissism to object love, one would expect that object relations would have already been firmly established. However, the point is that Freud is, in effect, positing a programmed natural unfolding of infantile sexuality—as well as of narcissism—in which one becomes increasingly object relational. One might say that the developmental move from narcissism to object love is paralleled by the move from the autoerotic to the object relational nature of infantile sexuality.

OBJECT RELATIONS AND NARCISSISM

The reluctant status, so to speak, of object relations is apparent not only in Freudian drive theory but also in the context of Freud's discussion of narcissistic development. In his essay *On Narcissism*, Freud (1914b) proposes that early in life, libido is cathected only on the ego and not at all on objects. As Freud puts it, there is

> an original libidinal cathexis of the ego, from which some is later given off to objects, but which fundamentally persists and is related to the object-cathexis much as the body of an ameba is related to the pseudopodia which it puts out. (p. 75)

Furthermore, although part of one's libido is "yielded up to objects," much like the amoeba that repeatedly turns back to itself the pseudopodia it puts out to the world at the sign of danger, we are characterized by a fundamental tendency to withdraw libidinal cathexis from objects and return it to the ego. For Freud, a consequence of excessive libidinal cathexis of the object (as in being in love) is depletion of the ego.[5]

However, despite our reluctance to cathect objects, Freud (1914b) writes, rather poetically, that "in the last resort we must begin to love in order not to fall ill, and we are bound to fall ill if, in consequence of frustration, we are unable to love" (p. 85). This lyrical statement is then immediately explicated in decidedly nonpoetic metapsychological language: "We have recognized our mental apparatus as being first and foremost a device designed for mastering excitation which would otherwise be felt as distressing or would have pathogenic effects" (p. 85).

Invoking the constancy principle at this point makes clear Freud's view that one must cathect objects with libido (i.e., one must love) in order to avoid the danger of the excessive excitation that results from cathecting the ego with excessive libido. In short, just as is the case in his early views regarding the hunger drive and hallucination of the breast, one must turn to objects in order to avoid the danger of excessive excitation. In both cases, we are forced to turn to objects because they are necessary for reduction of excitation. However, it should be noted that in the context of narcissistic development, the need to turn to objects is impelled, not by the object's role in drive gratification but by the necessity of, so to speak, draining away libido from the ego in order to avoid the danger of it being harmed by excessive excitation. Once again, we see the fundamental role given to the constancy principle in both Freud's conception of mind and of object relations.

There is an interesting irony in the view of object relations expressed in *On Narcissism* (Freud, 1914b). On the one hand, as noted, the basic idea that we reluctantly turn to objects because they are necessary to avoid excessive excitation is retained. On the other hand, despite our reluctance and despite the circuitous route of its development, the capacity for object relations (in particular, the capacity to love the object) assumes its place at the center of healthy functioning. If one is not to fall ill, Freud tells us, one must begin to love. In this sense and quite ironically, at least in the context of narcissistic development, Freudian theory becomes not only an object-relations theory but one in which the capacity for object love is at its

---

[5] Freud's (1914b) contention that falling or being in love depletes the ego flies in the face of the common observation that most people who are in love feel enhanced and energized (particularly if their love is returned) rather than depleted. It is a good example of a formulation that is mainly dictated by a theoretical assumption (i.e., that, because of a limited supply, libido directed toward an object is necessarily taken away from the ego or self) and has little or no connection with empirical observation.

center.[6] Thus, despite the reluctant origin, so to speak, of object relations, the capacity to love the object is at the center of optimal development.

EGO PSYCHOLOGY AND OBJECT RELATIONS

As we saw earlier, a central claim of ego psychology was that ego functions (e.g., thinking) develop autonomously of drive gratification. Thus, contrary to Freud's insistence that thinking is only a roundabout or detour method to achieve drive gratification, the ego psychologists maintained that in an "average expectable environment," thinking, as well as other ego functions, develops independently of drive gratification (Hartmann, 1958). What is striking is that a similar claim was not made in relation to the development of object relations. After all, as we have seen, the Freudian accounts of the origin of both thinking and object relations are pretty much identical. In these accounts, both thinking and object relations develop because hallucinatory wish fulfillment does not succeed in reducing drive tensions, and yet, whereas ego psychology proposed the autonomy of thinking, it did not extend that claim to the autonomy of object relations.

Apparently, one could argue for the autonomy of ego functions and still view oneself and be viewed by most others, at least in the American psychoanalytic establishment, as a loyal Freudian.[7] Indeed, one of the arguments the ego psychologists frequently made is that their ego psychological formulations were already implicit in Freud's later writings (particularly the elaboration of his structural theory) and would have been made explicit by Freud had he continued to develop his theory. To argue, however, for the autonomy and the independence from drive gratification of *object relations* would truly constitute heresy. Not only, according to Freud, are our very conception of and interest in objects propelled by the push for drive gratification but object relations are the main arena in which drive gratification is pursued. Recall that Freud (1915a) characterizes instincts in terms of their source, aim, and *object*. That is, whereas the aim of instinctual wishes is discharged, the object is the means by which this aim is achieved. The object becomes a component of the instinct. Given the embeddedness of object relations in drive gratification in Freudian theory, positing the

---

[6] Quite ironically, as we will see in Chapter 7, it is Freud's excessive emphasis on object relations, his insistence that healthy development is characterized by the move from narcissism to object love that is rejected by Kohut (1971, 1977, 1984), a rejection that constitutes the theoretical starting point for the development of self psychology. In effect, and quite ironically, Kohut's objection to Freud's view of narcissistic development is that it is excessively object relational

[7] Because the French psychoanalytic establishment never did accept the theoretical formulations of ego psychology, French analysts did not need to concern themselves with the autonomy of either ego functions or object relations.

autonomy of object relations would be seen as equivalent to renouncing a central tenet of Freudian theory. This Hartmann and other ego psychologists were not prepared to do.

THE IRONIC CENTRALITY OF OBJECT RELATIONS IN FREUDIAN THEORY

As we can see from the above discussion, as far as Freudian theory is concerned, although we may have originally turned only reluctantly to objects, and although the tendency to bypass and withdraw from them persists, our ability to emotionally invest in objects and to relate to them in certain ways constitutes the core of healthy functioning. This is expressed, as we have also seen, in a number of ways. Freud writes that if one is to both achieve drive gratification and not fall ill, one must libidinally invest in objects, and even if the relationship between the instinct and the object is contingent and a variable, the object "as the thing in regard to which the instinct achieves its aim" (p. 122) is an essential component of the instinct. One must keep in mind that the object is not simply an external thing. It is also as a libidinally invested thing that the object serves the instinct in achieving its aim. Hence, it is an object relation. Furthermore, as noted earlier, according to Freud, right from the beginning the infant wishes for the object—not only for satisfaction but for the object that is associated with satisfaction.

Freud's basic insight in *On Narcissism* is that one must love in order not to fall ill; he then "metapsychologizes" this insight by referring to the ego's need to avoid inundation with excessive ego libido. If, as I am suggesting, the latter is tacked on, why then must one love in order not to fall ill? It seems to me that Freud is dressing up in metapsychological language and assimilating to the constancy principle the basic insight that psychic integrity is not possible without cognitive and emotional links to objects in the world—quite apart from whether or not the objects are sources of drive gratification. Keep in mind that in *On Narcissism* when Freud insists on the vital importance of libidinally investing in objects, he says little or nothing about drive gratification. Although the specific object one cathects may be the one associated with gratification and pleasure, the need to invest libidinally in some object outside oneself appears to be a psychobiological imperative. To fail to do so, Freud tells us, is to risk grave psychic consequences.

If my interpretation of Freud is correct, one finds then in *On Narcissism* that to an important extent Freud had, in effect, abandoned the classical mainstay of the Nirvana principle and replaced it with the assumption that psychic functioning depends on object relations—indeed, that our very psychic survival depends on libidinal investment in the world, that is, on object love in its most general sense. The subtlety and seeming paradox here is that only loving the object for its own sake can keep us from falling ill and maintain our psychic integrity. To put it perhaps somewhat differently, it is as much in affirming the object as in being affirmed by the object that psychic integrity is rooted. Although the former carries vulnerabilities and risks of loss and narcissistic injuries—that is one way of interpreting Freud's claim that we are ever ready to draw our libido back to the ego when danger is present—it is nonetheless the case that the absence of object love carries the greatest risk of all. That, I believe, is the central insight to be found in Freud's *On Narcissism*.

From the perspective I have been describing, a central conflict and struggle within the individual is between, on the one hand, libidinally withdrawing from objects and resorting to the autoerotic modes of wish fulfillment that bypass the actual object (the model for which is hallucinating wish fulfillment) and, on the other hand, libidinally cathecting the object (that is, object love). The centrality of this conflict is implicitly recognized by the French Freudian analysts I discussed earlier. That is, in distinguishing between ties to objects in the real world and the autoerotic nature of infantile sexuality, characterized by a "general hedonic tendency to produce pleasure by hallucinating satisfaction" (p. 22), Widlöcher (2002) is identifying a central tension between forces in the individual that struggle to establish ties to real objects, that is, to achieve object love, and forces, embedded in infantile sexuality, that attempt to "produce pleasure by hallucinating satisfaction" (p. 22). As I have tried to show, it is not that objects are absent in hallucinatory satisfaction. It is rather that the object is "only ... called upon to play a role in an imaginary scenario" and thus cannot lead to real satisfaction. As we have seen earlier, from Widlöcher's perspective, what psychoanalytic theory sheds light on and what psychoanalytic treatment focuses on is the constant "conflictual interweaving of love for the other and the quest for auto-erotic pleasure" (p. 31) in the realm of fantasy.

The profound theoretical lacuna in classical theory, as I have tried to show, is that although the capacity for object love is viewed as an essential aspect of psychic integrity and health, there is no systematic rationale for why this should be so. The only account that Freud provides for why we must love in order not to fall ill is the one derived from the constancy principle and one in which the object is entirely a utilitarian and instrumental object and one in which a consequence of object love is ego depletion. As we have seen, this gap in classical theory is implicitly acknowledged by the French Freudians who construe as the main arena for psychoanalysis an examination of the impediments located in autoerotic infantile sexuality to the capacity for object love. One can say that in this view, clinical psychoanalysis is a treatment of impediments and barriers, not a direct route to object love. Once the impediments are ameliorated, the latter is a matter of the individual's constitution, vicissitudes of life, and other factors outside the clinical situation. And perhaps that is the way it should be.

One can say that from a Freudian perspective, the goal of psychoanalysis, both as a theory and as a treatment, is to identify and understand the aspects of psychic life that interfere with the achievement of object love. In that sense, Freudian theory is, ironically, both a profoundly object-relations theory and yet, a theory without an adequate account of the origins and necessity of object relations. According to Freudian theory, early in life, we resist commerce with objects and cathect them only reluctantly. We soon learn, however, that objects are vital in various ways. However, the early tendencies to bypass or do without the object, as reflected in fantasy and primary process thinking, persist and conflict with our attempt to reach the actual object. From this perspective, Freudian theory can be understood as a description of the individual's struggle to reach and relate to the actual object in the real world rather than the fantasied one in an imaginary scenario. In this regard, despite positing a reluctant turn to objects, forced upon us by both inner demands and the nature of reality, Freudian theory can be seen as a theory in which object relations are central.

Chapter 4

Conceptions of psychopathology in Freudian theory

My purpose in this chapter is to highlight what is essential in the Freudian theory of psychopathology as a foundation for a later discussion of the departures from Freudian theory that constitute much of the contemporary psychoanalytic conceptions of psychopathology.

Before discussing specific features of the Freudian theory of psychopathology, I want to note that the primary focus and arena of that theory were the psychoneuroses. As Waelder (1960) writes in his *Basic Theory of Psychoanalysis*:

> One should ... keep in mind that this theory refers to hysteria, phobia, and obsessive-compulsive neurosis, not, or at least not necessarily, to cases of diffuse maladjustment and quiet desperation as they are described by many authors today. (p. 46)

Even earlier, Anna Freud (1954) noted that "the particular relationship between id and ego ... on which our technique rests, is valid for neurotic disorders only" (p. 48n). It is important to keep this in mind in order to be able to evaluate to what extent differences between Freudian and contemporary theories of psychopathology are true differences in the sense of representing differing accounts of the same phenomena (i.e., the neuroses) rather than mainly the product of targeting different phenomena (e.g., neurotic conflict versus self-defects), in which case, there are perhaps good reasons to expect differing accounts. In any case, insofar as this chapter deals with the Freudian conception of psychopathology, it will necessarily focus on neurosis rather than other forms of psychopathology.

INNER CONFLICT

From his earliest writings on hysteria, Freud identified unresolved inner conflict as a central component in the development of psychopathology. As we saw in Chapter 1, hysterical symptoms were brought about by the occurrence of "an incompatibility between the ego and an idea presented to it" (Breuer & Freud, 1893–1985, p. 22) and the individual's attempt to deal with that incompatibility by an act of repression. Although repression may provide relief from the conscious experience of the incompatibility, it leaves the individual burdened with a "parasite" lodged in the mind, and, most importantly, it threatens the unity and integrity of the personality, as reflected, for example, in "splits in consciousness." The personality of the hysteric, as well as the neurotic, is an unintegrated and divided one.

This early basic idea is more fully spelled out, elaborated, and integrated into Freud's mature theory of the neuroses, which includes the following features:

1. The ideas that are incompatible with the ego now have mainly to do with infantile anxiety-laden sexual and aggressive wishes and desires that are repressed because they are associated with the "danger situations" of loss of the object, loss of the object's love, castration, and superego condemnation.
2. Despite repression, drive-related wishes and desires continue to strive for expression and gratification.
3. When conflicted drive-related wishes and desires threaten to reach consciousness (and gain control of motility), a small dose of anxiety (signal anxiety), functioning as a signal of danger, is triggered, which then automatically instigates repression and prevents these dangerous contents from reaching consciousness; in turn, this repression serves to prevent development of full-fledged anxiety—all of this operating as a negative feedback system.
4. When, for whatever reasons, repression fails and there is a serious threat of the "return of the repressed," that is, when conflicted infantile wishes and desires threaten to reach consciousness as well as gaining access to motility, the anxiety that was warded off by repression can no longer be held in check, with the consequence that signal anxiety may erupt into traumatic anxiety (i.e., an anxiety attack).
5. Neurotic symptoms such as phobias, compulsions, and obsessions represent attempts to bind anxiety, that is, function as a "secondary line of defense" following failure of primary defenses such as repression. They also constitute (maladaptive) compromise formations that are characterized by partial and disguised gratification of the forbidden wishes. Thus, both the wishes and the defenses against them receive their due. Although neurotic symptoms serve the adaptive purposes of binding anxiety and permitting partial drive discharge, they exact the cost of compromised functioning and the presence of ego-alien experiences in one's psychic life. Having to resort to a "secondary line of defense" reflects a more regressed level of functioning.

6. Along with Freud, one can employ the analogy of two armies, one the superior first line of defense and a second, the less effective army behind the first army. When the first army has been routed, the second army enters the battle.

DRIVE THEORY AND INNER CONFLICT: A DRIVE-DEFENSE MODEL

Following the centrality given to drive theory, inner conflict deemed to be implicated in neurosis mainly had to do with unacceptable and repressed universal sexual and aggressive impulses. The prime example of such a conflict involving both sexual and aggressive wishes is, of course, the oedipal one, consisting of incestuous wishes toward the opposite-sex parent and hostile wishes toward the same-sex parent. In the context of drive theory, the account of neurosis as well as general psychic functioning is now understood from the vantage point of a drive-defense model, in which functioning is viewed in terms of conflict between drive impulses, such as oedipal wishes, and defenses against these wishes and impulses, that is, against their emergence into consciousness and implementation in action. Insofar as drive impulses emanate from the id and defense is an ego function, the drive-defense model can be understood as a conflict between two structures of the personality, the id and the ego. Putting it this way makes it clear that from a Freudian perspective, neurosis entails disunity of the personality, that is, the existence of warring factions within the individual. Given this conception of pathology, it follows that the primary goal of psychoanalytic treatment would be to help restore the unity and integrity of the personality through resolution of inner conflict or through more adaptive compromise formation (see Brenner, 1994). (The means by which this is presumably accomplished will be discussed in Chapter 5).

OEDIPAL CONFLICTS AND THEIR VICISSITUDES

Although the drive-defense model encompasses more than strictly oedipal wishes and defenses against them, oedipal conflicts and the nature and adequacy of their resolution are at the center of the Freudian theory of neurosis. Freud (1924/1925) writes that "increasing experience showed more and more plainly that the Oedipus complex was the nucleus of the neuroses" (p. 55). Why should this be the case? Freud (1916–1917/1917) tells us that neurosis is caused by the interaction between fixation of libido (the internal factor) and frustration (the external factor). Oedipal incestuous wishes are a quintessential example of the operation of these two factors. Also, the Oedipus complex constitutes a main arena in which conflictual sexual and aggressive wishes trigger anxiety in response to the "danger situations" of threat of castration and superego attack (as punishment for incestuous and hostile wishes) (Freud, 1923).

Freud describes various specific symptomatic and other pathological consequences of failure to resolve oedipal conflicts. For example, he attributes "psychical impotence" in men to "an incestuous fixation on mother or sister, which has never been surmounted ... " (Freud, 1912a, p. 180). He also describes the individual's inability to experience both sexual desire (the "sensual current") and love (the "affectionate current") toward the same person, with the result that "where they love they do not desire and where they desire they cannot love" (p. 183). Freud makes clear that in his view this pattern is not limited to men but also includes women. He writes "of the capacity of [some] women for normal sensation as soon as the condition of prohibition is re-established by a secret love-affair; unfaithful to their husband, they are able to keep a second order of faith with their lover" (p. 186). For both sexes, Freud (1905) writes, "a normal sexual life is only assured by an exact convergence of the affectional and the sensual current both being directed toward the sexual object and the sexual aim" (p. 207). In other words, a normal sexual life is made possible by an adequate resolution of oedipal conflicts that is marked by the integration of the affectional and sensual currents, that is, by the capacity to experience both love and desire toward the same object.

In Freud's view, adaptive resolution of oedipal conflicts is characterized by relinquishment of incestuous wishes toward the opposite-sex parent and identification with the same-sex parent—a development that is critical in the formation of the superego. It should be noted that insofar as the Oedipus complex consists not only of incestuous wishes but also hostile wishes, identification with the same-sex parent also entails relinquishment— relinquishment of hostile wishes. Success in relinquishing incestuous wishes sets the stage for finding a love object outside the family, and success in relinquishing hostile wishes sets the stage for enabling the individual to pursue competitive and ambitious strivings without fear of retaliation, that is, without castration anxiety. Hence, one can say that adequate resolution of oedipal conflicts serves as a foundation for relative satisfaction in love and work. One can also understand that, in this view, inadequate resolution of oedipal conflicts would constitute a primary factor in the development of neurosis—which ultimately consists in failures in love and work.

FROM EXTERNAL TRAUMA TO ENDOGENOUS WISHES AND FANTASIES

Despite an early emphasis on trauma, at the core of inner conflict are universal endogenous wishes and fantasies (e.g., incestuous wishes) that are unacceptable to both the individual and society. Or perhaps one should say that they become unacceptable to the individual through the internalization of societal prohibitions that are conveyed by parental figures. In replacing his seduction hypothesis with the positing of fantasy and endogenous wishes as the primary source of neurosis, Freud moved from a trauma theory of neurosis in which an external event (e.g., seduction) constitutes the trauma to an inner conflict theory of the etiology of neurosis. In doing so, he moved further away from a Janet-like theory of pathology to a distinctive psychoanalytic theory. In other words, Freud not only rejected Janet's assumption of a constitutional weakness as a primary factor in hysteria—the usual emphasis in discussions of the differences between Janet and Freud—but also rejected Janet's emphasis on the role of external trauma and replaced it with an emphasis on the role of inner conflict—a rift in the personality that is mainly the product of neither constitutional weakness nor external trauma but rather conflict between different aspects of oneself.[1]

Although Freud rejected trauma theory in which discrete external events constitute the trauma, he introduced his own version of what one might call an inner trauma theory, one embedded in conflict and in the nature of the relationship between the id and the ego. Recall that for Freud (see Chapter 1) the primary danger confronting the organism is being overwhelmed by excessive excitation. Indeed, for Freud, the essence of trauma is precisely being overwhelmed by a quantity of excitations beyond the individual's ability to cope. Recall also that, according to Freud, the primary source of such danger lies in the excitation generated by drives. Putting all this together, one can see that the Freudian inner conflict model also implicitly entails a particular kind of trauma theory, albeit a trauma theory in which the source of the trauma is inner rather than outer events. That is, because inner conflict prevents the discharge of excitation, it increases the likelihood that one will be traumatically overwhelmed by the buildup of excessive excitation. Furthermore, the need to avoid such buildup plays a role in the formation of neurotic symptoms insofar as they enable a partial "draining away" of excitation.

RELATIONSHIP BETWEEN ID AND EGO

Freud is somewhat ambiguous regarding the ultimate sources of inner conflict. On the one hand, both he and Anna Freud describe the relationship

---

[1] Although Freud (1905) rejected constitutional weakness as the main causal element in hysteria, he did leave room for the role of hereditary factors in neurosis in his concept of "complemental series" (pp. 239–240), which, in effect, is a diathesis-stress model characterized by the interaction between dispositional or predisposing and precipitating factors in generating pathology.

between the id and the ego as one of, to use Anna Freud's (1954/1968) phrase, "primary antagonism." That is, insofar as id impulses always carry the threat of overwhelming the ego with excessive excitation, the id is, so to speak, a natural enemy of the ego—and a natural enemy of society. As Mitchell (1988) puts it, using the phrase "metaphor of the beast" (p. 67) to describe Freudian drive theory, "Freud regards what is distinctively human and special mankind as a tenuous overlay upon a rapacious bestial core, which is only with great difficulty brought under the control of civilized motives" (p. 74). Thus, repression is necessary for both the individual and society to function, and neurosis is an inevitable cost exacted by civilization (Freud, 1929/1930).

On the other hand, at various times Freud describes the conflictual relationship between id and ego as environmentally induced. Consider Freud's (1923) important idea that repression and other defenses are motivated by the attempt to avoid the danger situations of loss of the object, loss of the object's love, superego attack, and threat of castration. These danger situations are largely *external* ones. That is, the child represses certain feelings, thoughts, and impulses and experiences them as threats to the ego, not because or not only because they represent *inherent* threats to the ego but because they are associated with prohibitions, punishment, and threats from parental figures.

Thus, from this perspective, certain thoughts, feelings, and impulses are not inherently threatening, that is, are not inherently inimical to adequate ego functioning and are not inherent threats to society but rather come to be experienced as forbidden because of parental (and societal) reactions. In this view, repression and other defenses are essentially brought about by the pressures of parental threats, punishments, and prohibitions. However, it should be noted that even in his formulations of environmentally induced danger situations, Freud retains the central idea that id impulses are a potential natural enemy of the ego. Thus, according to Freud, ultimately, the danger situations are dangerous because each of these situations— loss of the object, loss of the object's love, castration threat, and superego attack—entails the risk of being left with the buildup of need tensions that leave one at the mercy of excessive excitation. That loss of the object or loss of the object's love is, so to speak, not bad enough in itself but is viewed as dangerous mainly because it leaves the individual at the mercy of excessive excitation dramatically indicates the centrality of the constancy principle in Freud's thinking.

Despite posting an inherent antagonism between the id and the ego because an "excessive strength of instinct can damage the ego" (Freud, 1938/1940, p. 199), Freud (1937a) also writes that "id and ego are originally one" (p. 240). So, in effect, Freud presents two different and somewhat contradictory models of the relationship between id and ego and of the nature of the origins of inner conflict. In one of his last works, Freud (1398/1940) acknowledges that he is positing two different models and suggests that both may operate in neurosis. He writes:

> [The] id is a source of ... danger [to the ego], and that for two different reasons: In the first place, an excessive strength of instinct can damage the ego in the same way as an excessive "stimulus" from the external world.... In the second place, experience may have taught the ego that the satisfaction of some instinctual demand that is not in itself unbearable would involve danger in the external world. (p. 199–200)

However, the incompatibility is not fully resolved. For if the id is a source of danger to the ego and if there is an "inherent antagonism" between the two, how can it be that in health there is no division between them? As far as I know, this incompatibility in Freud's views of the relationship between id and ego, and therefore of the ultimate source of inner conflict, is not fully resolved in his writings.

MEANINGFUL NATURE OF NEUROTIC SYMPTOMS: TWO LEVELS OF DISCOURSE

A central point that emerges from the Freudian theory of neurotic symptoms is their purposiveness and *meaningful nature*. And here we come to a conceptually distinctive feature of the Freudian perspective, not only on psychopathology but generally on psychological functioning. As Ricoeur (1970) has noted, Freudian theory is a hybrid theory characterized by descriptions at both the level of meaning and the level of mechanism. Quite consistently, Freud attempts to account for psychological phenomena at two different levels of discourse. One is the level of meanings, intentions, aims, desires, beliefs, and so on—that is, the level of ordinary discourse. At this level of discourse, psychoanalytic descriptions can be seen as an extension of common sense folk psychology. The other level of discourse is in the language of energy transformations, buildups and discharge of excitation, distribution of libido, and so on. The former language is generally associated with Freud's clinical case studies, whereas the latter is employed in his theoretical formulations.[2] A similar contrast has also been drawn between Freud's clinical theory and metapsychology and between experience-near and experience-distant descriptions.

Freud's descriptions at two different levels of discourse have been there from the very beginnings of his writings. At the same time that he is writing his case studies, he is attempting to formulate a quasineurological account

---

[2] Indeed, Freud complained that his case studies read more like literary products than scientific treatises.

of mental function in his *Project for a Scientific Psychology* (1895). A good example of Freud's style of writing and thinking about phenomena at two levels of discourse is seen in his formulation of the necessity of object love (Freud, 1914b) discussed in Chapter 3. On the level of ordinary discourse, Freud writes poetically that "one must love in order not to fall ill." This statement is immediately followed by the language of distribution of ego libido and object libido.

Consider as another example the Freudian hypothesis that both over-deprivation and over-gratification at a given psychosexual stage lead to fixation at that stage. From the perspective of ordinary discourse, this is equivalent to stating that one continues to long for gratifications in areas in which one has been excessively deprived and that one finds it difficult to relinquish gratifications of that which one has been excessively indulged. However, Freud's account of fixations is formulated, again, in the language of distribution of libido.

Consider also the Freudian account of neurotic symptoms as compromise formations. At one level of discourse, the concept of compromise formation includes the idea that insofar as neurotic symptoms entail partial gratification of repressed wishes, a function of the symptom is to permit partial discharge and thereby serve as a safety valve in preventing the buildup of excessive excitation. This level of discourse is an entirely mechanical one based on a hydraulic model of buildup and discharge of excitations. However, the neu-rotic symptom not only entails partial gratification but also gratification that is sufficiently *disguised* to bypass the ego censor and to avoid the anxiety that would be experienced were the gratification not sufficiently disguised. Once one employs the language of disguise, though, one has entered the realm of meaning rather than mechanism. Invoking the homunculus-like censor can-not obscure the fact that talk about needing to disguise one's gratification in order to avoid anxiety puts one squarely in the realm of meaning. Similar considerations arise when one thinks of the compromise formation aspects of neurotic symptoms as attempts to resolve what seems to be an unresolv-able conflict. The very locution "attempt to resolve a conflict" is stated in the language of a person planning and doing things, and yet neurotic symptoms are certainly not understood in the ordinary sense of intended acts. Rather, they are experienced as unintended, ego-alien happenings over which one has no control. Let me provide one or two examples from my own clinical experience. Before presenting this material, let me make clear that there are other interpretations of the material than the ones I provide. I select these clinical vignettes because they seem to me to especially lend themselves to a Freudian account of the symbolic meanings of symptoms, as well as their function as compromise formations and a second line of defense.

The patient, a 26-year-old man, S.T., came to treatment complaining of the following symptom: He was plagued with the obsessive thought that he was homosexual. He would spend much of his time "testing" himself by imagining a homosexual scene and then monitoring his reaction. If he felt that he did not experience any trace of sexual arousal, he would feel relieved, but only until the next test. If he detected any hint of sexual thoughts or feelings, he would become anxious and despairing. This would go on for much of his waking life. The symptom first appeared when his girlfriend put pressure on him to become formally engaged and to set a wedding date. This young man, who was not very psychologically minded, reported during one session that he told his girlfriend about his symptom and then added—without seeming to be aware of the underlying meaning of what he was saying—that he certainly could not get married as long as the symptom remained because it would be unfair to his girlfriend. It certainly does not require great clinical acumen to form the hypothesis that, whatever else was involved, the symptom served to protect my patient from the danger that engagement and marriage represented to him. It also represented an attempted solution to his seemingly insoluble conflict between his desire for and fear of closeness and commitment.

During one session, S.T. reported a striking series of events. After he and his girlfriend had a fight and made up, she turned to him and said: "I love you. You're my best friend." He reacted by feeling trapped. That night he had the following dream: Half of an eraser tip appeared, got bigger and bigger, and threatened to "smother" him. The dream ended with his "slipping into black nothingness." This is obviously a disturbing dream, but what I want to focus on here are the primitive fears of engulfment and of being erased that are portrayed in the dream following his waking experience of feeling trapped in response to his girlfriend's "I love you." This striking sequence of events lends dramatic support to the clinical hypothesis regarding the purposive nature of S.T.'s symptom. That is, all the material taken together suggests that the obsessive thought that he is homosexual, as disturbing and distressing as it is to him, protects S.T. from the greater danger posed by heterosexual intimacy, of being "smothered" and "slipping into black nothingness." I do not begin to adequately understand the mechanism or process that can generate a symptom that is experienced as unbidden, unintended, and involuntary and yet can be purposive (i.e., designed to protect S.T.). However, the evidence seems to point in that direction.

There is further evidence supporting the hypothesis that S.T.'s symptom represented an attempt to resolve a conflict and served to protect him from overwhelming danger. Although S.T.'s symptom abated somewhat in the course of treatment, it continued to plague him. After a period of time, S.T.'s girlfriend tired of his procrastination and left him. Although he was unhappy and felt loss and rejection, his symptom was dramatically reduced. Indeed, for S.T., it was sufficiently reduced that he terminated treatment. His sole purpose in seeking treatment, he informed me, was to get relief from his symptom; now that he had, he felt little interest in more prolonged and intensive exploration of his underlying conflicts.

A couple of years had passed when I received a call from S.T. informing me that his symptom had returned and asking for an appointment. I learned that he had a new girlfriend and was faced with the same situation he faced with his previous girlfriend. The new girlfriend also wanted a commitment from him, and it was at that point that his symptom returned in full force. In my experience, it is rare that one gets such compelling and cumulative evidence for a clinical hypothesis, namely, that the symptom of obsessive homosexual thoughts served to protect S.T. from what, at some level, he experienced as a greater danger. In other words, in accord with a classical view, the symptom represented a purposive attempt to deal with what was experienced as an insoluble conflict.

The meaningful nature of neurotic symptoms is also seen in the situations that not only triggered but also exacerbated these symptoms. In one session S.T. reported that his obsessive symptom worsened immediately following his mother's request that he return a baking dish to a top shelf that she could not reach (S.T. was quite tall). When I asked for his further thoughts, he said that this task was something "my father would do for my mom." He also recalled that his symptom also exacerbated when his mother asked him to mow the lawn, again something "my father used to do." When I asked S.T. about other situations that made his symptom worse, he responded that the most extreme exacerbation of his symptom occurred when he received a job promotion.

Of course, there are many ways of interpreting the above data and many possible inferences as to the common link among these quite different situations. As we know, theory is always undetermined by data. In any discipline, for any given set of data, there are an indefinite number of theories that would account for them (Duhem, 1954). However, given all the available information on S.T., a highly plausible inference is that the element that is common to all three exacerbating situations is that S.T. is put into an adult role that is associated with what his father "used to do." What is striking is that S.T.'s reaction of exacerbation of his symptom to these different situations occurred without any seeming conscious awareness of their underlying meaning. This sort of phenomenon lends weight to G. S. Klein's (1976) understanding of repression in terms of failing to understand connections among experiences and to understand their personal significance.

SECONDARY GAIN

Although Freud (1901, p. 115; 1920, pp. 158–159) used the term *secondary gain* associated with symptoms and illness sparingly, as he noted, secondary gain can serve an important function in maintaining neurotic symptoms. As the term *secondary* suggests, Freud distinguishes between the factors involved in the formation of the symptom and the gains provided by the symptom once it has been formed. Although this distinction makes theoretical sense, it is not always easy to make in practice. Let me provide an example, however, where the distinction was relatively clear on both a theoretical and practical level.

I treated a young woman, O.E., who had become severely agoraphobic after the birth of her first child. Her first anxiety/panic attack occurred when she and her husband drove to look at a house in a city some distance from the city in which they lived. They were living in an apartment near her parents, and after the new baby arrived, they were considering renting or buying a house that provided enough room for the three of them in a new city where the husband had taken a job. A couple of additional attempts to drive to the new city resulted in having to turn back because of O.E.'s anxiety attacks. From the very first session, it was apparent that O.E. did not want to move to the new city.

Given O.E.'s reluctance to move to the new city, it became clear that the agoraphobic symptom served the secondary gain function of preventing this move. It seemed to me that this aspect had to be dealt with if treatment was to be successful, and it was dealt with in the following way: O.E. and her husband agreed that they would give up the plan of moving to the new city and that he would get relocated in his work to the city in which they were living. Of course, her agoraphobia was not ameliorated once this agreement was reached. The point here is this: Although the agoraphobia served a secondary gain function in preventing the move, the removal of that issue had little or no direct effect on the symptom. This was so because other primary factors, not the reluctance to move, were instrumental in the formation of O.E.'s agoraphobia (see Eagle, 2009, for a further discussion of this case). However, dealing with the secondary gain issue did have the effect of facilitating the work of psychotherapy.

Although secondary gain factors may not be instrumental in the formation of neurotic symptoms, they may nevertheless exert a powerful role in the continuation and persistence of the symptom and may interfere with dealing with the more primary factors. I was struck by this fact during my work at Department of Veterans Affairs hospitals. Veterans who received disability payments would be subject to reduction in their disability pay if their symptoms improved, a situation that served to maximize the influence of secondary gain associated with their symptoms.

PSYCHOSEXUAL DEVELOPMENT AND NEUROSIS

From the perspective of Freud's theory of psychosexual development, fixation at a particular psychosexual stage, leading to the persistence of infantile wishes, can be, but need not be, a key factor in the development of neurosis. Fixations can influence character formation and can contribute to the development of, say, an oral or an anal character, but this in itself is not a neurosis. Infantile wishes associated with different psychosexual stages can also be integrated into genital sexuality. As I understand Freudian theory, the persistence of infantile wishes into adulthood contributes to the development of neurosis when these wishes are embedded in inner conflict. The persistence of infantile wishes per se may or may not be problematic in other ways. If they are unrealistic and cannot be gratified, they may result in some frustration and unhappiness.

However, such frustration and unhappiness do not themselves constitute a neurosis. Furthermore, some people find means of gratifying so-called infantile wishes when they are not especially conflicted about them. One must keep in mind that in neurosis, the individual persists in pursuing *repressed unconscious* wishes, which according to the logic of Freudian theory means that they are embedded in inner conflict. If there is no repression or inner conflict and the individual consciously pursues infantile wishes and fantasies that are unrealistic and difficult to gratify, he or she may be quixotic and foolish or perhaps courageous (Waelder, 1960), but this situation is not necessarily neurosis.

CHARACTER NEUROSIS

Character neurosis is a term that at one time had been used but then dropped out of the psychoanalytic literature. I think this is so partly because it was assimilated into the later concept of personality disorder. As the term suggests, character neurosis is intended to convey the basic idea that neurotic tendencies, rather than leading to the development of ego-alien symptoms, become absorbed into the individual's personality as ego-syntonic character traits that are experienced as part of oneself. The benefit is that the individual does not experience ego-alien symptoms, inner conflict, and the anxiety associated with such conflict. The costs may include a certain degree of ego restrictions, avoidance of certain danger areas, and a degree of rigidity of character structure. A typical example would be the integration of strong obsessional trends into rigid orderliness or the choice of jobs that may be below the individual's abilities but that do not clash with the obsessional trends.

In my experience, character neurosis can be maintained so long as it is not challenged by environmental events. I once treated a young man, J.K., who provided the following account: He dated frequently, and his pattern with women was early intensity of interest and then, when intimacy began to develop, a loss of interest. This pattern was not especially troubling to him. In each relationship, J.K. identified something wrong with the woman that accounted for his loss of interest, and in any case, there were always other women available. Furthermore, his pattern was not too different from that of his circle of single male friends with whom he had enjoyable relationships. After some years, the circle of single male friends dwindled as many of them married and had families. At this time in his life, J.K. began to feel a bit isolated and periodically wondered whether he "might have a problem with women." He was not overly concerned, though; he continued to enjoy his dating and felt relatively content with his life.

At this point, his best friend was planning to get married and asked J.K. to serve as his best man. During the wedding ceremony, while he was standing there as best man, J.K. fainted, a disturbing and humiliating experience for him. At first, he explained away his fainting as due to low blood sugar level attendant upon not having eaten enough. However, he failed to find this explanation convincing, and he generally felt uneasy and experienced a good deal of anxiety for, he reported, the first time in his life. The fainting episode and the subsequent anxiety led him to seek treatment.

The above account represents a clear example of a character neurosis, characterized by the ego-syntonic assimilation of neurotic tendencies into one's character; under the pressure of certain precipitating events, these tendencies become transformed into a psychoneurosis, characterized by distressing ego-alien symptoms. Until that precipitating event, J.K. could avoid the experience of full-blown inner conflicts (e.g., around heterosexual intimacy and unconscious homosexual fantasies) through his way of life. When that way of life became problematic and no longer worked, a symptomatic neurosis erupted, leading him to seek treatment.

The received wisdom in classical psychoanalysis is that in treating character neurosis, it is necessary to transform it into a psychoneurosis so that the patient will experience certain formerly ego-syntonic aspects of himself or herself as ego-alien and consequently will experience sufficient subjective distress to motivate self-exploration and desire for change. As J.K.'s experience indicates, the transformation of a character neurosis into a symptomatic psychoneurosis can occur prior to treatment under the impact of precipitating events. My impression is that this is quite often the case. People with a character neurosis generally do not seek treatment if their way of life works. They do so under the pressure of someone else (e.g., the spouse) or, as in the case of J.K., when the way of life represented in the character neurosis becomes problematic.

The idea of transforming a character neurosis into a psychoneurosis, insofar as it entails transformation of the ego-syntonic into the ego-alien, seems, on the surface, to contradict the dictum "where id was, there shall ego be"—that is, where ego-alien was, there shall ego-syntonic be. However, I believe the contradiction is only an apparent one. For one thing, "where id was, there shall ego be" is mainly applicable to psychoneurosis, at the center of which is inner conflict. In the character neuroses, the neurotic tendencies have become part of the ego. If change is to occur, these tendencies must become ego-alien, modified, and then the re-assimilated as ego-syntonic.

In the case of J.K., the ego-syntonic way of life that led to the state of affairs in which he found himself needs to be viewed as a substitute for a neurotic symptom. That is, underlying and motivating his way of life was the need to avoid experiencing an inner conflict, and the degree to which it succeeded in doing so was the degree to which it was experienced as ego-syntonic. As we have seen, when circumstances interfered with J.K's adaptation, the character neurosis was transformed into a symptomatic psychoneurosis. This meant that J.K's way of life had become sufficiently uncomfortable and distressing, that is, sufficiently ego-alien, to motivate him to engage in self-exploration. The conflict that was avoided by the character neurosis was now experienced as an inner conflict. One way of putting this is to say that J.K's ego-syntonic way of life needed to be made ego-alien in order to explore the ego-alien and conflicted desires, wishes, and fantasies that contributed to the character neurosis and rendered them ego-syntonic. In other words, only when hitherto J.K's ego-syntonic way of life was rendered ego-alien could one pursue the goal of "where id was, there shall ego be."

APPLICABILITY OF FREUDIAN THEORY TO NONNEUROTIC PATHOLOGY

As noted earlier, the Freudian theory of psychopathology developed mainly in the context of accounting for the neurosis and is mainly applicable to that form of pathology. The question that arises is the applicability of a theory that was intended to account for the neuroses and at the center of which is the primacy of inner conflict to apparently nonneurotic forms of pathology where repression and inner conflict do not seem to be at the center. If, as Gitelson (1963) has argued, today's patients are not characterized by the prominence of inner conflict and the use of repression, how applicable is a theory in which inner conflict and repression are cornerstone concepts? Indeed, as we will see, much of the contemporary psychoanalytic literature is characterized by the identification of and preoccupation with expressions of psychopathology that are not characterized by the primacy of repression and inner conflict. For example, according to Kohut (1984), whereas Freudian theory may be applicable to pathology characterized by structural conflicts, it is not especially applicable to pathology marked by self-defects.

FREUDIAN CONCEPTIONS OF PSYCHOPATHOLOGY AND THE ENLIGHTENMENT VISION

Before ending this chapter, I want to locate Freud's conception of psychopathology in a broad historical and philosophical framework. The Freudian emphasis on inner conflict as the core of neurosis and its resolution as a primary goal of treatment reflects a convergence between philosophical–moral ideals and clinical goals. By placing inner conflict at the core of neurosis and resolution of conflict at the core of treatment, Freud aligned psychoanalysis with the age-old idea that spiritual malaise lies in disunity in the self and spiritual peace lies in devotion and unity. As Kierkegaard (1886/1948) puts it, "Purity of heart is wanting one thing." When Confucius wrote that the dictates of his heart and sense of right and wrong were one and the same, he was essentially equating wisdom and spiritual health with the replacement of inner conflict with inner unity. Broadly speaking, the Freudian theories of psychopathology and of treatment reflect both philosophical traditions. That is, a greater inner unity of the self is achieved both by undoing self-deceptions through awareness and self-knowledge and by the confrontation with and resolution of inner conflict that such self-knowledge makes possible.

Although written in the clinical language of medical disorder and therapeutics, the Freudian conception of neurotic illness is essentially a description of the individual who is both deceiving and at war with himself or herself, and the Freudian conception of mental health is essentially a description of the greater self-knowledge and experience of a degree of inner harmony. Freud (1918/1919) writes: "In actual fact, indeed, the neurotic patient presents us with a torn mind divided by resistances. As we analyze it and remove the resistances, it grows together; the greater unity which we call his ego fits into itself all the instinctual impulses which before had been split off and held apart from it" (p. 161). In this sense, Freudian theory is truly a "one-person" psychology, but one that need not offer any apologies. That is, from this perspective, the psychoanalytic ideal is inner harmony or being at peace with oneself. Although interactions with others are, of course, necessary to achieve this goal, the goal remains the intrapsychic one of inner harmony. Furthermore, in that view, without some progress toward achieving that intrapsychic goal, there can be no meaningful two-person psychology. That is, to the extent that repression, other defenses, and inner conflict hold sway, there can be no fully separate other to whom to relate. Indeed, from this perspective, one can think of the goal of psychoanalytic treatment as enabling a true two-person psychology to develop through the one-person psychology work of undoing of repression and the resolution of inner conflict.

Chapter 5

Conceptions of treatment
in Freudian theory

My aim in this chapter is to identify certain core ideas in Freud's approach to psychoanalytic treatment. As is the case with most of Freud's ideas and formulations, his conception of treatment evolved over many years. I think it is important to trace the development of Freud's ideas on treatment, not only for its historical and scholarly interest but because such an effort is likely to help one better understand contemporary approaches to psychoanalytic treatment. Without such contextualization, that is, without understanding the aspects of classical theory to which contemporary views constitute a reaction, there is an appearance of a helter-skelter quality to theoretical developments in psychoanalysis.

Before presenting a brief historical overview, I want to note that just as the Freudian theory of psychopathology is applicable mainly to the psychoneuroses (see Chapter 4), so similarly is its theory of treatment. Although an "expanded scope" (Stone, 1954) was envisioned for psychoanalysis, as Waelder (1960) observed, neuroses are "the home base of psychoanalysis" (p. 35), and "psychoanalytic therapy stands and falls with the psychoanalytic theory of the neuroses" (p. 212). This observation echoes Freud's (1932/1933) reference to the "radical inaccessibility of the psychoses to analytic treatment" (p. 154) and his statement that

> the field in which analytical therapy can be applied is that of the transference-neuroses, phobias, hysterias, obsessional neuroses, and besides these such abnormalities of character as have been developed instead of these diseases. Everything other than these, such as narcissistic and psychotic conditions, is more or less unsuitable. (p. 155)

At the center of the psychoneuroses is the presence of inner conflicts for which neurotic symptoms constitute an attempted solution. As Waelder (1960) writes, the indications for psychoanalytic treatment are the following:

1. That the condition to be treated is either altogether due to the interruption of inner communications through repression or related mechanisms, i.e., is due to inner conflict not faced but evaded—"the dust has been swept under the carpet"—or that repression has at least a major part in its psychodynamics (i.e., that we have to do with a psychoneurosis or at least with a condition involving a significant neurotic component);
2. That the inner conflicts at stake permit a viable solution without prohibitive cost; and
3. That the patient is able to understand the psychoanalytic method and willing and able to cooperate with it. (pp. 216–217)

HISTORICAL OVERVIEW

As is well known, in what one might call his prepsychoanalytic period, Freud treated hysteria with hypnosis; moved on for a brief period to the pressure technique in which, in order to recover traumatic memories, pressure was applied to the forehead of the patient; and then settled on what has come to be known as the psychoanalytic method, characterized by free association, the use of the couch, and interpretation. What is to be noted here is that although the techniques used by Freud vary, all these approaches have in common the goal of bringing unconscious material into consciousness. Although Freud's conception of the nature of mental contents that are rendered unconscious varied (e.g., traumatic memories versus infantile wishes), although his understanding of why mental contents are unconscious varied (e.g., hypnoid state versus repression), and although the means of bringing these mental contents into consciousness varied (e.g. from hypnosis to free association), what remained constant was his assumption that bringing repressed unconscious material to consciousness—making the unconscious conscious through undoing repression—was therapeutic and was a primary goal of psychoanalytic treatment. This raises a fundamental question as to why bringing unconscious material to consciousness should be therapeutic. There is no single or simple answer to this question in Freud's writings. Rather, as we have seen in Chapter 1, there is a series of interlocking answers.

Abreaction of strangulated affect

Insofar as hypnosis or the pressure technique enables the patient to remember and abreact (i.e., reexperience) the affect that was triggered but not adequately expressed in the original traumatic situation, it will permit discharge of the patient's strangulated affect—the source of hysterical symptoms. That is, insofar as hypnosis or the pressure technique permits an abreaction of the strangulated affect, it has a cathartic effect. Such cathar-sis, in turn, eases the danger of excessive excitation (see Chapter 1 for a discussion of the constancy principle), and once the strangulated affect is abreacted, it is not available to be converted into hysterical symptoms. To be noted here is that according to this early conception of therapeutic action, the function of bringing unconscious material to consciousness has little to do with awareness and insight. Rather, employing the model of a hydraulic system, the therapeutic effect of hypnosis is attributable to the fact that it permits adequate abreaction of affect originally associated with the traumatic situation.[1]

Also to be noted here is the distinction between the use of hypnosis for the purpose of therapeutic *suggestion* and the use of hypnosis as a cathartic method, that is, as a means to enable abreaction of affect. It is the latter, not the former, that characterizes Freud's use of hypnosis. As noted by Freud, the usual use of hypnosis was for the purpose of making the patient "more susceptible to a therapeutic suggestion" (Breuer & Freud, 1893–1895, p. 7, Footnote 1). An example of such a therapeutic suggestion would be to sub-stitute a benevolent event for the traumatic event. Although Freud cites this use of hypnosis approvingly, the fact is that it is very different than the use of the hypnosis in order to abreact affect. Indeed, immediately after the footnote citing Binet and Delboeuf, Freud disputes the idea that the patient's symptom relief is due to "unconscious suggestion" (p. 7). I make much of this distinction between the use of hypnosis for "therapeutic suggestion" versus abreaction of affect in order to stress the point that right from the beginning, Freud's therapeutic purpose was to bring unconscious warded off material to consciousness rather than to remove it through suggestion.

Associative rectification

As we have seen in Chapter 1, according to Freud (Breuer & Freud, 1893–1895), abreaction of affect is not the only means of dealing with trauma. Another means at the disposal of the individual is "rectification by other ideas" (p. 9). As also noted in Chapter 1, isolation of mental contents, including traumatic memories, through repression, prevents them from entering the "great complex of associations" (p. 9) that normally permits mental contents to "come alongside other experiences, which may contra-dict [them], and … [subject them] to rectification by other ideas" (p. 9). Although, as Breuer and Freud (1893–1895) note, such associative recti-fication can reduce the affect associated with trauma, it does not do so through abreaction of affect but rather through what one might understand

---

[1] Janov's (1970) "primal scream" theory is a good example of a therapeutic approach, obvi-ously based on Freud's early formulations, that was almost exclusively focused on abreac-tion, that is, expression of bottled up trauma-linked affect.

as putting the traumatic experience into perspective. Thus, in Breuer and Freud's examples, "after an accident ... the memory of the danger and the (mitigated) repetition of the fright becomes associated with the memory of what happened afterwards—rescue and the consciousness of present safety" (p. 9), and "a person's memory of humiliation is corrected by his putting the facts right, by considering his own worth, etc." (p. 9). In effect, Breuer and Freud are commenting on the value of reflecting upon and working through the memory of a traumatic experience as an adaptive means of dealing with its impact, including its affective impact.

Of course, when the memory of a traumatic experience is repressed and therefore not available to consciousness and isolated from the dominant mass of ideas, it cannot be subjected to associative rectification. Hence, here we see still another rationale for the therapeutic importance of making the unconscious conscious. We also see here that such formulations as the rectification by other ideas are clear precursors to the fundamental psychoanalytic emphasis on the central therapeutic value of insight. In contrast to the virtual disappearance of reference to abreaction of strangulated affect as a central psychoanalytic goal from the later psychoanalytic literature, the concept of associative rectification was assimilated into the later primacy given to the therapeutic importance of insight and working through.

A major reason that the use of hypnosis as a primary technique was relinquished by Freud was not because it failed to make the unconscious conscious—he believed it did—but because simply bringing an unconscious mental content into consciousness via hypnosis does not, in itself, guarantee that it will enter the great complex of associations, that is, does not guarantee that it will be truly *integrated* into the rest of the personality. Indeed, quite apart from the context of hypnosis, this problem continued to confront psychoanalytic treatment as expressed in the emergence of such concepts as resistance, intellectualization, and working through and as reflected in the frequently heard comment from patients, "Yes, I understand and am aware of. ... But that hasn't changed anything about how I feel." Indeed, as we will see, making the unconscious conscious turned out to be an incomplete and inadequate description of the goal of psychoanalytic treatment.

LATER CONCEPTIONS OF TREATMENT

I turn now to a description of the Freudian conception of treatment that followed his relinquishment of hypnosis and the pressure technique. The description focuses on the following three aspects of treatment:

1. The nature of the therapeutic stance
2. The nature of therapeutic action
3. The nature of therapeutic goals

There are no hard and fast distinctions among these categories. For example, a particular analytic stance, say analytic neutrality, is recommended because it is believed to contribute to therapeutic action. However, for the purpose of exposition, it is useful to present these categories separately.

The nature of therapeutic stance

Perhaps the most obvious example of changing conceptions of psychoanalytic treatment is the shift in the analyst's role. In order to understand this shift, I will begin by describing the different components and the accompanying rationales of the classic analytic stance. In the face of its near-wholesale rejection in contemporary psychoanalysis, it is useful to remind oneself that although it is subject to cogent criticisms, the classic analytic stance was not an arbitrary one but was rather based on a clear set of rationales, even if these rationales are now seen by many as misguided. An identification of these rationales should contribute not only to a rational assessment of the tenability of the classic analytic stance but also to an understanding of later shifts in conceptions of the appropriate role of the analyst.

Rule of abstinence

One component of the classic analytic stance was what came to be called "the rule of abstinence." The rationale for the analyst's abstinence, that is, his or her refusal to gratify the patient's transference wishes, was that it would contribute to the patient's motivation to do analytic work and to change. As Freud (1914/1915) puts it,

> analytic technique requires of the physician that he should deny to the patient who is craving for love the satisfaction she demands. The treatment must be carried out in abstinence.... I should state it as a fundamental principle that the patient's need and longing should be allowed to persist in her, in order that they may serve as forces impelling her to do work and to make changes. (pp. 164–165)

Freud is clearly expressing the view that transference gratification—the opposite of abstinence—although it might make the patient feel better in the short term, would interfere with the analytic work necessary to lead to insight, resolution of conflict, and more lasting therapeutic change. According to this view, the frustration of the patient's wishes and the discomfort it generates serve to motivate the patient to carry out the difficult analytic work necessary for lasting change.

Another rationale provided by Freud for the rule of abstinence is that it protects the analyst (and the patient) from succumbing to his or her own temptations as well as to the patient's seductions. The reasoning implicit in the rule of abstinence is the prevention of boundary violations by imposing strict limits on gratification. As we will see next, this same rationale is given for recommending the analyst's emotional coldness.

The analyst as opaque

Another component of the analytic stance is the opaqueness of the analyst, or what has come to be known as the "blank screen." Freud (1912b) writes, "The doctor should be opaque to his patients and, like a mirror, should show them nothing but what is shown to him" (p. 118). There are a number of rationales for this component of the classic analytic stance. One is that the analyst's opaqueness would constitute a screen onto which the patient could project his or her conflicts, wishes, defenses, and so on in pure form, uncontaminated by the analyst's personal contribution. That is, the analyst's opaqueness would minimize the role of suggestion. It will be recalled that right from the beginning, even when he was relying mainly on hypnosis, Freud contrasted therapeutic suggestion, which, so to speak, swept the traumatic experience under the rug, with catharsis and abreaction, which led to an adequate response to the trauma. Also, Freud was extremely sensitive to the criticism that psychoanalytic interpretations were largely suggestions and that psychoanalysis worked mainly through suggestive influence. Thus, when Fliess accused Freud of being a "thought reader" who put his own thoughts into the mind of his patients, Freud (1954) wrote to Fliess: "You are ready to conclude that the 'thought-reader perceives nothing in others but merely projects his own thoughts into them' ... you must regard the whole technique as just as worthless as the others do" (p. 337).

Freud believed that just as is the case with transference gratification, change brought about by suggestive influence would not be lasting change because it would not entail insight, awareness, resolution of conflict, and integration into the personality.

Emotional coldness: The surgeon metaphor

Freud (1912b) writes:

> I cannot advise my colleagues too urgently to model themselves during psychoanalytic treatment on the surgeon, who puts aside all his feelings, even his human sympathy, and concentrates his mental forces on the single aim of performing the operation as skillfully as possible.... The justification for requiring this emotional coldness in the analyst is that it creates the most advantageous conditions for both parties: for the doctor desirable protection for his own emotional life and for the patient the largest amount of help we can give him today. (p. 115)

Here, too, there are a number of rationales for this component of the classic analytic stance. One rationale is that emotional coldness protects the analyst's own emotional life. Just as is the case for the surgeon, were the analyst to become emotionally involved with the suffering of each of his or her patients, he or she would become emotionally drained and unable to do useful work and be helpful to the patient. A related rationale, as Hamilton (1996) puts it, is to "protect both patient and analyst from the analyst acting on his own passions" (p. 167), that is, to discourage boundary violations on the part of the analyst. Still another possible meaning and rationale for the surgical metaphor is that the analyst's interventions, like the surgeon's, may cause necessary pain and suffering in order to help the patient. As Lohser and Newton (1996) put it, "at times analysts have to ignore their feelings of compassion and sympathy. In other words, their kindness must ultimately be subordinated to the task of the analysis, which by its very nature involves suffering on the patient's part" (p. 21; see Stepansky, 1999, for an excellent discussion of the appearance of the surgical metaphor in the psychoanalytic literature).

Although not stated explicitly, an additional implicit rationale for the analytic stance of emotional coldness is the assumption that such a stance will contribute to the analyst's greater objectivity in relation to the patient. That is, the analyst's understanding of the patient will be more likely to be objective insofar as it not colored by the analyst's emotional involvement.

Some commentators (e.g., Ellman, 1991) have argued that Freud's surgical metaphor should not be taken all that seriously and have cited, in support of their position, the fact that Freud provided his patient (the Wolf Man) a meal when he thought that he might have to go hungry. However, that fact is not an entirely compelling argument for a number of reasons. For one thing, although Freud may have given the Wolf Man a meal, his general demeanor during analytic sessions may well have conformed to the surgical metaphor. Second and more important, Freud's occasional (or even frequent) behavior may well have contradicted his own prescriptions and proscriptions. However, that did not lead him to ever retract the strong statement, "I cannot advise my colleagues too urgently to model themselves during psychoanalytic treatment on the surgeon ..." (Freud, 1912b, p. 115). Furthermore, it is this rather clear and explicit prescription, rather than this or that anecdote of providing a meal to a patient, that influenced the stance of future analysts. Many classical analysts modeled themselves not after the Freud who provided the Wolf Man with a meal but after the Freud who urgently advised emotional coldness and provided a clear psychoanalytic justification for it.

Finally, it was inevitable that the latter rather than the former Freud would constitute the model for the classical analytic stance. This is so because one does not have to read Freud or be an analyst in order to have the impulse to feed someone when he or she is hungry. One *did* need to read and internalize

Freud in order to feel that if one were to legitimately consider oneself a real analyst, one needed to adopt a stance of emotional coldness. To do otherwise was to risk transference gratification and the other dangers cited by Freud that would undermine the treatment and keep it from constituting a real analysis. Although one could argue, as Holzman (1976) does, that the aloof and cold behavior of some classical analysts constituted a caricature of a classical analytic stance, the fact is that such behaviors did seem, to some extent, to accurately reflect prescriptions offered by Freud.

Analytic neutrality

Analytic neutrality has been interpreted in a variety of ways and has been, mistakenly I believe, equated with the other components of the classical analytic stance that I have discussed. Freud used the German word for indifference, which Strachey translated as "neutrality." It is interesting that the first meaning given to *indifferent* by *Webster's New American Dictionary* (1995) is "unbiased or unprejudiced." A translation of *indifference* that more accurately captures Freud's intentions is "disinterest." The dictionary definition of *disinterest* is "not influenced by personal interests and selfish motives." In the psychoanalytic situation, the limits of "personal interests and selfish motives" are adequate remuneration and the satisfaction derived from doing good professional work. Everything that is done must be done with the patient's best interests in mind—that is, one must take a *disinterested* stance.

From the classical psychoanalytic point of view, keeping the best interests of the patient in mind means carrying out the analytic work and not taking sides in the patient's conflicts, or, as Anna Freud (1966) puts it, remaining equidistant among id, ego, and superego. The core of analytic neutrality is not only not taking sides in the patient's conflicts but taking a disinterested position regarding how the patient chooses to live his or her life. The primary rationale for a neutral or disinterested analytic stance is the valuing of the patient's autonomy. This is in keeping with the idea that the goal of psychoanalytic treatment is not to direct the patient's life in this or that direction but to remove the barriers (e.g., conflict, defenses) that limit his or her autonomy in pursuing a meaningful and gratifying life.

As Poland (1984, 2000) puts it, a position of analytic neutrality entails a respect for the essential separateness and otherness of the patient. Once relatively unencumbered by neurotic conflicts and maladaptive defenses and therefore more autonomous, the patient may choose a way of life that is very different from the goals, values, and patterns that characterize the analyst's life. This rationale for analytic neutrality is quite different from the ideas that the opaqueness of the analyst will contribute to the purity of the patient's projections onto the blank screen or that abstinence will impel analytic work. The fact is that one can adhere to analytic neutrality—understood as not taking sides in the patient's conflicts and not allowing one's own values to direct the patient's way of life—while at the same time expressing interest, concern for the patient, lively affect, and so on.[2] In short, analytic neutrality is not equivalent to a stance of blank-screen opaqueness or abstinence, and it is in no way incompatible with the analyst's lively interest in and caring for the patient. One may reject the desirability or even possibility of an analytic neutral stance, which, as we will see, is a position taken by many contemporary analysts. However, if one is to do this, it is important that one accurately understand the concept of analytic neutrality and the rationale for it in the classical psychoanalytic literature. Otherwise, critiques of the concept are critiques of a straw man.

Overall rationale for analytic stance

Although I have discussed the different rationales for each of the components of the classical analytic stance, it should be noted that the general and overriding rationale that they all have in common is the facilitation of the patient's ability to confront, become aware of, and resolve his or her conflicts, fantasies, wishes, and defenses in the best way possible. Each of the components of the analytic stance—abstinence, opaqueness, emotional coldness, and neutrality—is designed to facilitate these processes in a way that is uncontaminated by the analyst's suggestions, countertransference biases and barriers, and inappropriate personal contributions.

The nature of therapeutic action

As is the case with therapeutic stance, the Freudian conception of therapeutic action can be understood in terms of its different components.

Associations and the "fundamental rule"

I begin with free association, not because it is a component of therapeutic action but because it constitutes a precondition for the carrying out of psychoanalytic treatment and for the implementation of interventions that, according to Freudian theory, comprise the therapeutic action of the treatment. The analytic patient's sole task or assignment, other than coming to sessions and paying for them, is to adhere as fully as possible to the "fundamental rule" (Freud, 1912b, p. 107), that is, to say whatever comes to mind, however irrelevant it may seem or however embarrassing it may be. This is

---

[2] A fourth meaning for *neutral* as an adjective listed in *Webster's New American Dictionary* (1995) is "having no hue: gray." One wonders whether those who equate analytic neutrality with opaqueness and "blank screen" are thinking of neutral in line with this rarer meaning, that is, blank, without emotion. This definition, however, has little to do with the specifically psychoanalytic meaning of neutrality.

easier said than done, and patients can generally comply with this rule with only varying degrees of success.

The rationale for the fundamental rule is that relaxation of censorship will facilitate the emergence of "unconscious derivatives." These unconscious derivatives are then subject to interpretation—much like the manifest content of dreams—which will contribute to the patient's awareness of his or her unconscious wishes, conflicts, anxieties, and defenses. The patient's prone position on the couch and the spatial arrangement in which he or she does not face the analyst are designed to facilitate free association. The assumption is that associations are more fluid and more characterized by a primary process when one is lying down than when sitting up, and it is easier to give voice to something potentially embarrassing when not facing the person with whom one is communicating.

The idea that free associations will be meaningful and will lead to unconscious derivatives is clearly based on the assumption of psychic determinism, that is, the assumption that what enters the mind is never random but is determined by psychological meanings and motives, and by a psychoanalytic version of an associationist theory of mind, more specifically, a theory of how sequences of thoughts enter into consciousness. According to the association psychology dominant at the end of the 19th century and the beginning of the 20th century, ordinarily the sequence of mental contents is determined by a set of factors such as contiguity and similarity among these contents. However, in the context of free association and the psychoanalytic situation, *unconscious* motives and meetings play a larger role in determining the individual's sequence of thoughts. Without this assumption, there would be little sense in the use of free association in the clinical situation (see Chapter 2).

Resistances

As noted, free association does not flow seamlessly and smoothly; the fundamental rule is only partly followed by the patient. There are many hesitations, blank states where the patient reports nothing on his or her mind, instances of chit-chat over organized and intellectualized thoughts and narratives, and so on, all of which are understood as expressions of the patient's *resistances*. The reason that certain mental contents are rendered unconscious (via repression and other defenses) is to avoid the anxiety (and other noxious affects) that their becoming conscious would elicit. There is every reason to expect that this defensive process does not simply evaporate but rather continues to operate in the clinical situation. Indeed, insofar as free association is likely to touch on unconscious derivatives and insofar as the analytic situation is focused on bringing unconscious material to consciousness, that is, on undoing defenses, it is likely to trigger anxiety and mobilize defenses.

Transference

Underlying the concept of transference is the basic idea that in the course of treatment the patient transfers onto the analyst wishes, desires, fantasies, anxieties, and defenses that originated in his or her relationships with significant figures, most often parental figures, in early childhood. Freud (1912b) described transference as a "new edition of an old object relationship" (p. 116). Greenson (1967) defined transference as the

> experience of feelings, desires, attitudes, fantasies, and defenses toward a person in the present which do not befit that person but are a repetition of reactions originating in regard to significant persons of early childhood, unconsciously displaced onto figures in the present. (p. 155)

As Greenson's (1967) definition makes clear, transference reactions are not limited to the analytic situation but rather are assumed to be ubiquitous, especially in regard to emotionally significant figures in one's life. Greenson's definition also suggests that transference reactions most frequently entail inaccurate and distorted attributions to the person toward whom the transference reactions are directed. One should note here that insofar as the analyst has maintained an opaque, blank screen stance, one can more comfortably assert that the patient's transference reactions constitute pure projections from his or her earlier experiences.

According to Freudian theory, the regressive features of the analytic situation, including the patient role, the anonymity and authority of the analyst, the patient's supine position, and so on facilitate the emergence of a transference neurosis, which is understood as a recapitulation of the patient's infantile neurosis. In analyzing and treating the transference neurosis, one is treating and hopefully resolving the patient's neurosis that brought him or her to treatment. Thus, the primary foci of analytic interpretations are the patient's resistances and transference reactions. Although resistance and transference are distinguished as separate concepts, Freud viewed transference as a form of resistance. That is, instead of remembering and bringing infantile wishes to awareness, the patient instead continues to push for their gratification from the analyst. Rather than gratify these wishes, the analyst interprets.

Countertransference

Given the importance it has assumed in the contemporary psychoanalytic literature, there are remarkably few references to countertransference in the corpus of Freud's writing. Indeed, I could find only one instance where Freud (1910b) actually uses the term "counter-transference." He writes:

We have become aware of the "counter-transference," which arises in [the physician] as a result of the patient's influence on his unconscious feelings, and we are almost inclined to insist that he shall recognize this counter-transference in himself and overcome it.... We have noticed that no psychoanalyst goes further than his own complexes and internal resistances permit. (pp. 144–145)

In the other three instances where Freud (1914/1915) points to the dangers of the analyst returning and acting upon the patient's transference love, he is obviously discussing countertransference, but he uses the actual term in only one of these instances. In any case, Freud's suggestion is that when the analyst encounters countertransference problems in himself, he needs to engage in self-analysis. Although, as Strachey (Freud, 1914a, pp. 20–21, Footnote 2) points out, Freud expressed skepticism toward self-analysis and emphasized the importance of being analyzed by a separate person, he never explicitly linked these experiences of skepticism to the question of dealing with countertransference.

As we will see in Chapter 9, beginning with a paper by Heiman (1950), culminating in the work of Racker (1968), and continuing to the present day, not only was the concept of countertransference redefined, but its role in psychoanalytic treatment was radically altered. As we will also see, paralleling the reconceptualization of countertransference was an equally radical reconceptualization of transference.

Interpretation, self-awareness, and insight

As noted earlier, even when patients free associate successfully, insofar as defenses and resistances continue to operate, rarely does repressed material emerge into consciousness in an undisguised form (except in psychosis). Rather, what appear in consciousness are disguised derivatives of repressed wishes and fantasies. Hence, the analyst's interpretations are necessary to reveal the nature of repressed material, as well as the defenses against this material. It is interpretation—leading to insight and awareness—that is viewed as *the* primary carrier of therapeutic action in the classical conception of treatment.

What is it that the analyst interprets? Freud remarked that if a therapist interprets and analyzes the patient's resistances and transference, then whatever else he or she may be doing, he or she is engaged in psychoanalysis. As noted, Freud (1912b) viewed transference itself as a form of resistance insofar as it entails the patient's attempt to gratify rather than remember. However, analysis of the transference occupies a place of special importance in Freudian theory (and, as we will see, continues to do so in contemporary psychoanalysis) for a number of related reasons. (a) More than any other aspect of the patient's free association productions in the analytic situation, the patient's transference reactions reveal the core of the patient's neurosis.[3] Hence, by analyzing these reactions, one is targeting that core. (b) Because the patient's transference reactions occur in the here-and-now, becoming aware of them through the analyst's interpretations is likely to possess a greater emotional immediacy and cogency than other interpretations and is, therefore, more likely to lead to emotional insight and change. This is a point emphasized by Strachey (1934) in his classic paper on the therapeutic action of psychoanalysis and is also implicit in Freud's (1912b) comment that "when all is said and done, it is impossible to destroy anyone *in abstentia* or *in effigie*" (p. 108).[4]

Therapeutic or working alliance

Although Freud never used terms such as "therapeutic alliance" (Zetzel, 1956) or "working alliance" (Greenson, 1965), he did recognize the importance of rapport between patient and analyst and wrote about the positive transferring that need not be analyzed (Freud, 1912b), which one can think of as a precursor to these later concepts. Bach (2006) also notes:

> In a famous letter to Carl Jung, Freud wrote: "The [psychoanalytic] cure is effected by love" and a little more than a month later, at a meeting of the Vienna Psychoanalytic Society, he again commented, "Our cures are cures of love." (p. 125)

However, "cures of love" does not refer to the analyst's love for the patient but rather to the patient's love for the analyst, his or her desire to please the analyst, which, according to Freud, facilitates his or her acceptance of the analyst's interpretations. The point is that whether Freud was writing about the importance of rapport, positive transference, or cures of love, he was quite consistent and clear in noting that the importance of these relationship factors lay not in their direct therapeutic impact but in the degree to which they enabled and facilitated the therapeutic action of interpretation and insight. Thus, as the context makes clear, when Freud wrote about cure through love, he was referring not to the analyst's love for the patient but the patient's (transference) love for the analyst. Furthermore, the patient's love for the analyst contributed to cure

---

[3] Some analysts have maintained, in effect, that there are no other aspects of the patient's productions, only transference reactions. Thus, Gill (1982) and Gill and Hoffman (1982) have suggested that one view *all* of the patient's productions as either direct or indirect allusions to the analyst.

[4] Despite the widespread assumption regarding the special therapeutic stance of transference interpretation, there is little consistent empirical evidence that transference interpretations are uniquely or uniformly associated with a positive therapeutic outcome.

because it paved the way for and facilitated the patient's acceptance of the analyst's interpretations.

Working-through

Freud employs the term "working-through" for the first time in his 1914c paper "Remembering, Repeating and Working-Through." It is invoked in the context of commenting on the patient's continued resistance even after it has been interpreted and analyzed. Freud writes:

> One must allow the patient time to become more conversant with the resistance with which he has now become acquainted, to *work through* it, to overcome it, by continuing, in defiance of it, the analytic work according to the fundamental rule of the analytic work according to the fundamental rule of the analysis. (p. 155, italics in original)

It is clear that Freud formulated the concept of working-through partly as a way of dealing with the frequently observed clinical phenomenon of patients seeming to have insight and yet showing no significant therapeutic change. It is likely that there is no clinician or patient who has not addressed this question. Freud's response to this question in the passage cited above is, in effect, that one cannot reasonably expect the deeply rooted resistance to change or evaporate on the basis of the first interpretation or the patient's first experience of insight. Rather, the patient (and analyst) must repeatedly work through the resistances that, as Greenson (1967) puts it, "prevent insight from leading to change" (p. 42).

It is not entirely clear what Freud means by working-through. In the above cited passage, he suggests that it consists mainly in "continuing, in defiance of [resistance] the analytic work according to the fundamental rule of the *analysis*," that is, continuing to free associate. However, this is quite unconvincing. I doubt that any analyst believes that merely continuing to free associate overcomes resistance and/or leads to therapeutic change. I think that there are more clinically meaningful ways of understanding working-through. One such way is provided by Freud's analogy between working-through and "abreacting of the quotas of affect strangulated by repression—an abreaction without which hypnotic treatment remained ineffective" (1914c, p. 156). By analogizing between working-through and abreacting quotas of affect, Freud is suggesting that in order for insight to lead to change, it must be accompanied by affect, an issue that soon came to the fore in the psychoanalytic literature in discussions of emotional versus intellectual insight. In this context, working-through can be understood as the struggle to have one's insights take on emotional meaning and conviction.

Working-through has also been compared to the work of mourning (Chodorow, 2007; Greenson, 1967) in, say, the death of a loved one.

Although one cognitively knows that a loss has occurred, there is at the same time an emotional refusal to accept the reality of the loss. That reality is fully accepted only slowly, over a period of time, in sort of a titrated way. One can view this slow process as a working-through of the reality of the loss, knowing and accepting that reality not only cognitively but also emotionally. It is interesting to observe that in this regard, in contrast to cognitive or intellectual knowledge, emotional knowing is inherently personal, that is, inherently part of oneself. Another way to put this is to say that whereas cognitive or intellectual knowledge is often third-person knowledge, emotional knowing (e.g., "I desire," "I fear") is inherently first-person knowledge. From this perspective, one essential aspect of working-through is the continuing process of rendering insights part of oneself, that is, transforming third-person knowledge into first-person knowledge and experiencing the affect that the latter entails (see Moran, 2001).

The mourning involved in working-through is due to the experience of loss in the recognition that one needs to let go of unfulfillable cherished wishes and fantasies or early object ties. In this regard, relinquishing wishes, fantasies, and early object ties is often experienced as a loss, and working through the reality is not unlike the mourning of any other loss. Waelder (1960) describes this process with great clarity. He writes:

> The situation is comparable to all weaning processes and to the process of mourning. After the loss of a loved person, the longing for the lost one breaks out time and again, and the realization that the beloved no longer lives or is no longer available, and that longing is therefore in vain, renews the pain each time. The persistently returning desire meets an equally persistent answer: "it is impossible"; and under the influence of this often repeated experience the longing is gradually blunted and the survivor eventually turns his interest to new objects. (p. 226)

One can also relate working-through to the associative rectification in regard to trauma identified by Freud in his early writings. Trauma, including loss, is often experienced as a foreign body that takes over all other mental activity for a long period of time. Gradually and slowly, the memory of the trauma takes its place along "the great complex of associations" (Breuer & Freud, 1893–1895, p. 9) and slowly becomes absorbed as part of oneself. Freud referred to the "wearing away" (p. 37) function of this associative rectification process. That is, the memory of the trauma takes its place alongside other memories and associations that constitute one's personality. In an odd way, one can think of the working-through of insights as similar in certain respects to the associative rectification of trauma. Both entail the *assimilation* of experiences and the slow transformation of experience from not being fully part of oneself to being fully part of oneself.

The nature of therapeutic goals

Like any other form of psychotherapy, the goal of psychoanalytic treatment is to relieve distress, particularly distress accompanying neurotic symptoms. However, the factors that distinguish the psychoanalytic perspective from other therapeutic approaches are the lack of a direct focus on distressful symptoms; the belief that a focus on certain process goals, such as conscious awareness of and insight into one's inner conflicts, will in the long run lead to more adaptive compromise and therefore to a more effective therapeutic outcome, including symptomatic relief as a byproduct; and the claim that because psychoanalysis, when successful, leads to structural change in the patient's personality, it provides greater protection against succumbing to neurosis in the future than other forms of psychotherapy.

There are various ways of describing the process and outcome goals of psychoanalytic treatment. Although I have not been able to track down the reference, Freud presumably summed up the outcome goals of psychoanalysis as the increased capacity for love and work, which, in a theoretical context, can be stated as an enhanced capacity for satisfying and mature object relations and more effective ego functioning. A basic assumption of Freudian theory is that when the impediments of unconscious conflicts, anxiety, guilt, and defenses are more adequately dealt with, the capacity for love and work will be enhanced.

Making the unconscious conscious

From the earliest days of psychoanalysis, a central goal of treatment was to make repressed unconscious mental contents conscious. Early on, the primary technique used to achieve this goal was hypnosis. As noted earlier, it soon became apparent that merely making a repressed mental content conscious does not guarantee that it will be integrated into the patient's personality. However, the same issues arise with regard to the use of free association and interpretation, as evidenced, for example, by distinctions between intellectual and emotional insight and invoking the concept of working-through. In light of these considerations, as well as the supplementation of the topographical model with the structural model, the therapeutic goal of making the unconscious was supplemented by the goal of "where id was, there shall ego be" (Freud, 1932/1933, p. 80).

Where id was, there shall ego be

A central feature of neurosis is not simply the unavailability to consciousness of repressed mental contents but also the experience of drivenness and compulsion. One feels driven and compelled by forces that are experienced as alien to oneself and to one's conscious intentions and aims. An overriding goal of psychoanalytic treatment is to transform this experience of drivenness and compulsion into an enhanced sense of agency and autonomy. Indeed, one can understand the goal of "where id was, there shall ego be" as essentially equivalent to "where drivenness and compulsion were, there shall agency and autonomy be."

How, according to Freudian theory, are the above outcome goals achieved? The broad answer to this question is through awareness and insight-promoting interpretations of the patient's resistances and transference reactions as they are revealed in his or her free associations and dreams. The expectation is that well-timed and reasonably accurate interpretations will help the patient become aware of and gain insight into his or her unconscious conflicts, anxiety, guilt, and defenses, including their expression in the transference and their roots in childhood. The making conscious of what has been rendered unconscious, it is further expected, will enable the patient's ego to consciously confront what he or she had warded off through repression. The safety of the accepting and nonjudgmental analytic situation, the titrated, well-timed, and tactful nature of the interpretations, and the adult status of the patient's ego also contribute to the patient's capacity to consciously confront warded off material without overwhelming anxiety. The patient's capacity to consciously experience hitherto warded-off material, in turn, strengthens the patient's sense of agency and better enables him or her to exercise greater choice regarding how the patient wants to pursue his or her life.[5]

Implicit in the above account is the idea that simply making the unconscious conscious is not sufficient to achieve therapeutic goals, for if the material that has been made conscious continues to be fraught with intense anxiety (or guilt), pathogenic defenses will remain in place or be reinstituted, and symptomatic compromise formation will continue or recur. After all, it is the anxiety consequent upon the return of the repressed that led to the outbreak of the neurosis in the first place. This suggests not only the importance of a safe, accepting, and nonjudgmental analytic attitude but also the equal importance of the detoxifying function of interpretation. As Friedman (2008a) puts it, the analyst brings the good news that the danger situations—loss of the object's love, castration, and superego condemnation—against which the patient is so avidly defending are no longer realistic dangers.

Thus, making the unconscious conscious is only one step in the therapeutic process. There is no therapeutic virtue in rendering repressed unconscious material if it remains unintegrated into the personality and continues

---

[5] It is interesting to observe that in their translation of Freudian theory into learning theory terms, Dollard and Miller (1950) write about the therapeutic value of lifting repression in terms of permitting the application of the individual's higher mental functions to the resolution of conflicts and problems.

to be experienced as an ego-alien foreign body, as, say, a consciously experienced obsessive thought. Hence, there is the supplementation of making the unconscious, with "where id was, there shall ego be" as the goal of psychoanalytic treatment. The latter speaks to the importance of successfully integrating into the ego the material that had been warded off from conscious experience. Such integration results in a more unified personality rather than one sundered and driven by conflicting aims, and it enhances one's sense of agency through expanding the province of the ego. As Freud (1918/1919) puts it,

> the neurotic patient presents us with a torn mind divided by resistance. As we analyze it and remove the resistances, it grows together; the greater unity which we call his ego fits into itself all the instinctual impulses which before had been split off and held apart from it. (p. 161)

Relinquishment of infantile wishes and fantasies

When a wish or desire is avowed as one's own, that is, when "it" is transformed into "I," the patient has the options, in Waelder's (1960) words, of attempting (a) "a solution of a conflict between instinctual drives and opposing forces ... in favor if the instinctual drives" (p. 225); (b) "a solution in favor of the opposing forces" (p. 225); (c) "a solution that is a compromise between the two" (p. 225) (of course, Waelder refers here to a nonsymptomatic compromise); or (d) a solution "through a sublimation of the drives ..." (p. 225). Waelder observes that any of the above

> non-neurotic solutions might have occurred, in the course of development, had repression not intervened and, by pushing the drive underground, prevented it from direct expression, on the one hand, and protected it from the influence of experience, on the other. (p. 225)

Waelder goes on to state that although "in a great many instances, the decision will fall against the gratification of the instinctual drive" (p. 225), "a solution in favor of the instinctual drive" may occur if the "opposition [to gratification of the instinctual drive] had been due to fear of dangers which frighten us no longer," thus rendering "opposition to the drive no longer justified or no longer necessary" (p. 225). Waelder then makes the very interesting comment that the latter solution "reflects, for better or worse, increased *courage*" (p. 225, emphasis in original).

Why should the option of pursuing gratification of hitherto repressed wishes be viewed as courageous? Why, if repressed infantile wishes cannot be reasonably gratified in reality, is it courageous to pursue them? Why not futile or foolhardy? Waelder's remark about courage and his comment that repression keeps drive impulses from being "influence[d] by experience" (p. 225) suggests that he, along with Fenichel (1945), believes that infantile wishes and fantasies can be influenced and transformed by experience and by virtue of becoming conscious and that rather than renunciation constituting a primary goal of psychoanalytic treatment, pursuit of these (somewhat transformed) wishes and fantasies is a reasonable option, indeed even a courageous one.

Waelder's range of solutions seems quite different from Freud's emphasis on the patient's renunciation and relinquishment. For Freud, given the "timelessness of the unconscious" (Freud, 1915b, p. 187), repressed wishes and fantasies are largely infantile and remain infantile and therefore leave the patient with little realistic choice but renunciation and relinquishment. Indeed, as we have seen, mourning and loss are experienced in response to the presumed necessity of relinquishment of cherished wishes and fantasies.

There are a number of questions and problems with the above formulation that need to be addressed. One question that arises is whether it is indeed the case that infantile wishes are, so to speak, immutable, that is, remain infantile despite the passage of time. As Apfelbaum (1966) has pointed out, it is this assumption that logically leads to the view that the only realistic aim of treatment is relinquishment (or increased ego control) of infantile wishes and fantasies rather than an alteration or growth in the wishes and fantasies themselves. Fenichel (1945), himself a Freudian and the author of the most authoritative systematic presentation of Freud's thoughts, writes of the possibility of repressed wishes "attain[ing] a belated maturation" (p. 569).

However, as I have tried to demonstrate, it is not at all clear that the logic of Freudian theory allows for the possibility that unconscious infantile wishes can develop and mature. Indeed, Fenichel's (1945) proposal that once repression is lifted and hitherto repressed infantile wishes become conscious, they can belatedly mature seems to run contrary to Freud's view, for if belated maturation were possible, why would Freud emphasize the necessity of the patient's condemnation and renunciation? The clear implication of Freud's emphasis on condemnation and renunciation is that because infantile wishes (and fantasies) can neither be realistically gratified nor transformed into realistic mature wishes, the only choices available to the patient are either to continue to pursue them or to relinquish them. It is clear that Freud views the latter choice as the more realistic one. Indeed, as we have seen, it is the necessity of renunciation that has led psychoanalytic theorists to stress the inevitability of mourning in a successful analysis.

Although Freud emphasized the necessity of renunciation, he contradicts that position in at least two ways. First, as noted in Chapter 1, at one point Freud suggests not only that repression is necessary because of the inherent nature of instinctual wishes themselves but also that repression itself allows the instinctual wish to develop "in a more unchecked and luxuriant fashion," to "ramif[y] like a fungus, so to speak, in the dark" and "to take extreme forms of expression" that are alien to and terrify the individual because of "the way in which they reflect an extraordinary strength of instinct. This *illusory strength of instinct is the result of an uninhibited development of it in phantasy* [emphasis added] and of the damming-up consequent on lack of real satisfaction" (Freud, 1915c, p. 149).

The other way in which Freud seems to contradict his position regarding the necessity of renunciation is his suggestion that it is the danger situations associated with infantile wishes and fantasies, rather than the wishes and fantasies themselves, that account for their association with anxiety and guilt and their repressed status. In both of these views, the danger attributed to instinctual wishes is more fantasy than reality. This is so in at least two ways. First, although parental punishment and disapproval in relation to these wishes may have carried considerable dangers at one time, that is no longer the case in adulthood. Second, it is not so much that repression is made necessary by the actual dangers of instinctual wishes but rather that repression itself, through preventing contact between these wishes and the light of experience, leads to fantastic exaggeration of their danger and power.

The very idea of condemning or *renouncing* infantile wishes and fantasies needs unpacking. Does it mean continuing to harbor certain desires and fantasies but not acting on them? Or recognizing (intellectually or emotionally) that they cannot be fulfilled but nevertheless continuing to desire? Does it mean that over a period of time and through a working-through process, one no longer continues to have these desires and fantasies or has them only in attenuated form? Does it mean sublimating them? Or are all of these possible outcomes of treatment?

Waelder (1960) writes that

> what usually happens is that over a certain period of time a wish that is persistently denied satisfaction is gradually given up; just as people forced to follow a diet, or to give up smoking, after a time—usually not a very short time—lose their craving. Such people may search for, and find, new gratifications instead. (p. 226)

It is not always the case that individuals, including analysands, necessarily give up wishes that are persistently denied satisfaction and cravings and longings that are renounced. Consider Waelder's reference to giving up smoking in the above passage. One needs to distinguish between former smokers who no longer smoke but continue to crave cigarettes and those who not only no longer smoke but no longer have a desire to smoke. Despite no longer smoking, in an important psychological sense, the former individuals remain smokers—in the sense that one's desires partly define one's identity; the latter individuals, though, are no longer smokers—their identity has altered. In that sense, one can say that they have experienced a deep change.

A similar distinction is relevant in the clinical situation. One needs to distinguish between therapeutic outcomes characterized by changes in the individual's desires and wishes themselves from outcomes character- ized mainly by greater ego control, including greater capacity to reflect on, desires and wishes that continue to be experienced and that need to be resisted. As an example of the latter, Eagle and Wolitzky (2009) discuss a patient who was repeatedly attracted to the "wrong man"—described as a "party animal"—who brought short-term excitement but also, in the long run, grief. In the course of treatment, she came to better understand the basis for her attraction, to reflect on and resist her temptation to become involved with this type of man. However, her spontaneous attraction remained essentially unchanged. One can compare her to the former smoker who no longer smokes but continues to desire to smoke. Although greater reflection and control may constitute good enough outcomes, I would view as a deep change a therapeutic outcome in which my patient was no longer spontaneously attracted to the wrong man but rather to someone who was more likely to play a more satisfying and constructive role in her life.

Actual wishes or symbolic equivalence?

One needs to introduce another consideration to the above discussion. If, because of repression, infantile wishes take on a fantastic form, a question that arises is the degree to which anxiety and conflict associated with these wishes are due to their actual, say, oedipal nature (e.g., incestuous and death wishes) or whether these wishes are unconsciously experienced as *symbolically equivalent* to oedipal wishes and therefore fraught with anxi- ety and conflict. For example, there is a question of whether conflictual and anxiety-laden ambitious strivings necessarily entail an unconscious fantasy to kill off and replace father, or whether these strivings are experienced as symbolically equivalent to killing off father based on parental communica- tions to the effect that "if you succeed in your ambitions and outdo me, you will be castrated," or "you will be destroying me." In the former account, because the individual harbors actual death wishes, therapeutic goals (as well as developmental processes) include conscious awareness, acknowl- edgment, and ultimately renunciation and relinquishment of these wishes. In the latter account, because, based on parental communications, the indi- vidual experiences normal strivings *as if* they were equivalent to killing off father, renouncing and relinquishment would hardly seem to be appropri- ate therapeutic goals. Rather, an appropriate therapeutic goal would consist of the patient becoming aware of and freeing himself or herself from an "unconscious pathogenic belief" that ambition and success are equivalent to killing or destroying father (see Eagle, 1987a; Weiss, Sampson, and the Mount Zion Psychotherapy Research Group, 1986; see further discussion of this issue in Chapters 8 and 11).

Integration of infantile sexuality into adult sexuality

From the perspective of Freudian theory itself, there are both implicit and explicit "mature" alternatives to renunciation and relinquishment of infantile wishes in Freudian theory. One alternative is the integration of various elements of infantile sexuality into adult genital sexuality. As Fenichel (1945) puts it, "the undoing of repression enables the infantile sexual strivings to participate in the development of the personality and to turn into satisfied adult sexuality" (p. 556). He also writes that after "warded-off pre-genital sexuality ... is free from entanglement in the defensive struggle, its forces are included into the genital organization" (p. 572). Indeed, that alternative is already present in Freud's (1905) description of genital sexuality. The question that arises is why renunciation of infantile wishes is viewed as a therapeutic goal when the alternative of integration is available. Implicit in certain aspects of Freud's own formulation, particularly his early predrive theory formulations, is the idea that it is the isolated and unintegrated status of infantile wishes rather than their inherent character that renders them problematic. If this is so, it would argue for replacing the therapeutic goal of renunciation with the goal of integration. That, I believe, is the true meaning of "where id was, there shall ego be."

Sublimation

Enhancing the capacity for sublimation is also identified as an important goal of psychoanalytic treatment. Freud (1905) defines sublimation as the diversion of sexual aims "to higher asexual aims" (p. 50) and observes that one possibility[6] "for remaining healthy when there is a persistent frustration of satisfaction ... is by renouncing libidinal satisfaction, sublimating the dammed-up libido and turning it to the attainment of aims which are no longer erotic and which escape frustration" (Freud, 1912d, p. 232). However, Freud (1912c) warns that because "not every neurotic has a high talent for sublimation," (p. 119) therapeutic efforts "to bring about sublimation of instinct are, though no doubt always laudable, far from being in every case advisable" (p. 119). One could add that the importance of sublimation is lessened when one does not place great emphasis on the necessity of renunciation.

---

[6] The other possibility "is by transforming the psychical tension into active energy which remains directed towards the external world and eventually extorts a real satisfaction of libido from it" (Freud, 1912d, p. 232).

Softening of the superego

According to Freudian theory, one of the goals of psychoanalytic treatment is the softening of the harshness of the superego. Its centrality as an outcome goal of psychoanalytic treatment has been most fully treated by Strachey in his classic 1934 paper. A question that arises, however, is the relationship between the therapeutic goals of softening the harshness of the superego and condemning and renouncing infantile wishes and fantasies. Are they compatible with each other? Terms such as *condemning* and *renouncing* do seem to connote, if not denote, a moralistic stance that one normally associates with a harsh superego[7] (see Kohut, 1984).

One could argue that softening the harshness of the superego and renouncing or condemning infantile wishes and fantasies are really not incompatible therapeutic goals but simply a poor choice of terms, insofar as the latter is—or should be—motivated by reality considerations rather than moralistic judgments. That is, in this view, one renounces and relinquishes the pursuit of infantile wishes and fantasies, not because they are morally bad but because insofar as they cannot be realistically satisfied, one's pursuit of them dooms one to frustration and neurotic misery. One can say, then, that in successful treatment, renunciation and relinquishment of these wishes and fantasies is a product of the ego's reality-testing rather than of the condemnation exercised by a primitive and harsh superego.

Although this distinction is often not entirely clear in the psychoanalytic literature, it is one that it is important to make, for the goal of softening the harshness of the superego seems especially pertinent, not only with regard to infantile and presumably unfulfillable desires and wishes but also in relation to realistic and age-appropriate desires and wishes that are subjectively experienced as bad and therefore elicit guilt and superego condemnation. Consider someone who, on the basis of early experiences and learning, guiltily experiences any sexual feelings, including age-appropriate ones, as sinful and worthy of condemnation. This is an obvious example where softening the harshness of the superego is particularly relevant. It is also an obvious example where the goals of renunciation and relinquishment make little sense.

Compare this example with someone for whom the persistence of incestuous wishes and fantasies is a prominent feature of his or her pathology. Here, too, the goal of softening the harshness of the superego is an appropriate one to the extent that these desires, wishes, and fantasies elicit paralyzing guilt, anxiety, and other neurotic symptoms such as "psychical impotence" (Freud, 1912a, p. 179). However, in contrast to the above example, the goals of renouncing and relinquishment would seem to make

---

[7] Talk about renouncing and condemning infantile wishes is undoubtedly one aspect of classical theory that leads Kohut (1984) to conclude that classical theory imposes an "adult morality" in the patient (see Chapter 10).

much more sense in view of the unrealistic and unfulfillable nature of these desires, wishes, and fantasies and in view of the fact that they interfere with the individual's capacity to experience sexual gratification and to engage in mature relationships.

It is this latter example that is more representative of a classical perspective. An account that attributes inhibition and guilt in relation to realistic and age-appropriate desires, wishes, and fantasies exclusively or mainly to early experiences would likely be viewed as superficial from the perspective of Freudian theory. From that perspective, an exclusive emphasis on early learning experiences would omit the role of presumably universal, inherently conflictual and problematic desires, wishes, and fantasies in accounting for sexual inhibitions, guilt, and anxiety. That is, as we have seen, according to at least one strand of the Freudian view, conflict, anxiety, and defense in relation to sexuality are not simply or mainly a product of having had the bad luck to have experienced early parental disapproval in relation to expressions of infantile sexuality but are also due to the inherent challenges represented by infantile sexuality, particularly by oedipal wishes and fantasies. From a Freudian perspective, repression of infantile sexuality is a precondition for functioning as an adult in a civilized society. Furthermore, if adult functioning is not to be compromised, the individual needs to renounce and relinquish infantile desires, wishes, and fantasies. Insofar as differentiated adult functioning is incompatible with the continued pursuit of incestuous wishes and fantasies, they need to be renounced and relinquished—quite independently of the degree of punitiveness of parental reactions.

Even in the latter case, however, the question arises of whether, in the Freudian view, the persistence of infantile wishes inimical to ego functioning is uniformly a feature of neurosis. As we have seen, Freudian theory essentially presents two not entirely compatible views of the relationship between id and ego that have implications for how one thinks of the entire question of renunciation and relinquishment and for how one understands the goals of psychoanalytic treatment. In one view, insofar as instinctual wishes are always a threat both to the ego and to the demands of civilization, they need to be condemned by the superego. On the second view, there is considerably less need for superego condemnation. Indeed, it is the condemnation itself, including its harshness, that needs to be altered in treatment. Once these wishes are exposed to the light of consciousness and reflection, the patient may learn not only that they are not monstrous and worthy only of condemnation but that they may be subject to belated maturation and integratable into his or her psychic life. In this latter view, it is not so much the wishes one harbors that are pathogenic in neurosis but their embeddedness in conflict, anxiety, defense, and above all, superego self-condemnation. It would seem that this assumption is at the center of

Strachey's (1934) emphasis on superego modification as one of the primary goals of psychoanalytic treatment.

Questions of human nature are very much implicit in this entire discussion of treatment goals. If one adopts, in Mitchell's (1988) words, the "metaphor of the beast" (p. 67) to capture one's conception of human nature, then renunciation and relinquishment of infantile wishes (forms of greater ego control) would appear to be appropriate treatment goals—as well as accurate descriptions of psychological development—insofar as renunciation and relinquishment are held to be necessary for adult functioning in civilized society. If, however, one rejects the metaphor of the beast conception of human nature, it is not at all clear that renunciation and relinquishment can stand as important treatment goals.

It is true, as we have seen in previous chapters, that in Freud's dominant view of human nature, drives and instinctual wishes are inherently threats to the ego and to functioning in a civilized society. Hence, they must be ever subject to ego control. Thus, it follows that renunciation and relinquishment, as well as delay and stimulation—all forms of ego control—are appropriate treatment goals. However, as I have also shown, in what one might call Freud's less dominant view, it is not so much instinctual wishes themselves that are threatening and pathogenic but the individual's anxiety-ridden and conflictual *attitudes* toward these wishes. In this view, the neurotic is not an explosive individual, likely to be overcome with the passion and aggression linked to infantile wishes, but rather is an overcontrolled and overcivilized character who is anxiety and guilt-ridden over ordinary sexual wishes and aggressive wishes having to do with assertion, competiveness, and ambition.[8] In this latter view, the appropriate goal of psychoanalytic treatment is not renunciation and relinquishment but rather self-acceptance and moderation of superego self-condemnation.

SOME CONCLUDING REMARKS

I want to summarize and highlight a number of goals of psychoanalytic treatment that have already been discussed but seem especially important.

If repression entails a "persistent expenditure of force" (Freud, 1915c, p. 151), the undoing of repression should result in the freeing of energy that had hitherto been devoted to repression. In other words, according to the logic of Freudian theory, not only greater self-understanding but greater vitality should be an outcome of successful psychoanalytic treatment.

---

[8] It is not at all clear that a classical analysis is the appropriate treatment for the former kind of individual, for whom the expression of instinctual wishes is not especially embedded in inner conflict, defense, and anxiety.

If the now adult patient becomes emotionally convinced that the danger situations are no longer dangerous, not only should this persuade "the ego to accept on trial something formerly repulsed" (Fenichel, 1945, p. 570) but one should see a marked reduction in anxiety.

Perhaps the most superordinate goal of psychoanalytic treatment is to enhance the patient's sense of unity of the personality. At the core of the classical psychoanalytic theory of neurosis is a riven personality at war with itself. From the beginning of his writings, Freud viewed as the essence of psychopathology the experience of aspects of oneself as an unintegrated, ego-alien foreign body. Hence, no psychoanalytic treatment can be considered successful unless hitherto excluded and unintegrated aspects of oneself become integrated into the personality.

When one combines "making the unconscious conscious" and "where id was, there shall ego be," the overriding psychoanalytic goal is one that encompasses a self-knowledge that is fully internalized, an expansion of awareness and consciousness, an enlargement of one's identity, and a greater convergence between what one knows and believes and what one feels and desires. The latter has been an age-old ideal and is captured by Confucius' testimony that at the age of 70, his sense of right and wrong and the dictates of his heart were one and the same.

Finally, no psychoanalytic treatment can be viewed as fully successful unless it includes at least a partial replacement of a chronic experience of drivenness and compulsion with a sense of greater autonomy, choice, and agency.

Part II

Contemporary psychoanalytic theories

Chapter 6

Conceptions of mind in contemporary psychoanalytic theories

If one can say that the essence of the Freudian conception of mind lies in the idea that the function of the mental apparatus is drive discharge, one can equally say that the essence of contemporary psychoanalytic theories of mind lies in the idea that the main function of mind is to establish, maintain, and preserve ties to others. Many of the differences between Freudian and contemporary conceptions of mind to be discussed in this chapter follow from these divergent starting points.

I should note another difference. Unlike Freudian theory, contemporary psychoanalytic theories do not offer a systematic exposition of the origin and nature of mind. There appears to be little interest in the systematic exploration of such topics as the origin of thinking, perception, reality testing, or primary and secondary process. Rather, the contemporary psychoanalytic literature focuses on limited aspects of mind, and it is these aspects I will discuss in this chapter.

The organization of this chapter is as follows: I begin with a contemporary critique of the classical view of the dynamic unconscious and the cornerstone concept of repression and then discuss alternative views of unconscious processes and defenses. A good deal of time is spent on presenting and critiquing a reconceptualization of unconscious processes as unformulated experiences. I then turn to a discussion of a conception of unconscious processes and contents as interactional representations. Finally, I present a lengthy section on the social nature of mind where I discuss and evaluate its different meanings in the context of the work of Mitchell, Stolorow and his colleagues, and others.

CRITIQUE OF FREUDIAN CONCEPT OF THE DYNAMIC UNCONSCIOUS AS A FULLY FORMED HIDDEN REALITY

A central critique of the Freudian concept of the dynamic unconscious is directed toward the view of it as a storehouse of repressed mental contents that are fully formed and that, when uncovered and brought to consciousness, appear unchanged from their original form. Fingarette (1963) refers to this view as a "hidden reality" conception of unconscious mental contents. According to this view, a mental content, such as an idea or a wish, remains essentially the same fully formed idea or wish whether conscious or unconscious. The appropriate analogy is that of a hidden object that then becomes visible—whether hidden or visible, it remains the same object. Mitchell's (1998) specific analogy is of overturning a rock and finding insects hidden underneath. These analogies are apt ones insofar as they fit Freud's (1926) perceptual metaphor of consciousness as a sense organ that perceives mental contents (see also Rapaport's 1967 elaboration of Freud's idea that it is the deployment of attention cathexis—hypercathexis—to mental contents that renders them conscious). Freud proposed that mental contents are inherently unconscious and gain access to conscious awareness through the illumination or perceptual function of consciousness. According to this view, just as perception of an external object does not change the object but reveals it, so similarly does perception of an internal object (a mental content) not change but reveal that object.

Implied in the hidden reality view is not only the idea that the object (i.e., a wish) remains the same whether conscious or unconscious but also that when unconscious, it is fully formed and not just a fragment or a vague or unformulated state of the object. To return to Mitchell's (1998) image of finding insects under the overturned rock, to say that the insects that were hidden are the same insects that are now revealed is also to say that all along they were fully formed insects, not simply fragments or vague outlines of insects. Similarly, the idea that once repression is lifted the wish or idea that becomes conscious is the same as the hidden wish or idea that was unconscious implies that the wish or idea was as fully formed when it was hidden as it is when it becomes conscious. Because we attribute beliefs, desires, wishes, and other mental contents to people even when they are not aware of or do not acknowledge them, we are led to think that these mental contents or entities are contained or reside somewhere in the mind—the unconscious part of the mind. When these mental contents are uncovered and enter consciousness, they do so fully formed and unchanged. This, in essence, is what Fingarette (1963) refers to as the hidden reality view.

This view, as well as the entire conception of the unconscious as a storehouse of repressed mental contents to be uncovered, has been radically altered in contemporary psychoanalysis on a number of grounds. For one thing, with the rejection of Freudian drive theory, there has been a marked deemphasis on repressed drive-related ideas and wishes. Also, quite apart from the issue of repressed contents, the very idea of the unconscious as a storehouse of fully formed mental contents of any kind is seen as untenable in the contemporary psychoanalytic and cognitive psychology literature and has been replaced by an alternative set of formulations and reconceptualizations.

Unconscious processes as implicit

One approach to reconceptualizing unconscious processes was proposed quite some time ago by the philosopher Fingarette (1963, 1969), who was influenced by Jean-Paul Sartre's thinking, has been elaborated more recently by Stern (1989, 2003), and has gained currency because of interest in empirical work on implicit processes in cognitive psychology. According to Fingarette (1969), many of the phenomena attributed to the operation of repression (as well as other defenses) and self-deception can be understood in terms of our avoidance of "becoming explicitly conscious of our engagement, [and avoidance of] becoming explicitly conscious that we are avoiding it" (p. 42). In other words, in these situations, we do not *"spell out"* "some feature of [our] engagement in the world" (p. 46). Furthermore, not spelling out is not a matter of a defect or incapacity but a policy motivated by the desire to avoid anxiety, guilt, or aspects of oneself that one does not want to acknowledge or confront. Fingarette presents an example of someone who has been a failure in realizing a particular ambition and then adopts the policy of not spelling out this assessment of the situation, as well as of having adopted the policy of not spelling out.

Sartre (1956) provides a similar example of a married woman who, seemingly unaware of the import of her behavior, permits her hand to remain in the hands of a man who is trying to seduce her. When his intention is made more explicit (in part because he is encouraged by her seemingly acquiescent behavior), she reacts with surprise and outrage. Sartre describes the combination of allowing her hand to remain in the man's hand and reacting with surprise and outrage as being in bad faith (*mauvaise foi*). From Fingarette's point of view, the woman has failed to spell out both her partial acquiescence to the seduction and her policy to not spell out her acquiescence. From both Sartre's and Fingarette's perspectives, this is a more useful and accurate formulation of what is going on than invoking the concept of repression. Or perhaps one should say that this formulation is intended to account for many of the phenomena that prompted the concept of repression.

Consider Freud's (Breuer & Freud, 1893–1895) own case history of Lucy R., which he cited to illustrate the workings of repression. Without going into the details of the case, Freud links Lucy R.'s conversion symptoms (the smell of burnt pudding and a smell of cigar smoke) to her repressed love for the employer and wishful fantasies that he returned her love. At one point, Freud says to Lucy R.: "I believe that really you are in love with your employer, the Director, though perhaps without being aware of it yourself." Lucy R.'s response is: "Yes, I think that's true." Freud queries further: "But if you knew you loved your employer why didn't you tell me?" Lucy responds: "I didn't know—or rather I didn't want to know—I wanted to drive it out of my head and not think of it again; and I believe latterly that I have succeeded" (p. 117). However, although "she even allowed herself to dwell on the gratifying hopes," once she realized the futility of her hopes, she "decided to banish the whole business from her mind" (p. 118). The point to be emphasized here is that although Freud refers to Lucy R.'s repression, she is certainly not totally unaware of her feelings of love for her employer and her fantasy that he will ask her to marry him (see Erdelyi, 1990; Macmillan, 1991).[1]

Deployment of attention and unconscious processes

What kept Lucy R.'s feelings and fantasies from becoming fully conscious was the fact that when she experienced certain thoughts and feelings related to her employer, she would divert her attention from them and push them out of her mind. (We all have various ways of pushing thoughts out of our mind, for example, by distracting ourselves with other thoughts and concerns.) This meant that these thoughts and feelings were relatively fleeting and likely were permitted to remain vague, that is, were not permitted to be further processed.

The deployment of the individual's attention plays a central role in determining both the length of time the mental content occupies conscious awareness and the degree to which it has been processed. In general, in regard to any mental content, one can experience the extremes of a vague, fleeting sense of certain thoughts and feelings or a clearly delineated set of thoughts and feelings (often verbalized) that are the center of one's attention. In the above example, Lucy R.'s experience can range from vague and fleeting feelings and thoughts in relation to her employer to a fully articulated or spelled out "I love my employer and I think and hope he might want to marry me."

The situation is similar for Sartre's woman who allows her hand to remain in the man's hand. Her experience can range from fleeting feelings and thoughts of sexual interest, flattery, and so on to a fully articulated

---

[1] Erdelyi (1990) notes the following exchange between Sandler and Anna Freud regarding repression, which suggests that they thought that it might not be an entirely unconscious process:

> Anna Freud: "Heinz Hartmann would say that it can become automatic."
> Sandler: "I still think there must be an awareness of the impulse to evoke the response."
> Anna Freud: "Hartmann and I discussed it at the time in 1936 and 1937. There must be momentary awareness."
> Sandler: "An unconscious awareness?"
> Anna Freud: "It could even be a momentary conscious awareness." (pp. 13–14)

"I know this man is trying to seduce me and I know that I am both tempted and reluctant at the same time." And finally, the experience of the man in Fingarette's example can range from vague and fleeting thoughts and feelings of disappointment, failure, and so on to the spelled-out thought (and accompanying feelings), "I realize that I have failed to accomplish X and I have great difficulty in accepting that this is the case." In each of the above examples, the individual's experience is characterized by minimal attention and minimal spelling out. However, it is important to note that in each of the above examples, the individual's experience could have ranged at any point on a continuum from minimal and fleeting awareness to full articulation. In other words, deployment of attention and spelling out (or processing) are not all-or-none matters but *matters of degree*. If this is so, it would suggest that with much clinical material, it is more useful and accurate to replace thinking in terms of a sharp dichotomy between conscious and unconscious or between repressed and nonrepressed with thinking in terms of "fuzzy categories" that are distinguished by matters of degree. As we have seen, if one asks whether Lucy R. was conscious of her love for her employer, the answer would have to be both yes and no. Similarly, if one asked whether Lucy R. was *un*conscious of her love for her employer, the answer would also have to be both yes and no.

Freud (1900) clearly recognized the role of attention (or as he puts it, "attention-cathexis"; see also Rapaport, 1951) in determining whether or not a mental content is in awareness. However, he did not seem to leave room for degrees of attention or, therefore, for degrees of conscious awareness. Rather, for Freud, if a mental content received attention-cathexis, it became conscious; if it did not or if attention-cathexis was withdrawn from the mental content, it remained or became unconscious.

Although degree of attention plays an important role in spelling out, it seems to me that implied in Fingarette's concept is an additional critical factor, namely, the extent to which one acknowledges a mental content as one's own. A mental content can be in conscious awareness and fully processed and yet not be part of what Talvitie and Tiitinen (2006) refer to as the individual's "narrative self-consciousness." That is, it can be disowned or at least not fully owned as part of oneself, as part of one's project and engagement in the world (see Eagle, 1984c). Thus, Sartre's woman may be able to describe fully every detail of what took place and might even be able to do so without acknowledging her interest and acquiescence in the seduction (i.e., articulate the possible meaning of allowing her hand to linger). Would not that kind of awareness, unaccompanied by personal ownership, be the kind of thing we mean by intellectualization? What Sartre's woman does not do is spell out the nature of her project, that is, her sexual interest and her desire to engage in the seduction while at the same time taking no responsibility for doing so. Although Freud (1915c) defines the essence of repression as the banishment of mental contents from consciousness, the kinds of phenomena the term is often applied to have as much to do with disowning these mental contents as part of oneself. Banishment from consciousness can be seen as one primary *means* of disowning unacceptable ideas, wishes, desires, and so on rather than constituting the essence of repression (see Eagle, 1984c).

Failure to make connections and unconscious processes

G. S. Klein (1976) has written that a central aspect of repression lies in the individual's failure to make connections among and to understand the personal import of certain mental contents that are themselves fully conscious. In other words, for Klein, what is unconscious or repressed is not necessarily a specific mental content but the *personal meaning* of that mental content. One can be even more precise. In a psychoanalytic context, to say that the personal meaning of a mental content is unconscious or out of awareness is to say that one is not aware of what that mental content points to with regard to one's desires, aims, defenses, and engagements in the world. Note, however, that this is equivalent both to Fingarette's notion of failure to spell out and failure to acknowledge a particular desire, aim, or engagements as one's own.

Before continuing this discussion, let me sum up what has been presented thus far:

1. The idea that the dynamic unconscious is a storehouse of fully formed mental contents that, when uncovered, appear in consciousness, unchanged in their original form—what Fingarette (1963) refers to as the hidden reality view—has been rejected in much of the contemporary psychoanalytic, cognitive psychology, and philosophical literature.

2. A conception of unconscious processes as implicit has characterized current views. In particular, I have discussed Fingarette's (1969) account of various phenomena that have been attributed to repression in terms of a motivated policy of not spelling out one's engagements in the world. In the course of this discussion, I have highlighted the roles of attention and acknowledgment of personal ownership in determining, respectively, the degree to which and the form in which a mental content occupies consciousness and the degree to which one's projects and engagements are experienced as one's own. Finally, I have noted G. S. Klein's (1976) reconceptualizations of repression in terms of a motivated failure to make connections and to understand the personal import of certain mental contents.

THE UNCONSCIOUS AS UNFORMULATED EXPERIENCE

I turn now to Stern's (1989, 2003) recent reconceptualization of unconscious processes as unformulated experience, which, in many respects, is quite similar to Fingarette's idea of the not spelled-out. I spend a good deal of time on these formulations because, as we will see, they constitute a radical alternative to the Freudian dynamic unconscious, an alternative that Freud appeared to consider and reject.

According to Stern, to say that a mental content is unconscious is to say that it is unarticulated, given neither definite shape nor clarity. As Stern (1989) puts it, unconscious mental contents can be understood as "thoughts not yet thought, connections not yet made, memories one does not yet have the resources or willingness to construct" (p. 12). In this way of thinking, it is not uncovering a fully formed mental content but rather formulating what was unformulated, articulating what was inarticulate, and giving shape through words to the inchoate and nonverbal that render the unconscious conscious.[2]

Hence, in contrast to the view that the unconscious consists of fully formed contents waiting to be uncovered and brought to consciousness in their original form, according to Stern's (1989) conception, "unconscious material must ... change in form in order to enter consciousness" (p. 12). The change, of course, is from the unformulated to the formulated, from the inarticulate to the articulate, from the not spelled-out to the spelled-out. The primary means, according to Stern, through which this change occurs is *language,* that is, through giving words to the wordless. Thus, one can say that for Stern, the unformulated is essentially equivalent to experience that has not been given words, and the formulated is essentially equivalent to experience that has been formulated through language. The Freudian unconscious as a "cauldron full of seething excitations" (Freud, 1932/1933, p. 84) has been replaced by a conception of the unconscious in terms of the unformulated, the wordless raw experience prior to its representation and formulation in language.

This latter unconscious is characterized by "feelings of tendency," "indefinable, extremely rapid sensations" (James, 1890), "felt meanings" (Gendlin, 1962), fleeting, momentary experiences that may or may not go on to be formulated or completed, and, if formulated or completed, can be

---

[2] Stern's notion of unformulated experience bears a family resemblance to Bion's (1967) formulation that the raw data of sensory experience—the "beta" elements—need to be synthesized by the mind—the "alpha" function—for ordinary experience to occur. From a Bionian perspective, the failure to formulate can be understood as "an attack on linking." Similar to the motivated failure to formulate, the failure to synthesize beta elements results in fragments or particles of experience rather than the already formed experiences banished from consciousness by repression.

done so in many different ways, depending particularly on the relational context of the experience. Hence, in this view, to formulate or complete the unformulated is more a matter of *constructing* than uncovering or discovering preexisting meaning. In this view, to make the unconscious conscious is not to uncover and bring to awareness a clear and determinate preexisting mental content (e.g., a particular wish of desire or intention) but rather to interpretively construct or complete a fleeting and indeterminate experience.

One can understand the affinity between this view and relational psychoanalysis or a so-called two-person psychology insofar as how the unformulated is formulated or completed—what it, so to speak, becomes—is determined mainly by the interactional context in which the experience occurs. Thus, there is nothing to be uncovered or discovered, only something (i.e., the unformulated experience) to be completed and *coconstructed* in interaction with another. In the therapeutic context, the patient's unformulated experience is formulated, that is, coconstructed in interaction with the therapist. This point of view fits very well not only with a general relational perspective but also with what one might think of as an offshoot of that perspective, namely, a near-exclusive emphasis on the choreography of the transference-countertransference interaction—with both transference and countertransference redefined to reflect an interactional perspective.

The interactional or relational motivational influences on the process of formulating the unformulated is reflected in the central ideas that anxiety plays an important role in determining whether or not one formulates unformulated experiences and that a primary source of such anxiety lies in the need to preserve certain relational connections. In other words, in this view, the failure to formulate the unformulated takes its place as a primary defense against the experience of anxiety. In this regard, the affinity between failure to formulate and "selective inattention" (Sullivan, 1956) should be noted.

Unpacking the concept of unformulated experiences

I believe that Stern's (2003) concept of unformulated experience constitutes an interesting and important contribution to understanding and conceptualizing defensive processes. However, I think it needs to be unpacked and clarified. According to Stern, a primary defense against dealing with threatening material is avoidance of further formulating or further encoding of this material. As discussed earlier, one primary means of avoiding further encoding or formulating is through not directing attention to the mental content, with the result that it remains vague and unclear. However, this is not the only way that selective inattention (Sullivan, 1956) can work.

There are at least three ways that one can defensively deal with unwanted mental contents and experiences. One, a person can fail to formulate them so that they remain unformulated and unclear. Two, a person can fully formulate them but, once they are formulated, give them only fleeting attention so that they occupy conscious awareness only momentarily and then remain absent from consciousness because attention is kept away from them.[3,4] Three, they may be fully formulated but not permitted to enter consciousness at all. This third alternative, it will be recognized, is the fully formed, hidden reality view rejected by Fingarette as well as Stern as untenable.

Consider again the example of Lucy R. Her feelings and thought about loving her employer and hoping that he wanted to marry her were certainly not unformulated and vague. They were fully formulated even if only fleetingly experienced in consciousness. As she reports, when she had these feelings and thoughts, she immediately pushed them out of her mind.

What about the acquiescence of Sartre's woman in her seduction? Were her feelings and thoughts unformulated and vague (alternative one)? Or did she have a fully formulated unconscious knowledge of her desire and role in the seduction that was never permitted her conscious awareness (alternative three)? Or, as seems most likely, did she have fully formulated feelings (sexual desire, feeling flattered) and thoughts ("I am acquiescing in the seduction") that, as in the case of Lucy R., were only fleetingly experienced and then banished from conscious awareness (alternative two)?

For Stern, the essence of defense is failure to formulate; for Fingarette, it is failure to spell out. However, there are some people who *do* formulate their experiences and *do* spell out their engagements but nevertheless defend against these experiences and engagements in other ways, for example, through intellectualization. They do not turn attention away from "forbidden" thoughts, nor do they fail to spell them out. In fact, they may dwell on these thoughts and may be virtual experts at spelling out their engagements. What is missing in these instances is not formulation or spelling out but *feelings and affects, as well a sense of personal ownership of their thoughts and engagements.*

---

[3] It may be difficult to distinguish between failure to formulate or encode—the consequence of which is a vague and unclear experience—and failure to attend to an already formulated or encoded experience—the consequence of which is a clear and fully formulated but fleeting experience. This is so because once the fleeting mental content has been banished from consciousness, it may then seem to have been vague and unclear. Nevertheless, the two alternatives are conceptually different.

[4] In certain respects, the two alternatives are reminiscent of James's (1890) distinction between fleeting and momentary states of consciousness, on the one hand, and unconscious mental states, on the other. As is well known, James rejected the latter and maintained that claims regarding unconscious mental states are better understood as instances of momentary conscious states.

The story may get even more complicated. For, as Rubinstein (1974) has argued, one can *mislabel* emotions and feelings. Rubinstein presents an example of a woman whose behavior clearly shows anger but nevertheless gives a different label to her feelings. This does not seem to be a matter of failing to formulate unformulated experience but rather of formulating an experience in a particular way—a way that appears to be defensively determined. It is likely that defensive operations are not limited to failure to formulate or spell out. Consider the defense of rationalization and, as a hypothetical example, someone who, along with his wife, is invited to a party and insists that they go although his wife is not interested in going. He may have strong feelings about going to the party, which he attributes to such reasons as not being rude, the importance of being social, and the like. Now, let us further assume that he knows, but has given it no more than fleeting attention, that a woman to whom he is attracted and with whom he has flirted in the past is likely to be at the party. We have here a complex combination of possible defensive operations: failing to formulate vague thoughts having to do with his knowledge regarding the woman's presence at the party, failing to attend to clear but fleeting thoughts about the woman's presence at the party, failing to link his strong feelings about going to the party to the woman's likely presence at the party, failing to formulate or spell out feelings and fantasies about what will happen at the party, and mislabeling the reasons and motives for his strong feelings about going to the party. In short, it seems doubtful that the concepts of unformulated experience and not spelling out cover all instances of defensively motivated behavior. In view of these considerations, not formulating and not spelling out should be viewed as just one category of defense.

Unformulated experiences and indeterminate content

Perhaps the most serious problem with Stern's concept of unformulated experiences is his (and others') view of them as indeterminate and therefore subject to many different possible formulations, depending primarily upon the interpersonal context of the experience. Stern (2003) defines unformulated experience as "the uninterpreted form of those raw materials of conscious, reflective experience that may eventually be assigned verbal interpretations and thereby brought into articulate form" (p. 39). He also characterizes unformulated experience in the context of defense in the following way:

> Instead of positing the intentional removal and continuing exclusions of content from awareness, as the repression hypothesis does, lack of formulation as defense means never allowing ourselves to interpret our experience in the first place. The refusal to formulate is quite simple;

one just restricts one's freedom of thought, and the "offending" experience is never created. (p. 63)

Why do these characterizations of unformulated experience constitute a problem?

If unformulated experiences are indeterminate, entirely uninterpreted, never created, and subject to many different possible formulations or conceptions, why would they elicit a defensively motivated failure to formulate? There must be some determinate content—whether characterized as "feelings of tendency" (James, 1890) or "felt meanings" (Gendlin, 1962)— that, at some level, the individual experiences as threatening in order for the unformulated material to trigger a defensively motivated failure to formulate further. To respond to a vague felt meaning as threatening, as something requiring the defense of refusing to formulate further already indicates some interpretation of the experience, some determinate content. However, if there is some determinate content, then the further interpretation or formulation of the experience is more a matter of a completion of the experience, that is, a formulation of what it points to rather than entirely a matter of an *interpretive construction* of it. It is answerable to the more or less determinate content of the felt meanings or feelings of tendency.

In short, although the experience may be vague or fleeting, in order for an individual to respond to some content defensively, he or she must have experienced some determinate content. And further, if this is so, then adequately interpreting or formulating the unformulated is not primarily (or only) a matter of *constructing* an experience but primarily a matter of *completing* an aborted experience, which, of course, when accomplished, is itself a new experience. This is another way of saying that if the interpretation or formulation is an interpretation or formulation of *this* unformulated experience, it is answerable to it. If the interpretation or formulation is not answerable to the unformulated experience or does not correspond to it in some way, then it is not a completion of *this* unformulated experience but, indeed, a construction of an entirely new experience. In that case, however, if the unformulated experience is so utterly vague and so without determinate content that it can be completed or formulated or coconstructed in virtually an indefinite variety of ways, then why talk about formulating or completing a particular unformulated experience? Why talk about refusal to formulate as a defense? What content is being defended against?[5]

---

[5] In taking the time for an extended discussion of this issue, I am partly motivated by the defense of a version of Freud's (1916–1917/1917) insistence that interpretations "tally with what is real [in the patient]" (p. 452) even if one no longer takes for granted that what is real in the patient is a set of fully formed mental contents waiting to be uncovered and brought to consciousness. I am, in effect, suggesting that insofar as unformulated experiences have *some* determinate content—even if vague or fleeting—then interpretations and

The paradox of unconscious defense

There is a seeming paradox that arises in regard to any concept of unconscious defense. That is, how can one defend against threatening content unless *some* threatening determinate meaning was experienced and unless one has some knowledge of the content being defended against? How can one know what not to know? One answer provided by Freudian structural theory is that the ego or censor unconsciously keeps certain threatening material from reaching consciousness. This answer, however, comes perilously close to positing a subpersonal homunculus that knows things that I, as a person, do not know. Another answer, provided by Sullivan (1956) is that the self-system prevents certain mental contents from reaching consciousness through the use of selective inattention. But again, how does the self-system—Sullivan's version of the ego—know what and what not to attend to? One can direct the same or similar queries to conceptions of defense in terms of not formulating and not spelling out. How does one know what not to formulate or spell out? As noted earlier, at some level, one must have formulated *some* determinate content in order to have made the decision not to formulate further.

I think one solution to the above seeming paradox lies in the following considerations: There are likely to be fleeting experiential cues that elicit what Freud (1925/1926) referred to as "signal anxiety" and trigger a "do not encode further" or a "do not attend further" response. Operating as a negative feedback system, the aborting of encoding and of attending then removes the anxiety, which reinforces the defensive responses. As Stern (2003) notes in his discussion of Sullivan, the fleeting cues can refer to a class of experiences, such as unfamiliar versus familiar. Because these cues elicits anxiety, one can fail to encode or formulate further any experience or mental content that has been processed only to the level of unfamiliar. In other words, one does not need to have fully processed stimuli in order to defend against them, nor does one need to know or experience everything about the material one does not want to know or experience. One just needs to know or experience enough so that the defensive response of "do not encode further" or "do not attend" or "do not think about" is automatically triggered.

An issue similar to the one I am discussing arose in debates some years ago about so-called "perceptual defense" and subliminal perception. An early finding in this area of research was that people generally showed heightened recognition thresholds for taboo compared with nontaboo material. That is, longer exposures for taboo stimuli were required before subjects recognized them. Did this mean that subjects unconsciously processed and

---

formulations of these experiences need to tally with that determinate content, that is, need to tally with what is real in the individual.

identified the stimuli in order to be able to defensively delay recognition? Was this evidence of unconscious perception more sensitive than conscious perception? A number of alternative explanatory accounts of the perceptual defense phenomenon were offered. However, one, in particular—the partial cue hypothesis—seems most relevant to the current discussion. According to that hypothesis, subjects needed only to discriminate partial cues rather than have fully encoded the stimulus in order to account for the results obtained (Guthrie & Wiener, 1966; Golberg & Fiss, 1969). For example, let us assume that the taboo stimulus word is *fuck*. Only the partial cue "fu" or even "something like fu"—which has a higher probability of being associated with *fuck* than other partial cues—needs to be processed or encoded in order to elicit a defensive response. This entire process, particularly, the implicit calculation of probability associated with partial cues, suggests the intelligence of certain implicit or unconscious processes. But it does not suggest a super subpersonal unconscious perceiver who precedes and is more sensitive than the conscious perceiver.

As another example of partial cues, in my doctoral dissertation (Eagle, 1959), a subliminally presented aggressive scene contained more jagged, angular lines than a subliminally presented benevolent scene, which contained more rounded and curved lines. Thus, before recognizing the meaning of the stimuli, the partial cues of jagged versus rounded could generate differential responses to the stimuli. The point here is that unformulated—the full meaning of the stimuli had not been encoded—does not mean indeterminate. Jagged versus rounded constitutes determinate meaning.

There are other possible processes and heuristics entailing determinate content of some kind that can influence the decision as to whether to formulate unformulated experiences. For example, as noted above, Sullivan (1953, 1956) proposed that the self system maintains its sameness by filtering out from consciousness and not further formulating fleeting experiences that are new and unfamiliar and therefore dangerous and allowing only familiar and therefore safe fleeting experiences to reach consciousness and to be fully formulated. Combining the partial cue hypothesis with Sullivan's proposal, one can see that instantaneous judgments of old versus new, familiar versus unfamiliar can be made on the basis of partial and minimal cues. In short, and to reiterate the main point, any notion of defense understood as not formulating unformulated experiences necessarily implies some determinate content requiring defense, even if that determinate content consists of partial cues or permits only such general judgments as old versus new, safe versus dangerous.

Fleeting experiences as guides to authentic feelings

It is a common view that unformulated, fleeting, felt meanings may constitute the most accurate guide to what is real in the patient, that is, to his or her true feelings and inner state. For example, it is redolent of Rogers's (1951) position that one's true feelings and attitudes are often more accurately revealed by one's visceral experiences—what we colloquially call our "gut feelings"—than by fully conscious and articulated thoughts. The latter, according to Rogers (1951) are more subject to "conditions of worth," that is to the condition of having met with parental approval and therefore are allowed to become articulated in consciousness. Thoughts and feelings that have been met with parental disapproval (in particular, withdrawal of love) remain fleeting and unformulated. Hence, it is precisely those fleeting and unformulated experiences, those nonverbalized visceral sensations, that reveal feelings and thoughts that have escaped the constraints imposed by conditions of worth. In this conception and in contrast to Stern, only a narrow set of interpretations and formulations will be true to the important meanings inherent in the unformulated experiences. Only a particular set of interpretations and formulations of the unformulated will be faithful to the individual's true feelings, that is, in Freud's (1916–1917/1917, p. 452) words will "tally with what is real" in the individual.

Whatever other differences between them—and there are, of course, many—both Rogers and Freud can be said to be psychological realists. That is, they both believe that there are real meanings to which fleeting, unformulated experiences point. Despite many differences, there is something that Rogers's visceral sensations and Freud's fleeting free associations have in common. Both point to inner states that have not been permitted to reach consciousness. In interpreting, labeling, formulating, or spelling out fleeting and often fragmented thoughts, feelings, and sensations, one sheds light on the individual's inner states and facilitates their entry into consciousness. In this view, only those particular interpretations that are faithful to the inner states that have been prevented from being formulated—by conditions of worth or by anxiety or by superego prohibitions—constitute veridical formulations or completions of the unformulated. Contrary to Stern's (2003) suggestion that the vagueness and fleetingness of unformulated experiences render them susceptible to a virtually unlimited range of interpretations in principle, in this latter view, only a narrow set constitutes completions and formulations of a particular set of unformulated experiences. In other words, only a narrow set of interpretations and completions tallies with what is real in the individual—that is, are more accurate—while the rest of possible interpretations, although perhaps plausible, do not tally with what is real—that is, are less accurate—and therefore do not adequately spell out or formulate the meanings pointed to by unformulated experiences.

As Stern (2003) notes, the early interpersonal theorists also essentially took the position that unformulated experiences serve as guides to what is real in the individual. He observes that "for Fromm, Schachtel, and Tauber and Green, truth, or value, resides more often in direct apprehension or immediacy; less often in verbal communication" (p. 8). For these theorists, "once experience is organized and worded, its truth value has probably been irreversibly diluted or irretrievably lost, a casualty of the 'social filter'" (p. 8). From a somewhat different perspective, these theorists, like Rogers and Freud, also appear to take the position that fleeting and unformulated experiences, the unverbalized, the unworded, and the unarticulated may be far more revealing of who one is, of one's true feelings and attitudes than fully articulated and formulated experiences, which are more likely to be corrupted or diluted by the social filter (their version of Rogers's conditions of worth).

This conception of unformulated experiences represents what might be called a romantic view of the unconscious in which it is seen as a source of an unspoiled mode of experience that has not yet been shaped by the social filter, is devoid of guile and deliberation, and is therefore a source of truth and authenticity most revealing of who one really is and of one's true feelings and attitudes—a kind of noble savage of the mind.

Interestingly and ironically, in certain respects—but only in certain respects—this conception of the unconscious is not too different from Freud's view. Freud (1932/1933) remarks that the id represents the individual's real or true self, that is, his or her true wishes and impulses, unchecked and unmodified by the exigencies of reality and defense (ego) and social inhibitions and expectations (superego). For Freud, too, modes of experience that have not been screened through the social filter (i.e., the censor) are most revealing of the individual's true self. Of course, a central difference between Fromm's and Freud's views, however, lies in what they believe constitute the individual's real or true self prior to being shaped by the social filter. For Fromm, Schachtel, and Tauber and Green, the presocial self and presocial cognition and feelings are fresh, guileless, unspoiled, and innocently truthful.

For Freud, what lies beneath the social or socialized self are sexual and aggressive drive impulses, an image that Mitchell (1988) refers to as the "metaphor of the beast" (p. 67). It is a self that is inimical to and cannot be tolerated by society and needs to be tuned and socialized. For Fromm and others, what lies beneath the social self is the guileless self of the innocent child, which, for different reasons, also cannot be tolerated by society and needs to be, if not tamed, certainly socialized (one is reminded of the innocence of Dostoevsky's Prince Myshkin, ironically referred to as "The Idiot"). Without such socialization, neither the beast who knows neither inhibitions nor rules, nor the innocent who knows no guile can be tolerated by society or can survive in a complex society. Therefore, in both cases, the presocial—sexual and aggressive impulses in the one case, and unformulated experiences in the other—is relegated to the unconscious. In the former case, it is banished from consciousness, that is, repressed; in the latter case, it is left unformulated and not permitted to reach the level of verbalized explicit consciousness. If it does reach that level of formulation, we are told by Fromm, Schachtel, and Tauber and Green that it is likely to have already lost its innocence, immediacy, and capacity to reveal truth and authenticity.

There seems to be somewhat of a paradox in the latter view. For if one is to reflect on and avail oneself of the presumed wisdom and value potentially inherent in unformulated experiences, one must have some kind of conscious access to them, but this means formulating them and subjecting them to words. However, if Fromm, Schachtel, and the others are correct, once experience is organized and worded, its truth value is likely to have been irreversibly diluted or irretrievably lost, a casualty of the social filter (Stern, 2003, p. 8).

Perhaps the paradox is resolved if one takes the position that one can allow gut feelings, intuitions, and similar unformulated experiences to enter consciousness without immediately and prematurely subjecting them to verbal formulation and screening by the social filter. Isn't this what we mean when we advise ourselves to listen to our gut feelings? Such listening is not simply a matter of formulating the unformulated but also of attending to and reflecting on what the unformulated tells us.

It is true (at least in part) that attending to and reflecting on unformulated experiences, such as gut feelings, entails some steps toward formulating them, but not entirely. For, in attending to and reflecting on unformulated experiences, in, so to speak, capturing them, one wants to preserve the integrity and specialness of the immediate and direct experience. There is a special cogency about visceral responses that is often lacking in fully formulated, reasoned experiences. It is the very qualities of their fleetingness, their intuitive and visceral feel, their *non*verbal and *non*fully formulated nature that make them potentially valuable guides to where we stand. This, of course, is precisely that point the Fromm, Schachtel, and the others must have in mind. The preservation of these qualities is what distinguishes openness to these experiences and authentic heeding of them from navelgazing and intellectualization. Whereas one can intellectually understand oneself in a third-person mode (what Moran, 2001, refers to as theoretical understanding), a gut feeling is inherently first-person; it is experienced in one's body.

Consider as an example, Mr. X's experience of a fleeting "sinking feeling" in anticipating accepting a job offer. Let us also imagine that when offered the job he thought it was something he should accept and, if asked or if he asked himself how he felt about the job offer, his response would be something like "wonderful," "terrific." At the very least, the fleeting sinking feeling tells us and tells Mr. X that the story is more complex than simply what the "wonderful" and "terrific" responses suggest. The issue here is not simply or perhaps not primarily that Mr. X needs to verbally formulate the unformulated experience and put it into the words sinking feeling. Mr. X probably already knows how to describe that visceral sensation.

Let us further assume that Mr. X is not severely alexythymic, that is, he is not someone who cannot find words for his feelings and sensations, and that he does not have a repressive style, that is, he is not someone who does not allow physiological sensations to be consciously experienced. In short, let us assume that Mr. X does consciously experience a visceral sensation that he can identify as a sinking feeling. What is not fully formulated is what the sinking feeling *means*, that is, its possible connection to Mr. X's feelings regarding the prospect of accepting the job offer. Mr. X is not fully exploiting the adaptive value of the visceral sensations of a sinking feeling in pointing to an inner reality in the same manner that perception points to an outer reality (Damasio, 1994).

Mr. X could go on to formulate and describe the sensation of sinking feeling itself in great detail, which would very likely be of little use to him. Indeed, such behavior could serve as an example of what I referred to above as navel-gazing and intellectualization. It would take Mr. X away from focusing on the meaning of the sinking feeling, what it is telling him about his fears, ambivalences, fantasies, and so on that are omitted from and conflict with the responses of "wonderful" and "terrific." What Mr. X needs to do is allow the sinking feeling to be captured *without* a change in form and then be able to reflect on the meaning of the unformulated fleeting experience.

This example indicates that, at least the way I understand the conception of the unformulated, formulating the unformulated is not always a matter of completing the vague and incomplete but of reflecting on, articulating, and explicating the meaning of fleeting nonverbalized experiences that themselves cannot and need not be formulated any further. After all, how does one more fully describe or formulate a fleeting sinking feeling?

As noted above, G. S. Klein (1976) has argued that much of what is called repression consists in not being able—or willing—to make connections among experiences each one of which may be fully conscious and fully formulated. What is unformulated and needs to be formulated is an awareness of the meanings that are generated by seeing the connections among these different experiences. As we have seen in the hypothetical case of Mr. X, what needs to be formulated is the possible connection between the sinking feeling and the job offer. What is significant about the fleeting nature of the sinking feeling is not its fleetingness per se but its connection to those of Mr. X's attitudes and feelings regarding his new job that are not represented in his explicit and articulated conscious verbal response.

The emphasis on formulating the unformulated may come from the recognition that fleeting experiences, such as a momentary sinking feeling, can easily be ignored and sloughed off. As I noted above, one needs to capture them by attending to them and perhaps labeling them before they disappear altogether from experience—much as one needs to attend to and rehearse items in short-term memory before they decay and are no longer accessible to recall. However, as I have already noted, much of the important work of formulating the unformulated consists in interpreting the meaning and information contained in these experiences regarding our feelings and attitudes, what Fingarette (1963, 1969) refers to as our "engagements" in the world.

If one wants to preserve the immediacy, directness, and, so to speak, the presocial-filter authenticity of unformulated experiences and yet have access to them, one does not want them entirely to "change in form to enter consciousness" (Stern, 1989, p. 12), for were they to do so, they would lose their ability to serve as a guide to how we really feel and where we really stand. The trick is to both allow spontaneous unformulated experiences to enter consciousness—without prematurely formulating them and without too much change in form—and at the same time to be able to attend to and reflect on them.

This "trick" is relied on in the use of free association in the psychoanalytic situation. The rationale underlying free association is that following the fundamental rule of saying whatever comes to mind, without concern for propriety or rationality, will increase the likelihood of the emergence of unconscious derivatives. In the present context, one can say that following the fundamental rule will increase the likelihood that unformulated experiences will gain access to consciousness in a relatively unwilled and spontaneous way. The further assumption, the one that makes free association relevant to therapy to begin with, is that one's spontaneous and unwilled thoughts and feelings that emerge are purer indications and guides to what we really think and feel—to our true nature—than thoughts and feelings that are fully formulated and under our control. The latter are more subject to being screened by defense—that is, propriety, the social filter.

The assumption that what is unwilled and spontaneous is especially revealing of ourselves is not limited to fleeting and unformulated experiences. With regard to all experiences, both formulated and unformulated, we generally assume that spontaneous and unwilled behaviors that are not under the individual's conscious, volitional control can be most revealing of his or her true attitudes and sentiments or at least of hidden attitudes and sentiments that are not normally expressed. For example, accepting the wisdom of *in vino veritas*, we rightly react to say, someone's anti-Semitic rant while drunk (as was the case with the actor Mel Gibson)—that is, when his volitional controls were loosened by alcohol—as revealing his true attitudes and feelings that would not be directly espoused were he in better control.

The issue of unformulated versus formulated may then devolve partly into the basic issue of spontaneous and unwilled versus volitional and controlled. In other words, the authenticity of the unformulated noted by Fromm, Schachtel, and Tauber and Green, may be partly due to the frequent confluence between the unformulated and the spontaneous and unwilled.

Fleeting, unformulated experiences such as gut feelings or free associations are not the kinds of things that are under full volitional control, and to that extent, they may constitute a guide to those attitudes, feelings—to those aspects of one's inner state—that are *not* revealed in the formulated, the verbalized, and the volitional.

There is a good deal of research in psychology that supports the well-established assumption that responses that are not directly under one's control and/or that have a meaning of which one is not fully aware can be revealing of aspects of oneself that are not expressed by fully volitional responses and/or responses with a known meaning. For example, recent work on unconscious prejudice indicates that people who deny being consciously racist may still show a longer reaction time when asked to press the *good* key when viewing a photo of a Black person than when asked to press the *bad* key. The opposite results are obtained when the photo is of a White person. This occurs even when the Black figure is admired. Thus, conscious attitudes notwithstanding, implicit underlying negative attitudes out of one's conscious control are operating and influence reaction time (see Banaj & Greenwald, 1994).

It is worth noting the contrast between, on the one hand, Fromm, Schachtel, and Tauber and Green's emphasis on the authenticity of presocial experiences and, on the other hand, the position that the main task of psychoanalytic treatment is, through the use of language, to transform the subsymbolic into symbolic coding and the unformulated to the formulated (Bucci, 1997; Stern, 2003). It seems to me that the therapeutic value of attending to the subsymbolic and the unformulated does not reside merely in transforming or translating the subsymbolic and unformulated experience itself into the symbolic and formulated, that is, in finding words for the experience but also in grasping the significance of the experience, what it points to about one's feelings, conflicts, fears, desires, and so on. Although language may be helpful, at times necessary, to accomplish these tasks, it is not necessarily therapeutic in itself but is a means to an end.

What conception of the unconscious and, indeed, of conscious processes emerges from the above ideas of unformulated experience? In one sense, in this view, there is no clearly delineated category of unconscious but rather, as James (1890) argued (and, as Freud, 1915b, disputed), only fleeting and momentary conscious states, which may or may not go on to become formulated, depending on a variety of circumstances. It seems to me that implicit in Stern's (and Fingarette's) formulation is a basic distinction between a first order of prereflective consciousness—which is equivalent to unformulated experience—and a second order of reflective consciousness—which is equivalent to formulated experience. Looked at from the perspective of Freudian theory, this is essentially equivalent to the distinction between the conscious and the preconscious, with no category corresponding to the system *Ucs.*

UNCONSCIOUS AS REPRESENTATIONS

One approach taken in contemporary psychoanalysis, quite different from thinking of unconscious processes in terms of unformulated experiences and failure to spell out, has been to conceptualize unconscious processes and contents in terms of self, object, and interactional *representations* that are closely linked to beliefs, expectations, and affects and that have been acquired early in life in interaction with parental figures. Examples of representation include: Kernberg's (1976) object, self and affect units; Stern's (1985) representation of interactions generalized (RIGs); Beebe, Lachman, and Jaffe's (1997) "interactional structures"; Schachter's (2002) "habitual relationship patterns"; Bowlby's (1973) "internal working model"; the attachment patterns of Ainsworth, Blehar, Waters, and Wall (1978); the "unconscious pathogenic beliefs" of Weis, Sampson, and the Mount Zion Psychotherapy Research Group (1986) (which are essentially beliefs about the relationship between oneself and parental figures), Mitchell's (1988) "relational configurations"; and Fairbairn's (1952) internalized objects and internalized object relations.[6]

Accompanying the descriptions of unconscious processes in the above terms are an increasing number of references to concepts taken from cognitive psychology, such as "procedural memory," procedural knowledge," and "implicit relational knowing" (Lyons-Ruth, 1999). If one brings together all these different terms and concepts, they point to and convey the following set of ideas and formulations.

On the basis of repeated interactions early in life with parental figures, one forms implicit (unconscious) representations that constitute abstractions or generalizations of prototypic interactions. This is the basic idea intended by such terms as RIGs, interactional structures, and habitual relationship patterns. The RIGs or interactional structures we form are an expression, in the context of social interaction, of a basic tendency of mind, noted by cognitive psychologists, to abstract out general representations from repeated specific episodes and experiences. These representations reflect the contingencies of events and function as models or rules regarding what to believe and what to expect. Consider Nelson and Gruendel's (1986) concept of general event representations, which can be considered as the general category of which RIGs constitute a subset, and take as a simple example of such a structure the rules and representations involved

---

[6] Although there are important differences between the above concepts and Fairbairn's (1952) concepts of internalized objects and internalized object relations, one can legitimately include the latter as an early expression of an emphasis on unconscious representations in psychoanalysis. An internalized object is, of course, not literally an object but an internalized representation of an early parental figure; internalized object relations can be understood, in part at least, as internalized representations of prototypic interactions with early parental figures.

in the ordinary event of going to a restaurant. Even a young child who has been exposed to going to a restaurant a sufficient number of times will acquire implicit rules regarding what one can and cannot do and will be able to deal with a wide range of contingencies associated with going to a restaurant.

The RIGs or interactional structures one has formed early in life strongly influence one's expectations and representations regarding significant others, as well as one's corresponding self-concept. For example, if one has experienced repeated rejections, one's concept of the other would be of someone who rejects or does not meet one's needs, and one's concomitant self-concept would be someone who is unworthy and unlovable. It is likely that interactional structures precede differentiation between representations of self and other. The former can be thought of as analogous to conditioned responses insofar as they constitute a record of the contingencies between one's behavior and the environmental response. As conditioned responses—which even simple organisms are capable of—they do not require a delineated concept of self or other. The concept of interactional structure can be seen as an example of Mitchell's (1988) view that mind can be understood as "transactional patterns and internal structures derived from an interactional interpersonal field" (p. 17).

Although interactional, self, and object representations are described in the relatively cool cognitive terms of expectations and beliefs, they are suffused with strong affects and affective themes and concerns centering on such deeply emotional issues as love and rejection, self-esteem, abandonment, vulnerability, engulfment, intimacy, and autonomy. These issues and concerns are often also suffused with conflict (e.g., between seeking intimacy and fears of abandonment or engulfment) and defenses against the experience of dysphoric affects.

Because these representations have been acquired nonverbally early in life, they are often unconscious. However, they are unconscious not in the dynamic sense of being repressed but rather in the sense of being implicit. In this regard, they are more like habits or motor skills (e.g., riding a bicycle) that have been etched into the behavioral procedures in the body. In the language of cognitive psychology, they belong to the category of "procedural knowledge" rather than "declarative knowledge" (see also Lyons-Ruth, 1999, who has coined the term *implicit relational knowing*, which can be understood as procedural knowledge in the context of relationships).

Whereas, according to traditional theory, repressed wishes are recoverable once repression is lifted, insofar as early representations function similarly to procedural knowledge, they are not recoverable in the same way that repressed wishes and memories are. That is, one does not directly experience, in a first-person sense, a representational structure the way one would a desire or wish or memory. Rather, one can come to discern implicit repetitive relationship patterns in one's life (which is often the reason that people come for treatment). However, insofar as recognition of one's repetitive relationship patterns could just as easily be about another person as oneself, it is based on a third-person epistemology of observation, evidence, and inference and, as such, does not have the first-person authority of immediacy and avowal (see Moran, 2001). Rather than leading to direct access to representational structures or the repeated early experiences from which they were abstracted, treatment often facilitates recognition of, awareness of, and reflection on the patient's representational structures. It is the more or less direct, here-and-now experience of the patient's repetitive pattern in the transference that is presumed to provide the concrete first-person access to his or her representational structures (Strachey, 1934).

The emphasis on representations reflects the reduced importance given to the recovery of repressed memories in contemporary psychoanalysis (Fonagy, 1999). Patients can and do remember specific past episodes that often serve as a model or prototype of inferred repeated early experiences that are assumed to have played a formative role in the development of their representational structures. However, from a contemporary perspective, the therapeutic significance of recovering such memories lies less in the direct curative role of recovering memories per se and more in the fact that such memories instantiate the kinds of experiences that constituted the basis for the patient's representational structures.

Let me provide a concrete example of the kind of representational structure I have been discussing. Some years ago, I attended a presentation given by Beatrice Beebe, who showed a videotape of a mother asked to make eye contact with her 5-month-old infant. Each time the mother attempted to make eye contact, the baby turned his head away from her. However, mother persisted and, at one point, the infant's head was turned away from mother's looming face at such an extreme angle that it looked like it was swiveling, but mother persisted and finally, the baby suddenly went limp, losing all muscle tonus.[7] Now, imagine that an experience with the same structure—responding to the looming mother by going limp—occurs repeatedly, in age-appropriate ways throughout the child's life. Imagine further that as an adult, this young man seeks treatment because he cannot sustain intimate relationships and reports that when he gets close to a woman, he feels emotionally trapped and empty, and he becomes sexually impotent (limp).

According to the perspective being discussed here, one can say that, on the basis of repeated early experiences, the patient has abstracted out an interactional structure that can be characterized in the following way: When I am close to a woman, I experience her as looming and intrusive,

---

[7] As Rita Eagle (personal communication, August 20, 2010) has pointed out, why the baby refuses to make eye contact with mother is not clear; there may already be some difficulties in the relationship.

and I become emotionally dead.[8] Now, it is, of course, highly unlikely that the patient will be able to recover the experience he had at 5 months of age that represents a prototype of the above interactional structure. Of course, there will likely be many other specific experiences at later ages that have the same structure and that may be now available to episodic memory. However, as I understand the contemporary perspective, the therapeutic significance of recovering these episodic memories lies mainly in the fact that they instantiate the patient's dominant interactional structures and give concrete autobiographical and emotional content to what can otherwise remain as an abstract, third-person description.

That is, the patient can observe and infer the third-person description representations, interactional structures, and rules that may dominate his or her life in the same way that another (e.g., the therapist) can. Although this kind of insight and self-knowledge may be important and useful in treatment, it is essentially cognitive in nature. The memory of a concrete instantiating episode or the experience of a specific here-and-now interaction with the therapist may be necessary to provide the affective feel, the emotional conviction, the sense of "me-ness," and the authenticity necessary to give self-knowledge the first-person authority (Moran, 2001) often necessary for change.

What picture of unconscious processes emerges from all this? Most strikingly, one can observe a radical shift from the classical unconscious of repressed wishes, dominated by irrational primary process thinking, to a contemporary unconscious of essentially *cognitive* representations, which, although cognitive, are associated with strong affects. Any distinction between the "cognitive and dynamic unconscious" (e.g., Burston, 1986; Eagle, 1987a; Kihlstrom, 1987) becomes increasingly blurred. The contemporary unconscious is essentially a rational and reality-oriented unconscious. RIGs, interactional structures, and so on, are understood as pretty much accurately reflecting actual events, that is, as abstracted records of actual interactions with the caregiver. Thus, the unconscious representations of contemporary psychoanalysis, although reflecting the immature cognition of the child (Eagle, 2001), are not based on endogenous fantasies but are rather the result of implicit and explicit parental messages and communications. In other words, given the limits of the child's developmental level, unconscious representations reflect actual events in a reasonably accurate way. Indeed, what Bowlby felt was the excessive Freudian and Kleinian emphasis on fantasy and the neglect of the role of actual events in the life of the child was one of his main criticisms of psychoanalytic theory and one of his main motives in developing attachment theory.

---

[8] There is evidence that caregiver intrusiveness is, indeed, associated with avoidant attachment.

There is a position somewhere between exclusive emphasis on fantasy and exclusive emphasis on actual events as determinative factors. For one thing, as already noted, the child's encoding of events is limited and shaped by his or her developmental level, a factor that leaves room for the role of fantasies in the child's construal of actual events, even if the fantasies are not those posited by Freudian and Kleinian theory. The issue of the kinds of fantasies that influence the child's construals and experiences of events is one not to be determined *a priori* by one's favorite theory but by empirical evidence. For example, there is evidence that young children often react to traumatic events (including maltreatment) egocentrically by blaming themselves (Putnam, 2003), a finding that is congruent with Fairbairn's (1952) formulation regarding the young child's tendency to take the badness of the parent into himself or herself.

The fact of individual differences in temperament also suggests that the formulation that the child's representations accurately reflect actual events is oversimplified. For example, an infant with a high frustration tolerance is likely to encode, say, waiting X number of minutes to be fed as a good experience, whereas an infant with low frustration tolerance is more likely to encode the same wait as a bad experience. In short, temperamental differences are likely to play a role in the infant's psychic reality (Eagle, 1995).

As noted earlier, the unconscious status of representations is not mainly due to repression but rather is largely the result of their early *nonverbal* and implicit nature. Hence, unlike repressed unconscious wishes and desires, unconscious representations are not striving for expression in consciousness, and there is no counterforce requiring a "persistent expenditure of force" (Freud, 1915c, p. 151) to keep them from reaching conscious awareness. In short, they function like learned cognitive structures rather than dynamic motives. However, to some degree, the unconscious status of these representations may be the result of defensive processes that are similar to repression. That is, one may resist becoming aware of representations (as well as the episodes that instantiate them) because awareness would trigger noxious affects. Indeed, Bowlby (1984) refers to this process as "defensive exclusion." Also, as Bowlby and others have pointed out, failure to become aware of certain representations may be partly due to subtle family prohibitions against becoming aware and the consequent threat to object ties that awareness would entail. For example, becoming aware of parental rejection not only would evoke painful feelings associated with rejection but also would threaten an idealized parental image and ties to early parental figures (see Fairbairn, 1952, for a further discussion of these issues).

In summary, the unconscious of contemporary psychoanalysis is a very different construct from the Freudian unconscious. It is primarily a cognitive unconscious of beliefs, self, object and interactional representations, and implicit assumptions and expectations regarding how significant others will behave toward oneself (see Eagle, 1987a; Burston, 1986). One can say that we have witnessed a shift from an unconscious of infantile wishes to an unconscious of infantile *representations*. That is, rather than psychopathology being maintained by the persistence of infantile wishes, in contemporary psychoanalysis, psychopathology is maintained by the persistence of representations that were at one time adaptive but are now maladaptive. In the Freudian vision, psychopathology is characterized by the continued pursuit of infantile wishes that are unlikely to be gratified in the real world and that are in conflict with both other aspects of the personality and society, as well as by defenses against the conscious experiences and acknowledgment of these wishes. In the contemporary view, psychopathology is a product of such factors as negative self-representations that produce dysphoric affect, fixed and stereotyped representations of oneself and others that are based in early experiences with parental figures and that make satisfying adult relationships more difficult, and expectations and pathogenic beliefs regarding the kind of life one must lead if one is to maintain ties to objects. These views will be elaborated in subsequent chapters.

THE SOCIAL NATURE OF MIND

A central characteristic of contemporary psychoanalytic theories is their conception of the social nature of mind. This view is expressed in the contemporary psychoanalytic literature in at least two forms. One, as we will see in the next chapter, lies in contemporary conceptions of object relations. In contrast to classical theory, contemporary psychoanalytic theories are distinguished by their insistence on our inherent rather than derivative social or object-seeking nature. The second form lies in the assertion that the mind is socially constructed. These two views are not identical and should not be equated. To say that we are inherently social or object-seeking is to say that these tendencies are innate, that is, not socially constructed. Indeed, to say that our social and object-seeking tendency is innate is equivalent to saying that this tendency is relatively independent of social influences, as indicated by its transcultural, transhistorical, and even transspecies nature.

Bowlby's (1969/1982) account of the hard-wired attachment system as selected out in the course of evolution serves as a good example of an insistence on the biologically based innateness of our own social nature. The disjunction between asserting our inherent social nature and the claim that mind is socially constructed is also made clear by the following consideration: Imagine that in a given society, early socializing influences resulted in the construction of a mind that was primarily oriented to achieving gratification of sexual and aggressive wishes and that was not especially tuned to object relations beyond that function. In this hypothetical case, the social construction of mind would result in a mind that is not especially social. Now imagine, in contrast, that our social nature is virtually entirely innate rather than socially constructed and that this innate propensity is relatively immune to social influences. Here is a case in which our social nature is independent of social construction. In these hypothetical examples, ironically, the social construction of mind would result in an asocial mind, whereas an insistence on the innate social nature of mind would result in a conception of mind as relatively uninfluenced by social forces.

Mind as socially constructed

What does it mean to say that mind is socially constructed? One obvious and widely shared meaning lies in the recognition that one's mind is shaped by repeated early interactions with others, primarily but not limited to caregivers. Indeed, most would agree that one would not develop what we would normally call a human mind without being immersed in repeated human interactions. So, in that sense, mind is—almost literally—socially constructed.

However, the contemporary claim that mind is socially constructed goes beyond the recognition that, in a developmental sense, social interactions make possible the emergence of mind and shape the form in which it emerges. The claim that mind is socially constructed has been extended to include the more radical assertion that in its adult function—beyond infancy and childhood—mind is a product of ongoing and often varying social (intersubjective) interactions. In this view, mind is conceptualized not as a relatively stable inner structure but rather as fluid and ever-shifting responses to social influences and interactions. This view of mind is reflected, as Friedman (1998) has observed, in the focus of many contemporary analysts on the momentary and the fluid. In this context, to say that mind is socially constructed is equivalent to saying that mind is constantly being constructed by ongoing and ever-changing social interactions.

The social content of mind

I noted earlier in this chapter that in contrast to the classical view that the basic unit of mind is a wish or impulse (see Holt, 1915) and that the unconscious mind can be understood as a "cauldron full of seething excitations." The basic unit of mind in contemporary psychoanalytic theories is some form of interactional representation accompanied by representations of self and other. Thus, whereas in classical theory the contents and processes of mind consist in the intrapsychic vicissitudes of drive-related wishes, the representational contents and processes of mind in contemporary psychoanalytic theories have to do with *social interactions* between oneself and others. In other words, in the latter view, the contents that populate the mind and that centrally influence its concerns and operations are interactional representations. Mitchell's (1988) assertion that mind is made up of "relational configurations" (p. 3), Fairbairn's (1952) conceptualizations of personality structure in terms of internalized objects and object relations, and Kernberg's (1976) view of personality in terms of self and object representations linked by affects serve as good examples of theories of mind in which the components of mind are social-interactional structures.[9]

Intersubjective perspective of Stolorow and colleagues

The view that mind is constructed and constituted by ongoing social interactions is seen in the writings of Mitchell and of Stolorow and his colleagues. I begin with some representative passages regarding the nature of mind in the writings of Stolorow and his colleagues:

> Psychoanalysis is pictured here as a science of the intersubjective, focused on the interplay between the differently organized subjective worlds of the observer and the observed. (Atwood & Stolorow, 1984, p. 41)

> The concept of an intersubjective system brings to focus both the individual's world of experience and its embeddedness with other such worlds in a continual flow of reciprocal mutual influence. (Stolorow, Atwood, & Orange, 1992, p. 18)

> All of the collaborators of intersubjective systems theory have continued to work toward a fundamental and far-reaching shift in the concept of the human, from isolated minds and punctual selves ... toward a system embedded, context-conscious sense of experiential worlds. (Stolorow, Atwood, & Orange, 2002, p. 32)

According to Stolorow et al. (2002), the patient's experiential world is shaped by a "network of convictions, rules, and principles that prereflectively organize [his or her] world and keep [his or her] experiences confined to its frozen horizons and limiting perspectives" (p. 46). Furthermore, these rules and

---

[9] As will be discussed in Chapter 11, there were theoretical developments within a more classical drive theory tradition that also essentially, even if less explicitly, proposed the idea of the inherently social nature of mind but did so by reformulating the concept of drive and its relationship to objects. Freud's view of the relationship between the drive and the object is that it is a contingent one. Freud (1915a) writes that the object "is what is most variable about an instinct and is not originally connected with it, but becomes assigned to it only in consequence of being peculiarly fitted to make satisfaction possible ..." (pp. 122–123). In contrast to this view, Klein (1930/1964) maintains that there is no drive without an object; the drive and the object are inherently linked. However, it should be noted, as Greenberg and Mitchell (1983) point out, that the inherent link between the drive and the object is based on a concept of innate object images that are "wholly phantastic" (Klein, 1930/1964, p. 238). They also point out that it is Isaacs (1943) who makes explicit the ideal that desire always implies an object of that desire (see also Sandler, 1976).

principles have been acquired in childhood in the context of a relational field that, quoting from Stern (2003), "structures the possibility of knowing—the potential for what we can say and think and what we cannot" (p. 31). When the child perceives that certain experiences are unwelcome or damaging to the caregiver, "these regions of experience are sacrificed to safeguard the needed tie" (Stolorow et al., 2002, p. 47). When the child's experiences are not validated, they never become articulated, that is, in Stern's (2003) terms, they remain unformulated. Thus, for Stolorow et al. (2002), as for Stern (2003), the child's early interactions with his or her caregivers determines what contents or regions the individual will be capable of experiencing and what contents will be excluded and precluded from conscious experience.

For Stolorow et al. (2002), the influence of the interactional on what one can and cannot experience is not limited to childhood but is also operative in adulthood, for example, in the analytic situation. According to them, the patient assesses the analyst's receptivity to the patient's experiences, which, if deemed to threaten ties with the analyst, are kept from further encoding or processing. They do not attempt to describe the specific cognitive operations through which all of this occurs. However, one can bring to bear the earlier discussion and assume that the patient, both consciously and unconsciously, picks up cues from the therapist regarding his or her attitudes toward certain "regions of experience" and, when judging that defense is called for, institutes defensive operations such as failure to process further.

There is a curious inconsistency in how Stolorow et al. (2002) view the role of factors other than early interactions with parents in shaping experience. On the one hand, they appear to assume that the horizons and limiting perspectives created by early interactions with parents are frozen and remain in place thereafter. On the other hand, seemingly in direct contradiction of that assumption, they write that "the horizons of awareness are fluid and ever-shifting products both of the person's unique intersubjective history and of what is or is not allowed to be known within the intersubjective fields that constitute his or her current living" (pp. 46–47). Were the horizons of awareness so fluid and ever-shifting, why would it be so difficult to change them in treatment?

The work of Mitchell

I come now to the work of Mitchell, who also rejects the traditional view of mind as a stable structure and instead conceptualizes mind as the fluid, socially constructed product of ever-shifting social interactions. The following passages are representative of Mitchell's point of view:

> The basic unit of study is not the individual as a separate entity ... but an interactional field within which the individual arises and struggles to make contact and to articulate himself. (Mitchell, 1988, p. 3)

Mind has been redefined from a set of predetermined structures emerging from inside an individual organism to transactional patterns and internal structures from an interactional interpersonal field. (Mitchell, 1988, p. 17)

Human minds are fundamentally social phenomena that become focalized and secondarily elaborated by individuals. (Mitchell, 2000, p. xii)

An individual mind is an oxymoron. To say that an "individual mind" is oxymoronic is to say that no individual human mind can arise *sui generis* and sustain itself totally independent of other minds. (Mitchell, 2000, p. 57)[10]

That the very possibility of developing a human mind depends on human interactions seems indisputable and, today, relatively noncontroversial. That the mind is composed of "relational configurations" (internalized object relations in Fairbairn's terms) is perhaps somewhat more controversial and less clear, but also defensible. However, somewhat puzzling is the assertion that "the basic unit of study is not the individual as a separate entity ... but an interactional field" (Mitchell, 1988, p. 3). Although analysts are certainly interested in the interactional field, for example, between analysand and analyst, for most analysts the basic "unit of study" is indeed the individual as a separate entity. Certainly, the patient coming for treatment comes "as a separate entity" and is the major focus of the analyst's interest.

If Mitchell means by "the individual as a separate entity" the individual uninfluenced by anyone or any social interaction, then, of course, the individual is not the basic unit of study in psychoanalysis (or anywhere else). First, though, who would maintain that such an individual exists? Second, to maintain correctly that there is no such entity as an individual or an individual mind uninfluenced by social interaction does not mean that the interactional field *rather than* the individual is the unit of study.

It is likely that Mitchell's emphasis on the interactional field reflects, in part, his reaction to what he perceives to be the neglect of the interaction between patient and analyst in classical theory. However, the fact remains that when Mitchell discusses patients he writes about the patient as a basic unit of study who, for example, struggles both to maintain ties to others and to differentiate himself from others (Mitchell, 1998)—although the patient's struggle may have arisen in an interactional field and may find expression in current interactions, including the interaction with the analyst.

One should not confuse and conflate, on the one hand, the claims that minds are shaped by early interactions with others and that much that goes

---

[10]Mitchell then acknowledges that "individual psyches with subjectively experienced interior spaces" (p. 57) do, in fact, develop.

on in our mind has to do with our relationships with others and representations of these relationships and, on the other hand, the claim that "the basic unit of study is not the individual as a separate entity" (Mitchell, 1988, p. 3). We may not develop a mind without being embedded in human interaction, the mind we develop may be shaped by these interactions, and we may be vitally concerned with relationships with others throughout our lives. However, none of these truisms implies that the basic unit of study in psychoanalysis is an interactional field rather than the individual as a separate entity. Indeed, insofar as the individual mind is the product of and reflects in its very structure the human interactions in which it arose and is embedded, it is the appropriate unit of study.

Perhaps Mitchell intends to say is that the individual and the individual mind cannot be studied *as a separate entity* in the sense that it cannot be studied apart from early and current interactional influences and apart from embeddedness in an interactional field. One can gain some insight into Mitchell's position by noting the influence on him of Sullivan's ideas regarding the concept of an individual personality. In declarations quite similar to Mitchell's skeptical statements regarding the individual as a separate entity and his striking assertion that the "individual mind is an oxymoron," Sullivan (1953) wrote that "the overweening conviction of authentic individual selfhood ... amounts to a delusion of unique individuality." He adds that "no such thing as the durable, unique individual personality is even justified. For all I know, every human being has as many personalities as he has interpersonal relations" (p. 221). As Mitchell (1988) writes, "in Sullivan's way of thinking, people are not separate entities, but participants in interactions with actual others and with 'personifications' (or 'representations') of others derived from interactions with actual others" (p. 25).

I must confess that I find this passage totally confusing and virtually incoherent. How can one be a participant in an interaction with actual others without being a separate entity? And how can one interact with actual others without these others also being separate entities? Is the puzzle due to the equation of a separate entity with something like "totally self-enclosed and isolated entity"? Of course, one can be a separate entity without being totally self-enclosed and isolated.[11]

One can make a similar point with regard to Mitchell's (1998) rejection of the traditional claims "that the central dynamics relevant to the analytic process are preorganized in the patient's mind and that the analyst is in a privileged position to gain access to them" (p. 18). In this statement, a rejection of certain aspects of the classic analytic stance has become transformed into the claim that the patient–analyst interaction constitutes and organizes the patient's mind, as if there were no stable organization prior

---

[11] I react in a similar manner to Winnicott's often cited statement that there is no such thing as a baby but only a mother–baby unit.

to and independent of these interactions. Or, to put it simply, the legitimate idea that the analyst constantly emits cues that may *influence* the patient's state of mind is radically extended and transformed into the proposition that the analytic interaction totally *organizes* the patient's mind. Mitchell's position has led Meissner (1998) to comment that

> [i]t seems odd ... that one would think of the patient, as he enters the consulting room for the first time, as without a history entirely of his own without a developmental background, without a psychology and personality that he has acquired and developed in the course of a life-time, all; accomplished before he had any contract with the analyst. (p. 422)

Mitchell (2000) has noted that he is arguing against "the assumption that there is a static organization that manifests itself *whole cloth* across experiences" (p. 155, emphasis added) and has distinguished between pre-existing and preorganized. However, it should be perfectly apparent that one can argue against a conception of mind as static and entirely uninflu-enced by differential situations and interactions and yet recognize that the patient's mind is preorganized (what would a mind that is *not* preorga-nized look like?) and that the central dynamics that partly constitute that organization are entirely relevant to the psychoanalytic process. Indeed, a straightforward and legitimate critique of the idea of mind as static and unsusceptible to interactional influence would obviate the need for the pur-portedly clarifying—but actually incomprehensible—distinction between preexisting and preorganized.[12]

Some contemporary theorists attempt to support their social constructiv-ist conception of mind by drawing on developmental evidence suggesting that social interactions shape the infant's mental states and even the very possibility of developing any mental states at all and apply such evidence to adult mental functioning. However, they draw on developmental data very selectively. Yes, the developmental literature strongly suggests that social interaction influences the infant's mental states. However, an important

---

[12]It is far from clear that traditional theory assumes a static organization of mind. Indeed, a basic rationale for the blank-screen role of the analyst rests on the assumption that the patient's mind (and the association he or she produces) is anything but static and would all too easily be influenced by the analyst (i.e., would be too subject to suggestion) were the latter not to take a blank-screen stance. Also, although traditional theory may posit certain stable and inherent structures and motives (e.g., drives and drive gratification, defenses, conflicts), it hardly follows that mind is characterized as having a static organization. Indeed, the interplay of and compromises among different forces, motives, and structure of the mind, as well as what is elicited by different meanings of interactional situations (e.g., oedipal fantasies, fear of or opposition to authority), suggest anything but a static organization of mind. It seems to me that the criticism that traditional theory posits a static organization of mind is somewhat of a straw man.

distinction is made in that literature between caregiving that is characterized by a sensitive and attuned responsiveness to the infant's actual signals and caregiving characterized by the imposition and projection of the
caregiver's mental states on to the infant (e.g. Lieberman, 1999). In both
cases, the caregiver is helping to shape the infant's mental states. In one case,
though, the caregiver is responding relatively accurately and sensitively to the
infant's actual signals; in the other case, the caregiver is unable to distinguish between his or her own and the infant's mental states and imposes
those mental states on to the infant.

Even in infancy, there are limits to social influences that, when exceeded,
violate the integrity and inner nature of the infant. The infant is not a
tabula rasa, infinitely malleable to social influence. Although some contemporary theorists may be uncomfortable with anything that smacks of essen-
tialism, each infant possesses essential characteristics to which the sensitive
caregiver responds and the insensitive caregiver does not. Furthermore, if
there are limits to social influence in infants, there certainly are such limits
by the time one gets to be an adult, when one has developed relatively stable
mental structures that are certainly not unlimitedly malleable and unlimitedly susceptible to being shaped by social interaction.

One is reminded here of Winnicott's (1965) concepts of true self and false
self, implicit in which is a distinction between sensitive and insensitive caregiving. It will be recalled that for Winnicott the false self is a self of social
compliance. That is, it is the product of compliance with the caregiver's
impositions—a kind of "I will be who you want and need me to be." By
contrast, the true self flows from the spontaneous organic impulse of the
infant. For those who emphasize the thoroughgoingly social construction
of mind, any distinction between true self and false self becomes entirely
blurred. Indeed, the concept of true self is too essentialist and therefore
anathema to a thoroughgoing social constructivist view. Implicit in the
concept of true self is the idea that in optimal development, certain areas
of the personality need to be relatively *unsusceptible* to social interactional
influence. There is no room for this idea in a radical social constructivist
view of mind. From that point of view, not only is there no meaningful
distinction between true self and false self, but, to put it more sharply,
Winnicott's description of a false self is virtually equivalent to the social
constructivist's normative conception of the development of mind and self.

It seems to me that one can draw a useful analogy between the importance of a caregiver's accurate and attuned responsiveness to her infant's
signals—which partly depends on genuinely knowing his or her baby—
and the importance of the traditional idea that the analyst's interpretations
need to "tally with what is real [in the patient]." In either case, if mind is
entirely constituted by social interaction, then there are no independent
mental states in the infant for the caregiver to be accurately responsive
to, or, in the adult, nothing corresponding to the phrase "in the patient's

mind" for the analyst (or the patient) to be right or wrong about—a position we have seen taken by Mitchell (1998).

In rejecting drive theory, some contemporary theorists have also rejected any semblance of the idea of endogenous (i.e., not entirely shaped by social interaction) properties of mind—as if to leave room for these endogenous properties is equivalent to reintroducing some form of drive or instinct theory, or to put it more broadly, equivalent to adopting an essentialist conception of mind.[13] It is interesting to note that in his conceptualization of the two sources of ego autonomy, Rapaport (1957/1967) observed that the external environment (which, of course, includes social influences) enables relative autonomy from the inner drives and that the drives enable relative autonomy from the environment. In other words, for Rapaport, it is the endogenous drives that place limits on social influence. What Rapaport seems to be saying, more broadly, is that there are essential properties of the human mind that are relatively unsusceptible to social influence. Furthermore, when these essential properties are invaded or violated by social influence, to that extent, we lose our humanity and become social robots. Thus, in direct contrast to the contemporary perspective, and quite ironically, Rapaport locates the essential properties of being human in the endogenous drives rather than entirely in social influences.

One should remember that in George Orwell's *1984* (published in 1949), it is the private, drive-related arena of sexual love that represents the primary escape from social influence and is therefore a major threat to a totalitarian society. One should also remember that the word *totalitarian* as a description of a certain ideology and form of society is an apt one. It is intended to convey the idea of the *total* domain of the social, the total dominance of the social over the personal and the inner. In a totalitarian ideology, the Winnicottian idea of an inviolable inner private aspect of the self cannot be tolerated. In a certain sense, the aim of a totalitarian society is to shape and produce false selves, that is, selves of compliance.

Situationism, social behaviorism, and social construction of mind

The contemporary emphasis on momentary and fluid states of mind that fluctuate with each interpersonal interaction, noted by Friedman (1998), is curiously reminiscent of a theoretical position know as "situationism" that was influential in personality theory some years ago. As the term suggests,

---

[13] One should note that a thoroughgoing social construction of mind theory would seem to be hostile to *any* drive or instinct theory, whether it is Freud's dual instinct theory or Bowlby's positing of an inborn attachment instinctual system. It is irrelevant that in contrast to the asocial nature of Freudian drives, Bowlby's system entails an instinctual basis for our social behavior, for insofar as Freudian drives and the attachment instinctual system are endogenous and inborn, they are not wholly constituted by social construction.

the central claim made was that the situation the individual is in is a more robust predictor of behavior than supposedly stable inner traits. For example, in a classic study, it was found that variations in external situations accounted for more of the variance in predicting honest versus cheating behaviors in children than measurement of the trait honesty (Hartshorne & May, 1928). Not surprisingly, after hundreds of studies and papers were published on the trait versus situations debate, a consensus emerged to the effect that behavior is a product of the *interaction* between inner traits and external situations.

My point in citing this period in personality research and theory is to draw a parallel between situationism and the contemporary emphasis of relational psychoanalysis on the social construction of mind, as well as its more specific emphasis on and interest in the fluid states of mind that vary with fluctuations in interpersonal interactions. It should be clear that the role played by interpersonal interactions (or what Sullivan, 1953, called the "interpersonal field") in the psychoanalytic context directly parallels the role played by external situations in the context of personality theory. Both converge on skepticism toward the role of stable inner structures, and both emphasize the role of varying situations in determining behavior. Interestingly, not only was situationism generally opposed to trait theory but it was specifically critical of psychoanalytic theory of personality as a prime example of a theory that emphasized the overriding influence of inner stable structures, such as unconscious wishes, conflicts, and defenses on behavior.

Sullivan's (e.g., 1953) interpersonal theory—which has clearly influenced relational psychoanalysis to a far greater degree than is perhaps acknowledged—can be understood as an evident, even extreme, formulation of situationism in a psychoanalytic context. The most obvious expression of Sullivan's situationism is his statement that there is no such thing as an individual personality, only an interactional field. One could not find a clearer expression of situationism linked to the social construction of mind thesis. Recall that Sullivan was strongly influenced by the social behaviorist philosopher G. H. Mead (e.g., 1934), as well as social role sociologists, such as Cooley (1902). For Mead and Cooley, much of what is understood as mind and personality is a matter of social roles rather than inner structures.

There is much more to be said about this whole area, but the main point I want to make here is to show the historical intellectual lineage of the social construction of mind thesis in contemporary psychoanalysis—from Mead and Cooley to Sullivan to Mitchell and relational psychoanalysis. Mitchell's replacement of uncovering and discovering with "interpretive construction" and organizing of experience as psychoanalytic goals, his insistence that there are no clearly discernible processes corresponding to the phrase "in the patient's mind" about which either patient or analyst can be right or wrong, and his discomfort with the idea that the patient's mind is preorganized all can be related to both Sullivan's interpersonal theory and Mead and Cooley's social behaviorism.

UNCONSCIOUS MENTAL CONTENTS AND MOTIVATION

As noted, a central question that arises in considering the above view is the motivational force of unconscious mental contents. At the core of the classical conception of mind are the ideas that the major part of mental life goes on outside awareness and that unconscious mental contents exert motivational force in influencing mental functioning. With regard to the latter, more specifically, a core psychoanalytic assumption is that unconscious, repressed ideas, wishes, and desires continue to strive for satisfaction and expression in consciousness (and that such striving is opposed by other forces). Although this formulation has usually been described as a drive-defense model, the central idea that wishes and desires banished from consciousness may continue to be active does not require retention of drive theory—just as a focus on inner conflict in mental functioning does not depend on drive theory.

In any case, what I want to note here is that in the contemporary view I have been discussing, unformulated mental contents and experiences—the contemporary version of the unconscious—have little or no motivational role. Motivation enters the picture only in the form of the decision to not formulate. The contents themselves that remain unformulated, however, have no motivational role; they exert no motivational force on behavior or on mental functioning. What motivational force could a fleeting, unformulated experience that, if not formulated, attains no lasting representational status and therefore decays into oblivion have? Thus, the axiomatic psychoanalytic claim that unconscious mental contents and processes exert a major influence on personality functioning is absent in these contemporary views. Again, I spell out these implications not because these departures from traditional psychoanalytic theory invalidate them but to indicate the radical nature of these departures, which, in turn, raises the question of whether these formulations constitute theoretical developments in psychoanalytic theory or essentially replacements for that theory. Thus, one can legitimately ask whether a theory of mind that essentially replaces the dynamic unconscious with momentary states of consciousness and that assigns no major motivational role to nonconscious processes and contents remains a psychoanalytic theory of mind or whether it is best thought of as constituting an alternative theoretical framework. The virtue of the latter position is that it may better encourage looking to empirical data to adjudicate between alternative theoretical views.

Communicating versus experiencing

In the formulations presented, there is no discussion of a distinction between what is not experienced versus what is not *communicated*. As we have seen, Stolorow et al. (2002), along with Stern (2002) and Weiss et al. (1986), focuses on the influence of the relational field on what the patient is able or not able to fully *experience*. Surprisingly, for those who view themselves as intersubjective theorists, there is little emphasis on what the patient is willing or not willing to communicate to the therapist. If a patient judges that the therapist will not be receptive to certain experiences or, even more, that certain experiences—if communicated to the therapist—will threaten ties to the therapist, then the patient may decide not to communicate that experience. However, this is primarily a matter of the assessment of the therapists' receptivity and attitudes influencing what the patient communicates, not what the patient formulates or fails to in experience. Certain experiences may be fully formulated and yet not communicated because of the patient's assessment that the communication, in one way or another, will not be well received by the therapist.

I have noticed, as a therapist, that when I am not handling certain matters well, that is, when I feel and sound awkward or somewhat anxious, the patient will often change topics, as if he or she is giving me something I can manage better. I think this is often done in order to protect the therapist and the therapeutic relationship from what the patient assesses as a threat to it. Mutual exploration of these interactions is likely, I believe, to yield rich clinical material. However, it is also a fertile ground for collusion insofar as both patient and therapist are motivated to avoid the discomfort that such exploration might generate. In the present context, the point I want to make is that the interactions I am describing are mainly a matter of the patient not communicating certain experiences rather than failing to encode or formulate them.

Stolorow et al. (2002), Stern (2003), and other contemporary theorists appear to assume that when certain experiences are not reported in treatment, it is because they have not been formulated or encoded rather than because, although they are encoded, the patient has reasons not to communicate them—to this particular therapist. I think this is also the case in the study of Weiss et al. (1986). As noted above, they assume that the new material that emerges following the passing of tests by the therapist has not been experienced before rather than not being communicated before because it was experienced as unsafe to do so. In other words, although using different language and a different theoretical context, Weiss et al., along with Stolorow et al. (2002) and Stern (2003), assume that the therapist's attitudes and behaviors (e.g., receptive versus nonreceptive) will directly determine whether or not certain contents will be consciously experienced. They also assume that the new contents that appear following test-passing are new experiences or, at least, newly available experiences (i.e., unrepressed or formulated) rather than already available experiences that are *newly communicated* because it is now safe to do so.

It is surprising that Stolorow et al. (2002) and Stern (2003) minimize the role of communication insofar as a truly interactional or relational conception of defense need not be limited to elucidating the influence of the other (i.e., parent, therapist) on what the individual may or may not formulate or permit to enter consciousness—which, although influenced by interaction, is essentially an intrapsychic process—but may also include what the individual feels free to communicate to the other—which is inherently an interactional process.

Chapter 7

Conceptions of object relations in contemporary psychoanalytic theories

As we have seen in Chapter 1, according to Freudian theory, we develop an interest in objects and object relations mainly by virtue of the demands of drive gratifications and the need to avoid excessive excitation. More specifically, because hallucinatory wish fulfillment does not succeed in reducing the hunger drive, we are forced to turn to objects. As Freud (1915a) makes clear, in his view, the relationship between the drive and the object is a loose one, contingent on the fact that the object is "the thing in regard to and through which the instinct achieves its aim" (p. 122). A fundamental divergence from this point of view is at the center of contemporary psychoanalytic conceptions of object relations.

WHAT IS THE OBJECT?

Before elaborating on the nature of this divergence, which will constitute the bulk of this chapter, I want to first address Laing's comment that "it is still objects not persons, that are written of" (Guntrip, 1969, p. 387). Laing's comment raises the question of why we use the terms *object* and *object relations* rather than *humans* and *human relations* or *interpersonal relations*. I think that trying to respond to Laing's question may yield some important insights into what we mean by the terms *object* and *object relations*.

As Compton (1986, 1987) has elaborated in a series of papers, the term *object* (and, therefore, by extension, the phrase *object relations*) has diverse and complex meanings in psychoanalytic theory. From a strictly historical point of view, the use of the term *object,* as in object relations, seems to follow the tradition begun by Freud (1915a) who uses the term *object* (rather than, say *person*) as "the thing in regard to which and through which the instinct achieves its aim" (p. 122). In addition to historical precedent, there are substantive reasons to refer to object rather than human or interpersonal relations. One reason is based on the assumption that the young infant does not, as yet, have a conception of a person and does indeed respond to the object (i.e., the breast) rather than the whole person of the caregiver. As

Anna Freud (1971) puts it, the assumption is that the infant moves from love of the feeding situation to love of the breast to love of the caregiver; relating to "part objects" such as the breast does not end with the passing of infancy. All one needs to do for this to become apparent is to spend some time in a men's locker room and hear self-descriptions of being a "tit man" or "ass man" or "leg man." And, indeed, there is evidence that certain features of female bodies, including breast protrusion and a particular hip to waist ratio, for example, are more likely to elicit sexual interest in men across a wide range of cultures studied.

Another substantive reason to refer to objects and object relations is that it is literally the case that inanimate objects can play a vital role in the development and regulation of the infant. A striking finding reported by Harlow (1974) is that the mere inclusion of a piece of cheesecloth in the otherwise bare cage of the monkeys raised in isolation reduced their mortality rate. This is a remarkable testimony to the importance of, literally, the object in serving regulating function. Also, as the phenomenon of the transitional object (Winnicott, 1958) indicates, in the course of development, we relate to inanimate objects and rely on them to serve psychological functions also provided by persons. As Winnicott observes, in adulthood, transitional phenomena become spread out over the world of culture. What I take that to mean is that cultural artifacts and phenomena (e.g., music, art) become capable of serving the regulating functions originally served by the transitional object and the caregiver. As I have discussed at length elsewhere (Eagle, 1982), interests and values serve object relational regulating functions. That this is so suggests the wisdom of using the broader term *object relations* rather than *human relations* or *interpersonal relations*.

For the purposes of this chapter, I want to distinguish three different meanings:

1. Object as actual physical object, which can refer to people and other animate beings, as well as inanimate objects. In this context, to speak of object relations means that one has some connection to an actual and external physical object. This, in turn, implies that one has developed the capacity to have the concept of things separate from oneself. For example, although mother's breast may, in fact, satisfy the infant's hunger drive, there is no object relation unless the infant has developed a conception of the breast as a separate entity and has developed some connection to that object.
2. Object as a mental representation of an external other. This meaning needs some clarification. It has been argued that we relate not to the actual external object but to our mental representations of the object. This formulation, however, is, I believe misleading. It is intended to convey the idea that our experience of the object—and therefore of the object relation we form—is a function of our representation of

the object. For example, let us say that our representation of object X seriously distorts X's actual characteristics. It is then tempting to say that in relating to X we are relating to our (distorted) representation of X. However, it is not the case that we are relating to our representation but rather to *our version of X*. That is, however inaccurate our representation may be, our relating is pointed outward, not inward. We do not develop an affective connection to an inner representation of X but to an external X as represented by us.

Consider this issue in the context of transference. Let us say that I relate to my analyst as if he or she were a parental figure. One can say that I am relating to my analyst in terms of my parental representations of him or her rather than to who he or she actually is. However, I am still relating to this external analyst rather than to my inner representations. The problematic nature of my object relating lies not in my affective connection to my own representations—that would be truly solipsistic—but in the fact that I am relating to a version of my analyst that is saturated with parental representations. However, I note again that my relating is outwardly directed toward an object, not inwardly directed toward my representation.[1]

3. Internalized object. Obviously, one does not literally internalize or incorporate an actual external object the way one would swallow a piece of food. What, then, does one internalize when one internalizes an object? Fairbairn (1952) has remarked that the idea of an internalized object is based on Freud's concept of the superego. One can think of the superego as a set of prohibitions, beliefs, rules, values, attitudes, and so on—that is, a set of cognitive–affective representations—that are linked to early parental figures and that have been internalized. Much hinges on how one understands the process of internalization. Internalizing in the sense of acquiring a set of prohibitions, values, and so on from parental figures can be understood as ordinary learning and modeling. One can adequately describe this sort of internalization process without any reference to internalized objects. Why, then, internalized objects?

---

[1] The contrasts I have drawn seem quite relevant to Freud's (1915b) distinction between "transference neuroses" and "narcissistic neuroses" (pp. 196–197). He viewed the former treatable by psychoanalysis because, however distorted their transference reactions might be, these patients were capable of forming a relationship to an external object. Contrastingly, as the very term suggests, the narcissistic neuroses, he believed, were untreatable by psychoanalysis because such patients could not relate to external objects. Their libidinal investments were directed inward, not outward. I refer to Freud's discussion of the transference neuroses and narcissistic neuroses not because he was necessarily correct in his assertion that the latter could not be successfully treated by psychoanalysis but to note his recognition of the distinction between libidinal investment in external objects versus libidinal investment in oneself.

The answer lies in the consideration that the superego is often understood as an introject rather than a fully assimilated part of oneself. For example, many people refer to their conscience as an external object, a homunculus often depicted standing on their shoulder, telling them what to do and what not to do. This reflects the experience of the superego as both part of oneself and also not part of oneself, that is, an external object.

WE ARE INHERENTLY OBJECT RELATIONAL

Rather than viewing human nature as secondarily and derivatively object relational, according to contemporary psychoanalytic theories, we are *inherently* object relational, as Mitchell (1988) puts it, object relational "by design" (p. 21). This claim finds its clearest psychoanalytic expression in Fairbairn's (1952) dictum that "libido is primarily object-selecting rather than primarily pleasure-seeking (as in the classic theory)" (p. 82); one specific example of which is Bowlby's (1969/1982) positing of an inborn attachment system.

In the psychoanalytic context, an essential initial theoretical step taken in the development of this view was M. Klein's (1930/1964) insistence that drive and object are inherently rather than contingently linked.[2] However, to the extent that Klein retained the centrality of drives, her theory was largely rejected by Fairbairn and relational theorists. For example, Fairbairn replaced drive-related wishes with ego structures and internalized objects as central components of mind. In other words, a drive impulse or wish always entails a particular kind of object relation, that is, a role of oneself in interaction with a role for the other (see Sandler, 1976).

To say we are inherently object relational means, of course, that we are inherently *social* rather than asocial creatures. In the former view, infants do not need to be forced to turn to objects because presumed hallucinatory wish fulfillment does not work. Rather, they are immediately interested in objects, curious about them, show preferences for certain object configurations, and so on (see Eagle, 1984c, for a description of studies in this area). In short, we are immediately and inherently oriented toward objects in the real world, both human and inanimate.[3] This is a fundamental shift from a conception of human nature in which our earliest mental state is an object-less narcissistic encasement (Freud, 1915a, p. 137), a state in which our earliest reaction to objects is "repulsion" and "hate" (see Chapter 3) and in which we are reluctantly pulled toward objects by the exigencies of drive

---

[2] Given her origins in the Hungarian school, it is very likely that the influence of Hermann and the Balints played an important role in Klein's linking of the drive and the object.

[3] This is not to say that reality-testing capacities and functions do not develop over time. However, infants show a greater reality-testing capacity than is suggested by Freudian theory.

demands and the dangers to the ego of excessive excitation emanating from drive and from "narcissistic cathexis" (Freud, 1914b).

PRECURSORS TO CONTEMPORARY VIEWS

The claim that we are inherently object relational or social is hardly new and, in that sense, is not entirely contemporary. As early as 1933, Hermann, of the so-called Hungarian school, postulated a primary component instinct to cling in primates. And in 1935, Suttie had already disputed Freud's drive theory and insisted on our inherent relational nature. However, I refer to that claim as contemporary because it has finally been fully assimilated as a central unifying theme in contemporary psychoanalysis. There is a straight line from Suttie (and other early figures, such as Hermann and Michael and Alice Balint) to the American relational psychoanalysis of Mitchell and his colleagues.

There is a long history within psychoanalysis of objections to the view that object relations are secondarily contingent on drive gratification accompanied by an insistence on the autonomous and inherent basis for object relations. In the 1958 paper "The Child's Tie to His Mother: Review of the Psychoanalytical Literature" published in the *International Journal of Psychoanalysis* (and, with only a few changes, republished as an appendix in his 1969/1982 *Attachment* book), Bowlby presents an excellent summary of that literature, one that remains extremely useful and informative.

There is no point in repeating Bowlby's review. I do not think it can be improved upon. However, I believe it is useful, in understanding current views, to provide some sampling and a brief overview of the formulations and concepts of these early object relational theorists. As noted above, as early as 1935, Suttie disputed Freud's secondary drive theory and maintained that we are inherently object relational. A few years later, M. Balint (1937), of the Hungarian school, acknowledging his indebtedness to Hermann and to Ferenczi's concept of "passive object love," rejected Freud's theory of primary narcissism and proposed the idea of an autonomous "primary object-relation" that is present from birth. He writes, "This form of object relation is not linked to any of the erotogenic zones, it is not oral, oral-sucking, anal, genital, etc. love, but is something on its own ..." (Bowlby, 1969/1982, p. 372; see also A. Balint, 1949). In 1943, Ribble referred to the infant's "innate need for contact with the mother" (p. 273). However, as Bowlby (1969/1982) notes, she relates this innate need to satisfactory functioning of physiological processes, such as breathing and circulation and not to social bonding.[4]

---

[4] The work of Hofer (e.g., 2008) and others suggests that the mother's role in regulating the infant's physiological processes may constitute an important basis for later attachment.

As Bowlby (1969/1982) points out, one can find passages in the writings of Freud, Anna Freud, and Klein that suggest an independent and autonomous basis for object relations. Some examples: In distinguishing between the "affectionate and the sensual current," Freud (1912) writes:

> The affectionate current is the older of the two. It springs from the earliest years of childhood; it is formed on the basis of the interests of the self-preservative instinct and is directed to the members of the family and those who look after the child. From the very beginning it carries along with it contributions from the sexual instincts—components of erotic interest—which can already be seen more or less clearly even in childhood and in any event are uncovered in neurotics by psycho-analysis later on. It corresponds to *the child's primary object-choice*. We learn in this way that the sexual instincts find their first objects by attaching themselves to the valuations made by the ego-instincts, precisely in the way in which the first sexual satisfactions are experienced in attachment to the bodily functions necessary for the preservation of life. (p. 180)

Burlingham and Freud (1944) describe the child's need "for early attachment to the mother" as an "important instinctual need" (p. 22). And in a 1952 paper, in describing the infant's "unmistakable signs of love and a developing interest in the mother at a very early stage," Klein et al. observe that "such behavior implies that gratification is as much related to the object which gives food as to the food itself" (p. 239).

Although the above passages do point to a serious flirtation with the possibility of an autonomous object relational and attachment system, they are isolated thoughts and observations that are not further pursued or developed. Also, the ideas contained in these passages are incongruent with, indeed contradicted by, the main theoretical positions taken by these theorists. Contrast, for example, Burlingham and Freud's (1944) above brief comment with the following formulation by Anna Freud (1954):

> In the struggle for satisfaction of the vital needs and drives the object merely serves the purpose of wish fulfillment, its status being no more than that of a means to an end, a "convenience." The libidinal cathexis at this time is shown to be attached, not to the image of the object, but to the blissful experience of satisfaction and relief. (p. 322)

Thus, although Anna Freud and other ego psychologists, such as Hartmann and Rapaport, could accept the idea of the relative autonomy of cognitive ego functions from drive gratification, they did not take a similar step with regard to the relative autonomy of object relations.

However, as we have seen, others were prepared to take this step. This was true not only within psychoanalysis but also outside it. In academic psychology, Harlow's (1958) famous experiment with wire and terry cloth surrogate mothers—perhaps the most well known experiment in the history of psychology—was designed to test and ultimately refute Hull's (1951) secondary drive theory of the basis for infant-mother attachment. Harlow's reasoning was simple: If reduction of the hunger drive is the basis for the infant's attachment to mother, than the infant monkey should become attached to the wire surrogate mother, which provides milk. However, although the infant monkeys went to the milk-providing wire mother when they were hungry, they clearly became attached to the terry cloth mother, as expressed in such behaviors as sheer amount of time spent with clinging to it, returning to it when frightened or distressed, and using it as a base from which to explore. According to Harlow, the results decisively demonstrated that the "contact comfort" provided by the terry cloth surrogate rather than the hunger drive reduction provided by the wire surrogate mother constituted the basis for the infant's attachment—thus refuting Hull's claim that infant attachment to mother is based on the latter's association with tension-reduction resulting from satisfaction of the hunger drive (I will return to a discussion of the Harlow study later in the chapter).

OBJECT RELATIONS IN CONTEMPORARY PSYCHOANALYSIS

I turn now to an examination of the origin and function of objects and object relations in psychic life as viewed in the psychoanalytic theories of the British object relations school (primarily the work of Fairbairn), relational psychoanalysis (primarily the work of Mitchell), attachment theory, and self psychology. With the exception of self psychology, each of the theories can be viewed as some form of object relational theory. As Mitchell (1988) has also pointed out, "relational models" in psychoanalysis draw from a number of diverse sources, including the work of Fairbairn, Sullivan, Winnicott, Loewald, and Bowlby. And, as Mitchell (1988) has noted, despite these diverse sources, relational models have in common a perspective "which considers relationships with others, not drives, as the basic stuff of mental life" (p. 2). As noted, they also have in common the assumption that we are *innately* object-seeking rather than object-seeking as a function of the object's role in drive gratification.

The work of Fairbairn

I will spend a great deal of time on Fairbairn's formulations because they represent the most systematic exposition of object relations in the psychoanalytic literature. Fairbairn's concept of internalized object plays a key role in his formulation of the nature of object relations. The above reference to the superego as an introject helps one understand Fairbairn's concept of internalized object. The core idea is that one has internalized a set of interactional (negative) experiences that one has not been able to fully assimilate as part of oneself. One can use the analogy of swallowing a piece of indigestible plastic, which is now inside one's body; rather than being digested and thereby becoming part of one's body, it remains as a foreign object. Thus, for example, let us say that a child has been subjected to repeated experiences of criticism and rejection. Because they are so painful and traumatic, these experiences cannot be fully assimilated and, like the piece of plastic, are internalized as a foreign body, as a set of devaluing "voices" and felt "presences" within oneself—what Fairbairn (1952) refers to as an "internal saboteur" (p. 101). One can understand this idea as the child internalizing a critical and rejecting parent as an internalized object.

Although the inability to fully assimilate traumatic experiences is sufficient to account for the process of internalizing the object, Fairbairn (1952) also provides an additional motive for the process when he writes that the child takes the "badness" of the parent into himself or herself in order to keep the representation of the parent as good. The child needs to do this, according to Fairbairn, because to experience one's parents as unconditionally rejecting and unloving is intolerable. As Fairbairn (1952) puts it, "It is better to be a sinner in a world ruled by God than to live in a world ruled by the Devil" (pp. 66–67). If being rejected and unloved can be attributed to one's badness, then there is hope that by being good, one can earn parental love. If, however, rejection is unconditional, there is no hope.

In effect, then, Fairbairn offers a two-factor theory of the processes involved in internalizing the object. One factor is the child's inability to fully assimilate traumatic experiences, and the other factor is the motive to keep intact a representation of the object as good by viewing oneself as bad.

The two factors seem inconsistent with each other for the following reason: On the one hand, because the traumatic experience cannot be fully assimilated, the object is internalized as a bad object; on the other hand, because the child takes the badness of the object into himself or herself, the child is able to maintain a representation of the object as good. This formulation suggests that the object is both bad (and therefore not fully assimilated and internalized qua object) and good (and therefore, presumably, fully assimilable). The seeming inconsistency is, however, resolved by the considerations that the (idealized) representation of the object as good in response to traumatic negative experiences is due to defensive processes, and that, according to Fairbairn, the bad object is not only rejecting but also alluring and exciting. Indeed, according to Fairbairn, what makes the object truly bad is the combination of rejection and allure and the fantasy and hope that one can overcome the rejection and that the object's love will be earned and forthcoming. It is this fantasy and the inability to relinquish it that plays a major role in maintaining the individual's connection to the object. Taking the badness into oneself in order to maintain the object as good is one expression of this fantasy. As noted earlier, if one has been rejected because of one's own rather than the object's badness, then there is at least some hope that one may earn the object's love. One may say, then, that the representation of the object as good is a defense designed to ward off despair and hopelessness. One consequence of this defensive process is "splitting in the ego" (Fairbairn, 1952, p. 8).

Fairbairn struggled with the question of whether a good object could also be internalized as an internalized object. Given his basic assumption that the bad object is internalized qua object because traumatic experiences are not assimilable, it would make little sense to propose that the good object is internalized qua object. Good experiences, Fairbairn tells us, are fully assimilable in the form of ordinary learning and memory (see also Guntrip, 1969). They become part of who we are. Again, the analogy of eating and digestion is useful. If one swallows a piece of food, it is digested, broken down into amino acids, and so on and becomes part of one's body. This process is analogous to good, "digestible" experiences that become part of one's memory system, learning repertoire, and identity. If, however, as discussed earlier, one swallows an indigestible object, it cannot be broken down into constituents of the body but rather resides in the body in its original form as a foreign object. This process is analogous to bad, "indigestible" experiences that cannot be assimilated as ordinary memory and learning.

What, then, does it mean to refer to the internalization of good objects? It seems to me that, given the logic of Fairbairn's object relations theory, the answer is relatively straightforward. Good objects and good object experience are internalized as ordinary cognitive–affective representations that Freud (Breuer & Freud, 1893–1895) once characterized as constituting the individual's "great complex of associations (p. 9). They are not internalized as felt presences that are experienced, at some level, as critics and persecutory "saboteurs" lodged within oneself. Rather, they are experienced as ego-syntonic aspects of oneself, as part of one's identity.

The distinctly different psychological status of good versus bad objects is also seen in Fairbairn's (1952) comment that an important aim of psychoanalytic treatment is to exorcise the internalized bad object. Insofar as the internalized object is not fully part of oneself, Fairbairn's use of the term *exorcise* evokes the association of an exorcist freeing the individual from being inhabited by a foreign body. It would make little sense to talk about exorcising the good object because there is no unassimilated object to be exorcised.

One needs to distinguish, then, between the good object that is defensively created as a means of coping with intolerable bad experiences and the representations of good object experiences that, as noted, become part of one's identity and one's learning and memory systems. A hallmark of the former is a defensive *idealization* of the object that is not easily linked to actual concrete experiences with the object. Kernberg (1975) observes that a motive for idealization is to counteract the aggression directed toward the object and thus preserve some sense of a good object. This is somewhat similar to Fairbairn's formulation regarding the need to preserve some semblance of a good object.

There is, indeed, indirect support from attachment research regarding the relationship between defensive parental idealization and early experiences of rejection. There is evidence that an avoidant attachment pattern is associated with repeated experienced of parental rejection. A defining characteristic of an avoidant attachment pattern on the Adult Attachment Interview (George, Kaplan, & Main, 1996) is a narrative in which the individual selects highly positive adjectives to describe his or her parents (e.g., "wonderful") but either cannot support the general description with specific instantiating episodes or reports specific episodes that contradict the general idealized description. In other words, the idealized description appears to be a defensive response to rejection experiences.

Let me turn to another issue raised by Fairbairn's formulation regarding the child taking the badness of the object into himself or herself in order to maintain a representation of the object as good. I have already discussed the defensive nature of the good object representation in this process. However, I have not fully discussed what the idea of taking the badness of the object into oneself might mean. It is a somewhat ambiguous idea that needs further unpacking. In Fairbairn's formulation, one views oneself as bad as a consequence of being subjected to the voices of an internal critic or internal saboteur telling one that one is bad—much like the experience of a primitive and harsh superego. One can say that in this case the experience of one's badness is not fully assimilated—one experiences the voice of a foreign body—an "internal saboteur"—telling one that one is bad.

A question that arises is whether it is possible to experience oneself as bad, not in the above form but in the form of an assimilated, even if negative, representation of oneself. That is, can one distinguish between experiencing a critical, rejecting presence within oneself, similar to the homunculus-like superego, and simply experiencing oneself in a negative way, that is, having a negative identity? The latter is captured by Sullivan's (1940, p. 22) idea that one's representation of oneself is, in large part, a product of "reflected appraisals" of significant others. Thus, if one has been viewed as unworthy or unlovable by significant others, one will come to represent oneself as unworthy or unlovable. One can say the same sort of thing about other concepts, such as internal working models or representations of interactions generalized. Implicit in these concepts is the idea that one's self-representation is more or less the product of straightforward learning based on early interactions with parents. There is nothing in these concepts that necessarily refers to an internalized object, only to the internalization processes of learning and generalizing. That is, the self as reflected appraisals of significant others does not carry the implication of the experience of being inhabited by a critical presence, a foreign body. Another way to sum up this distinction is to say that the product of a reflected appraisal internalization process is ego-syntonic—it is experienced as "me"—even if in Sullivan's (1953) terms, it is a "bad me," whereas the product of the internalization process underlying internalizing the object is, at least to some degree, ego-alien, that is, again in Sullivan's terms, "not me."

Internalized object relations

According to Fairbairn, much of one's affective life—more so as psychopathology increases in severity—is played out in the entirely inner arena of internalized object relations, where one is relating to internalized objects rather than actual others. Indeed, actual others are largely stand-ins for internalized objects, and although one may think one is relating to an actual other, one is, in fact, largely relating to one's own internalized object. Although Fairbairn does not put it this way, it seems to me that one can understand this process as one in which the individual *projects* his or her internalized object on to the other and then relates to these projections rather than to the actual other. The result is that object relations largely consist in relations among different (and conflicting) components of oneself rather than between oneself and an actual other. For Fairbairn, an important index of mental health is one's ability to relate to another, not as a representation of an internalized object but in terms of who that other actually is. Indeed, one can say that for Fairbairn, a critical measure of mental health is adequate functioning of the individual's reality testing, now extended from the arena of physical reality to the arena of object relations. Thus, a criterion of mental health is one's ability to recognize and relate to this other in terms of who that other actually is.

It is interesting to observe the convergence between Fairbairn's concept of internalized object relations and the Freudian concept of transference. Both share in common the idea that one is relating to the other in terms of one's projections. Hence, in analyzing the transference, one is not only helping the patient gain insight into his or her projections, wishes, defenses, etc., but through those insights, become increasingly able to be freed from these projections and relate to the other in terms of who that other actually is.[5]

---

[5] Because of the analyst's relative anonymity, at least in the context of the traditional conception of the analytic situation, the notion that an aim of the analysis of the transference is to enhance the ability of the patient to relate to the analyst in terms of who he or she actually is may seem odd. It raises the question of how that can be an aim when the analyst reveals so little of himself or herself. However, to the extent that interpretations of the transference

Relatedness and autonomy

Because contemporary theories often cast psychopathology in terms of clinging to early object ties or failure to move from symbiotic ties to separation-individuation, there is a tendency to assume an inherent conflict or incompatibility between relatedness and autonomy. Although I will elaborate on this issue in Chapter 8, I want to note here my view that there is no inherent and necessary conflict between relatedness and autonomy or between object relations and self-definition. Rather, persistent and chronic conflict between these two trends characterizes psychopathology rather than the outcome of optimal development. Indeed, as the perspective of attachment theory makes clear, there is a synergistic rather than a conflictual relationship between relatedness and autonomy. At the center of attachment theory is the relationship between the secure base (and safe haven) functions of the attachment figure and the individual's ability to explore the world and self relatively free of anxiety. If one thinks of exploration as an aspect of autonomy and self-definition, then it is clear that in linking exploration to the secure base provided by the attachment figure, Bowlby is articulating a reciprocal rather than a conflictual relationship between ties to others and self-definition. That is, one cannot comfortably engage in exploration (including self-exploration) without the ties to other (i.e., a secure base).

According to the logic of attachment theory, there is no inherent and necessary conflict between ties to others (attachment) and self-definition and autonomy in normal development (secure attachment). Rather, the conflict between the two develops when the attachment figure fails to provide an adequate secure base or safe haven in times of distress. Under these circumstances, conflict develops between autonomy and attachment; this conflict is maladaptively dealt with by either an excessive, defensive emphasis on autonomy (avoidant attachment) or an excessive, defensive emphasis on ties to others (preoccupied attachment). I am suggesting more generally that the conflict between relatedness and autonomy generally lies in the individual's defensive clinging to early object ties, which do, indeed, interfere with the development of autonomy—an issue to be discussed further in Chapter 8.

Self psychology and object relations

Let me turn now to the conception of objects and object relations in self psychology. As Bacal and Newman (1990), themselves self psychologists, note, Kohut's self psychology is not an object relations theory. Nowhere in

---

focus on the patient's projections, defenses, and the like, they reduce the impediments to the patient's ability and freedom to relate to the analyst in terms of who he or she actually is—within the limits of the nature of the interaction and of the information and cues available.

his writing does Kohut posit an inborn object-seeking, relational, or attachment tendency, as, respectively, Fairbairn, Mitchell, and Bowlby do. Indeed, the starting point for self psychology is Kohut's objection to Freud's (1914b) view that in the course of normal development one moves from narcissism to object relations. Kohut (1971, 1977) insists on narcissism as a separate line of development—from archaic to healthy or mature narcissism—and makes clear his view that satisfying and productive lives can be led without object relations at their center. The importance of developing a cohesive and productive self, not object relations, is at the core of the self psychology conception of psychological functioning.

One gains a basic insight into the conception and role of objects and object relations in Kohut's self psychology by observing that the central terms and concepts in that theory are not *object* and *object relations* but the neologisms *selfobject* and *self–selfobject relationships*. As Kohut defines it, the hybrid term selfobject is intended to refer neither to fully self nor to fully separate other but to the narcissistic function served by the other. Thus, in a self–selfobject relationship, one relates to the other not as an object but as a function, that is, in terms of the other's enhancement of oneself. Here we have a central distinction between Kohut's selfobject and the concept of object in the context of object relations theory. In the context of self psychology, relating to a selfobject is understood as relating to another in terms of his or her narcissistic function, that is, in terms of enhancing the self. Another way to put this is to say that the selfobject is a regulator of one's self-cohesiveness and self-esteem. From the perspective of object relations theory, the primary function of the object is to enable an inner affective connection. One might say that from the perspective of self psychology, the ultimate psychological disaster is a sense of utter worthlessness, whereas from the perspective of Fairbairn's object relations theory, the ultimate psychological disaster is an empty inner world devoid of any cognitive–affective connection to objects. It is no wonder that the early focus of self psychology was narcissistic disorders, whereas the early focus of object relations theory was schizoid disorders.

From the perspective of object relations theory, the most dire psychological condition one can face is not the failure to be loved by the object but one's inability to love the object, that is, to be incapable of any affective connection to the object—that is truly the ultimate schizoid disaster. One might say that on this view, unrequited love is far more preferable than the inability to love. To be noted here is the convergence between Fairbairn's view and Freud's (1914b) insistence that in normal development one moves from narcissism to object love and that "one must love in order not to fall ill" (p. 85). Also to be noted is Kohut's rejection of this point of view. Thus, with regard to the role of object love in psychic life, there is much greater affinity between the views of Freud and Fairbairn than between the views of either one and that of Kohut.

In Freudian theory, by however circuitous the route, an end point in optimal development is the individual's experience of the object as a whole object, that is, as a fully separate other with his or her own needs, feelings, and so on (which, as Benjamin, 1988, points out, would warrant the term *subject* rather than *object*). Contrastingly, in self psychology, optimal development proceeds from the experience of the other as an archaic selfobject to a mature selfobject. What remains unchanged is the experience of the other as a *selfobject*, that is the experience of the other in terms of his or her role in enhancing one's self-cohesiveness and self-esteem. As far as I can tell, there is nothing in Kohut's writings that suggests the eventual transformation of the selfobject into an experienced separate whole object. Kohut's theory belongs in the category of what one can call *self-realization* or self-actualization theories in the tradition of Rogers (e.g., 1951; also Maslow, 1952, 1968). In this tradition, the focus is on the conditions necessary—and these conditions include the necessary behavior of others—to foster clear identity, self-esteem, and a self that is productive and creative and that fulfills its potential—all characteristics that play a prominent role in Kohut's conception of a cohesive self.

In short, Kohut's theory is truly a self psychology, that is, a theory of narcissism and narcissistic development, rather than a theory of object relations. This should be no surprise, insofar as, as noted, the central theoretical motives for the development of self psychology begin with Kohut's rejection of, first, Freud's view regarding the imperative that one must move from narcissism to object love, and second, Freud's concomitant insistence on narcissism as a separate line of psychological development.

THE RELATIONSHIP BETWEEN SEXUALITY AND OBJECT RELATIONS IN CONTEMPORARY PSYCHOANALYTIC THEORIES

The object relations theory of Fairbairn, the relational psychoanalysis of Mitchell, and the self psychology of Kohut all share the view that the primacy given to sexuality in traditional theory is misplaced. For relational theorists, sex is emotionally loaded because the "sexual is regarded as a central realm in which relational conflicts are shaped and played out" (Mitchell, 1988, p. 66). As Mitchell (1988) puts it, "For Freud, object relations are the realm in which drive impulses are expressed, gratified, or defended against. For the relational-model theorist, sexual and other bodily processes are the realm in which relational conflicts are expressed or defended against" (p. 92). In other words, whereas for Freud, object relations develop and become important because they constitute the means to drive gratification, for relational psychoanalysis, sex becomes important because it is an arena in which object relational issues get played out. Another way to put it is to say that whereas for Freud, the object is a signpost to drive gratification, for Fairbairn (1952), "sex is a signpost to the object" (p. 33). In self psychology, too, the sexual motive is, so to speak, subservient to other motives, in this case, those having to do with strivings for self-cohesiveness. When sexual motives (as well as aggression) do become peremptory, they are viewed as products of fragmentation of the self. As Kohut (1984) puts it, the analyst demonstrates to the patient that when the oedipal self began to crumble, lust and destructiveness began to rise in consequence of the fragmentation of the oedipal self.

The oedipal situation

In the Freudian view, at the center of the oedipal constellation are incestuous wishes toward the opposite-sex parent and aggressive wishes toward the same-sex parent. In other words, the primary elements of the oedipal conflict are sex and aggression. From a relational perspective, apparently incestuous wishes are not inherently sexual but rather constitute expressions of the child's difficulties with separating and differentiating from parental figures. As Schafer (1978) puts it, seemingly incestuous wishes represent unconscious symbiotic wishes, and fear of incest represents "fear of being devoured by the first sexual object" (p. 157). In other words, incestuous impulses are not inherently sexual but represent wishes for merger, and correspondingly, fear of incest is not so much fear of sexual urges but rather fear of being engulfed. Although Schafer would certainly not view himself as a relational theorist, his above rendering of the nature of oedipal dynamics is entirely compatible with a relational perspective. According to this perspective, the importance of the oedipal situation lies in the fact that it is an arena for the playing out of such object relational issues as wanting exclusive parental attention, the fear of separation and differentiation, and the equal fear linked to fantasies of merging and engulfment. One can say that the oedipal situation entails a playing out of the conflict between, in Fairbairn's (1952) words, "the progressive urge toward separation from the object and the regressive lure of identification with the object" (p. 43). From an object relational perspective, an adequate resolution of oedipal conflicts is characterized by the individual's ability to relinquish early object ties and to move toward the "progressive urge toward separation" (this will be discussed more fully in Chapter 8). (See Loewald [1979] for a helpful discussion of the Oedipus complex.)

Oedipal conflicts and environmental factors

In general, whether stated by relational theorists or others, contemporary psychoanalysis is characterized by skepticism regarding the universality of oedipal incestuous wishes. Rather, such wishes, when they are present, are attributed to interactional environmental factors. For example,

Kohut (1984) maintains that the oedipal period is *not* normally character-ized by incestuous and aggressive wishes. When it is dominated by such wishes, it represents a pathological development resulting from inappropri-ate parental seductiveness and intergenerational envy and hostility. Miller (1997/2007) makes a similar point. Along with Kohut, she notes that par-ents often are envious of and hostile toward their children and points out that in the Oedipus story, Laius, the father, intends to kill his son, Oedipus. She suggests that we use the term *Laius complex* to describe the father's hostility toward the son.

Once Freud relinquished his environmentally based seduction theory and transformed it into a theory of endogenous and universal seduction fanta-sies, he had a curious blind spot regarding evidence of parental seductive-ness, envy, and hostility toward their children. Perhaps it is not curious, however, insofar as his assumption of the hard-wired nature of psycho-sexual development rendered oedipal wishes and fantasies universal and relatively independent of environmental vicissitudes. Why bother attending to parental variations when they do not matter that much anyway?

Both with regard to the oedipal situation and more broadly, contempo-rary psychoanalysis is characterized by a deemphasis on the role of geneti-cally programmed processes (e.g., psychosexual stages) and an increased emphasis on the role of environmental vicissitudes, including environmental failure and trauma. Although not limited to relational psychoanalysis, this general trend necessarily places increasing emphasis on relational factors, for the environmental factors that are of primary interest to psychoanalysis are, of course, object relational factors (i.e., relationship with parents).

A good example of a traditional psychoanalytic dynamic essentially reconceptualized in environmental relational terms is seen in Weiss et al. (1986) reformulation of castration anxiety.[6] According to traditional the-ory, the boy fears being castrated by the powerful father as a punishment for his incestuous and rivalrous wishes. In the reformulation proposed by Weiss et al. (see also Eagle, 1987a), the boy's fear of punishment at the hands of the father is often based on the latter's implicit communications that carry the following message: "Don't you dare try to outdo me. You will incur my wrath if you do." To be noted here is that in the above con-text, castration anxiety is not understood literally. Rather, although the term *castration anxiety* is retained, it is now being used symbolically, to refer to feared punishment in general and to powerlessness at the hands of a powerful figure.

Consider a symptom of a patient who experienced fear of a heart attack following an achievement, standing up to authority, or some other experi-ence of "oedipal victory" (e.g., winning a woman over a rival). According

---

[6] It should be noted that Weiss et al. (1986) do not view themselves as relational theorists, nor do they view their control-mastery theory as a relational theory.

to Freudian theory, the heart attack symptom is interpretable as a symbolic expression—a sort of displacement upward—of the real, underlying, unconscious anxiety about literally being castrated. For a contemporary theorist, particularly a relational theorist, the heart attack symptom would likely be interpreted as a general fear of punishment arising out of guilt in relation to the fantasy of surpassing father. Indeed, from a relational point of view, if a patient actually reported literal castration anxiety, it would probably be interpreted as symbolic of a fear of general powerlessness and impotence.

WHY DO WE NEED OBJECTS?

One can gain an insight into different psychoanalytic theories by examining how each of them addresses the question of not only the origin but also the function of objects and object relations. As we have seen in Chapter 3, from the perspective of both Freudian drive theory and the Freudian theory of narcissism, we need objects in order to prevent the ego from being overwhelmed with excessive excitation—either excitation emanating from undischarged drive tensions or from failing to direct libido toward objects. With regard to the former, if the object is the thing in regard to which the instinct achieves its aim, then it follows that the unavailability of the object leaves the organism at the mercy of undischarged drive tensions, that is, at the mercy of excessive excitation.[7]

Common to contemporary psychoanalytic theories is the rejection of these fundamental ideas and their replacement by alternative answers to the questions of why we need objects and what dangers we face when deprived of the object. From the perspective of Mitchell's (1988) relational theory, objects are necessary "to preserve the continuity, connections, familiarity of one's personal, interactional world" (p. 33). Mitchell goes on to say: "There is a powerful need to preserve an abiding sense of oneself as associated with, positioned in terms of, related to, a matrix of other people, in terms of actual transactions as well as internal presences" (p. 33).

From the perspective of Fairbairn's (1952) object relations theory, we need objects for ego support and in order to avoid the ultimate psychological disaster of an empty inner world with no connections to objects. With regard to the former, Jones writes in his preface to Fairbairn's 1952 book:

> If it were possible to condense Dr. Fairbairn's new ideas into one sentence, it might run somewhat as follows. Instead of starting, as Freud

---

[7] An expression of how utterly seriously this formulation is taken by Freudian is seen in Spitz's (1960) conclusion that the marasmus condition of the orphaned infants he studied was attributed to the absence of an object upon which to discharge sexual and aggressive drives.

did, from stimulation of the nervous system proceeding from excitation of various erotogenous zones and internal tension arising from gonadic activity, Dr. Fairbairn starts at the centre of the personality, the ego, and depicts its strivings and difficulties in its endeavour to reach an object where it may find support. (p. v)

From the perspective of self psychology, empathic mirroring from objects—more accurately, selfobjects—is necessary for the development and maintenance of a cohesive self. The traumatic absence of empathic mirroring puts one at risk for self-defects and a proneness to "disintegration anxiety" (see Chapter 8).

And finally, from the perspective of attachment theory, the function of objects can be understood in both a distal and proximal sense. From the standpoint of the former, object-seeking or proximity-seeking is a hard-wired tendency that has been selected out in the course of evolution because it protects the infant of the species from predators. As for proximal psychological function, "felt security" in relation to the object is an important factor in optimal functioning and in one's ability to engage comfortably in the exploration of the physical and social world that is necessary for the development of various competencies. One can see that the concepts of felt security and a secure base (particularly, an internalized secure base) bear a strong family resemblance to Winnicott's (1965) emphasis on the importance of introjecting an ego supportive environment in facilitating the capacity to be alone—Winnicott's version of exploratory activity.

Objects are necessary for physiological and emotional regulation

There is a good deal of empirical research from both animal and human studies demonstrating the function of the object in regulating vital physiological and behavioral systems in the infant. In the psychoanalytic context, this work begins with Spitz's (1945; Spitz & Wolf, 1946) report of marasmus in maternally deprived infants and is also reflected in the work of Ribble (1944). As for animal studies, the work of Hofer (2008) demonstrating that different stimulus inputs from the caregiver regulate different physiological systems in the rat pup stands out. For example, the mother rat regulates the pup's heart rate by the amount of milk she provides (which operates by the intestinal tract communicating to the brain, which results in a certain level of sympathetic autonomous tone to the heart); thermal stimulation regulates the level of activity and growth hormone by tactile stimulation (see Shanberg & Kuhn, 1980); the modulation of extreme emotional states by vestibular stimulation (Hofer, 1995), something mothers do intuitively when they engage in gentle rocking of distressed infants;

the control of behavioral reactivity by the temperature level; and so on.[8] Hence, and as Hofer and his colleagues have demonstrated, when a rat pup is deprived of its mother, it is subject to the loss of a wide range of stimulus inputs that regulate different physiological and behavioral systems.

One of the striking aspects of Hofer's work (and other similar work) is the demonstration that one can prevent or ameliorate the dysregulating effects of maternal deprivation by plugging in the various stimulus inputs that are lost with mother's removal. For example, one can regulate heart rate by providing milk; one can ameliorate the apathy and inactivity characteristic of rat pups who are separated from mother by keeping the pups warm, something the mother normally does; one can reduce hyperactivity by providing tactile stimulation; and most strikingly, one can correct the drop in production of ornithine decarboxylase, a biochemical index of tissue maturation or so-called growth hormone, that normally occurs following maternal deprivation and keep the hormone production at a normal level by stroking the rat pups with a wet camel hair brush that is similar to the texture of the mother's tongue (Schanberg & Kuhn, 1980). And it has been shown that distressed infants can be quieted by kinesthetic, vestibular, and auditory stimulation independent of maternal presence. The above results suggest that the regulation of endogenous needs through the provision of various stimulus inputs is the primary function of the object, whatever relational aims are served are byproducts of that regulation of endogenous needs.

The above work provides one answer to the questions posed earlier of why we need objects and the functions they serve. In the light of Hofer's and other related findings, the caregiving object can be understood as someone who, through the provision of an array of stimulus inputs, functions as a regulator of the infant's physiological and behavioral systems. One short answer, then, to the question of why we need objects, at least early in life, is that we need them in order to be regulated, for as we have seen, without them and without their regulating function, we become dysregulated, and adequate functioning is impaired. Although the regulating function of objects and object relations is most evident in infancy and childhood, as Hofer (1995) notes, there is evidence that objects also serve regulating functions in long-term adult relationships. The psychological reactions, such as grief and despair, that frequently accompany the loss and disruption of long-term adult relationships are evidence of physiological dysregulation, leaving the individual at greater risk for somatic illness and even death.

---

[8] One can think of Hofer's work, as well as other similar work, as providing an empirical basis as well as an animal model for Spitz's (1965) concept of "auxiliary ego," which pointed to the caregiver's role in regulating the young infant's functions and states.

Chapter 8

Conceptions of psychopathology in contemporary psychoanalytic theories

THEORIES AND TYPES OF PSYCHOPATHOLOGY

One of the issues that complicate a discussion of contemporary psycho-analytic theories of psychopathology is the question of whether different psychoanalytic theories selectively emphasize a particular component of psychopathology and therefore provide different perspectives on the same kind of pathology or whether each theory attempts to account for a different form and expression of psychopathology. Are some forms of psychopathology especially characterized by, say, unconscious pathogenic beliefs or relational conflicts, whereas other forms of psychopathology are mainly characterized by self-defects? Are there still other forms characterized mainly by conflicts around drive impulses? Or, in line with Pine's (1990) perspective, are each of these—pathogenic beliefs, relational conflicts, drive conflicts, and self-defects—different features of the individual's overall maladaptive functioning—which each theorist elevates to a complete theory? This set of questions, posed with regard to differences among different contemporary theories, is also relevant in the context of the relationship between contemporary and classical theories of psychopathology. Do contemporary theories deal with new forms and expressions of psychopathology that were not addressed by traditional theory? Or do contemporary theories constitute mainly new perspectives on old and familiar clinical phenomena that are essentially the same or similar to the ones with which Freud and other classical analysts were concerned?[1]

This last set of questions also raises the issue of the range of applicability of psychoanalytic conceptions of psychopathology (as well as of treatment). As noted in Chapter 4, despite forays into the application of psychoanalytic concepts to psychosis—as in the Schreber case (Freud, 1911)[2]—classical

---

[1] The former alternative raises the interesting questions of whether forms and expressions of psychopathology change in different cultural–social historical eras or whether it is mainly ways of describing and understanding them that change.

[2] Although it should be noted that Freud's discussion of the Schreber case focuses on a psychoanalytic elucidation of the dynamics of Schreber's psychosis, he does not suggest that a psychoanalytic approach is the appropriate treatment for Schreber's psychosis.

psychoanalytic theory, with its emphasis on inner conflict, is essentially a theory of the psychoneuroses (see Waelder, 1960; Fenichel, 1945). However, given the challenge of presumably more disturbed patients coming for treatment as well as the development and increasing prominence of ego psychology, psychoanalytic conceptions of psychopathology (as well as of treatment) expanded in an attempt to account for these more serious forms of psychopathology. Examples of such attempts include Knight's (1953a, 1953b) classic paper on borderline conditions and Bellak's (1958) comparison of deficits in ego functions between neurotic and schizophrenic individuals.

One approach taken to the range of applicability issue is what one might call a partitioning one. For example, in his early work, Kohut (1971) proposed that whereas classical theory was applicable to "structural conflicts," self psychology theory accounted for pathology characterized by self-defects (see also Stolorow & Lachmann, 1980, as another example of a partitioning strategy in regard to inner conflicts versus defects and developmental arrests). However, by the time his 1984 book was published, Kohut was essentially proposing that self-defects rather than conflicts around sex and aggression are at the core of all psychopathology—even when the patient presents with the former set of problems.

Thus, although early in his 1984 book Kohut appears to accept the existence of "the structural-conflict neuroses" (p. 10), side by side with narcissistic pathology, this is not really the case, for Kohut also writes: "Issues that are traditionally considered genetically primary and structurally central in the neuroses (the *content* of the Oedipus situation, the conflicts of the child) are now, without denying their importance, considered secondary and peripheral" (p. 27). He also writes:

> Self psychology is now attempting to demonstrate, for example, that all forms of psychopathology are based either on defects in the structure of the self, on distortions of the self, or on weakness of the self.... Stated in the obverse, by way of highlighting the contrast between self psychology and traditional theory, self psychology holds that pathogenic conflicts in the object-instinctual realm—that is, pathogenic conflicts in the realm of object love and object hate and in particular the set of conflicts called the Oedipus complex—are not the *primary* cause but its result. (p. 53)

The clear implication is that self psychology conceptions of psychopathology should *replace*, not merely supplement, traditional theories of psychopathology at the center of which are inner conflicts around sex and aggression. Another way to put this is to say that, in effect, Kohut's later 1984 claim is that self psychology theory is not simply a supplemental theory but a superior and more comprehensive theory because it can account for the clinical phenomena dealt with by traditional theory (i.e., inner conflicts) plus clinical phenomena that cannot adequately be dealt with by traditional theory (i.e., self-defects).

Pretty much the same thing can be said of other contemporary theories, such as object relations theory and relational psychoanalysis. Thus, when Fairbairn (1952) states that the neurotic configurations that are the focus of classical theory can be understood as transitional defenses against ultimate schizoid dangers, he, like Kohut, is claiming hegemony for his theory, namely, that at the core of *all* pathology is the schizoid fear of a cognitively and affectively empty and void inner world. Also as with Kohut's claim for self psychology, Fairbairn essentially maintains that object relations theory is a superior and more comprehensive theory because it can account for clinical phenomena dealt with by traditional theory, as well as clinical phenomena not dealt with by it.[3]

COMMON THEMES IN CONTEMPORARY PSYCHOANALYTIC THEORIES OF PSYCHOPATHOLOGY

Despite the above issues and despite the fact that contemporary psychoanalysis is not a monolithic entity with a unitary conception of psychopathology but is rather characterized by a plurality of different theories, one can identify some common themes.

The centrality of relationships and the role of environmental failure

One such theme, constituting a negative consensus, is the rejection of the classical view that the essence of psychopathology lies in inner conflict around infantile sexual and aggressive wishes. The corresponding positive consensus is that lives are shaped, made, or broken as a function of object relations. As Mitchell (1988) puts it, "relationships with others, not drives [are] the basic stuff of mental life" (p. 2).

---

[3] Greenberg and Mitchell (1983) take the position that different psychoanalytic theories constitute different worldviews and different paradigms in the Kuhnian sense, a position similar to Schafer's (1983, 1992) discussion of different narratives. In this view, it makes little sense to claim greater validity or superiority for one paradigm over another or to attempt to integrate these incommensurable worldviews. Rather, one, so to speak, chooses the one with which one is most comfortable. However, Greenberg and Mitchell's apparent ecumenicism is belied by their sharp and sustained criticism of Freudian theory and their strong arguments in favor of their own relational perspective, suggesting that they believe the latter to be a more valid and superior theory.

A sort of corollary of this view, another consensus, is the emphasis on parental failures of one kind or another as at the etiological core of psychopathology. Thus, whatever other differences there may be among them, contemporary theories of psychopathology, in one way or another, constitute what one may call *environmental failure* models. Psychopathology is attributed mainly to various deprivations and deficiencies of early parental care, ranging from subtle failures of attunement to gross and outright rejection, abuse, and neglect. In this sense, environmental failure models are akin to trauma theories with the degree of trauma varying along both quantitative and qualitative dimensions.

Although different contemporary theories emphasize the role of environmental failure in psychopathology, they differ with regard to how they understand the nature of the failure and how they conceptualize the consequences of such failure. For example, whereas Weiss et al. (1986) focus on the role of early parental communications in the development of unconscious pathogenic beliefs—which they hold to be central to psychopathology—Kohut (1984) focuses on the effect of parental failures in empathic mirroring on the development of self-defects—which, for Kohut, is at the core of psychopathology.

Psychopathology as persistence of early modes of relating

The persistence of early modes of relating that may at one time have been adaptive but are now maladaptive is another common theme in contemporary psychoanalytic conceptions of psychopathology. As an altricial species, our long periods of helplessness and being cared for entail at least two factors that exert strong influences on subsequent development: one, the early formation of intense emotional bonds to our caregiver(s); and two, being subjected to long periods of social influence and interactions that serve as an arena for the acquisition of social skills, competencies, and templates for modes of relating to others. Thus, in addition to the obvious link between receiving caregiving and physical survival, the prolonged social interaction that is part of receiving caregiving enables us, in a more long-term way, to survive and function as social beings. Indeed, Fonagy et al. (1995) have argued that learning how to understand and interpret other's behaviors and how the other's mind works is an adaptive function of the attachment bond equal in importance to its function of protection from predators posited by Bowlby (1969). They have suggested that one adaptive function of extended attachment is to facilitate the development of what they refer to as an interpersonal interpretive mechanism.

Although the formation of strong emotional attachments to our caregiver and the acquisition of templates for modes of relating are integrally related, they can be conceptually distinguished. In the context of psycho-pathology, one can meaningfully distinguish between the effects of the persistence of early emotional bonds on functioning—which I will discuss in the next section—and the effects of having learned maladaptive modes of relating. Whereas a primary consequence of clinging to early object ties is interference with the individual's ability to form new object ties—in Freud's (1916–1917/1917, p. 348) metapsychology, the individual's libido has adhered to early objects—a primary consequence of the persistence of early modes of relating is that although the individual may be relatively capable of developing emotional ties to new objects, the mode of relating to these new objects is stereotypic, a variation of an early mode of relating.

Maladaptive representations

As noted above, learning how to relate to others is one major adaptive aspect of prolonged attachment. One of the ways we learn to relate to others is through the formation of representations and expectations that abstract out prototypic features of countless and repeated interactions with caregivers early in life. As noted in Chapter 7, this process is an expression in the relational arena of what appears to be a basic tendency of mind to form general event representations (Nelson & Gruendel, 1986), that is, to represent the invariant features of repeated specific episodes and events. Through representing prototypic interactions, we learn what to expect from others and how to relate to others. Although this representational capacity is a highly adaptive property of mind, it can have maladaptive consequences. This occurs when our learned expectations and ways of relating that emerged from coping with early experiences are rigidly clung to and do not adequately take account of current new realities. Rather, new realities are assimilated to early acquired representations and expectations. Thus, paralleling a contemporary conception of mind as a set of representations of prototypic interactions between self and other is a conception of psycho-pathology largely formulated in terms of *maladaptive* representations of interactions between self and other (and associated representations of self and other).

Although the form in which it is expressed may vary with different theo-ries, a basic assumption common to contemporary theories of psychopathol-ogy is that based on early experiences with parental figures, the individual has acquired a set of representations that may have been adaptive at one time but are now maladaptive in that they bring distress and interfere with the possibility of gratifying and enriching relationships. Specific expres-sions of this basic idea include the concept of internal working models of attachment theory (Bowlby, 1973), the unconscious pathogenic beliefs of control-mastery theory (Weiss et al., 1986), the "relational configurations" of relational psychoanalysis (Mitchell, 1988), the self-object-affect units of Kernberg (1976), the emotional convictions and organizing principles of intersubjective theory (Stolorow et al., 2002), and the internalized objects and object relations of Fairbairn (1952).

Consider as an example of an early representation underlying an avoidant-dismissive attachment pattern that developed in response to repeated experiences and consequent expectations of rejection. Although this pattern may have constituted an adaptive strategy at one time, in the sense that it spared the infant the pain of repeated rejections and permitted whatever fulfillment of attachment needs was available from the caregiver, when continued later in life, it prevents the individual from experiencing his or her attachment needs and from developing satisfying intimate relationships. In another example, early in life an individual may have received repeated and often implicit parental communications to the effect that striving for certain satisfactions and for individuation and autonomy is damaging to and will threaten ties to the parent. If the individual carries over this pattern to subsequent relationships, the result is unhappiness and the aborting or sabotaging of developmental strivings.

The influence of unconscious representations on personality functioning is different in many ways from the influence of unconscious repressed wishes, desires, and impulses posited by classical theory. For one thing, as they are understood in the contemporary literature, representations are unconscious not only or not primarily because of defense (that is, because of dynamic motivations to remove them from consciousness) but because they have been acquired nonverbally early in life. In this regard, they are similar to habits or motor skills that have been etched into the behavioral procedures of the body. Hence, it makes little sense to think of these representations and procedures constantly striving for expression in consciousness and gratification in action, as one would in regard to repressed wishes and desires. Rather, as learned procedures, they implicitly and silently guide one's expectations and patterns of behavior.

The picture of psychopathology and of mental functioning in general that emerges from this account is very different from the traditional one. Without the primacy of unconscious motives and desires striving for expression and opposed by other structures of the personality, there would appear to be less room for the role of inner conflict, defense, and compromise formation in psychopathology. To the extent that psychopathology is largely a matter of the persistence of early maladaptive representations, it becomes quite difficult to draw a sharp distinction between these features of contemporary psychoanalytic theories and a sophisticated form of cognitive behavior theory or schema theory (e.g., Young, Klosko, & Weishaar, 2006). All have in common the central idea that at the core of pathology is the early acquisition of and persistence into adult life of representations, schemas, and belief systems that are maladaptive, that is, that interfere with adequate functioning.[4]

Were contemporary psychoanalytic accounts of psychopathology limited to maladaptive representations and belief systems, they would indeed not differ sharply from the cognitive behavioral emphasis on irrational beliefs or the emphasis of schema theory on early maladaptive schemas that are carried over into adult life. These formulations constitute, in essence, a straightforward learning theory. That is, they basically state that one has learned patterns of thinking, feeling, experiencing, and relating that are maladaptive. Why, however, are patterns learned early in life so resistant to change, even in the face of contrary evidence and the experience of much suffering? That is the classic question that needs to be addressed in thinking about the nature of psychopathology. It is in response to this question that contemporary psychoanalytic accounts can be distinguished from cognitive behavior or schema theories to the extent that they go beyond faulty learning and maladaptive representations and emphasize dynamic and motivational factors that are involved in the origin and maintenance of maladaptive patterns of behavior.

Psychopathology as clinging to early object ties

From a dynamic point of view, psychopathology is characterized not only by the persistence of early representations and modes of relating due to early learning but also by active emotional clinging to early objects. In discussing the nature of the child's tie to the attachment figure, Cassidy (1999) suggests that a tendency toward monotropy may have been selected out in the course of evolution because of its adaptive advantages, including an increase in the likelihood of being cared for through the "establishment of a relationship in which ... one attachment figure assumes principal responsibility for the child" (p. 15),[5] as well as permitting a quick, automatic response regarding whose help to seek when facing danger. In short, there are major adaptive advantages to our readiness to develop deep and persistent emotional ties to early objects. However, as can be the case with other patterns that have been selected out, our monotropic tendency may also potentially constitute the source of psychopathology.

---

[4] The idea that psychopathology entails the persistence of representations, beliefs, expectations that at one time may have been appropriate but are now maladaptive is similar, in important respects, to what Friedman (2008a) refers to as Freud's "second model" of pathology and treatment. In that model, the patient is held to be in the grip of unrealistic fears emanating from the early "danger situations" (e.g., loss of the object; loss of the object's love) that may at one time have been dangerous, but no longer are in the present. As Friedman (2008a) writes, "the analyst brings the good news that danger situations are not really dangerous" (p. 3).

[5] Monotropy does not rule out the possibility of a hierarchy of attachment figures. It does, however, imply a principal figure at the top of the hierarchy.

That the clinging to early object ties can be distinguished from the persistence of maladaptive representations and early modes of relating is made evident when one considers that it is possible to relinquish early emotional object ties and nevertheless continue to respond to others in accord with modes of learned relating early in life. In other words, as noted above, relating to others in terms of early modes may be, in part at least, a function of early learning (including procedural learning) and may not be entirely motivated by the need to cling emotionally to objects. However, just as the adaptive function of acquiring the rules of relating based on early experience can have maladaptive consequences, so similarly can this be the case with regard to emotional ties to early objects. That is, the very same adaptive capacity to form and maintain strong and prolonged affective connections, as expressed in prolonged attachment bonds, can have maladaptive consequences when the affective connections to early objects cannot be transformed in the course of development and cannot be transferred on to new objects.

Indeed, Fairbairn (1952) maintains that the patient's "devotion" and "obstinate attachment" to internal objects are a core feature of psychopathology and one that is the most difficult challenge to successful treatment. Similarly, Mitchell (1988) observes that "conflictual attachments to and identifications with archaic objects are universal [and] it is the alteration of those ties which constitutes the basic therapeutic action of the analytic process" (p. 278). It is also evident that Freud's (1916–1917/1917) concept of "adhesiveness of the libido" (p. 348) bears a strong family resemblance to Fairbairn's devotion and obstinate attachment and to Mitchell's conflictual attachment to archaic objects.

Although different psychoanalytic theories locate a central source of psychopathology in the persistence of early object ties, they conceptualize the nature of and motivation for these ties in somewhat different ways. According to classical theory, the persistence of early object ties is largely characterized by the adhesiveness of infantile wishes and desires, a quintessential example of which is the persistence of incestuous wishes characteristic of an inadequate resolution of the oedipal conflict. The persistence of these wishes interferes with the individual's ability to experience gratifying intimate relationships with appropriate objects. At the core of the control-mastery theory of Weiss et al. (1986) is the idea that perpetuation of early ties is motivated primarily by guilt. For example, if the parental communication has been, "If you pursue developmental strivings for autonomy and success, you will be abandoning me and therefore doing so at my expense," then pursuing autonomy and success will generate guilt and relinquishing and sabotaging these aims will constitute loyalty to and protection of early objects from harm. Modell (1965, 1971; Modell, Weiss, & Sampson, 1983) has referred to this dynamic as "survivor guilt" or "separation guilt." That is, for many people from trouble-ridden families, to survive and separate from these families through living a more successful life is experienced, at an unconscious level, as an egregious act of disloyalty that generates guilt.

The role of guilt in maintaining ties to early objects was made powerfully evident to me in the treatment of a Canadian Indian patient. He was a talented poet and had published a few poems. Any experience of success (e.g., having a poem accepted for publication, a fruitful therapeutic session) was almost always followed by self-destructive behavior (e.g., getting drunk and speeding). He was quite aware of this pattern and openly stated that success in the "white man's world" meant abandoning his people and his origins—and this he could not and would not do. (By the way, this vignette suggests the possible role of cultural factors in the negative therapeutic reaction.)

For Fairbairn, the motives for maintaining early object ties and clinging to early objects include not only guilt but also fear, even terror, at the prospect of living in an empty inner world devoid of object ties. As we have seen in Chapter 7, and as Mitchell (1988) has noted, Fairbairn's observation that mistreated and abused children not only maintain ties to their abusing parents but often idealize them, at the cost of viewing themselves as bad, had a strong impact on his theorizing. He concluded that the child's need for the object is so absolute that he or she cannot tolerate the idea of a bad—that is, a rejecting and unloving—object. To give up idealization and replace it with a more negative view of the object is experienced as equivalent to giving up all hope of receiving the object's love. It is less threatening and less conducive of despair to think of oneself as bad, as somehow deserving rejection. As noted in the previous chapter, this construal of one's rejection as contingent upon one's own badness at least keeps alive the possibility that there is something one can do (i.e., become good) to merit and elicit love and caring from the caregiver. Despite the above variations, it can be seen that a common theme that cuts across classical and different contemporary psychoanalytic theories is the central idea that the failure to relinquish emotional ties to early objects interferes with the individual's ability to pursue satisfying and age-appropriate goals and relationships and is a central factor in psychopathology.[6]

---

[6] Mitchell (1988) appears to reject a concept of psychopathology because presumably it is linked to a medical model that implies a "normative human mind," deviations from which are deemed to constitute illness requiring treatment. For Mitchell, there is no normative human mind. Rather, one develops an idiosyncratic mind and personality "only by adopting a highly specific, delimiting shape, and that shape is forged in interaction between the temperamental givens of the baby and the contours of parental character and fantasies" (p. 275). Thus, no one can escape being influenced and shaped by conflictual and delimiting bonds with parents. However, despite his disclaimer, Mitchell cannot avoid reference to psychopathology. Thus, two pages before the above passage, Mitchell writes: "Psychopathology in its infinite variation reflects our unconscious commitment to stasis, to embeddedness in and deep loyalty to the familiar" (p. 273). In other words, although no one can escape being shaped and delimited by parental influences, when these influences result in a certain degree of rigidity and a commitment to stasis, we are entitled to refer to psychopathology. Thus, despite Mitchell's eschewal of a concept of the normative human mind (presumably associated with a medical

Psychopathology and conflict between clinging to early objects and strivings for autonomy

Implicit in assigning pathogenic significance to clinging to early object ties is the idea that such clinging conflicts with the optimal pursuit of various developmental strivings, particularly the striving for separation-individuation (Mahler, 1968) and autonomy, one aspect of which is the development of new age-appropriate relationships. Fairbairn (1952) describes this conflict as one between "infantile dependence" and "mature dependence." As he puts it in his discussion of agoraphobia, the individual is conflicted between "the progressive urge towards separation from the object and the regressive lure of identification with the object" (Fairbairn, 1952, p. 43).

Similar to Fairbairn, Mitchell (1988) views the struggle "both to maintain our ties to others and to differentiate ourselves from others" (p. 3) as the central conflict facing the individual and as a central source of psychopathology.[7] For Mitchell, as for Fairbairn, people cling to archaic objects, even bad objects, because they "impart a sense of familiarity, safety, and connectedness" (p. 172). To feel connected in some way, even if it is suffused with conflict and distress, is preferable to the prospect of being without a sense of inner connectedness. Indeed, according to Mitchell, people willfully pursue "conflictual interactional patterns" (p. 172) as a means of experiencing a needed sense of familiarity, safety, and connectedness.

Mitchell describes the case of a young man who repeatedly becomes involved with depressed women. We learn that in his early life, the only occasions his social butterfly mother spent long periods at home and had time for him is when she was depressed. Thus, for this young man, seeking out depressed women was a way of reinstituting a familiar connection. It is not uncommon to see a similar pattern in women who, having been abused early in life, become involved with abusive men. By doing so, they maintain early object ties and ways of relating that for them constitutes connectedness.

---

model), he is, in effect, offering a model in which a certain degree of rigidity of connection and of commitment to stasis—that is, deviations from the normative—is deemed pathological.

[7] It may be the case that whereas the classical conception of the "danger situations" is more appropriate to one kind of pathology, for example, the neuroses, the contemporary views I have described are more etiologically applicable to other kinds of pathology. Thus, Masterson (1976) believes that parental negative responses to the child's strivings for separation and autonomy, along with reinforcement of the child's dependence and helplessness, are especially associated with borderline conditions. One wonders whether a pattern opposite to the above, that is, a combination of lack of parental emotional availability in the face of the child's dependence and positive response to autonomous behavior, will be associated with some other distinctive form of pathology. These are questions to be explored in future research.

In contrast to the traditional view that infantile wishes (e.g., incestuous impulses) are met with parental disapproval, according to contemporary views, particularly in the case of psychopathology, parental disapproval is often directed not toward the infantile and regressive strivings (that is, early object ties) but rather toward developmental strivings for autonomy. Hence, it is the latter that is often associated with anxiety. One consequence of this state of affairs is that insofar as developmental strivings for autonomy are experienced as threats to needed object ties, these strivings are abandoned or compromised because of the anxiety (and guilt) they entail.

A good example of this dynamic is provided by Masterson (1976). According to his etiological hypothesis, the early experiences of border-line patients are marked by parental emotional availability in response to the child's dependent and helpless behavior and emotional withdrawal and unavailability in response to the child's independent and autonomous behavior. Thus, for these patients, it is not the infantile, that is, helpless and dependent impulses, that are threatening, but rather strivings for independence and autonomy.

In these contemporary views, traditional theory is turned on its head, for it is not only the infantile that is held to be forbidden and suffused with anxiety but also normal developmental strivings for autonomy, what Fairbairn (1952) describes as the "progressive urge toward separation" (p. 43). Another way to describe this view is to say that it is not solely infantile wishes but also what one might call mature wishes and strivings for separation and autonomy, that evoke the "danger situations" of loss of the object and loss of the object's love. If one assumes that mental contents that elicit anxiety are banished from consciousness, that is, repressed, one would conclude that the unconscious of the contemporary views I have described does not consist solely of a "seething cauldron" of infantile instinctual wishes; it also includes repressed mature strivings for separation and autonomy. Of course, the fact that there are dangers associated with *both* regressive and mature strivings is what makes the conflict seem insoluble.

This is an important difference between classical theory and contemporary theories. From a classical point of view, given the oedipal child's harboring of incestuous and hostile wishes, his or her anxiety regarding the danger situations and fears of retaliation are, in some sense, warranted. From a contemporary perspective, the child's fears, anxieties, and guilt are more likely to be seen as based on parental communications than on universal endogenous wishes and impulses. That is, it is not that the child actually harbors, say, hostile wishes toward the parent. Rather, because of parental communications, the child comes to believe that developmental strivings that are not in themselves hostile are harming parents.

In the classical perspective, the primary parental communication is "If you persist in thinking and feeling such and such (primarily infantile sexual and aggressive wishes), I will withdraw my love from you or punish you."

In the contemporary perspective, on the other hand, the prototypic parental communication identified is "If you persist in thinking and feeling such and such (primarily striving for separation and autonomy), you will be harming or destroying me." In both contexts, the child accommodates the demands implicit in parental communications by strategies such as excluding certain possibilities of experience and relinquishing certain strivings in order to maintain needed ties to the object. However, in the former case, the demand is to relinquish infantile sexual and aggressive wishes, whereas in the latter case, the demand is to relinquish strivings for separation and autonomy.

In the classical view, one would say that the child fears that his or her sexual and aggressive wishes will result in being harmed by parents—through loss of the object and loss of the object's love. In the contemporary view, there is greater emphasis on the child's fears that his or her strivings for separation and autonomy will harm parents and therefore will also harm himself or herself. Another difference is that in the former case, the dominant emphasis is on *anxiety*, that is, anticipated danger, for example, fear of punishment. In the latter case, there is an equal emphasis on *guilt* linked to harming parents (Friedman, 1985a). Both perspectives, however, converge on the idea that the primary danger with which the child is concerned is the unavailability of the object, whether that comes about through expected parental withdrawal of love in response to the child's sexual and aggressive impulses or through the child's conviction that he or she has harmed or destroyed the object.

Psychopathology and failure to internalize a secure base

I have noted above that a common theme in contemporary psychoanalytic theories is that psychopathology is marked by clinging to early objects and consequent failure to achieve an adequate degree of autonomy. What accounts for this state of affairs? One answer to this question implicit in the above discussion is that because the individual has not been able to adequately internalize a secure base, he or she continues to cling to early objects and cannot autonomously explore the world (including the exploration of new relationships) without undue anxiety.

Winnicott (1965) observes that the capacity to be alone—which can be understood as an expression of autonomy—is vitally dependent on the individual's success in internalizing a supportive environment—which can be understood as virtually synonymous with a secure base. Winnicott's reasoning here is that the internalization of an ego-supportive environment enables one to be physically alone without undue anxiety because one is not psychically alone, that is, without a sense of connectedness. The internalization of an ego-supportive environment essentially means that one is relatively confident of one's ability to symbolically evoke the presence of the other as well as the actual availability of the other should the need arise.

A clear example of the relationship between the failure to internalize an ego-supportive environment (or safe haven and secure base functions) and impairments in the capacity to be alone (i.e., to explore the world) is the agoraphobic syndrome. It is commonly observed that the agoraphobic individual can tolerate otherwise anxiety-inducing situations if he or she is with, in Deutsch's (1929) words, a "trusted companion." Agoraphobic anxiety is likely to occur when the individual confronts anxiety-inducing situations when physically alone, that is, without the trusted companion.

Another question that arises is what accounts for the individual's failure to internalize a secure base or an ego-supportive environment. There is obviously no single answer to this question. As Mahler (1968) suggested, particularly in the case of severe pathology, constitutional factors may contribute to the individual's relative inability to make use of and internalize parental functions. Another factor, already identified above, lies in parental communications that encourage symbiotic ties and discourage normal strivings for greater autonomy and independence. As an example of this dynamic, one can cite Masterson's (1976) earlier noted hypothesis that an important factor in borderline conditions is parental emotional availability in response to the child's helpless and dependent behavior and parental emotional withdrawal and unavailability in response to the child's moves toward autonomy.

Psychopathology as self-defects

The conception of psychopathology in terms of an active and conflicted clinging to a way of being gives way in Kohut's self psychology to a conception of a passive victim, who, because of self-defects brought about by traumatic environmental failure, cannot help but relate to selfobjects in an archaic way. As Friedman (1986) has put it, according to self psychology, there is only a "stunted state," never a "preferred state." The aptness of Friedman's description is attested to by Basch's (1986) remark that once self-defects are repaired, the patient readily gives up archaic selfobjects and archaic modes of relating because they were never pleasurable in the first place, suggesting that relating to archaic objects is not a matter of active pursuit of certain aims but an expression of defects. As Kohut (1984) notes, at the core of psychopathology are self-defects. Once these defects are repaired, the individual automatically resumes developmental growth in accord with his or her biological design.

Although Kohut essentially removes "structural conflicts" from his conception of psychopathology, there is, however, a trace of the idea of inner conflict in the self psychology theory of self-defects, albeit, as we shall see, a somewhat altered conception of inner conflict. Kohut (1984) maintains that normal development is characterized by the move from archaic to mature selfobject relationships, the self psychology version of a model in which development is conceptualized in terms of the move from symbiotic embed-dedness and infantile dependence to increasing autonomy and mature rela-tionships. According to Kohut, although individuals with self-defects remain embedded in archaic self-selfobject relationships, they continue to strive to complete a normal developmental trajectory, as reflected, for example, in the spontaneous development of mirroring and idealizing transferences in treatment. That is, according to Kohut, the patient seeks from the analyst the empathic mirroring and opportunities for idealization missing in his or her development. Indeed, without such continued strivings, it would be dif-ficult to imagine that treatment could have any positive effect.

However, if the individual who is stuck in archaic self-selfobject rela-tionships nevertheless continues to strive to complete his or her develop-mental trajectory and to achieve a more mature form of relating, then we are, in effect, describing some kind of inner conflict—something akin to Fairbairn's (1952) description of the conflict between "the progressive urge toward separation from the object and the regressive lure of identification with the object" (p. 43).

An emphasis on defects puts a different cast, however, on the nature of the conflict and the form in which it is experienced. Thus, an individual with a particular deficit or defect may strive for autonomy and desire a mature relationship but may not be able to achieve these aims because of the limitations imposed by his or her defects. Thus, this is the kind of con-flict in which one wants to achieve X but cannot do so because, in Kohut's (1984) words, "the nuclear self ... may be composed of structures that are riddled with defects" (p. 99). In this kind of conflict, the issue is not primar-ily ambivalence or guilt about the aims being pursued. Rather, the conflict is between one's aims and one's capacities. It is this sort of fundamental situation that, I think, leads Kohut to speak of "tragic man," in contrast to the "guilty man" of classical theory. What makes man tragic for Kohut it that the individual's suffering is not due to guilt or conflict about his or her aims but the incapacity to carry out these aims.[8]

Kohut's account here is identical in structure to one that would obtain were we talking about someone who although wanting to achieve X, can-not do so because of, say, brain damage or, in Janet's (1907) terms, "con-stitutional weakness." In short, in contrast to the view that certain aims and desires cannot be successfully pursued because they conflict with each other and elicit anxiety and guilt, according to self psychology, certain aims cannot be pursued because of the limitations imposed by the individual's defects and deficits—the stunted state to which Friedman (1986) refers.[9]

---

[8] Although I understand Kohut wanting to make the point that, in his view, the issue is defects rather than guilt over impulses, it is not clear why suffering due to guilt is any less tragic than suffering and failure due to defects.

[9] As we will see in Chapter 9, these different views of the nature of psychopathology have implications for how one understands therapeutic action and the nature of treatment.

It should be noted that although the individual's stunted state, that is, defects, is attributed to environmental failure in self psychology rather than to constitutional weakness, the structure of its etiological theory, that is, the emphasis on defects and its eschewal of the role of inner conflicts, seems to constitute a return to prepsychoanalytic thinking. One simply needs to substitute defects caused by environmental failure for defects caused by constitutional weakness.

Wishes versus needs

The centrality of defects brought about by environmental failure naturally leads Kohut to identify the patient's *unmet needs* rather than *conflictual wishes* as the source of psychopathology and the focus of treatment. using Friedman's language, one can say that whereas conflict theory focuses on the pathogenic role of the patient's preferred state, that is, his or her conflictual wishes, Kohut's self psychology focuses on the pathogenic role of the patient's stunted state, that is, his or her unmet *needs* (see Eagle, 1990, for a further discussion of needs and wishes in self psychology).

As Kohut (1984) has made clear, he eschews talk about the patient's wishes largely because he associates such talk with what he views as the "adult morality" implied in the traditional notion of relinquishment of infantile wishes. For Kohut, the idea that the patient needs to relinquish infantile wishes comes perilously close to viewing the patient as a willful and spoiled child who refuses to give up certain infantile pleasures rather than as someone whose "faulty structures" leave him or her no option but to function in archaic and pathological ways.

One would conclude from the above discussion that there is a sharp distinction between a conception of psychopathology that focuses on conflictual wishes and one that places defects and unmet needs at the center. One emphasizes (conflicting) aims, intentions, and "willful commitments"—a preferred state—and the other emphasizes faulty structures that leave the individual with no options—a stunted state. It seems to me, however, that further analysis suggests that the differences between these two points of view are not as great as they seem.

Consider again Mitchell's view that the individual clings to and makes a willful commitment to the pursuit of early object ties and early modes of relating. Consider also Mitchell's view that the willful commitment to these early ties and modes is motivated by the sense of familiarity, safety, and connectedness these ties provide. To relinquish these ties would be to threaten the individual's sense of familiarity, safety, and connectedness.

Because, in Kohut's view, the individual's successful pursuit of developmental strivings is impeded not by conflict about them but rather because of defects or "faulty structures," treatment does not focus on resolution of conflicts but on repair of faulty structures.

Consider also Fairbairn's (1952) formulation that threats to one's sense of connectedness raises the terrifying prospect of living in an inner void. Hence, although one may use the language of active pursuit and willful commitment—which implies some choice in the matter—if indeed, relinquishing early ties is as terrifying as Fairbairn suggests, there is, in reality, not much of a choice. That is, there is not much of a choice when the alternatives are, on the one hand, some sense of familiarity, safety, and connectedness—even if costs are entailed—and, on the other hand, the terrifying prospect of an inner void.

If the individual clings to early objects because the alternative is experienced as a terrifying void, then the distinction between a preferred state and a stunted state becomes blurred. As noted, although willful commitment and active pursuit are the language of choice, there is not much of a choice. In other words, despite the language of willful commitment and active pursuit, there is no real preference here in any meaningful sense. Or, to put it paradoxically, the individual experiences no choice but to prefer clinging to early ties. It is the peremptory nature of the preference that renders it a stunted state as well as a preferred state.

Thus, in important respects, Mitchell's (and Fairbairn's) accounts are not that different from Kohut's. In both cases, the individual clings to early objects and early modes of relating because the alternative is experienced as impossible and terrifying. As we will see in Chapter 9, in both cases, one important aspect of treatment is enabling the patient to become more capable of relinquishing early object ties through the experience of a different kind of relatedness and different sense of safety and connectedness with the therapist. In short, early ties and early modes of relating can be relinquished only when the alternative is not a void but a new sense of connectedness and a new way of relating.

As noted above, Kohut (1984) has objected to the adult morality that he believes is inherent in the emphasis in traditional theory on the relinquishment of infantile wishes. That is, he suggests that this emphasis smacks too much of a moralistic importuning that the patient give up his or her pursuit of early pleasures. Kohut is intent on replacing the purported attitude of adult morality with the empathic understanding that, because of faculty structures, the patient cannot help but doing what he or she does, demanding what he or she demands, and wanting what he or she wants. The patient's mode of behavior (clinging to archaic selfobject relationships), Kohut (as well as Basch) tells us, is not to be understood as a matter of indulgence in early pleasures but as a matter of preserving some degree of self-cohesiveness and of warding off self-fragmentation.[10]

---

[10]Because it is associated for him with the instinctual infantile wishes emphasized by classical theory, Kohut has no room for the role of preference or pleasure in conceptions of psychopathology. However, although the patient's mode of behavior, say, grandiosity, may

To the extent, however, that an attitude of adult morality has crept into an understanding of the nature of infantile wishes, it constitutes a misunderstanding of that concept and the role it is assumed to play in psychic functioning. That is, the persistence of infantile wishes is not a matter of a self-indulgent pursuit of infantile pleasures or a willful refusal to relinquish these pleasures. Rather, as I have noted elsewhere (Eagle, 1990), infantile wishes and desires are frequently experienced as vital to one's psychic life and psychic functioning. They would not persist were that not the case. In this regard, they are not especially different from the role played by early object ties. Indeed, it seems to me that infantile wishes can only be meaningfully understood as wishes for actual and fantasied early object ties that are experienced as vital to one's life. That is the only plausible clinical meaning that "adhesiveness of the libido" can have. To say that early ties impart a sense of familiarity, safety, and connectedness and to recognize, as Chodorow (2007) does, that the relinquishment of these ties is inevitably accompanied by the experience of loss and mourning, is to grasp in a deep way the concept of infantile wishes in classical theory and to recognize that the pursuit of infantile wishes is not a matter of self-indulgence.

Psychopathology as restriction of range of experience

In the above section, the focus has been on the individual's rigid clinging to early object ties and to early modes of relating as a central aspect of psychopathology. Implicit in this formulation is the idea that these maladaptive patterns also entail rigidities in regard to how one experiences others and oneself and restrictive limitations on the range of one's experiences. The idea that one relates to current objects as if they were stand-ins for earlier objects already clearly implies a rigidity and narrowing of experience. That is, one cannot experience the current object in any other way than through fixed experiential categories formed early in life. New experiences are assimilated to preexisting and fixed structures, with little accommodation of these structures (Piaget, 1954).

The influence of early relational interactions, particularly negative interactions, on limiting the individual's range of awareness and experience has been explicitly addressed by Mitchell and, in particular, by Stolorow and his colleagues. I turn to the latter's work now. According to Stolorow et al. (2002), the child's interactions with parental figures determine his or her "horizons of awareness." That is, those "regions of experiences" that are

---

serve to ward off self-fragmentation, this does not preclude the possibility that there are pleasurable feelings associated with grandiosity. Furthermore, from the perspective of the pleasure principle, the warding off of the danger of self-fragmentation would itself be understood as adhering to the pleasure principle. Thus, once again, one can see that there is no hard and fast distinction between a preferred state and a stunted state.

rejected or invalidated by parental figures or threaten ties to them are sacrificed and remain unformulated and unsymbolized (see discussion of Stern, 2003, in Chapter 6). This is true, according to Stolorow et al. (2002), not only in childhood but also in the individual's current interactions with significant others, including interactions with the therapist. In short, in this view, interactions with others determine "what is or is not allowed to be known"—one's horizons of awareness (p. 47).

It seems to me that the formulation of Stolorow et al. (2002) implicitly identifies two factors involved in the restriction of the individual's range of experience. One factor is a straightforward learning one. That is, certain regions of experience drop out of the child's repertoire because they have not been validated—in the language of learning theory, have not been reinforced. This process serves to shape one's horizons of awareness in a way that is not, in itself, pathogenic in the sense that all socialization entails a sort of culling process in which certain regions of experiences are discouraged, not reinforced, and therefore drop out of one's repertoire.[11] This kind of socializing process becomes pathogenic when it selectively reinforces primarily maladaptive experiences and/or when it restricts the individual's horizons of awareness to the point that experiences necessary for adult competence (including interpersonal competence) and an adaptive and satisfying life are excluded.

The other factor involved in the restriction of the individual's horizons of awareness is not simply a matter of reinforcing a particular set of experiences but has to do with active motives for avoiding certain regions of experience because they threaten ties to objects. In other words, the restriction of experience is not simply the consequence of selective reinforcement

---

[11]The culling of regions of experience in early life as a function of environmental input is part of a normal developmental process. For example, English-learning infants under 6 months of age can discriminate sounds in other languages that English-speaking adults cannot normally discriminate. However, because these sounds of other languages are not provided by the input from the environment, by 1 year of age, the English-learning infants can no longer distinguish these sounds. Their regions of experience have been narrowed by the pattern of environmental input (see Pinker, 2003; Pinker & Bloom, 1992).

A striking experimental example of the shaping of the nervous system and therefore of regions of experience during a critical period by environmental input is found in the work of the Nobel Laureates Hubel and Wiesel (see Wiesel, 1982), who raised kittens that were selectively deprived of experiencing certain line orientations. For example, in one set of experiments, by wearing particular goggles, kittens were raised for the first few months of life experiencing only horizontal lines. When the goggles were removed, the kittens were and remained blind to vertical or oblique lines, that is, to all but horizontal lines. A comparable pattern of results was obtained when kittens were raised in an exclusively vertical or oblique environment. When kittens are raised in an environment with only one orientation, say a horizontal orientation, columns of cells in the primary visual cortex that would have responded to vertical or oblique lines shrink in size or are recruited to represent and respond to horizontal lines. In other words, the input provided by the environment strongly influences the regions of experience that are possible for the organism.

and validation but also the product of implicit and explicit parental communications to the effect that certain regions of experience must remain unformulated and unarticulated because to formulate them would threaten vitally needed ties to parental figures.

Thus, whereas the first factor is a straightforward learning factor, the second factor points to the process of defense. That is, certain experiences are defensively kept from full articulation in consciousness because they elicit fear and anxiety associated with threats to object ties. Thus, the restriction of the range of experience and horizons of awareness that Stolorow et al. (2002) place at the center of psychopathology can be seen as reflecting a special emphasis on one central aspect the experiential aspect, of clinging to early object ties and early modes of relating. That is, whereas the theorists discussed above may focus on the influence of early objects ties and early modes of relating on later relational patterns, Stolorow et al. (2002) emphasize their impact on the range and nature of phenomenal experience. As Brandchaft (2007) puts it in a recent paper, "when the child is required preemptively to adhere to an inflexible personality organization that caregivers bring to its needs for psychological distinctness, these earliest attachment exclude or marginalize spontaneous experience and second thought metacognitive processes of self-reflection" (p. 668).

An important question that one can address to both Freudian and more contemporary views is why defensively excluding certain mental contents from consciousness, however it is accomplished, either through repression or failure to formulate, should be pathogenic. Why assume that narrowing the range of the individual's experience or horizons of awareness is necessarily pathological? After all, under certain circumstances, the exclusion of mental contents from consciousness may enhance rather than compromise adaptive functioning. Indeed, Freud (1929/1930) maintained not only that a certain level of repression—which entails a narrowing of experience—is necessary for functioning in a society but also its corollary, that the *failure of repression* (that is, the threat that certain mental contents will not successfully be excluded from consciousness) leads to the outbreak of neurotic symptoms (see Chapter 4; Eagle, 2000b).

For Freud, that repression narrows the individual's range of experience does not, in itself, render it pathogenic. As we have seen in Chapter 1, its pathogenic significance lies in other reasons having to do with hypotheses about how the mind works. For example, as discussed in Chapter 1, in Freud's early writings, the pathogenicity of repression lay in the fact it prevents discharge of quotas of affect, which are converted into somatic symptoms.

From a Freudian perspective, a critical consideration that links repression to psychopathology is that, given our psychobiological nature, when an instinctual wish or desire is repressed, it does not disappear from psychic life. Rather, it continues to make demands upon the mind that must be dealt with in some way. When these demands cannot be met directly through gratification (i.e., discharge), indirectly or through sublimation, wishes will find partial and disguised expression in neurotic symptoms. Thus, in traditional theory, it is not simply the narrowing of the range of experience that gives repression its pathogenic significance but the fact that certain wishes and desires that are linked to our biological nature need to find some form of discharge.

In contrast to this picture, Stolorow et al. (2002) tend to focus directly on restriction of the range of experience itself as a primary factor in psychopathology. Thus, as we have seen, in the view of Stolorow et al., the main pathogenic consequence of parental failure to validate the child's experience is that certain regions of experience are sacrificed, with the result that one's horizons of awareness become limited and restricted. Indeed, they write that the essence of pathology is "a kind of freezing of a person's experiential horizons" (p. 46) that shuts out certain possibilities of experiencing and relating as well as sense of self and forms of being. Given this view of pathology, it is no surprise that for Stolorow et al., the aim of treatment is to expand the patient's horizons of awareness and to open up the possibility "of an enriched, more complex, and more flexible emotional life" (p. 46).

One should note here that although most observers would agree that the restriction of horizons of awareness or of regions of experience is not desirable, there may not be widespread agreement that it constitutes a primary criterion of psychopathology, nor would there be universal agreement that expansion of the patient's horizons of awareness constitutes a primary goal of treatment. Kohut (1984), for example, maintains

> that with regard to all forms of analyzable psychopathology, *the basic therapeutic unit of the psychoanalytic cure does not rest on the expansion of cognition* [emphasis added] .... Rather, it is the accretion of psychic structure ... that constitutes the essence of the cure. (p. 108)

Ironically, although early on Stolorow viewed himself as a self psychologist, his conception of psychopathology in terms of restrictions of regions of experience and his conception of treatment in terms of expansion of horizons of awareness are closer in spirit to the classical emphasis on the expansion of cognition that Kohut rejects as a goal.

PSYCHOPATHOLOGY AND SELF-REGULATION

Common to both contemporary and classical perspectives is a focus on dysfunctions in self-regulation of negative affects and tension states as a core feature of psychopathology. Although the term *self-regulation* is a relatively recent one in the psychoanalytic literature, the ideas it conveys are already present in classical psychoanalytic theory in the form of the relationship between defense and anxiety, including signal anxiety. As we have seen in Chapter 1, the basic function of defense is to prevent the eruption of anxiety, as well as other dysphoric affects, that is, to regulate affect. In that view, when defenses fail, anxiety and other dysphoric affects erupt into conscious experience. Hence, the failure of defense can be understood as a disorder in self-regulation of negative affect. In classical theory, neurotic symptoms constitute attempts to "bind" the more diffuse anxiety that results from failure of defense. That is to say, they constitute a second line of defense, an attempt at self-regulation that is more maladaptive and exacts a greater cost.

Beyond the psychoanalytic context, there is a good deal of evidence from both animal and human research that the experience of early failures in regulation by the caregiver, for example, through maternal separation, results in subsequent failures in self-regulation lasting into adulthood. To cite but a few findings, rat pups, as well as primates, subjected to maternal disruption show later dysregulation of their stress response systems. For example, separation of the rat pup from mother for more than 3 hours appears to have permanent effects on the rat's reactivity to later external stressors (Francis, Caldi, Champagne, Plotsky, & Meany, 1999). In contrasting, rat pups reared by mothers high in licking and grooming are less fearful in adulthood (Francis & Meany, 1999). There is also evidence that women who were maltreated as children show a 6-fold greater ACTH response to laboratory stress than controls (Heim et al., 2002).

It should be noted that the earlier discussion of failures in internalization of safe haven and secure base functions and of an ego-supportive environment could well have been placed under the heading of self-regulation. That is, the consequences of such failures include inadequate regulation of tension and negative affect states. Recall that when the infant or child is distressed, he or she seeks physical proximity to the attachment figure for comforting and soothing. In the course of development, as one internalizes safe haven and secure base functions, although physical proximity to one's attachment figure may continue to be sought during times of distress, one can increasingly rely for comforting and soothing on one's ability to psychologically evoke one's attachment figure. This is one aspect of an increasing capacity for self-soothing and self-comforting. It is impairment in this capacity that Adler and Buie (1979) and Buie and Adler (1982–1983) identify as a central factor in borderline conditions. It is also an impairment in this capacity that, as we have seen, is central in agoraphobia, where only the actual physical presence of the trusted companion (Deutsch, 1929) serves to regulate the anxiety accompanying exploration.

Self-regulation and object relations and relational theories

As discussed earlier, from the perspective of object relations theory and relational psychoanalysis, clinging to early objects is motivated by the terror of being without a sense of inner connectedness. In the present context, one can say that these early ties constitute a basic means of regulating affect and to relinquish them is to risk serious dysregulation of such negative affects as anxiety, depression, terror, and inner emptiness. That is, the adhesiveness of early object ties serves regulating functions. In this sense, it serves the same basic regulatory function as the defenses of classical theory and the archaic self–selfobject relationships of self psychology theory.

Earlier, I noted the contemporary emphasis on the anxiety-eliciting potential of normal developmental strivings (e.g., for autonomy) rather than of infantile wishes and desires. That is, contemporary theories tend to focus on parental punishment and withdrawal of love in response to strivings for separation and autonomy rather than, as in traditional theory, in response to regressive infantile wishes. I have made much of this point because, as noted, it turns traditional theory on its head and highlights a sharp contrast between contemporary and traditional conceptions of the factors that are at the center of psychopathology. However, I do not want to leave the impression that early object ties are not associated with their own class of dangers.

Although regressive ties to early objects ward off the danger of a feared inner void, they are also associated with other dangers, such as fear of engulfment, and with dysphoric affects, such as depression and shame. Thus, many patients are caught in a seemingly unresolvable conflict in which ties to early objects carry the cost of stasis and the danger of engulfment and dedifferentiation (Schafer, 1983) and breaking of these ties carries the danger of a terrible inner isolation. A frequent compromise formation solution to this dilemma is to maintain these early ties, but at just that distance that minimizes the fears of engulfment on the one hand and of aloneness on the other. This solution, although unsatisfactory and seemingly unstable, can remain unstably stable over a long period, sometimes over a lifetime. This is so because either alternative—clinging to early ties or separation—is dysregulating and is experienced as an intolerable danger. Hence, the compromise solution is maintained.

Another compromise solution is captured by Guntrip's (1969) description of the "in and out program" (p. 36), characterized by an oscillation between moving toward and away from the object. As Guntrip puts it, the individual trapped in the "in and out program" "when separated ... feels utterly insecure and lost, but when reunited ... feels swallowed, absorbed, and loses his separate individuality by regression to infantile dependence" (p. 36). Although Guntrip locates this pattern in the context of schizoid phenomena, one should not understand that to mean that it only characterizes schizoid individuals. Rather, it should be understood, in Guntrip's terms, as a schizoid phenomenon or compromise that is present in a wide range of individuals.

To the extent that the other is a stand-in for an early object, the above compromise solutions will be played out with current figures. Neither real intimacy and closeness, which are experienced as engulfment, nor actual separation, experienced as terrifying inner aloneness, will be possible. Instead, either an "in-out" oscillation or a stable, safe stance between distance and closeness that avoids either catastrophe of engulfment or utter aloneness will be implemented.

Two patients with whom I have worked have shown the above patterns in a strikingly clear way. In one case, the patient had been separated from her abusive and sadistic husband for more than 20 years but could not either end the relationship or fully engage in it. Moves in either direction were met with severe depression, despair, and suicidal thoughts. My patient's solution was to live apart from her husband but spend one or two weekends a month with him. Although this solution was of more than 20 years' duration, it was stably unstable. That is, when she arrived at her husband's house, she would immediately feel anxious and want to return home. However, as soon as she returned home after the weekend, she would call her husband and feel the urge to visit him again. It was stably unstable in another way. Despite the maintenance of this pattern for more than 20 years, my patient continued to expect that she was going to make a clear-cut decision as to whether she would reunite with or divorce her husband.

In the second case, discussed in Chapter 4, in which the patient's symptom consisting in very troubling obsessive thoughts that he might be homosexual protected him from the terrible danger of engulfment—of "black nothingness"—that heterosexual intimacy represented for him. As long as he could maintain an optimal distance, which was challenged by the girlfriend's pressure, he maintained his equilibrium. After the girlfriend got fed up with his procrastination and failure to commit to her and left him, his symptom abated. The nature of the compromise reached and the degree of distance maintained will vary with whether engulfment or aloneness is experienced as the greater danger. Some patients experience aloneness as the greater danger and others experience engulfment as the greater danger.

According to Guntrip (1969)—and I am inclined to agree with him, by and large—the former is generally experienced as the greater danger. As he puts it:

> My own experience of patients suggests that the fear of isolation, of the ego being emptied by feeling completely cut off from all object-relationships is deeper and more overpowering than the fear of the ego being violated or smothered in object-relationships. (p. 267)

PSYCHOPATHOLOGY AND VIEWS
OF HUMAN NATURE

The contrasting conceptions of psychopathology I have described are derived not only from different theories of its etiology but also from different conceptions of human nature and its relationship to society. As noted earlier, on the Freudian view, we harbor *endogenous and universal* infantile sexual and aggressive wishes, impulses, and fantasies that are inherently inimical to the rules and demands of civilized society. It is this inherent conflict that constitutes the foundation for neurosis, the inevitable "discontents" generated by civilization (Freud, 1929/1930). In disapproving and punishing infantile sexual and aggressive wishes, parental figures are merely fulfilling their socializing role as agents of society. Were they not to carry out their role, other aspects of society (e.g., teachers, authorities) would do so. Hence, it is not merely the happenstance of parental disapproval that results in the conflictual and anxiety-laden status of infantile sexual and aggressive wishes. It is, rather, the inherent and inevitable conflict between these wishes and the demands and requirements of living in a civilized society. So, in a certain sense, from the point of view of traditional theory—although this may perhaps be overstating the case—it does not matter that much what parents do, how disapproving and punitive they are. The roots of neurosis mainly lie not in the vicissitudes of environmental failure but in the nature of human nature or, more accurately, in the inevitable clash between human nature and society. As Mitchell (1988) observes, for Freud, "sexuality is a vestige of our bestial ancestry, always a threat to our superimposed civilized demeanor" (p. 76). In his later writings, Freud (e.g., 1927) also adds aggression as a vestige of our bestial ancestry and as a threat to civilization.

In contrast to the above view, in the contemporary theories I have been discussing, neurosis is not inherent in human nature but, as we have seen, is attributable to one form or another of parental failure early in life. For Winnicott (1965), parental failure consists in not providing a good enough "facilitating environment" for optimal unfolding of "maturational process." For Weiss et al. (1986), parental failure consists in parental communication that engenders "unconscious pathogenic beliefs." For Fairbairn (1952), parental failure consists in deprivation and frustration that lead to splits in the ego.[12] For Kohut (1984), parental failure consists in traumatic lack of empathic mirroring. For Stolorow et al. (2002), parental failure

---

[12]The concept of self-defects shares in common with the notion of ego weakness formulated in ego psychology the central idea of failures in self-regulation of negative affects. Insofar as defense is an ego function, failure of defense and the flood of dysphoric affects experienced in its wake can be understood as a failure of self-regulation due to ego weakness.

consists in rejection and invalidation of the child's experiences, resulting in restrictions in the individual's range of experience.

Mitchell's views on psychopathology are more complex and nuanced and therefore more difficult to simply place in the category of parental failure theories. On the one hand, similar to Freud, Mitchell suggests that given our prolonged helplessness and dependence on parents and the powerful parental influence on development, some degree of psychopathology is inevitable. He writes:

> In my view, *all* children are bent out of shape (or more accurately, *into* shape) in their early significant relationships, and this is a result neither of inherent bestiality nor of faulty parenting, but of the inevitable emotional conditions of early life. (p. 275)

He also writes that "conflictual attachment to and identification with archaic objects are universal" (p. 278). On the other hand, he states that "the more rigid the connection provided by the parents, the more the child is forced to choose between the limited forms of relation or total isolation, and the more compulsive are the residues of these relationships" (p. 278). In other words, although "identification with archaic objects [is] universal," the degree of "difficulties in living" one is likely to experience will be a function of one's "degree of adhesion" to one's early relational matrix, which in turn will be strongly influenced by the rigidity of connection provided by the parents. In short, although more nuanced, Mitchell's theory of psychopathology or, as he prefers to say, "difficulties in living," also constitutes a parental failure model. In Mitchell's scheme, parental failure consists in providing so rigid a connection that the child is forced to choose between limited forms of relation and total isolation.

The emphasis in contemporary psychoanalysis theories on parental failure was preceded by an earlier parallel view, associated with the work of Fromm (e.g., 1955/1990, 1973/1992) and others, to the effect that the essential goodness and essential soundness that characterize human nature are contaminated not so much by parental failure as by the evil and sickness of society. In contemporary theories, parental failure has replaced societal failure as the primary etiological agent of psychopathology. Consider, for example, Fairbairn's (1952) proposal that the infant is born with a pristine unitary ego that is then subjected to splits due to parental rejection and deprivation. For both Fromm and Fairbairn, our fall from grace is brought about by, respectively, societally and parentally induced depredations of postnatal life. It should perhaps be no surprise that for Fromm, the Marxist analyst, it is the evils of (capitalist) society that are responsible for our suffering, whereas for Fairbairn, the object relations psychoanalyst with a religious background, it is parental rejection and failure to love adequately that transform our God-given unity into a state of disunity and distress. One also wonders whether it is modern disillusionment with the possibilities of altering society that, at least in part, accounts for the shift from a focus on societal failure to a focus on parental failure.[13]

There is another shift worth noting. It has been a long time since one heard Frommian talk about the essential goodness or essential soundness inherent in human nature. Instead, what characterizes at least some contemporary psychoanalytic theories is a view of human nature as *essentially socially malleable*. This perspective is apparent in Hoffman's (e.g., 1991) espousal of "social constructivism" and, as we have seen in Chapter 6, is especially characteristic of Mitchell's (e.g., 1998) more recent views.

RECAPITULATION

In contrast to the classical view that psychopathology is the product of conflict between sexual and aggressive wishes and prohibitions and defenses against them (drive-defense model), contemporary psychoanalytic theories locate psychopathology in "relationships with others ...[,] the basic stuff of mental life" (Mitchell, 1988, p. 2). A corollary of this view is that psychopathology is the product not of the conflict between endogenous wishes and defenses against them but of environmental failure, that is, failures in early relationships with others. To the extent that inner conflict remains a central concept in contemporary psychoanalytic theories of psychopathology, it is not the conflict between instinctual drives and defense but the conflict between early object ties and early modes of relating, on the one hand, and more adaptive object ties and modes of relating, on the other. Indeed, clinging to early object ties and the persistence of early modes of relating, based on early interactional representations, emerge as central factors in contemporary psychoanalytic theories of psychopathology.

Other issues discussed in this chapter include the concept of self-defects centrality of wishes versus needs, limitations in the range of experience as a function of parental prohibition and invalidation, the role of self-regulation in conceptions of psychopathology, and the relationship between theories of human nature and conceptions of psychopathology.

---

[13]However, Fairbairn (1952) also notes that because it is impossible to altogether escape deprivation and frustration in the course of development, the original "pristine unitary" status of the ego cannot be maintained, and some degree of ego splits is inevitable. In this regard, although from an entirely different theoretical vantage point, Fairbairn, like Freud, suggests that given the nature of social reality, some degree of *pathology* is inevitable.

Chapter 9

Conceptions of treatment in contemporary psychoanalytic theories: Therapeutic goals and analytic stance

Before attempting to identify various themes in contemporary conceptions of treatment and therapeutic action, I want to reiterate some observations made earlier. Contemporary conceptions of psychoanalytic treatment are not only a function of such factors as clinical experience, the changing nature of psychopathology, widened scope, and empirical findings but also reflect socioeconomic factors and broad philosophical changes in the larger culture. The classical psychoanalytic emphasis on the therapeutic value of insight, awareness, and self-knowledge reflect, at least in part, the influence of the Enlightenment vision. "Know thyself," an Enlightenment value, was also identified as the way to cure oneself. Perhaps more than any other factor, it is deep skepticism toward the Enlightenment assumption that self-knowledge and learning truths about oneself are curative (the truth shall set you free) that represents a challenge to the classical conception of treatment. Such skepticism is but one specific expression of a more general questioning attitude regarding the value and even the possibility of pursuing truths, either about the external world or about oneself.

This attitude is very clearly expressed in, for example, Rorty's (1991) critique of the idea of pursuing truths and his favoring of solidarity over objectivity as a cultural value to be pursued. He writes:

> The tradition in Western culture which centers around the notion of the search for truth, a tradition which runs from the Greek philosophers through the Enlightenment, is the clearest example of the attempt to find a sense of one's existence by turning away from solidarity to objectivity. The idea of truth as something to be pursued for its own sake, not because it will be good for oneself, or for one's real or imagined community, is the central theme of this tradition. (p. 21)

If one thinks of solidarity, which is defined as "unity and mutual support" (*Compact Oxford English Dictionary*, 2000), as generally equivalent to privileging relationships and objectivity as equivalent to privileging the pursuit of truths, one can understand the deemphasis of insight and self-knowledge and concomitant strong emphasis on relationship factors as clear expressions of the favoring of solidarity over objectivity in contemporary conceptions of treatment.

Freud, a product of the Enlightenment vision, clearly believed in the apparently extraordinarily fortunate convergence between knowing oneself and curing oneself. Thus, he could insist that he was not injecting his Enlightenment *Weltanschauung* into his conception of treatment. Rather, he could maintain that it happened to be objectively the case that insight and self-knowledge are curative. However, once this claim is questioned and the convergence between *know thyself* and *cure thyself* is no longer taken for granted, the issue of values and *Weltanschauung* comes to the fore. That is, it becomes more difficult to base one's justification of the traditional psychoanalytic emphasis on awareness and self-knowledge primarily on its claims of clinical cure. Rather, the grounds for valuing self-knowledge, knowing oneself, and leading an examined rather an unexamined life become somewhat independent of their clinical efficacy.[1]

Whatever *Weltanschauung* characterizes contemporary psychoanalysis, it is certainly not the Enlightenment one that influenced Freud's thinking. That *Weltanschauung* is no longer a central aspect of the zeitgeist. Indeed, many contemporary psychoanalytic theorists not only are skeptical about the clinical efficacy of self-knowledge and learning truths about oneself but, as we will see, are also deeply skeptical about their very possibility. The goals of enhanced self-understanding and self-knowledge are replaced by such goals as constructing more coherent narratives, reorganization of experience, interpretive constructions, retellings, new perspectives, new experiences, an empathic bond, and so on—anything but self-understanding and self-knowledge.

SOME COMMON THEMES IN CONTEMPORARY CONCEPTIONS OF TREATMENT

The above paints contemporary conceptions of treatment in broad strokes. I turn now to a more detailed description and an attempt to identify some common themes. I have organized my discussion of contemporary psychoanalytic conceptions of treatment into the same categories used in Chapter 5

---

[1] Alan Stone (1997), a former president of the American Psychiatric Association, has remarked that although it has turned out that psychoanalysis may not be an appropriate treatment for major mental illness, it is the best means of learning about the "otherness" of oneself. Furthermore, even if the content implanted by the analyst's interpretation did accurately correspond to what is going on in the patient's mind, the patient's response to the interpretation could still represent succumbing to suggestion rather than reflecting greater self-understanding. Indeed, I suspect that much of what we think of as intellectual insight can be understood as the product of the patient's response to suggestion.

(although the order of the discussion of each topic is different). The topics are as follows:

1. Process and outcome therapeutic goals
2. Analytic stance
3. Therapeutic action and ingredients[2]

Process and outcome therapeutic goals

One needs to distinguish between process and outcome goals. The former term refers to goals within the treatment that are believed to facilitate the treatment process, whereas, as the term *outcome* suggests, the latter refers to the goals one would want to see the treatment achieve. For example, the lifting of repression is a process goal that, according to classical theory, will facilitate the outcome goal of more adaptive resolution of conflict. As another example, reorganizing one's experiences (Mitchell, 1998) seems primarily a process goal in the service of achieving the outcome goals of developing new perspectives and new coherent narratives about one's life— achievements that one would want the patient to take with him or her upon terminating treatment. Of course, it is not always possible to distinguish sharply between process and outcome because some goals belong to both categories. For example, strengthening of the patient's capacity for reflection and mentalization would clearly seem to constitute both a process and outcome goal in the sense that it both facilitates the ongoing treatment process and also represents an achievement (a "structural change") and end product of the treatment (see Fonagy & Bateman, 2006, for a description of the outcome of a mentalization treatment with borderline patients).

From a general and broad perspective, one would think that all forms of treatment would have a common limited set of outcome goals, such as relief of suffering and distress, increased capacity for love and work (which Freud is purported to have tersely summarized as the goals of psychoanalytic treatment), and increased pleasure and satisfaction in life. However, beyond these broad background aims, there is a bewilderingly long list of process and outcome goals identified in the psychoanalytic literature. I note only a partial list below:

1. Making the unconscious conscious (Freud, 1932/1933)
2. Where id was, there shall ego be (Freud, 1923)
3. Increased capacity for love and work (Freud, 1914b, 1929/1930)
4. Renunciation of infantile wishes (Widlocher, 2002)
5. Structural change (Wallerstein, 1988)

---

[2] Therapeutic goals and analytic stance will be covered in this chapter, and therapeutic action and ingredients will be covered in Chapter 10.

6. Enhancement of self-cohesiveness (Kohut, 1984)
7. Increased flexibility of defenses (Weiss & Sampson, 1986)
8. Meaning-making and reorganization of experience (Mitchell, 1998)
9. Enhancement of personal agency (Schafer, 1978)
10. Exorcising internalized objects (Fairbairn, 1952)
11. Reducing splits in the ego (Fairbairn, 1952)
12. Expanded range of experience (Stolorow Atwood, & Orange, 2002)
13. Internalization of therapeutic function (Wzontek, Geller, & Farber, 1995)
14. Greater capacity for sublimation (Freud, 1932/1933)
15. More coherent "retellings" and narratives (Schafer, 1992; Spence, 1993)
16. New perspectives (Renik, 1996)
17. Better affect regulation (Kohut, 1984)
18. Identification of maladaptive representations and interactional patterns (Mitchell, 1988)
19. Identification of unconscious pathogenic beliefs (Weiss & Sampson, 1986)
20. Disconfirmation of unconscious pathogenic beliefs (Weiss & Sampson, 1986)
21. Change in maladaptive attachment patterns (Levy et al., 2006)
22. Learning of new and more varied ways of relating (Mitchell, 1988)
23. Resumption of developmental growth (Guntrip, 1969; Kohut, 1984; Loewald, 1979)
24. Resolution of conflict (Freud, 1918/1919)
25. More adaptive compromise (Brenner, 1998)
26. Enhancement of the adaptive function of the ego (Freud, 1932/1933)
27. Enhancement of reflective capacity (Fonagy, 2006)

It is obviously beyond the scope of this chapter to discuss each of the above therapeutic goals. Further, I doubt that it would be profitable to even make the attempt. Some overlap with each other, some are vague, and some constitute different language for already familiar ideas. Instead, I will attempt to identify and discuss some common themes that emerge in contemporary psychoanalytic theories in the context of contrasting them with traditional theory.

From insight, self-understanding, and self-knowledge to coherent narratives, interpretive constructions, and an empathic bond

As noted above, at least some contemporary conceptions of treatment are characterized by a deep skepticism toward the therapeutic value of insight and self-knowledge. Freud's Enlightenment faith that the Socratic imperative to know oneself is also the route to clinical cure is not shared by many contemporary analysts. One consequence of this skepticism is that the rationale and justification for the former is, so to speak, left hanging. If self-understanding and self-knowledge cannot be entirely justified on clinical grounds (e.g., amelioration of symptoms), on what grounds can they be justified? The question is not only a conceptual or philosophical one but also a practical one. Imagine trying to justify an insurance payment primarily on the grounds that the treatment will enhance the patient's self-understanding and self-knowledge, or that the unexamined life is not worth living.

The contemporary skepticism regarding self-understanding and self-knowledge is expressed in a number of ways. As we have seen in Chapter 6, one such way is a rejection of the classical idea that the analyst uncovers or discovers what goes on in the patient's mind (Mitchell, 1998). The emphasis in treatment has shifted from learning truths about oneself that had not been accessible because of repression and other defenses to reorganizing one's experiences and developing new perspectives and new narratives.[3]

Another, more fundamental challenge to the therapeutic role of self-understanding and self-knowledge that flows from contemporary psychoanalytic conceptions of mind (see Chapter 6) lies in a virtual denial of their very possibility. This shift in the goals of treatment does not rest primarily on pragmatic grounds, that is, on an empirically based conviction that enhanced self-understanding and self-knowledge are not clinically effective. Rather, it appears to be based on the conceptually grounded rejection of the very possibility of self-understanding and self-knowledge. In other words, it is not that, say, the construction of coherent narratives has been shown to be more therapeutically effective than enhanced self-understanding and self-knowledge. Rather, the claim is that there exist only coherent narratives, interpretive constructions, and so on. To put it still another way, there is no kind of self-understanding or self-knowledge possible that can be distinguished from persuasive and coherent narratives (Spence, 1984), interpretive constructions (Mitchell, 1998), aesthetic fictions (Geha, 1984), and so on (see Eagle, 1984a, b).

Identifying and altering maladaptive self, other, and interactional representations

Given the focus on maladaptive representations and patterns as a core factor in contemporary theories of psychopathology (see Chapter 8), it is not surprising, first, that a central process goal of contemporary conceptions of treatment is the identification of these maladaptive representations and

---

[3] "Retellings," in Schafer's (1992) words, about one's life. See also Spence (1984); Eagle, Wolitzky, and Wakefield (2001); and Eagle, Wakefield, and Wolitzky (2003) for a critique of this view.

patterns, particularly as they are reflected in the relationship with the therapist, and second, that a central outcome goal is their modification and replacement by new, more adaptive and satisfying ways of relating to others.

This focus on identification of maladaptive representations as a therapeutic goal appears to be somewhat at odds with the above-noted contemporary skepticism regarding the possibility of uncovering and discovering mental contents in the patient's mind that will contribute to self-knowledge. Although Mitchell (1998) focuses his skepticism mainly on the possibility of uncovering repressed unconscious wishes, he does seem to suggest that uncovering of any kind is not possible. However, is not the identification of certain interactional patterns and of the unconscious beliefs and expectations that underlie them a kind of uncovering and discovering? And does not what is uncovered and discovered contribute to the patient's self-knowledge? It seems to me that the identification of self, other, and interactional representations does, indeed, constitute a kind of uncovering and discovering. However, it is not the kind of uncovering and discovering to which contemporary theorists such as Mitchell object. That is, it does not entail the discovery of repressed wishes waiting to be uncovered. Nevertheless, I believe that an emphasis on identifying the patient's representations and interactional patterns does present a challenge to a view that maintains that psychoanalytic treatment offers only or mainly interpretive constructions, narratives, retellings, and so on.

Analytic stance: Rejection of blank-screen role

Let me turn now to the question of analytic stance. Contemporary conceptions of treatment have in common a rejection of the so-called blank-screen role of the analyst and its replacement with a more active and interactional therapeutic role. This trend goes at least as far back as Ferenczi (e.g., Ferenczi & Rank, 1924/1956), is apparent in Sullivan's (1940) conception of the role of the therapist as "participant-observer," is implicit in discussions of "a widened scope" in analysis (L. Stone, 1954) and of "parameters" (Eissler, 1953) and finds a clear expression in the contemporary distinction between a "one-person" versus a "two-person" psychology (e.g., Gill, 1994). In contrast to the classical conception of the analyst as an opaque, relatively affectless, objective, neutral observer, the contemporary analyst is seen as a more active interactional participant who cannot help but react emotionally to the patient in various ways and whose views and interpretations of the patient are "irreducibly subjective" (Renik, 1998; see also Hoffman, 1994). Hence, for these contemporary theorists, it is not only the blank-screen role of the analyst that is rejected but also what to them seem related ideas such as analytic neutrality and the possibility of offering objective interpretations. (I will have more to say about the former later in the chapter.)

For contemporary theorists, a fundamental problem with the classic analytic stance is the assumption that the analyst can be a blank screen who contributes nothing to the interaction. As Gill (1994) and others have pointed out, being silent or nonresponsive is not equivalent to not contributing to the interaction or not emitting cues. Indeed, it is virtually impossible in any interaction between two people for either of them not to emit cues. Long periods of silence and a nonresponsive demeanor constitutes a particular and potentially powerful set of cues that will have different meanings to different patients—ranging from an experience of nonintrusive and quiet holding to an experience of sadistic withholding—depending upon, among other things, the patient's and analyst's individual histories, the nature of their relationship, and aspects of the analyst's tone and general demeanor.

Another problem with the classic analytic stance that has been identified by contemporary analysts and that has been pointed out by Holzman (1976) is that, unfortunately, it often became caricatured into emotional coldness, aloofness, and stodginess. Surely, these qualities do not simply constitute a neutral blank screen onto which the patient projects. Rather, they are likely to have a great, including an iatrogenic, impact on the patient. Furthermore, although it may be true that more disturbed patients would have greater difficulty dealing with these qualities, why would one expect them to be helpful and therapeutically useful for anyone?

Of course, it is possible that personal qualities of warmth, empathy, and concern rather than coldness and aloofness were communicated to the patient by classical analysts, despite theoretical endorsement of a blank-screen neutral stance. However, it would likely be more difficult for inexperienced analysts to trust their personal intuition and resist the strictures of the blank-screen stance. My impression is that when classical orthodoxy was predominant, that is, prior to the current pluralism and the loosening up of the analytic situation brought about by the advent of self psychology and relational psychoanalysis, many younger analysts, wary of being seen as not truly analytic by permitting so-called transference gratification, adopted an austere stance that was pretty close to what Holzman (1976) described as a caricature of analytic neutrality.

In a recent paper, Skolnick (2006) devotes a lengthy discussion to lending his patient an umbrella as a turning point in his perspective on the question of an appropriate analytic stance. What does this tell us about a discipline when so much self-doubt and torturous discussion are generated by the simple act of lending a patient an umbrella? In this regard, one wonders about the degree to which some developments that are hailed as advances, for example, greater freedom to do things like lend the patient an umbrella, are mainly commonsensical corrections (see Hoffman, 1998, for an interesting discussion of "ritual and spontaneity" in the analytic situation).

It has been frequently remarked that despite advocating a blank-screen neutral stance, Freud lent a patient money, gave food to a hungry patient, and the like. However, it was also Freud (1912c) who urged analysts

> to model themselves during psychoanalytic treatment on the surgeon, who puts aside all his feelings, even his human sympathy, and concentrates his mental forces on the simple aim of performing the operation as skillfully as possible.... The justification for requiring this emotional coldness in the analyst is that it creates the most advantageous conditions for both parties: for the doctor a desirable protection for his own emotional life and for the patient the largest amount of help that we can give him today. (p. 115)

It is likely that it was the latter that had a greater influence on generations of analysts than the anecdotes about lending money to a patient.

The problem of suggestion

Although suggestion was a major concern for Freud (Meehl, 1994), given contemporary conceptions of treatment and of the role of the analyst, it appears to be no longer viewed as a major issue. For one thing, there is the general recognition that however much one may try to be a blank screen, one cannot help but emit cues that are likely to reveal one's personal biases. Although these cues are not direct suggestions, they nevertheless can operate as subtle forms of indirect suggestion. Indeed, Renik (1998) has argued that given the analyst's "irreducible subjectivity" and inevitable personal biases, it would be more realistic and helpful to the patient for the analyst to openly express them, to acknowledge his or her aims for the patient and his or her interest in personally influencing the patient to pursue these aims. Renik's argument is that both patient and analyst can more adequately deal with personal biases and influences when they are, so to speak, laid out on the table then when hidden and unacknowledged. (That it is not a universal view is reflected in the comment by Friedman, 1998, that the fact that analysis is already so complex and noisy is no reason not to try to keep the complexity and noise down.)

There is another, deeper reason that suggestion is no longer seen as a major issue in contemporary conceptions of treatment. Indeed, I think it is fair to say that given contemporary psychoanalytic conceptions of mind and of the main tasks of analysis, rather than being problematic, suggestion is essentially, even if implicitly, embraced as a central component of analytic work. Recall that, as Meehl (1994) has pointed out, the classic issue of suggestion—the one that was of greatest concern to Freud—is that the analyst's interpretation constitutes "content implantation" rather than uncovering and identifying what is going on in the patient's mind, that is, "tallying with what is real in the patient" (Freud, 1916–1917/1917, p. 452). Thus, the suggestion critique went, when a patient accepts such an interpretation, he or she is not furthering self-understanding but is, rather, succumbing to the analyst's suggestion. These concerns about content implantation become far less relevant when the analytic task is understood not as uncovering and discovering what is going on in the patient's mind but in such terms as reorganization of experience, "interpretive construction," coconstructions, retellings that make a "beneficial difference," coherent narratives, and so on. In this latter view, there is no sharp demarcation line between what is there in the patient's mind and what is implanted by the analyst. All is constructed and coconstructed by patient and analyst in a complex negotiating process. There is no longer a clean-cut problem of suggestion and content implantation.

Empathic stance

Although most analysts recognize the desirability and importance of an empathic stance as a background factor in treatment, the role of empathic understanding has been pushed to the forefront as an active therapeutic ingredient, indeed, as the primary curative factor, in self psychology. I will discuss this more fully later in the chapter. Here, I merely want to note that in identifying empathic understanding as a therapeutic ingredient in itself, the analyst's focus is not on interpreting and uncovering repressed contents or on identifying maladaptive representations or on analyzing ego defenses but rather on establishing an empathic bond. In this regard, there is a clear convergence (although an unacknowledged one) between self psychology and Carl Rogers's (e.g., 1951) assumption that an empathic stance (along with other components of a therapeutic stance such as genuineness and authenticity) is itself therapeutic and growth-promoting.

Analytic neutrality

One of the difficulties in discussing the role of analytic neutrality in psychoanalytic treatment lies in the way it has been understood—in my view, misunderstood. Analytic neutrality has been equated, mistakenly, I believe, with the blank screen, anonymity, abstinence, objectivity, and the eschewal of subjectivity.

Therefore, for many contemporary analysts who view themselves as self psychologists or "relational" or "intersubjective," the idea of analytic neutrality deserves the same fate as these other remnants of a classical analytic stance. In this view, the analyst who espouses the value of analytic neutrality is precisely the analyst who is also impersonal, anonymous, silent, passive, a nonresponsive blank screen. It must be acknowledged that given the caricature of analytic neutrality and of other aspects of a classical analytic stance noted by Holzman (1976), it is understandable that analytic neutrality came to be equated with emotional coldness, aloofness, and so on. However, I think this is a mistaken view of the concept.

Let me first provide some examples of current attitudes and construals of analytic neutrality. In a recent panel on analytic neutrality, as suggested by the title of their paper, "Neutrality and Abstinence: Obstacles to an Analysis in Depth," Orenstein and Orenstein (2003) repeatedly pairs neutrality and abstinence and, in his presentation of clinical vignettes, contrasts talking *about* the patient—presumably associated with neutrality and abstinence—with talking *to* the patient—presumably associated with the relinquishment of neutrality and the assumption of an empathic position. Needless to say, in this view, the patient can be reached or helped only when the analyst adopts the latter stance.

As another example of how analytic neutrality is understood by some contemporary analysts, I cite Renik's (1996) comment that any claim to analytic neutrality is rendered untenable in the light of the analyst's irreducible subjectivity. Such presumed irreducible subjectivity leads Renik (1996) to reject the traditional claim that "the analyst addresses the patient's, rather than the analyst's own psychic reality" (p. 509) and argues that because of the analyst's irreducible subjectivity, the patient is given the "analyst's own idiosyncratic views" rather than finding "the patient's views" (p. 509). There is a good deal of confusion on Renik's part, for even if the analyst is presenting his or her "own idiosyncratic views," they are idiosyncratic views about the *patient's* psychic reality, not his or her own. What else would psychoanalytic (or any other) treatment be (see Eagle et al., 2001)?

Renik seems to confuse the necessary irreducible subjectivity of personal experiences with the phenomenon of subjective biases. It is a truism to say that all experiences are irreducibly subjective. My experiences are mine, they are not anyone else's. Stating that personal experiences are necessarily irreducibly subjective, however, is not equivalent to stating that they are subjectively biased. My experience of a chair in front of me is irreducibly subjective, but this does not mean that my experience cannot also be objective and unbiased (see Nagel, 1986; Searle, 1992, 1998). Furthermore, I am not necessarily helpless in the face of possible subjective biases. I can reflect on my experiences and views. I can report my experiences, as well as my beliefs, accounts, and so on, to people with different perspectives and perhaps different subjective biases. I can also attempt to subject my experiences and views to certain commonly agreed upon procedures and safeguards that have been proven to be relatively effective means of dealing with a wide variety of subjective biases. One such set of procedures constitutes the scientific enterprise. As Von Eckardt (1981) has pointed out, one can declare oneself helpless in the face of subjective bias, wallow in its inevitability and inescapability, and embrace its virtues, or one can adopt a set of agreed upon procedures that are designed to modulate the effects of subjective bias.

However, Renik's confusion aside, the point I want to make here is the distinction between, on the one hand, acknowledging one's biases and attempting to modulate them and, on the other hand, embracing a solipsistic position in which one proclaims that the analyst is addressing his or her own rather than the patient's psychic reality. Most important, that the analyst's, or anyone else's, experiences are irreducibly subjective—what else can first-person experiences be?—does not in any way mean that one cannot try to understand another's psychic reality, which is also irreducibly subjective, as accurately and objectively as possible (see Nagel, 1986), nor does the irreducible subjectivity of the analyst's experiences in any way mean that one cannot take a position of analytic neutrality in relation to the patient.

Although the analyst's subjective biases, suggestions, subtle selective reinforcements, idiosyncratic views, and so on may all be unavoidable, one can nevertheless pursue the ideal of analytic neutrality. In my view, it is important to do so because of the place of *autonomy* as a central value in psychoanalysis. When properly understood, analytic neutrality does not consist in being a blank screen or in being without affect and caring or in remaining cold and silent. Rather, at its core are the ideas of avoiding taking sides in the patient's conflicts and not telling the patient how to live his or her life—which, in turn, rest on the central valuing of the patient's autonomy. And by autonomy I do not mean autonomy as independence but autonomy as greater freedom to shape one's life. It seems to me that central to any psychoanalytic perspective are the core ideas that psychopathology of any kind (whether viewed as intrapsychic conflict or developmental defects) always impairs one's autonomy in some way, and that essential goals of psychoanalytic treatment include removing or ameliorating these impairments and enhancing the patient's ability to more freely choose how to live his or her life.

Renik (1996) is, of course, right in noting that as a therapist one wants to contribute to one's patients' increased happiness. However, there are many routes to increased happiness, and the patient has to find his or her own route, not adopt the analyst's route. The kind and degree of happiness the patient is capable of experiencing will not be determined by the analyst's zeal or intentions but by the patient's makeup and life circumstances. The analyst's job is not to *provide* the patient with happiness but, as much as possible, to remove impediments to the patient's ability to make choices that will at least provide the opportunity, certainly not the guarantee, for increased satisfaction and happiness.

One is reminded here of Freud's (Breuer & Freud, 1893–1895, p. 305) often misunderstood comment that a successful analysis replaces neurotic misery with ordinary human unhappiness. This has often been understood as an expression of Freud's gloomy and deeply pessimistic attitude toward life and toward the therapeutic possibilities of psychoanalysis. However,

I believe that Freud was attempting to be utterly realistic in pointing out that any psychoanalysis, including a successful one, cannot guarantee happiness. Life is filled with too many unexpected events such as illness and loss for that guarantee to have any meaning. In response to these events, unhappiness is an appropriate response. The goal of psychoanalysis, Freud is telling us, is not happiness but the amelioration of neurotic factors that guarantee misery and that serve as impediments to the realistic pursuit of those satisfactions that life has to offer.

As I see it, the analyst's role and the goal of psychoanalytic treatment are not to delineate the path to a more gratifying and more meaningful life but to enhance the possibility of the patient finding his or her own route. In discussing a particular patient, Renik (1996) remarks that what he wants for this patient is the same as what he wants for his daughter. However, the patient is not his daughter. Furthermore, it is not even necessarily the case that what he wants for his daughter is identical to what his daughter wants for herself. Renik's sentiment is perfectly understandable. He undoubtedly wants good things for both his patient and his daughter. However, although understandable, as countertransference, his statement is as subject to self-reflection as any other reaction. It cannot, it seems to me, serve as a legitimate goal for psychoanalytic treatment.

One of the central points made by Renik is that insofar as subjective biases and personal preferences are inevitable, the analyst might as well lay them out on the table rather than pretend that he or she is neutral. The latter, Renik (1996) argues, constitutes a more insidious influence insofar as it is not dealt with openly. I think that Renik has a legitimate point here. However, the issue is a more complex one. Given the power of the transference, the patient may be able to hear the analyst's position only as a directive rather than as something to be mutually examined. Although the analyst's biases are often expressed in thinly disguised ways (e.g., "I am puzzled by …"; "Why do you think that …"), there is, I believe, something to be said for the value of expressing one's biases indirectly rather than directly and openly. For one thing, the indirectness reflects one's own tentativeness, one's belief in the value of exploring further, and one's hesitation about encroaching on the patient's autonomy. The indirectness and even the poorly disguised way in which one's biases are expressed leaves greater room for the possibility that upon self-awareness and reflection, one will decide to back off and not go further in a particular direction.

Schafer (1983) also suggests that the analyst speak provisionally and in the first person (e.g., "I think," "It puzzles me," "I get the impression") as a way of avoiding addressing "the analysand in a controlling and alienating way as an object being scrutinized from on high" (p. 172). I agree with Schafer that if one's subjective biases are to be expressed, they should generally be done so in a modest and provisional and "meta" manner, rather than given directly. Something like: "I find myself wanting to encourage you to … and I thought we could talk about …"; Or, "I find myself worried that you might lose your job if you…." I think that this tentative mode is both honest, that is, one is not hiding one's biases, and, at the same time, avoids too blatantly offering directives to the patient. Perhaps this is the sort of thing that Renik has in mind when he talks about laying one's subjective biases on the table to be examined. If that is what he has in mind, this stance is not inimical to an attitude of analytic neutrality. Indeed, by using such locutions as "I find myself wanting …," one is preserving analytic neutrality in the sense that one is implicitly distinguishing between reporting an experience to be examined and directly favoring a direction to be pursued.

It is one thing to recognize that one's subjective biases may influence how one understands the patient. Such recognition should lead one to attempts to minimize these biases through increased self-awareness and self-reflection. It is another thing to take the position that because subjective biases are unavoidable, one should make no attempt to deal with them through one's own self-reflection but should rather lay them out on the table to be mutually examined by patient and analyst. Perhaps greater self-reflection regarding these biases would go some way toward mitigating them and thereby obviating the need to openly express them.

The core of analytic neutrality, as I understand it, is not only not taking sides in the patient's conflicts but taking a "disinterested" position regarding how the patient wants to live his or her life. In most relationships, particularly intimate ones, both parties have needs, wishes, and fantasies that they want and expect to have met and that entail each person in the interaction being, feeling, and behaving in certain ways. Failure to do so has consequences for the relationship. In short, there are few relationships outside psychoanalytic treatment where either party is disinterested. The closest one comes to it outside treatment is an enduring and mutual high level of friendship and, in principle, the parent-child relationship.

Why do I use the term *disinterested* and what do I mean by it? The dictionary definition of *disinterested* is "free from selfish motives or interest" (*Webster's New American Dictionary*, 1995). In the psychoanalytic situation, the appropriate personal interests and selfish motives are adequate remuneration and the satisfaction of doing good professional work for the patient's benefit. Of course, this is an ideal that may not always be fully achieved, but in my view it is important to accept and aspire to this ideal.

Affective presence

Let me turn now to other components of the analytic stance that have appeared in the contemporary psychoanalytic literature. The analyst's genuine caring and interest in understanding the patient—that is, his or her affective presence—has emerged as an important component of an appropriate analytic stance (Stechler, 2003) and, I believe, is entirely compatible with analytic neutrality when the latter is properly understood. As is the case in any other relationship, interactions dominated by boredom, affective withdrawal, and going through the motions are not likely to be productive unless these experiences are dealt with in a constructive way. When the analyst is not affectively present, the patient is very likely to experience and respond to this state of affairs whether or not he or she explicitly acknowledges it. Let me illustrate with a concrete clinical example.

I had been recovering from a flu; I was seeing my last patient of the day face-to-face and was feeling fatigued and sleepy. I had been seeing this woman for about four months. She began the session reporting how well she was doing in a number of areas in her life. Her account was presented in a droning voice and had a quality of going through the motions. Given my fatigue and my patient's droning, the session felt lifeless. About halfway through the session, eager for the session to end, I glanced off to the right where my clock rested on a book shelf. I then intervened with the comment: "I have the feeling that you are telling me what you think I want to hear." She responded by bursting out crying and then said that when she walked in I looked tired and she was worried that I would be bored, tried to please me and get my full attention by telling me how well she was doing. She cried following my remark because this experience brought to mind a familiar pattern of trying to please her father and the men in her life by telling them what she thought they wanted to hear. She then added: "You looked off to the right," to which I responded: "You mean where the clock is." (Note: She could not get herself to say directly: "You looked at the clock.") After this intervention and exchange, a session that had been lifeless came alive. My failure was replaced by active interest and affective involvement, and my patient's droning was replaced by affectively rich self-reflection.

The above interaction, intended to illustrate the importance of affective presence, can also be seen as an instance of what Safran and Muran (1996) refer to as "rupture and repair" or what Kohut (1984) describes as "optimal failure." No therapist can be affectively present at a high level of involvement all the time. However, occasions of a relative lack of affective presence need not be inimical to the progress of the treatment if one's affective absence is acknowledged (at the very least, to oneself), examined, and actively dealt with in some way. It seems to me that in the above vignette, had I allowed the session to end without some intervention, some attempt to understand and change its lifeless quality, the experience might have been a very discouraging one for my patient (and for me). It would likely have been one of rupture without repair and failure that could hardly be characterized as optimal.

I think it is important to resist the current tendency to too readily attribute one's lack of affective presence to the patient's behavior. That tendency, in my view, is one of the problems with the current readiness to invoke the concept of projective identification to account for one's own difficult and troubling feelings in the session. One's lack of affective presence (being bored, for example) is often understood as being induced or put there by the patient, or, as a specific variant of this formulation, the patient has induced boredom in the analyst in order to help the analyst understand the patient's chronic experience of boredom. I am not disputing the fact that this sort of phenomenon can occur. However, one needs clinical evidence beyond the fact that one is experiencing boredom. Also, I cannot resist noting that if one feels that the patient is unconsciously attempting to induce boredom as a way of trying to be understood, one would more likely experience empathy and compassion rather than boredom. The more general point I want to make here is the risk of not looking to oneself when one too quickly attributes one's lack of affective presence to what the patient has presumably induced.

Self-disclosure

One of the more dramatic and radical expressions of the departure from the traditional conception of the "proper" analytic stance in psychoanalytic treatment is the advocacy of the analyst's self-disclosure as a legitimate and useful component of the analytic stance (e.g., Davies, 1998; Ehrenberg, 1995). This advocacy is quite congruent with the shift from the conception of the analyst's role as an objective observer to that of an active participant. Of course, once again, one must note that whether self-disclosure is associated with a more positive therapeutic outcome is an empirical question. However, I want to comment on the relationship between affective presences and self-disclosure. First, I want to reiterate, in the present context, the earlier point that analytic neutrality is not inimical to affective presence or perhaps even to self-disclosure. One can be interested, caring, and affectively involved as well as disclosing aspects of oneself while at the same time leaving it to the patient to chart the direction of his or her life. Second, in my understanding, affective presence is not to be equated with self-disclosure. One can be affectively present with a patient without disclosing anything about oneself beyond the fact that one is interested, caring, and concerned—that is, affectively present. I have often wondered whether the impulse to self-disclose may, at least at times, constitute a way of dealing with some sense that one is not affectively present. By self-disclosing, one attempts to establish a quick affective connection that, at some level, one knows is not there or has been lost. It would be interesting to carry out an empirical study to test the hypothesis that at least certain kinds of explicit self-disclosure are more likely to occur when an affective connection (as rated by clinical judges) is relatively absent. The study would also investigate to what degree, in what circumstances, and what kind of self-disclosure, if any, succeeds in establishing or reestablishing affective presence and affective connection.

Chapter 10

Conceptions of treatment in contemporary psychoanalytic theories: Therapeutic actions and ingredients

THERAPEUTIC ACTION

I turn now to the third major category of contemporary psychoanalytic theories of treatment to be examined—conceptions of therapeutic action. A central aspect of any contemporary conception of treatment is what it takes to be the nature of therapeutic action, that is, the processes and factors that bring about positive change in treatment. Other aspects of a theory of treatment I have discussed, such as therapeutic stance, are subsidiary to the fundamental question of what brings about therapeutic change and are worthy of discussion only because they presumably subserve therapeutic change.

What one takes to be the nature of nature of therapeutic action will vary with how one understands the nature of psychopathology and what one takes to be central therapeutic goals. For example, because according to self psychology theory, lack of self-cohesiveness is viewed as a central feature of psychopathology, an equally central therapeutic goal in that theoretical perspective is strengthening of self-cohesiveness, and the therapeutic ingredients identified as constituting the core of therapeutic action are those (e.g., empathic understanding, "optimal failure") believed to accomplish this central therapeutic goal. When one identifies some other factor, such as inner conflict, as a core feature of psychopathology, a central therapeutic goal will be resolution of conflict, and one's conception of therapeutic action is likely to privilege interpretation and insight.

Let me turn now to a more systematic examination of the different conceptions of therapeutic action highlighted in contemporary psychoanalytic theories and then try to determine whether common themes emerge.

Empathic understanding

Earlier, in the section on analytic stance, I discussed a general acceptance of an empathic stance as a background factor in treatment, one that facilitates other therapeutic processes. Here, I discuss empathic understanding as a direct ingredient of therapeutic action. Given its central role in the self psychology theory of treatment, my discussion will perforce focus on that theory. It is, I believe, appropriate to devote much discussion to self psychology insofar as it constitutes the most radical departure from the traditional psychoanalytic theory of treatment.

One hardly needs a new theory to recognize that experiencing another person's empathic understanding can be comforting to someone in distress and can strengthen emotional bonds. However, it is quite another matter to assert that such understanding constitutes the essence of psychoanalytic cure. One can also understand, from a traditional perspective, that the analyst's empathic understanding may facilitate the formulation of interpretations that are conducive to the patient's insights into his or her unconscious conflicts and that facilitate the patient's reception of interpretations. However, in this way of thinking, the analyst's empathic understanding is mainly a vehicle for the facilitation of other fundamental curative factors and processes, namely interpretation and resulting insight, rather than being itself a primary curative factor. This is surely not what Kohut has in mind. In contrast to Freud's emphasis on insight-generating interpretations as the main vehicles for therapeutic change, Kohut places the therapist's empathic understanding at the center of therapeutic action. The fact is that despite all the talk about Freud having recognized the importance of empathy (*Einfühlung*) in understanding the patient, he never assigned it a direct therapeutic or curative role. Rather, its role was to help in facilitating the true therapeutic ingredient, namely insight-producing interpretations.

In what way or ways does empathic understanding bring about therapeutic change? What are the processes involved? Kohut's (1984) answer to these questions rests on basic assumptions about human nature and psychological development, assumptions captured by the comment, "We cannot exist unless we feel that we are affirmed by others, including, and especially, by our parents and those who later come to have a parental self object significance for us" (p. 190). According to Kohut, in order to develop a healthy and cohesive self, one must have experienced adequate empathic mirroring early in life. When this has not been the case, the individual is at risk for the development of self defects.

In this view, treatment is viewed as an arena for meeting unmet developmental needs, mainly the need for empathic understanding. According to self psychology theory, empathic understanding, the "basic therapeutic unit" (Kohut, 1984, p. 96), functions as a curative factor because the patient's experience of such understanding fulfills a presumably universal developmental need that was not adequately fulfilled in the patient's early life. In other words, the curative role assigned to empathic understanding derives partly from a general developmental-etiological theory in which early empathic resonance is necessary for the development of a cohesive self and the traumatic failure to provide such resonance increases the risk of the development of self defects.

This etiological theory is, then, so to speak, transferred onto a proposal that the patient's spontaneous development of transference (e.g., mirror transference) in the treatment situation represents his or her striving for developmental growth and for the fulfillment of needs that were not adequately met in the course of development. As Kohut (1984) puts it, in treatment there is a "reactivation of the thwarted developmental needs of the self ... in other words, the renewed search of the damaged self for the development-enhancing responses of an appropriately empathic selfobject" (p. 192). He also writes:

> The researcher who wishes to demonstrate the correctness of the hypothesis under scrutiny must show, with the aid of numerous detailed clinical illustrations, how analysands who had originally been restricted to archaic modes of self-selfobject relationships because the development toward maturity in this sector of their personality had been thwarted in childhood became, in the course of successful analyses, are increasingly able to evoke the empathic resonance of mature selfobjects and to be sustained by them. (p. 66)

Thus, to put it simply, the basic developmental theory of self psychology identifies certain needs, such as the need for empathic mirroring, as fundamental and universal and then proposes that people seek opportunities to have these needs met. Further, the spontaneous selfobject transferences that emerge in the treatment represent attempts to have unmet developmental needs met, and when these unmet needs are met in treatment, self defects are repaired.

Before continuing, I need to clarify the neologistic term *selfobject*, which Kohut (1984) defines "as that dimension of our experience of another person that relates to this person's functioning in shoring up our self ..." (p. 49). In other words, as a selfobject, the other person is experienced neither as a fully separate object nor as fully part of oneself but as something between the two—thus, the hybrid term selfobject. Another way to put it is to say that the other is experienced primarily in terms of his or her narcissistic function in relation to oneself (Socarides & Stolorow, 1984).

Explaining

In addition to empathic understanding, another therapeutic ingredient in analytic cure, from the perspective of self psychology, is explaining. What Kohut means by explaining is giving interpretations that focus on genetic reconstructions and dynamic formulations. One can assume that by genetic reconstruction, he means interpretations that link current selfobject relationships and transferences to relationships with early parental figures. As for dynamic formulations, I assume that a good example would be an interpretation that links the patient's defensive retreats to archaic selfobject relationships to his or her experience of the analyst's empathic failures.

The following passages reveal Kohut's (1984) conception of the role of explaining in treatment:

> The analyst's communication to the analysand and of his dynamic-genetic formulation of the patient's reactions, in other words, not only broadens and deepens the patient's own empathic-accepting grasp of himself, but strengthens the patient's trust in the reality and reliability of the empathic bond that is being established between himself and his analyst by putting him in touch with the full depth and breadth of the analyst's understanding of him. Whereas the analyst's more or less accurate empathic understanding of the current condition of the analysand's self (phase one of the basic therapeutic unit) promotes the movement toward health and leads to the laying down of new psychological structure, the result of this experience tends to be ephemeral. Well-designed verbal interpretations, on the other hand—which explain the patient's psychological reactions (in particular and par excellence his transference experiences) in dynamic terms (substep one of this explanatory phase of the basic therapeutic unit) and which, furthermore, refer to the genetic precursors of his vulnerabilities and conflicts (substep two of the explanatory phase of the basic therapeutic unit)—*will implant the wholesome but heretofore, ephemeral experience of having been understood into a broader area of the upper layers of the analysand's mind.* (pp. 105–106, emphasis in original)

> Formerly, the analyst had simply shared with the patient his grasp of what the patient experienced. Now, in moving toward the greater objectivity embodied in his explanations, however, the analyst provides the patient with the opportunity to become more objective about himself while continuing to accept himself, just as the analyst continues to accept him in offering the dynamic and genetic explanations. The movement toward greater objectivity during the analysis should therefore be seen as a sign of developmental progress; it parallels the replacement of one selfobject experience with another, namely, the replacement of an archaic selfobject experience by a mature one, the replacement of a merger experience with the selfobject by the experience of empathic resonance from the side of the selfobject. (pp. 184–185)

Although one might assume from the above passages that explaining is intended to generate the patient's insight and self-understanding, it should be clear that that is not its main purpose in the self psychology conception of treatment. Rather, the main functions of explaining are "to strengthen the patient's trust in the reality and reliability of the empathic bond that in being established [by empathic understanding] between himself and his analyst by putting him in touch with the full depth and breadth of the analyst's understanding of him" (p. 305).

The following passage makes it quite clear that for Kohut (1984), the role of interpretation and explaining in self psychology is quite different from that in classical theory:

> It is not what the self psychologically informed analyst does, that is, his "technique," that has changed, but how he views what he does. In contrast to those—including James Strachey (1934)—who believe, in harmony with the spirit of the Age of Enlightenment of which Freud was a true child, that it is the power of reason which cures, the self psychologically informed analyst holds that with regard to all forms of analyzable psychopathology the basic therapeutic unit of the psychoanalytic cure does not rest on the expansion of cognition. (It does not rest, for example, on the analysand's becoming aware of the difference between his fantasy and reality, especially with reference to transference distortions involving projected drives.) Rather, it is the accretion of psychic structure via an optimal frustration of the analysand's needs or wishes that is provided for the analysand in the form of correct interpretations that constitutes the essence of the cure. (p. 108)

In short, enhancing insight and self-understanding is neither the function of explaining nor the function of empathic understanding. Rather, the primary function of both understanding and explaining is the establishment and strengthening of an empathic bond between patient and analyst. Furthermore, the significance of the patient's move toward greater objectivity toward himself or herself lies not in its reflection of greater insight and self-knowledge but as a marker suggesting "the replacement of an archaic selfobject experience by a mature one" (Kohut, 1984, p. 185).

One can sum up much of Kohut's stance by noting that from a self psychology perspective, the key ingredients in treatment is *feeling understood* by the therapist rather than, as is the case in classical theory, understanding himself or herself. From a classical perspective, too, the analyst's understanding of the patient is important, but it is important in a different way. It is important insofar as it leads to accurate interpretations that undo repressions and generate awareness and insight. From a self psychology perspective, it is feeling understood rather than understanding that is critical.

I think it is fair to say that Kohut's theory of therapeutic action is essentially a theory of the role of "corrective emotional experiences" in bringing about therapeutic change. Indeed, Kohut's (1984) response to the charge that his conception of therapeutic change places corrective emotional experiences at the center is "so be it" (p. 78). He goes on to note that it is "but a single aspect of the multifaceted body of the psychoanalytic cure" and that the "valuable" and "perfectly serviceable term" of corrective emotional experience came into disrepute because it has been associated with Alexander's use of it in "brief analysis" and with "manipulation of the transference" (p. 78). There is an additional reason that the concept of corrective emotional experience was in disrepute in classical theory not noted by Kohut: it presumably implies that the analyst gratifies the patient's wishes in the treatment.

Gratification in the treatment

Kohut and other self psychologists are at pains to deny that a self psychology conception of treatment and therapeutic action entails gratification, a prime taboo in the classical theory of treatment. Kohut repeatedly notes that as far as procedure and technique are concerned, an analysis conducted from a self psychology perspective is no different from the way a classical analysis is conducted. In both cases, "the transferences are allowed to unfold and their analysis—the understanding of the transference reactions; their explanation in dynamic and genetic terms—occupies, now as before, the center of the analyst's attention" (Kohut, 1984, p. 208). In both cases, it is

> through interpretation, first of the need (i.e., to be perfectly mirrored and/or to merge with an idealized figure) and then of the origin of the need) [that] the analyst offers an empathic bond rather than one based on fulfilling the patient's wish to have the past replayed under more auspicious circumstances. (Basch, 1986, p, 411)

As I have discussed elsewhere (Eagle, 1990), the entire issue of gratification and fulfillment of the patient's wishes and needs in Kohut's and other self psychologists' writings needs to be unpacked. For one thing, the classical context for the stricture against gratification in the analysis is the assumption that the patient attempts to gratify primarily infantile sexual and aggressive wishes. When this assumption is relinquished, as it is in self psychology, and when the focus is not on infantile sexual and aggressive wishes but on presumably vital developmental empathic mirroring needs, as it is in self psychology, there would appear to be little reason for the taboo status of gratification in the analytic situation. Put very simply, if the need for empathic understanding is a vital developmental need that is activated in the transference, and if the analyst provides that empathic understanding, then that need is being gratified. In this context, it is not clear why Kohut and other self psychologists should be so much at pains to deny that gratification is involved in their conception of treatment. They seem to carry over the taboo on gratification formulated in one theoretical context to another theoretical context in which it is not especially pertinent.

The taboo on gratification in classical theory is derived primarily from two considerations. One is protection against the analyst's sexual acting out and emotional overinvolvement; the other concerns the hydraulic model rationale for the rules of abstinence, namely, that whereas gratification impedes, abstinence facilitates the emergence of repressed unconscious material in consciousness. Given self psychology's rejection of drive theory and of a hydraulic model and given its own conception of treatment, one would expect that neither consideration would play a very prominent role.

I think the (unwarranted) concern about gratification on the part of self psychologists lies, partly at least, in their eagerness to reassure the psychoanalytic community that analysis carried out from a self psychology perspective is still analysis and not just a matter of gratifying the patient's wishes and needs. Thus, as I have already mentioned, Kohut is at pains to state repeatedly that the procedures and techniques of self psychology are no different from those of classical analysis. Basch (1986), too, makes a similar point when he states that self psychologists use *interpretation* of the patient's need "to be perfectly mirrored and/or to merge with an idealized figure" rather than "fulfilling (i.e., gratifying) the patient's wish to have the past replayed under more auspicious circumstances" (p. 411). In short, both Kohut and Basch are telling us that like the classical analyst, the self psychology analyst interprets rather than gratifies.

I have argued elsewhere (Eagle, 1990) that what Basch refers to as "the [patient's] *need* to be perfectly mirrored" is essentially equivalent to "the patient's *wish* to have the past replayed under more auspicious circumstances" (emphasis added; see Chapter 7). Consider the following logic: According to self psychology theory, self defects are generated by the traumatic failure to receive (perfect?) mirroring in childhood. This unfulfilled need is activated in the transference as, to quote from Basch, "the need to be perfectly mirrored" (p. 411). Obviously, it is not possible for the analyst or anyone else to perfectly mirror another. Hence, the so-called need to be perfectly mirrored cannot possibly be met. However, if, as Basch maintains, being perfectly mirrored is a developmental need, if the nonfulfillment of this need produces self defects, and if this need cannot possibly be fulfilled, how are self defects to be repaired in treatment? Why would "interpretation, first of the need ... and then of the origin of the need," which "offers an empathic bond" (Basch, 1986, p, 411), serve to repair self defects? Surely, the *interpretation* of the need (to be perfectly mirrored), along with the empathic bond it constitutes, is not the same as meeting the need.

Were perfect mirroring a vital developmental need, it would be difficult to understand how and why less than perfect mirroring (that is, optimal failure; to be discussed below) would serve as a basic therapeutic ingredient. It becomes understandable only if one assumes that the patient's demand for perfect mirroring is based on a wish and on the fantasy that only if this wish is gratified can dire threats to self-intactness and self-esteem be averted.

Based on the patient's repeated experience of benefiting from good-enough empathic mirroring, that is, from optimal failures and how they are dealt with by the analyst, the patient becomes increasingly able to relinquish the fantasy that perfect mirroring is a vital need. Once one is able to give up the fantasy that only perfect mirroring will do, one becomes increasingly ready to experience the good-enough empathic understanding that is realistically available in the world as sustaining and enhancing. A benevolent circle is created whereby each experience of surviving and working through an episode of "optimal frustration" leads to a steady decrease in the patient's demand for perfect mirroring and a steady increase in his or her ability to feel sustained by less than perfect mirroring.

Thus, the interpretation of the so-called need to be perfectly mirrored is an interpretation of a wish or fantasy. In this sense, Kohut and Basch are correct in noting that in the emphasis of a self psychology analysis on interpretation, its technique and procedure are no different from the technique and procedure of a classical analysis—although the function of the interpretation is different. Insofar as that function is to provide an empathic bond that was not available early in the patient's life, it does, of course, constitute gratification.

Optimal failure or optimal frustration

In addition to empathic understanding and explaining, a basic ingredient or unit of therapeutic cure in self psychology is what Kohut variously refers to as optimal failure and optimal frustration. According to Kohut (1984):

> The quietly sustaining matrix provided by the spontaneously established selfobject transference to the analyst that establishes itself in the early phases of analysis is disrupted time and again by the analyst's unavoidable, yet only temporary and thus nontraumatic, empathy failures—that is, his "optimal failures." In response to the analyst's errors in understanding or in response to the analyst's erroneous or inaccurate or otherwise improper interpretations, the analysand turns back temporarily from his reliance on empathy to the archaic selfobject relationships (e.g., to remobilization of the need for merger with archaic idealized omnipotent selfobjects or remobilization of the need for immediate and perfect mirroring) that he had already tentatively abandoned in the primary selfobject transference of the analysis. In a properly conducted analysis, the analyst takes note of the analysand's retreat, searches for any mistakes he might have made, nondefensively acknowledges them after he has recognized them (often with the help of the analysand), and then gives the analysand a noncensorious interpretation of the dynamics of his retreat. In this way the flow of empathy between analyst and analysand that had been opened through

the originally established selfobject transference is remobilized. The patient's self is then sustained once more by a selfobject matrix that is empathically in tune with him. (pp. 66–67)

As the above passage indicates, inevitably, the analyst will periodically fail in the provision of empathic understanding. The patient's typical response to these failures, according to Kohut, will be to retreat to archaic modes of selfobject relationships, as well as experiencing rage and despair. However, so long as these failures are nontraumatic and the analyst tactfully interprets the dynamics of the patient's regression, the empathic resonance between patient and analyst will be reestablished. Furthermore, after repeated experiences of optimal failures followed by appropriate understanding, acknowledgment, and interpretation on the part of the analyst, the patient "will build up internal structures that allow him to turn toward an ever broadening spectrum of self objects for support, confirmation, and sustenance" (Kohut, 1984, pp. 78–79). The buildup of internal structures occurs through a process Kohut refers to as "transmuting internalization."

If one replaces terms such as *building up of psychic structures* and *transmuting internalization* with ordinary descriptive language, Kohut is suggesting that the following takes place: After the patient has repeated experiences that he or she can survive the optimal frustration of less than perfect understanding and can even benefit from the imperfect empathic bond represented by the analyst's acknowledgment of his her failure and interpretations of the patient's retreat in response to these failures, the patient gains strength and becomes more capable of benefiting from the less than perfect empathic understanding—from, to borrow a phrase from Winnicott, the good-enough understanding—that is realistically available in the world.

Bacal (1985) has objected to Kohut's terms *optimal failures* and *optimal frustration* and suggests that they should be replaced by the more positive term *optimal responsiveness*. However, it should be apparent that a careful examination of Kohut's terms suggests that they are, in fact, equivalent to optimal responsiveness. That is, of course, the analyst tries to be optimally responsive rather than intentionally trying to (optimally) fail or frustrate the patient.[1] The points that Kohut is making however, are that (a) even when one is trying to be as responsive as one can be, it is inevitable that one's empathic understanding will not be perfect; (b) therefore, the patient will, equally inevitably, experience the analyst's interventions

---

[1] I think there are a number of reasons that Kohut uses the terms *optimal frustration* and *optimal failure* rather than *optimal responsiveness*. One reason, I believe, is that he, (along with other self psychologists) wanted to avoid any possible implication that the analyst gratifies the patient's needs or wishes. Hence, whereas *optimal responsiveness* runs the risk of suggesting the taboo connotation of gratification, *optimal frustration* or *optimal failure* clearly does not.

as frustrating; and (c) so long as the interventions are nontraumatic, that is, are optimal rather than traumatic failures or frustrations, and so long as these failures and frustrations are dealt with in the way prescribed by Kohut (i.e., acknowledgment and so on), they will contribute to a positive therapeutic outcome.

There is an interesting and benevolent paradox here. Even when the analyst's interpretations miss the mark and constitute relative failures of empathy, his or her acknowledgment of these failures and his or her understanding of the patient's reactions to these failures themselves constitute successful empathic understanding. Although the analyst's failures of empathy are, of course, nonintentional, their (inevitable) occurrence offers the analyst an opportunity to transform an empathic failure into an empathic success—just as many ruptures in the treatment, if acknowledged, reflected on, and repaired, can offer an opportunity to further the treatment (Safran & Muran, 1996).[2]

I think a similar idea is implicit in other theoretical formulations. For example, in the context of control-mastery theory, Weiss et al. (1986) distinguish between test-passing and test-failing on the part of the analyst, and they have shown that whereas test-failing tends to be followed by retrenchment of defense and lack of therapeutic progress, test-passing tends to be followed by positive events such as emergence of new themes, lessened anxiety, and so on. They have not, however, investigated the possibly differential

---

[2] Although I have focused exclusively on the mirroring transference in the above discussion, Kohut also discusses other selfobject transferences, namely, idealizing and twinship transferences. All of these selfobject transferences are understood as the patient's attempts to elicit from the selfobject analyst those responses that were not forthcoming from parental figures. Thus, in a mirror transference, the patient attempts to elicit empathic mirroring and confirming-approving responses that were traumatically absent early in life. In an idealizing transference, the patient searches "for a self object that will accept [his or her] idealization," and in a twinship transference, the patient "seeks a self object that will make itself available for the reassuring experience of essential alikeness" (Kohut, 1984, p. 193). The essential points here are that, according to Kohut, the treatment situation spontaneously activates early developmental needs that the patient seeks to have met by the selfobject analyst. I have focused on the mirror transference because the role of empathic understanding as a curative agent is especially clear in the mirror transference and less clear in the idealizing and twinship transferences. Thus, in the idealizing transference, all the analyst needs to do is refrain from analyzing and interpreting the patient's idealization in order to enable it to develop. Of course, making the therapeutic decision not to interpret or analyze the patient's idealizing requires an empathic understanding of the patient's need for a self object that will accept his or her idealization (as well as an acceptance of Kohut's theory regarding the presumably universal need for an idealized figure). However, here empathic understanding functions as a general tool for decisions regarding therapeutic interventions rather than as a direct curative agent—as it does in the mirror transference. Thus, Kohut's formulation of the mirror transference and his discussion of the analyst's responses to the mirror transference represent the clearest expression of the role of empathic understanding as a central ingredient of therapeutic action. They also represent the clearest expression of Kohut's conception of treatment as an arena in which the meeting of unmet early selfobject needs results in the repair of self defects.

consequences of unacknowledged and unexamined test-failing versus test-failing that is acknowledged and mutually examined. One can hypothesize that in contrast to unacknowledged test-failing, the positive consequences of acknowledged and mutually examined test-failing will be largely indistinguishable from test-passing. This hypothesis is based on the reasoning that acknowledging and examining test-failing themselves constitute test-passing—something like a meta-test-passing or rupture and repair.

Analysis of the transference

When Kohut discusses with the patient his interpretation of the patient's rage and despair as reactions to experiences of the analyst's empathic failures, he is, of course, describing analysis of the transference. Indeed, a focus on analysis of the transference has been viewed as the common ground" among different psychoanalytic schools despite other theoretical differences (Wallerstein, 1990). As Kernberg (1993) puts it, the common ground should be understood "not in the sense of a common clinical theory, but in the evolution toward commonalities of technique, sometimes almost in spite of the differing underlying theories" (p. 52). Indeed, there is much truth in this claim. From Strachey's (1934) classic paper on therapeutic action to Gill's (1994) work to contemporary Kleinian and relational psychoanalysis, there seems to be widespread agreement with Freud's (1916–1917/1917) assertion that "the decisive part of the work is achieved by creating in the patient's relation to the doctor—in the 'transference'—new editions of the old conflicts" (p. 454). There also appears to be widespread agreement that it is the interpretations of these new editions of the old conflicts, that is, transference interpretations, that are especially conducive to therapeutic change.[3]

Although there may be widespread agreement regarding the centrality of the analysis of the transference, including the suggestion that transference interpretations are virtually the only ones worth making in the analytic situation (e.g., Gill, 1994), the confidence and certainty of these assertions notwithstanding, there is little consistent empirical support for them. As Weiss et al. (1986) have shown, therapeutic change can come about through the analyst's passing of the patient's unconscious tests, without analysis of the transference, indeed, without any interpretation at all. In accord with

---

[3] It should be noted that to the extent that contemporary psychoanalytic theorists also emphasize the centrality of analysis of the transference, they are, it seems, giving significant weight to the therapeutic value of discovering and identifying the patient's interactional patterns and the wishes and expectations associated with these patterns. That is, despite explicitly denying the possibility of uncovering and discovering (e.g., Mitchell, 1998) and despite explicitly minimizing the therapeutic value of awareness and self-knowledge (e.g., Kohut, 1984), an emphasis on the analysis of the transference implies a central therapeutic role for a process of uncovering and discovering that contribute to the patient's awareness, self-understanding, and self-knowledge.

these findings, I have presented a case study in which the dramatic disappearance of a chronic symptom occurred following test-passing, in which there was no interpretation of the interactions that constituted the test-passing (Eagle, 1993).

Most important, there is no consistent evidence in systematic psychotherapy research that a focus on analysis of the transference is reliably associated with positive outcome. Indeed, a number of studies have reported a negative impact of transference interpretations on treatment outcome (e.g., Connolly et al., 1999; Ogrodniczuk, 1999; Piper, Hassan, Joyce, & McCallum, 1991). Some recent studies have shown that the effects of transference interpretations on therapeutic outcome vary with level of interpersonal functioning. However, contrary to received clinical wisdom, for patients with a lower level of quality of object relations, transference interpretations were associated with positive outcome, whereas there was no significant association between transference interpretations and therapeutic outcome for higher functioning patients (Hogeland, 2004; Hogeland et al., 2007, 2008). Furthermore, although both treatment groups with and without transference interpretations showed improvement during treatment and after termination, "patients with a lifelong pattern of poor object relations profited more from one year of therapy with transference interpretations than from therapy without transference interpretations. This effect was sustained throughout the 4-year study period" (Hogeland et al., 2008, p. 763).

How does one account for these surprising findings? One suggestion is "that less resourceful and less healthy patients show transference patterns that are easier to identify and interpret for the patient" (Hogeland et al., 2006, p. 171). Another related possibility is that analysis of transference focuses on the very area—problematic interpersonal relationships—where the most therapeutic work is needed. Still another related possibility is that because poorer functioning patients may find it more difficult to establish a positive therapeutic relationship, more attention—as reflected in transference interpretations—needs to be paid to this aspect of the treatment. This line of reasoning tends to be supported by the relative success of Kernberg's transference-focused psychotherapy (TFP) with borderline patients (e.g., Clarkin, Levy, Lenzenweger, & Kernberg, 2007; Levy et al., 2006).

One question that arises with regard to the above finding is the impact they will have on clinical practice. One set of findings suggests that transference interpretations may not be especially helpful with higher functioning patients and may even have a negative impact on treatment outcome. Although these findings have been reported since the early 1990s, as far as one can tell, they have not had any impact on the general claim that transference interpretations represent the primary vehicle through which therapeutic change occurs. As noted, the second set of findings regarding the usefulness of transference interpretations with lower functioning patients does seem to have had a greater influence on practice, as reflected in the use of transference-focused psychotherapy with borderline patients. It is highly likely that Kernberg's development of his transference-focused psychotherapy approach was influenced by the early finding of the Menninger project that patients with ego weakness responded better to expressive therapy that was more likely to include transference interpretations than to supportive psychotherapy that was less likely to include transference interpretations (Kernberg et al., 1972).

Despite the great importance given to the analysis of the transference in the psychoanalytic literature, from Freud to contemporary analysts, we do not know to what extent analysts generally do, in fact, focus near exclusively on the analysis of the transference in their actual clinical work. Indeed, I suspect that there might be a problem obtaining accurate data (unless they were obtained from tape-recorded sessions) because, given the authoritative statements proclaiming the singular value of transference interpretations, younger analysts in particular might be loathe to acknowledge that they do not focus near exclusively on the transference in their clinical work.

Countertransference

When one includes in one's conception of transference cues emitted by the analyst, one essentially introduces the idea of the analyst's countertransference reactions to the patient, that is, his or her thoughts and feelings, as active coparticipants in the analytic process. Beginning with Heimann (1950) and more fully elaborated by Racker (1968), the concept of countertransference came to be more "totalistically" defined (Kernberg, 1993) as constituting the full range of the analyst's reactions to the patient. Furthermore, since Racker's seminal 1968 book, the central idea that the analyst's countertransference reactions (now totalistically defined), rather than being an impediment to the progress of treatment, can serve as an indispensable guide to the patient's unconscious mental states has become a hallmark of contemporary psychoanalytic thinking. Indeed, Gabbard (1995) has proposed that this idea constitutes a common ground of contemporary psychoanalytic conceptions of treatment despite other theoretical differences. One implication of the idea that one's countertransference reactions can serve as a guide to what is going in the patient's mind is that in trying to understand the patient, one attends not only to the content of the patient's productions but to the thoughts and feelings they evoke in oneself.[4]

---

[4] It should be noted that although the analyst's therapeutic use of his or her own thoughts and feelings in response to the patient's transference reactions was recognized by Freud, the concept of countertransference was reserved for instances in which the analyst's thoughts and feelings interfered with the therapeutic work, because of insufficient awareness and understanding of them and because of anxiety and conflict surrounding them (Freud, 1914/1915).

One can distinguish between the weak and strong version of the claim that the analyst's thoughts and feelings serve as a guide to what is going on in the patient's mind (Eagle, 2000a). The weak version states that the analysts' countertransference *may* (which, therefore, leaves open the possibility that it may not) serve as a guide to knowledge about the patient's mental states; the stronger version suggests that countertransference virtually always serves as such a guide. As I have also noted previously, although most observers would likely explicitly endorse the weak version as the more plausible claim, much of the contemporary literature on countertransference implicitly assumes the strong claim. Indeed, the endorsement of the strong claim need not be implicit but can be quite explicit. For example, Levine (1997) writes:

> I ... hope to demonstrate that there is a pragmatic value in assuming that even those thoughts and emotional experiences that clearly arise within the analyst from the analyst's own personal life and have seemingly little to do with the specific patient at hand—for example, when the analyst's personal life events intrude upon the hour to such an extent as to encroach upon or even override his/her capacities to analyze effectively—can be presumed to have a patient related component that contributes to their appearance in a given hour in a particular way. (p. 48)

The strong version of the countertransference claim essentially constitutes a return to, if not a blank screen, at least a blank *tabula rasa* mind or blank personality conception of the analyst. That is, if virtually all of the analyst's thoughts and feelings in the analytic session are assumed to be attributable to the patient's transference reactions, it follows that the analysts' own history, own personality, own dynamics, and own preoccupations contribute little or nothing. This is a blank screen with a vengeance!

Although, on the surface, this conception of countertransference appears to be a two-person interactional one—after all, the analysts' reactions are assumed to be interactively elicited by the patient—further thought suggests that there is a risk that it is a new version of a one-person perspective, save that the one person to be focused on now is not the patient but the analyst. To take this new perspective to its perhaps absurd but nevertheless quite logical extreme, one could say that in trying to understand the patient, it is less important—perhaps not important at all—to listen to and try to understand the content of the patient's productions than to listen to and monitor one's own cognitive and affective reactions to the patient.

Of course, in any human interaction, including the therapeutic one, it is frequently the case that one's fleeting thoughts and particularly affective reactions can serve as a guide to the other person's unspoken, or at least not fully spoken, meanings and intentions. Affective reactions often constitute implicit assessments and tell us what is going on, including what is going on interpersonally (see Damasio, 1994). There is also interesting work on mirror neurons and related systems suggesting a neural substitute for this process (see Gallese, Migone, & Eagle, 2007). These meanings and intentions are often unwittingly communicated paralinguistically, for example, by, what a jazz musician friend of mine referred to as the "music in one's voice." However, one's affective reactions can also mislead one as to the other person's meanings and intentions, particularly when these reactions reflect more one's own baggage—one's preoccupations, anxieties, conflicts, projections, and so on—than the meanings and intentions of the other. In short, one cannot automatically assume that the fleeting thoughts and affective reactions one experiences while listening to the patient necessarily serve as reliable guides to what is going on in the patient's mind. Rather, and this is perhaps an obvious conclusion, one needs to reflect on one's thoughts and feelings in order to sort out the various factors that contribute to them.

Projective identification

The above issue comes especially to the fore in the preoccupation with the concept of projective identification in the contemporary psychoanalytic literature. The concept is frequently invoked in the context of the analyst experiencing certain feelings, often unusual ones, which are then assumed to have been induced or put into the analyst by the patient.

As far as I can tell, in Melanie Klein's original references, projective identification is understood entirely in intrapsychic terms. At one point, Klein (1946–1963/1975) defines projective identification as entailing the projection of parts of oneself or one's impulses and feelings onto another and then identifying with that other on the basis of attributing to others the feelings, etc. that have been projected. At another point, Klein (1946–1963/1975) refers to the baby's projection of impulses to harm and control onto the mother and then experiences her as a persecutor. This, according to Klein, is the result of "identification of the object with hated parts of the self" (1946–1963/1975, p. 8). Finally, in her *Introduction to the Work of Melanie Klein*, Segal (1964) introduces an interpersonal element into the definition of projective identification. She writes: "In projective identification parts of the self and internalized objects are split off and projected into the external object, *which then becomes possessed by, controlled and identified with the projected* parts" (p. 14, emphasis added). Segal tells us nothing about how the external object becomes possessed and controlled or whether what she is referring to is a *fantasy* of controlling and possessing.

In the more recent literature, an attempt has been made to account for the interpersonal aspect of projective identification. One interpretation of this elusive concept (see Ogden, 1982; Tansey & Burke, 1995) is that the patient *projects* an internal object—say, an internal critic—onto the analyst; the patient then exerts *interpersonal pressure* on the analyst to feel and perhaps act critically, and the analyst is taken to have introjected and identified (*introjective identification*) with the patient's internal critic. This account of projective identification is virtually identical to Racker's (1968) concept of complementary identification and, indeed, is subject to the same criticism. If through interpersonal pressure, the patient induces the analyst to feel and perhaps behave critically, this does not necessarily indicate that the analyst has identified with the patient's internal object. There is nothing mysterious or nothing that requires a special concept such as projective identification to recognize that one person can induce another person to feel critical or hostile by emitting certain cues, often very subtle ones, of which neither party may be conscious. Furthermore, insofar as one can induce hostile or critical feelings in another by behaving in a particular way, this phenomenon does not necessarily indicate that the patient is projecting anything onto the analyst, although that may occur. However, to conclude that the patient is projecting anything onto the analyst, it is not sufficient simply to point to the analyst's feelings of hostility. That can occur without projection. One needs good additional clinical evidence for the inference of projection.

The concept of interpersonal pressure is somewhat ambiguous insofar as it could mean either that the patient's behavior—for example, sullenness and sarcasm—simply *elicits*, as an average respectable response, hostile and critical feelings in the analyst or that the patient is consciously or unconsciously *motivated to induce* hostile and critical feelings in the analyst. For example, in the case of the projection of hostile feelings onto the analyst, the patient may be motivated to induce hostile feelings as a means of supporting his or her projections. That is, if A projects his or her hostile feelings onto B and also manages to induce B to feel and act with hostility, then A's projections are supported by external behavior. B need not examine his or her own hostile feelings and thoughts. Or, as another example, the patient may be unconsciously motivated to induce hostile and critical feelings in the analyst to gratify an unconscious wish to be punished.

By invoking the concept of identification, either in the context of complementary or projective identification, the implicit claim is made that the analyst's emotional reactions are a *mirror* of some aspect of the patient's inner world rather than reactions *elicited* by the patient. The former, I have been arguing, is essentially a new version of the blank screen (or blank mirror) analyst, whereas the latter refers to an ordinary process in which two people interacting with each other elicit reactions in each other. In the analytic situation, both parties, patient and analyst, each for different reasons, have, or should have, a great investment in understanding the nature and source of these reactions. It is too easy for analysts to grab hold of a dogma or formula or buzz term such as *projective identification* that tells them that their reactions have been put into them by patients and that those reactions reflect identifications with the patients' inner object. Thus, if I as an analyst feel critical of my patient, the formula assures me that it is likely that my feelings constitute complementary identifications with the patient's internal critic. Hence, I need not view my critical feelings as my reactions, even if elicited by the patient (and try to understand what these feelings reveal about me), but rather as a mirror of the patient's inner world.

Defense analysis and understanding how one's mind works

In this section, I want to discuss a conception of interpretation that, in contemporary theories, as in classical theory, is also focused on the observing function of the ego, insight and self-understanding, but in a somewhat different way. I am referring to a conception associated with what can be called modern ego psychology, in which the primary function of interpretation is not so much uncovering particular repressed wishes and impulses but rather understanding how one's mind works. Self-knowledge and self-understanding, in this view, are not linked primarily to becoming aware of specific wishes and aims but rather to the characteristic ways that one deals with the affects associated with these wishes and aims. For example, as G. S. Klein (1976) has noted, when one is conflicted or anxious about particular aims or desires, one may fail to understand the personal significance of or fail to make connections among contents associated with these aims and desires. In this view, self-knowledge and self-understanding are not only a matter of learning that I have such and such a desire or aim but also of learning that when I am conflicted or anxious about a desire or aim, I do such and such (e.g., fail to make connections, engage in self-deception, dissociate). It will be recognized that, in effect, I have been describing a shift from id analysis to ego analysis, that is, from an emphasis on uncovering repressed wishes to an emphasis on analysis of defense (see, for example, the work of Gray, 1994; see also Busch, 2001). According to this perspective, a main function of interpretation is to enhance the patient's curiosity about and motivation for exploring how his or her mind works, for example, what he or she does, what maneuvers are engaged in when conflicted or anxious or ashamed or guilty about something, what implicit expectations and representations are held regarding significant others and himself or herself, or his or her understanding of and attributions about how the other's mind works.

It will be noted that this way of understanding the function of interpretation fits well into a contemporary theoretical and clinical context in which defense analysis and identification and alteration of implicit maladaptive representations, beliefs, and unconscious fantasies are viewed as the main functions of psychoanalytic treatment. For after all, what does defense analysis consist in if not an understanding of how the patient's mind works when he or she is conflicted or anxious or is trying to deal with other dysphoric affects and threats to self-esteem? And does not interpretation of fantasy, at least partly, consist in helping the patient understand how his or her mind works, for example, how his or her affects (i.e., wishes and fears) interact with his or her thinking and cognition (i.e., representations and beliefs) and the kinds of expectations he or she has or she has as well as the attributions made to others?

Enhancing capacity for reflective functioning

The therapeutic aim of helping the patient understand how his or her mind works bears a strong family resemblance to the classical psychoanalytic goal of enhancing the observing function of the ego, which in turn bears a strong family resemblance to the recently popular concepts of capacity for reflective functioning and mentalization (e.g., Fonagy, 2006). Indeed, all these concepts seem to be virtually synonymous with each other. They all emphasize a capacity to reflect on one's mental states—a capacity that is impaired in various degrees in various forms of psychopathology.

However, underemphasized in classical theory (though more adequately represented in contemporary theories) is the recognition that the capacity to reflect on others' mental states is also impaired in psychopathology. In any case, given this conception of psychopathology, it is not surprising that enhancement of the capacity for reflective functioning or, if one prefers, of the observing function of the ego is a central goal of psychoanalytically oriented treatment. Indeed, in the classical literature, achieving a strengthened observing function of the ego is viewed as a critical criterion for successful termination.

The goal of enhancing the capacity for reflective functioning and mentalization in the contemporary psychoanalytic literature is especially prominent in two contexts: one, treatment of borderline conditions (e.g., Fonagy & Bateman, 2006); and two, interventions with infant-mother dyads, an arena reflecting the synergistic relationship between attachment theory and psychoanalysis.

With regard to the former context, there is general agreement that borderline pathology is characterized, among other features, by a relative failure to reflect on one's own and others' mental states, one consequence of which is "an experience of self and others that is poorly integrated, unstable, idealized, or persecutory and often chaotic" (Caligor, Diamond, Yeomans, & Kernberg, 2009, p. 275). Patients with personality disorders, particularly borderline and narcissistic disorders, have a low threshold for construing the behavior of others as indicating rejection, humiliation, abandonment, and so on and also tend to react to their experiences with intense negative affect, including rage, despair, and retaliation fantasies. The experience of the others' behaviors is often taken as absolute, that is, there is no other way to construe those behaviors, and the intense negative affective reactions are also experienced as absolutely justified. As one might expect, these absolutist construals of others' behavior and the consequent intense negative affects have a destructive influence on the individual's interpersonal and intrapsychic life. Hence, it is understandable that enhancement of the patient's capacity to reflect on his or her own mental states and those of others would be a central goal of treatment (Kernberg, Yeomans, Clarkin, & Levy, 2008). An increased ability to reflect on one's own construals, as well as others' experiences and perceptions, when it leads to considering the possibility of different construals and attributions, can serve to dampen and regulate the intense negative affects that are generated by the rigid and repetitive experience of rejection, humiliation, abandonment, and so on.

In a recent paper, Gabbard and Horowitz (2009) present a garden-variety example of a borderline patient who reports feeling that she had made a spectacle of herself by an episode of shouting at a sales clerk because he would not accept her credit card. She also reported that the sales clerk was rude and discourteous to her. When the therapist inquired whether it was store policy not to accept credit cards, the patient felt that he was suggesting that she overreacted and exploded in rage and screamed: "You're not interested in empathizing with my feeling of humiliation—only in figuring out how I caused the whole incident" (p. 517). The therapist observes that the same thing that happened in the store is, of course, happening in the therapeutic session.

Gabbard and Horowitz (2009) describe different phases of therapeutic work that focuses on enhancing reflective capacity and that includes such steps as encouraging "the patient to see her distress as growing out of her particular perception of events rather than as a replica of reality" (p. 519) and "considering other possibilities that might explain the behavior of the clerk" (p. 520). Similar work is, of course, also carried out in relation to the patient's here-and-now transference reactions and may also include an examination of the developmental origins of the patient's habitual construals and attributions. Ideally, treatment would succeed in altering the patient's habitual and rigid expectations and construals. However, short of that, treatment can be very useful in helping the patient "be ready for the emergence of the habitual sense of grievance and to maintain alertness so she can detect prerage signals from herself and the trigger behaviors she expects from others" (p. 520).

I think it is fair to note that although Gabbard and Horowitz's (2009) paper refers to "dynamic psychotherapy," much of the description of borderline patients, as well as aspects of the therapeutic work with them (e.g., focusing on problematic and dysfunctional beliefs, construals, expectations, and attributions), would likely be quite acceptable to many cognitive behavior therapists. My impression is that transtheoretical convergence is more likely when descriptions (of both the nature of the psychopathology and of the treatment) are specific and closer to the actual clinical data.

In the context of work with infant-mother dyads, beginning with Fraiberg, Adelson, and Shapiro's (1975) classic paper "Ghosts in the Nursery," underlying interventions is a basic assumption—for which there is much evidence—that insecure attachment in the infant is associated with limitations in the caregiver's capacity to reflect on both her own and her infant's mental states (see also Lieberman, 1999). In a remarkable study, Fonagy et al. (1995) reported that the Reflective Functioning scores of pregnant women who were given the Adult Attachment Interview in their third trimester of pregnancy was successful in predicting what the attachment status of the as yet unborn infant would be at 1 year of age.

A number of studies have found that interventions that enhance the caregiver's reflective capacity in relation to her own and her infant's mental states are relatively successful in generating secure attachment in the infant. Given that insecure attachment is a risk factor and secure attachment a protective factor with regard to later difficulties, the reasonable assumption is made that increasing the likelihood of secure attachment will make subsequent pathology less likely. However, as far as I know, there are no longitudinal studies examining the long-term influence on the infant's development of facilitating secure attachment through enhancing the caregiver's reflective capacity.

The work of interpretations

In part, historical concern with the issue of accuracy of interpretation has been motivated by the need to counter the charge of suggestion. Freud (1916–1917/1917) argued that only interpretations that "tally with what is real (in the patient)" (p. 452), that is, only accurate interpretations, will effect therapeutic change (see Grunbaum, 1984). Over the years, a continued concern with the problem of suggestion (Meehl, 1994) has led to much discussion in the psychoanalytic literature of the issue of accuracy or veridicality of interpretation. I would suggest that much of the discussion is misplaced. Consider the basic methodological concepts of reliability and validity. One kind of reliability (interjudge) enters the picture when one tries to determine the degree of agreement among different clinical judges' interpretations of, say, the unconscious defenses or conflicts expressed in therapeutic sessions. As we know, there is little to boast about in this area. Interjudge reliability tends to be quite low. It is the question of validity, however, that goes to the heart of the issue of interpretation. Validity is defined in terms of whether a measure (e.g., a score on a test) does what it is supposed to do, as determined by a validity criterion (e.g., performance on the job).

What is an interpretation supposed to do in the psychoanalytic context? In the framework of traditional theory one answer to this question is that it is supposed to enhance self-awareness (make the unconscious conscious), self-understanding, and self-knowledge. Hence, the degree to which an interpretation is *valid* is determined by the degree to which it does what it is supposed to do, namely, enhance self-awareness, self-understanding, and self-knowledge. It can be seen from this analysis that a valid interpretation (that is, one that enhances self-understanding and self-knowledge can be inaccurate) and that an invalid interpretation (that is, one that fails to enhance self-understanding and self-knowledge) can be accurate. In effect, I am distinguishing between the accuracy and veridicality of an interpretation and its therapeutic effectiveness when the criterion for the latter is enhanced self-understanding and self-knowledge (see Eagle, 1980a). Although one would like to believe that the two are positively correlated, veridicality and validity are two different concepts.

Although much of the debate in the psychoanalytic literature has concerned itself with the thorny problem of determining the accuracy of the interpretations or has confounded accuracy with effectiveness, an equally formidable challenge is determining the degree to which an interpretation (or any other intervention) does what it is supposed to do. More specifically, if the job an interpretation is supposed to do is enhance self-understanding and self-knowledge, how does one determine the degree to which that job has been accomplished? What are the validity criteria for enhanced self-understanding and self-knowledge? What kind of stock should one place in the patient's self-report or in the therapist's judgment? What degree of reliability would one obtain among clinical judges? How much agreement would one find among different validity criteria? These are only some of the questions that arise in assessing complex outcomes such as enhanced self-understanding and self-knowledge, outcomes that go beyond checklists of symptoms or numerical ratings on an inventory (e.g., the Beck depression inventory).[5]

If a primary function of interpretation is not so much uncovering of repressed mental contents as facilitating the patient's understanding of how his or her mind works, it would seem to follow that one should evaluate an interpretation not primarily in terms of its accuracy—that is, how accurately it identifies the patient's repressed wish or desire—but rather primarily in terms of how well it serves the function of facilitating the patient's self-understanding—that is, how his or her mind works, for it is entirely possible that a precisely accurate interpretation will not further self-understanding, whereas an inaccurate or "inexact" interpretation will. As Glover (1931) noted, an inexact interpretation may have more of a therapeutic impact precisely because its very "inexactness" is less likely to evoke defensive reactions that reduce the therapeutic impact of the interpretation. A corollary of this observation is that under particular circumstances, a highly accurate interpretation that elicits strong defensive reactions may impede self-understanding, whereas an inaccurate or inexact interpretation

---

[5] The same set of questions arises in attempting to assess such complex outcomes as structural change.

that evokes fewer defensive reactions may enhance self-understanding (see also the discussion of this issue by Kohut, 1984).

In this view, the issue of the accuracy or veridicality of the interpretation itself is nowhere near as important as the accuracy or veridicality of the self-understanding it generates. In effect, the issue of accuracy or veridicality is shifted from the content of the interpretation itself to the nature of the self-understanding it facilitates. The relevant question becomes the degree to which the interpretation, whatever its degree of accuracy or inaccuracy, promotes genuine self-understanding rather than compliance or intellectualization. When the emphasis is on the impact of the interpretation (rather than primarily its content), factors such as tone and timing, the intuited intention behind the interpretation, and the context of the ongoing relationship in which the interpretation is given are likely to become increasingly important. Thus, as Mitchell (1998) has noted, certainly in the psychoanalytic context, an interpretation is truly a relational event.

In deemphasizing the veridicality of interpretation, I am not abandoning or dismissing the importance of accuracy and veridicality. Rather, as noted, I am shifting the concern from the accuracy of the content of the interpretation to the question of the veridicality and authenticity of the self-understanding it generates. I emphasize this point because I also want to make it clear that, contrary to some contemporary views, I believe that one can speak meaningfully about the accuracy or veridicality of self-understanding and that, however difficult it may be, one can, in principle, identify veridical, or perhaps one should say genuine, self-understanding and distinguish it from nonveridical and nongenuine expressions of presumed self-understanding. In other words, just as there are more veridical and less veridical forms of understanding events in the world, so similarly are there more veridical and less veridical forms of understanding oneself, and just as there is a legitimate distinction to be drawn between relatively veridical knowledge and what passes for knowledge of events in the world, so similarly is there a legitimate distinction to be drawn between relatively veridical and genuine self-knowledge and illusory and defensive accounts that pass for self-knowledge.[6]

I also want to make it clear that in deemphasizing the role of accuracy of interpretation, I am *not* adopting the contemporary view that the sole or primary function of interpretations is to construct or coconstruct a coherent and persuasive narrative or provide a new perspective. Indeed, I reject

---

[6] I am not commenting here on the question of whether, as suggested by the work of Taylor and her colleagues (e.g., Taylor & Brown, 1994; Taylor, Kemeny, Reed, Bower, & Gruenewald, 2000), illusory beliefs about oneself serve as a protection against dysphoric affects such as depression. I am only arguing that a legitimate distinction between illusion and self-knowledge can be made. Indeed, the finding that illusory beliefs about oneself are protective rests on the distinction between illusory and veridical self-knowledge.

that view because it is entirely possible to construct a persuasive and coherent narrative that is wholly fictional and that contributes little to understanding how one's mind works.

THERAPEUTIC RELATIONSHIP

Let me turn now to a factor that is heavily emphasized in the contemporary psychoanalytic literature, namely, the therapeutic relationship. Indeed, an emphasis on the therapeutic relationship as the central therapeutic ingredient in psychoanalytic treatment has become a hallmark of contemporary psychoanalytic theories.

I have already introduced the therapeutic relationship in my earlier discussion of the direct role of empathic understanding and the centrality of an empathic bond between patient and therapist in the self psychology conception of treatment. However, I want to discuss the role of the therapeutic relationship more broadly. Just what it is about the therapeutic relationship—the processes and mechanisms involved—that makes it central is not always clear. What is it that one means when one states that the therapeutic relationship is a primary therapeutic ingredient? Furthermore, the term *therapeutic relationship* itself may have many different meanings that need to be unpacked.

When one states that the therapeutic relationship is the primary ingredient of therapeutic action, one is going beyond the claim that it is a vehicle or arena for the operation of other active and primary therapeutic ingredients such as interpretation and insight. Rather, it is viewed as a direct therapeutic agent itself. However, in order for this view to have any coherent meaning, one needs to unpack it. In a certain sense, to say that the therapeutic relationship is a therapeutic ingredient is not very useful insofar as therapeutic relationship is a general, somewhat abstract, category that is constituted by a whole host of specific interactions and processes. It is these interactions and processes that define the therapeutic relationship and that constitute it as a therapeutic ingredient.[7] Hence, when one states that the therapeutic relationship itself is the therapeutic ingredient, one needs to ask: What goes on in that relationship that makes it therapeutic? Which specific interactions and processes that define that relationship are therapeutic? In what ways are they therapeutic?

---

[7] Ryle's (1949/2002) idea of "category mistake" comes to mind. Ryle's example is of someone who, taken to a university, is shown the building, students, syllabi, lectures, faculty, classrooms, and library but still wants to know where "the university" is. Of course, the university is an abstract category constituted by its various components that the visitor is shown. Similarly, the therapeutic relationship is constituted by what goes on in that relationship. There is no therapeutic relationship as a separate therapeutic ingredient apart from its specific constituents that, so to speak, carry the therapeutic action.

Corrective emotional experience

Let us consider some answers to the above questions that have been forth-coming. One general and influential answer has been that the therapeutic relationship provides a corrective emotional experience (Alexander, 1950; Alexander & French, 1946) based on the fact that the therapist's behavior and reactions are different from the patient's expectations acquired in early experiences with parental figures. Thus, the therapist's behavior tends to disconfirm or extinguish the patient's (maladaptive) expectations and hopefully slowly replace them with more adaptive expectations and representations. To take a garden-variety and perhaps trivial example, the patient's expectation, say, of rejection and punitiveness and the concomitant feelings of unworthiness and guilt are repeatedly disconfirmed by the therapist's nonjudgmental, accepting, and empathic attitude. With repeated experiences of this kind, these maladaptive expectations and representations in relation to significant others and self and their accompanying negative affects are replaced by more adaptive expectations, representations, and accompanying feelings. To be noted here is the good fit between this perspective on therapeutic action and the therapeutic goal discussed earlier, and emphasized in contemporary psychoanalytic theories, of altering maladaptive expectations and representations in relation to self, other, and prototypic interactions between self and other.

Many different conceptions of therapeutic action in the contemporary psychoanalytic literature, particularly those that emphasize the therapeutic relationship, can be subsumed under the general rubric of corrective emotional experience and can be understood as particular elaborations of that idea from a particular theoretical perspective. For example, as discussed earlier, after describing "the patient's increasing realization that, contrary to his experiences in childhood, the sustaining echo of empathic resonance is indeed available in this world" (p. 78), Kohut (1984) remarks that "if an ill-disposed critic now gleefully told me that ... I ... believe in the curative effect of 'corrective emotional experience' and equate such an experience with analysis, I could only reply: so be it" (p. 78).

Consider below other formulations of therapeutic action that focus on the therapeutic relationship. Each one, I believe, can be understood as a particular variant of the concept of the corrective emotional experience and to constitute a particular theoretical account of the processes through which the corrective emotional experience operates.

Disconfirmation of unconscious pathogenic beliefs and test-passing in control-mastery theory

According to Weiss et al. (1986), at the core of psychopathology are unconscious pathogenic beliefs and at the core of therapeutic action is the analyst's disconfirmation of these pathogenic beliefs through the process of passing tests presented to the therapist by the patient. It is not much of a strain to understand the analyst's test-passing and disconfirmation of unconscious pathogenic beliefs as a particular kind of corrective emotional experience. It should be noted, however, that unlike Alexander and French's (1946) stance, Weiss et al. do not propose that the analyst intentionally try to play a particular role in order to disconfirm the patient's unconscious pathogenic beliefs and expectations. Rather, most of the time, doing good analytic work—that is, being sensitive to the patient's communications, fears, goals, and tests; keeping the frame; and maintaining analytic neutrality—will, according to them, constitute test-passing and disconfirmation of the patient's unconscious pathogenic beliefs. Let me provide a few very brief clinical examples in which the therapist's test-passing is followed by progress in treatment and the appearance of new warded-off material.

A patient for whom a central aspect of her unconscious pathogenic belief is that defiance of parents is always followed by punishment and pain angrily defies my suggestion to use the couch. When I react with understanding and simply continue the treatment, a painful symptom is ameliorated. That is, the disconfirmation of the expectation that punishment will inevitably follow defiance serves to ameliorate the symptom (see Eagle, 1993, for a fuller description of this case). A patient suddenly announces her intention to terminate treatment. Following the analyst's reaction that her decision needs to be explored, the patient recovers a memory in which her mother sent her out to the grocery store during a gang fight in the neighborhood as if she had no concern for her welfare. A plausible interpretation of this sequence is that the recovered memory is made possible by the analyst's expression of interest and concern regarding her decision to terminate treatment. Following the analyst's tactful rejection of an expensive gift from a patient, the patient, who appears to be reassured regarding the analyst's seducibility, for the first time, talks about his homosexual fantasies. It is now safe to do so. There is, of course, much more that can be said about all these brief vignettes. However, the point to be noted is that in all three examples, the therapist's test-passing is followed by either the amelioration of a symptom or the emergence of new material.

One of the great virtues of the work of Weiss et al. (1986) is that they have subjected their formulations to systematic and ecologically valid empirical research. One of the main findings that has emerged from this body of research is that test failures on the part of the therapist, as rated by clinical judges, are reliably followed by defensive behavior and lack of therapeutic progress, whereas test-passing is more likely to be followed by such signs of therapeutic progress as emergence of new themes, greater flexibility of defenses, and reduced anxiety.

How does the patient experience the therapist?

An emphasis on corrective emotional experience seems to be at least partly based on the implicit assumption that when the therapist behaves differently from the patient's experience of his or her parents, that is, nonjudgmentally, accepting, empathic, passing tests, and so on, he or she is *experienced* that way by the patient. The assumption is that, in Fairbairn's (1952) language, the therapist is experienced as a good object. However, given the tenacity and assimilative power of expectations and representations established early in life, it is unlikely that the patient will simply and uncomplicatedly experience the therapist as a good object. Were the patient able to do so, he or she would be less in need of treatment, for surely there are potential good objects in the patient's life who cannot be experienced by the patient as such partly because they are experienced in terms of such early established bad object representations and expectations. In short, one's experiences of significant others is influenced by transference.

Consider, as an example, someone who is, say, avoidantly attached. There is evidence that avoidant attachment is often the outcome of early experiences of rejection and intrusion on the part of the attachment figure. Underlying this attachment pattern is a representation or internal working model characterized by an expectation of rejection from significant others. Let us say that this person comes to treatment. Given his or her avoidant attachment pattern and corresponding internal working model, it would be unrealistic to expect that at the onset, this individual will simply experience the therapist as a good object. Rather, it is likely that he or she will, at least in part, experience the therapist in accord with early representations and expectations. Were the individual able to fully experience the therapist as a good object, there would be little need for treatment. Indeed, from a psychoanalytic perspective, one can say that much of the treatment, particularly, the analysis of the transference, is taken up with analyzing and altering the impediments to the experience of the therapist as a good object (see Eagle & Wolitzky, 2009).[8] Hence, for many patients, the *potentially* corrective emotional experience of the therapist may need to be accompanied by an analysis of the factors that interfere with that experience. However, this is, of course, equivalent to saying that the analysis of the transference, as well as of the transference–countertransference interaction, may be necessary to enable the patient to experience the therapist as a good object in interaction with whom a corrective experience is possible.

---

[8] Implicit in Freud's (1922/1923) discussion of the distinction between the transference neuroses and narcissistic disorders is the idea that unless the patient has had some good object experiences in his or her life and therefore a potential template for experiencing the analyst in a benevolent way, psychoanalytic treatment may not be possible.

The therapist as a good object

Let me pursue somewhat further the question of why it is important that the patient experience the therapist as a good object. As we have seen, for Alexander and French (1946), the answer is that the experience of the therapist as a good object (i.e., essentially as someone who behaves differently from the parents) tends to extinguish and disconfirm ingrained maladaptive expectations and representations (e.g., expecting significant figures in one's life to be rejecting or punitive). For Kohut (1984), the answer is that through repeated experiences of optimal frustration and consequent "transmuting internalization," the patient is increasingly able to experience a sustaining empathic bond with the therapist and others outside the treatment. In other words, there is a slow transformation of the experienced therapist from a bad object who cannot provide perfect mirroring to a good object whose good-enough understanding and empathic bond can be sustaining.

Fairbairn (1952) presents another reason for the therapeutic importance of experiencing the therapist as a good object, namely, the assumption that in order for the patient to be able to relinquish early object ties—a central goal of treatment for Fairbairn—the patient needs to internalize the therapist as a good object. As we have seen (see Chapter 8), according to Fairbairn, the ultimate terror for the individual is living in a psychic world devoid of a sense of inner connections. Hence, from this perspective, even connections to bad objects are preferable to the absence of connections. This means that the patient cannot be expected to relinquish ties to early objects, including ties to bad objects, unless he or she can establish inner ties to a good object, and this is, according to Fairbairn, what the therapist as good object provides

Mitchell's (1988) view of the role of the therapeutic relationship is, in important respects, similar to Fairbairn's. For Mitchell, too, the basic goal of psychoanalytic treatment is to alter early object ties through a new experience with the analyst. As Mitchell puts it, "conflictual attachments to and identification with archaic objects are universal. It is the alteration of these ties which constitutes the basic therapeutic action of the analytic process" (p. 278) Further, it is the analyst's offering "something different, something new, another form of engagement and relationship" (pp. 305–306) and discovering "other channels through which to engage each other [that] is the crucible of analytic change" (p. 292).

Therapeutic importance of experiencing the therapist as a bad object

I commented above that given his or her history, the patient will inevitably experience the therapist as a bad object and that much of analytic work will focus on the impediments in the way of the patient experiencing the therapist as a good object.[9] I want to pursue that issue further. There is something of a paradox here. How can the patient feel safe enough to confront and explore early bad object experiences when he or she experiences the therapist as a bad object? One answer to this question is that along with the negative transference, there is also positive transference. Further, the patient wants and hopes to be able to experience the therapist as a good object. Indeed, if there is nothing in the patient's history and repertoire that makes possible the potential experience of the therapist as a good object, it is difficult to see how psychoanalytic treatment can work.[10]

Another answer to the question is that the experience of the therapist as a bad object itself is subjected to mutual examination. A good illustration of this is seen in Kohut's (1984) earlier noted description of the operation of optimal failure or optimal frustration in treatment. Because the patient's demand for perfect mirroring cannot possibly be met, it is inevitable that the therapist will be experienced as failing the patient, that is, will be experienced as a bad object. However, also according to Kohut, so long as the therapist acknowledges them and relates the patient's reactions to these failures, they will constitute optimal failures and will contribute slowly and cumulatively to the patient's increasing capacity to benefit from the less than perfect understanding.

In other words, an open-minded, nondefensive, and empathic examination of the patient's experience of the therapist as a bad object (e.g., not providing perfect mirroring) itself is likely to contribute to the patient's feeling understood and, therefore, to increasingly facilitate the transformation of the therapist from an experienced bad object to an experienced good object. Another way of putting this is to say that the therapist's tactful

---

[9] I have been emphasizing the sources of the impediments to experiencing the therapist as a good object in the patient, for example, in his or her history. This emphasis is consistent with a tendency in the psychoanalytic literature to attribute lack of progress in treatment mainly to the patient's resistance. However, given the contemporary interactional conception of psychoanalytic treatment, one should be able to recognize that the therapist's personality and behavior, as well as the nature of the match between patient and therapist, can also represent impediments to the patient's experience of the therapist as a good object.

[10] I am reminded of a young woman who was an inpatient at a clinical facility with which I was associated. On the usual psychiatric criteria, she was not the most disturbed patient at the facility. She was not psychotic, had no thought disorder, no hallucinations or delusions. However, despite initial optimism—after all, she was articulate, highly intelligent, nonpsychotic, and so on—she eventually came to be seen as the most hopeless patient at the facility. Treatments with a number of highly competent therapists at the facility all had the same outcome—the patient felt that each therapist could not possibly understand the depths of her inner emptiness and despair. After finding a therapist (who was now practicing outside the facility) who, the patient felt, could begin to understand her, and seeing the therapist for a period of time, she committed suicide after the therapist changed an appointment time for a session. I am reminded of this sad and depressing story in the present context because the patient's history seemed to provide no template for the experience of a good object. When the hope for the bare beginnings of such an experience seemed possible, it was immediately crushed by something as seemingly nontraumatic as a changed appointment.

examination and understanding of the patient's experience of him or her as a bad object, including an understanding and acknowledgment of the therapist's contributions to that experience, itself constitutes a good object experience and contributes to the evolving experience of the therapist as a good object.

Implicit in the above discussion is the seemingly odd and counterintuitive idea that an essential component of the treatment is the patient's experience of the therapist as a bad object. Of course, I am not suggesting that the therapist intentionally try to be a bad object, just as Kohut is not suggesting that the therapist intentionally try to (optimally) frustrate or fail the patient. Rather, I am suggesting that when the therapist is excessively concerned with warding off being experienced as a bad object (e.g., by using excessively compliant language or by being unable to set limits) and does not recognize that the patient's inevitable experience of him or her as a bad object represents an important arena of the treatment, he or she may fail to help the patient examine and work through critical issues.

As Mitchell (1988) observes, an examination of the patient's struggle to experience the therapist differently from his or her "predesigned categories" (p. 301) is a central aspect of the treatment. Mitchell writes that it is important that the therapist try to grasp the patient's experience of him or her as a bad object and then try to "free himself of this role, in his interpretive effort to clarify and understand the patient's insistence, offer[ing] something different, something new, another form of engagement and relatedness" (pp. 305–306). For Mitchell, discovering "other channels through which to engage each other is the crucible of analytic change" (p. 292). According to Mitchell, rather than reacting to the analyst solely in terms of a stereotyped template from the past, the patient is also trying to reach this particular analyst in an authentic and meaningful way. Initially, the patient may be able to reach the analyst only as a bad object. It is the understanding and working through of this experience and the cooperative and mutual struggle to move beyond that this experience that constitutes much of the analytic work. Without an affective experience of the analyst—even if the experience is one of a bad object—there is little emotionally compelling and meaningful to work through.

A number of analysts make a similar point. For example, Friedman (2008a) cites Fairbairn's description of the patient's placing the analyst in preset roles as "press-ganging," which "refers to the practice in the old English Navy of kidnapping men from local bars and streets, and 'impressing' them [into] service aboard warships" (p. 5, fn 4). As Friedman notes, according to Fairbairn, the analyst needs to deal constantly with the patient's press-ganging of the analyst into his or her relational world.

As another example, Loewald (1960) writes that through the analyst's interpretation of the patient's distorted experience of the analyst, he or she helps the patient to rediscover the developmental path of early object relations and ultimately to acquire a new way of relating to objects (as well as relating to oneself). When Loewald (1960) writes that the analyst interprets the patient's distorted experience of the analyst, he is, in effect, referring to the experience of the analyst as a bad object. That distorted rendering of the analyst as a bad object is precisely what needs to be interpreted. Furthermore, in Loewald's view, it is through the analyst's examination and interpretation of that experience that the patient both discovers or rediscovers the path of his early object relation and learns a new way of relating, for it is the analyst's tactful and empathic examination and interpretation of the patient's experience of him or her as a bad object that transforms the analyst into a good object and contributes to a new way of relating. In this process, Loewald tells us, the analyst must avoid falling into the role the patient has transferred onto him or her—in Fairbairn's colorful language, the analyst must avoid being press-ganged and instead must reflect back to the patient the role assigned. Further, as I have suggested, the analyst's effort to avoid falling into the transference role assigned and his or her interpretation of the patient's persistence in placing him or her in that role add up to being a good object. As Strupp and Binder (1984) put it, instead of responding in terms of what the patient's behavior "pulls for," the analyst and patient mutually examine the interaction.

Unless the patient can be sufficiently emotionally engaged to experience the analyst in his or her assigned role, that is, as a problematic figure from the past, there will be little opportunity in the treatment to meaningfully (i.e., in an affectively real way) explore and rediscover the developmental path of early object relations. As Loewald (1960) writes, the affective intensity of early object relations needs to be transferred onto the analyst if early modes of object relations are to make their appearance and to be interpreted in the treatment. From this perspective, one can understand why resistance to forming a transference would constitute the greatest impediment to treatment. One can also understand why under certain circumstances, the experience of the analyst as a bad object—in all the affective intensity that that implies—can be a vital component of treatment. An experience of the analyst as an all-good object would not facilitate access—indeed, can be seen as a resistance against such access—to the path of early object relations.

Let me return to Fairbairn once more. According to Fairbairn (1958), psychoanalytic treatment can be understood as a struggle between, on the one hand, the patient's persistent attempt to press-gang his or her relationship with the therapist into the closed system of the patient's inner world and, on the other hand, the analyst's determination "to breach the closed system and to provide conditions under which the patient may be induced to an open system of our reality" (p. 379). From this perspective, it is through this patient–analyst struggle that the primary goal of psychoanalytic treatment can be achieved, namely, the establishment of an open system in which the distortions of inner reality can be corrected by outer reality and true relationships with external objects can occur. In short, paradoxically, although one needs a good object to safely explore painful aspects of one's life, the patient's experience of the analyst as a bad object is a necessary component of the treatment, for it is through an examination of that experience that the analyst is transformed into a good object.[11]

If my reasoning is correct and conforms to clinical realities, it follows that corrective emotional experience, defined primarily in terms of the therapist behaving differently from early parental figures, would not likely be sufficient for therapeutic change. What may also be required is a mutual examination of the impediments (encompassing both transference and countertransference reactions) that are a barrier to experiencing the treatment as emotionally corrective. Of course, these issues need to be subject to systematic empirical investigation.

Interpretation and a "truth-seeking attitude"

I want to return once again to the question of interpretation in the context of the above discussion of the therapist as a good and bad object. We have seen that in one form or another and whether or not explicitly acknowledged, interpretation plays a critical role in the transformation of the therapist from a bad to a good object. Recall, for example, that for Kohut (1984), optimal failure or optimal frustration consists in the therapist acknowledging his or her failure and linking the patient's rage, despair, regression, and so on to these failures. Notwithstanding Kohut's distinction between understanding and explaining, this kind of intervention linking the patient's reactions to his or her experience of the analyst as failing him or her is clearly a garden-variety transference interpretation. Even the analyst's acknowledgment of his or her failures can best be understood as an interpretation. It states something like: "You experienced my doing (or not doing) X as failing you, not understanding you."

Mitchell (1988) also makes quite clear that a major intervention in the transformation of the analyst from a bad object to a good object is interpretation. Recall the previously cited passage from Mitchell in which he writes that in freeing himself or herself from the role of bad object, "the analyst's *interpretive effort* to clarify and understand the patient's insistence [i.e., on perceiving the analyst as a bad object], offer[s] something

---

[11] One can think of the classical ideas of the transference neurosis and its resolution as (a) an immersion in the experience of the analyst as a stand-in for an earlier object; (b) slowly learning—through interpretation and analytic neutrality—to represent the analyst more in terms of who he or she actually is, as well as learning to correspondingly represent oneself in terms of who one actually is; and (c) generalizing from the experience in the analytic situation to representations of and interactions with significant figures outside the analytic situation.

different, something new, another form of engagement and relatedness"
(p 306, emphasis added). In other words, there is no clear distinction
between the therapeutic relationship and interpretation insofar as, in
important ways, the analyst's interpretive effort partly constitutes the
relationship. As Loewald (1960) puts it, "the analyst through the objective interpretation of transference distortions, increasingly becomes
available to the patient as a new object" (pp. 228–229). In a similar
way, Mitchell (1988) writes that an interpretation is a *complex relational
event* ... because it says something very important about where the analyst stands vis-à-vis the patient, about what sort of relatedness is possible
between the two of them" (p. 295, emphasis in original). Thus, it is not
just the content of the interpretation, but, as Friedman (2008b) observes
in his discussion of Loewald, the "devoted and truth-seeking" attitude of
the analyst that has an impact on the patient. It is, Friedman tells us, the
reception the patient has been seeking. Further, it is this attitude, as well
as the interactions it generates, that, according to Friedman, is internalized and that guides the patient to an understanding of who he or she is
and has the potential to be.

In my view, the devoted and truth-seeking attitude noted by Friedman is
not conveyed—indeed, the opposite is the case—by clever and deep interpretations, nor is it compatible with such conceptions and locutions as
coherent narratives, "narrative truth," retellings, new perspectives, interpretive constructions, and the more extreme "aesthetic fictions." These
concepts reflect epistemological skepticism toward the possibility of analyst and patient discovering truths (and therefore toward the meaningfulness of pursuing them) and instead convey the epistemological conviction
that narratives, interpretive constructions, aesthetic fictions, and so on are
all there are. That is, I believe that a devoted and truth-seeking attitude is
more respectful of the integrity of the individual than the *attitude* inherent
in such concepts as narrative truth, interpretive constructions, aesthetic
fictions, and so on.[12]

I believe that these concepts—although they certainly are not intended
to do so—tend to violate the integrity of the individual to the extent that
they imply that the primary function of interpretations is not to be true
to the core aspects of the individual but rather to construct a new, more
coherent and more persuasive narrative of the individual's life or to reorga-
nize experience. What would it mean to be deeply understood by another
in the latter context? I can envisage a new perspective and a new narrative *following* or being generated by an understanding of core aspects of

---

[12]That this belief is implicitly held even by many of those who emphasize coherent narratives,
interpretative constructions, and so on is indicated in a number of ways, including the
frequently observed disjunction between, on the one hand, the conceptual–epistemological
position explicitly propounded and, on the other hand, the position implicit in the discussion of clinical material (see Eagle, Wolitzky, & Wakefield, 2001).

oneself, but I cannot envisage them as standing alone, as a replacement for a truth-seeking attitude. Of course, for those who reject the very notion of core aspects of oneself and replace that idea with one of multiple selves that are constructed by ongoing interactions and interpretations (e.g., Bromberg, 1996; Mitchell, 1995), there is far less reason to be concerned with whether or not the interpretation violates the integrity of the individual. This is so because, to put it perhaps too strongly, the interpretation constructs the self (or selves) rather than reflects it (or them).

In short, I am suggesting that an epistemological stance that is reflected in a "devoted and truth-seeking attitude" or, as Steingart (1995) puts it, in a desire to understand and appreciate the patient's psychic reality, is more likely to convey a deep motivation to understand the patient than a construal of one's analytic work as consisting largely in constructing or coconstructing persuasive and coherent narratives, reorganizing experience, providing aesthetic fictions, and so on. Of course, once again, one has to say that, in part at least, these are empirical issues.

Most people who come to psychoanalytic treatment expect to learn about and come to terms with core aspects of themselves. They do not, generally, have the aim of constructing more coherent narratives and aesthetic fictions or reorganizing experience. To the extent that their therapists construe the therapeutic situation in this way, there is the risk of a serious disjunction between patient and therapist regarding how they understand the therapeutic situation. Furthermore, it is unlikely that this disjunction would be confronted. As far as I know, analysts who in their theoretical papers conceptualize treatment in terms of coherent narratives, etc., do not share these views with their patients and do not disabuse them of their presumably mistaken assumption regarding the nature of the treatment. Regardless of what they write in theoretical papers, I do not know of any analyst who tells a prospective patient that a goal of treatment is to construct more persuasive and coherent narratives independently of whether they tally with what is real in him or her.

As noted above, Mitchell (1988) has commented that the patient relates to the analyst not simply in terms of an early stereotyped template but as someone who wants to find and relate to *this* particular analyst. One way of putting this is to say that the patient is struggling to relate to the analyst not as an "interpretive construction" or as an "aesthetic fiction" but in a way that tallies with what is real in the analyst. What is puzzling to me is the following: If Mitchell believes that it is possible for the patient to find and relate to *this* particular analyst, in terms of who he or she actually is, why does he not believe it is equally possible for the analyst to find and relate to *this* patient in terms of who he or she actually is? Why is it only the analyst who is limited to "interpretive constructions" in his or her understanding of the patient?

Therapeutic alliance

Any discussion of the role of the therapeutic relationship in treatment would be incomplete without reference to the concept of therapeutic alliance. The fact is that in the above discussion of such factors as empathic understanding, optimal failures, and therapist as secure base and as a good object, the therapeutic alliance has already been implicitly introduced, even if that term was not used. However, given its centrality in psychotherapy theory and research, it merits explicit reference and discussion. Unlike the relationship factors I have already discussed, which are embedded in specific theories (e.g., self psychology) and which are not especially associated with a research program (the secure base concept of attachment theory is an exception), the concept of therapeutic alliance is prominently present in psychotherapy research and has achieved transtheoretical status (Safran & Muran, 1996).

The terms *working alliance* and *therapeutic alliance* first appeared in the psychoanalytic literature (Zetzel, 1956; Greenson, 1965) and, as the term *alliance* suggests, referred generally to a cooperative working relationship between patient and therapist. It was largely understood as a background factor that facilitated other therapeutic processes (e.g., achieving insight) rather than constituting a primary therapeutic ingredient itself. Since its introduction into the psychoanalytic literature, it has been a controversial concept, with some psychoanalytic theorists arguing that there is no need for it. These theorists object to the implication that there is an aspect of the analytic relationship—the therapeutic alliance—that is not part of the transference and that therefore escapes the need for analysis of the transference (e.g., Brenner, 1979). In tracing the origins of the concept, one also needs to make reference to Rogers's (e.g., 1951) emphasis on the therapeutic role of such factors as unconditional positive regard and empathy. Finally, as far as I know, Bordin (1976) introduced the term *working alliance* to the general psychotherapy research community in the paper "The Generalizability of the Psychoanalytic Concept of the Working Alliance," which reflects his recognition of its psychoanalytic origins.

There have been various definitions of the term *therapeutic alliance*. The one that I believe is most useful (and that also incorporates the working alliance) includes three basic components: a collaborative and cooperative relationship between patient and therapist; an affective bond between the two; and patient–therapist agreement on treatment goals (Martin, Graske, & Davis, 2000). It should be apparent that perceptions of the therapeutic alliance can be made from three different perspectives that do not necessarily yield the same judgment: the patient's, the therapist's, and an outside observer's. It should also be noted that the therapeutic alliance can be fluid and vary across time, as expressed in such concepts as "rupture and repair" (Safran, Muran, Samstag, & Stevens, 2001). Finally, the therapeutic alliance is likely to vary with patient characteristics, therapist characteristics, and patient–therapist match.

One of the most consistent findings in psychotherapy research is that the strength of the therapeutic alliance is the single best predictor of treatment outcome (Baldwin, Wampold, & Imel, 2007; Horvath & Symonds, 1991; Martin et al., 2000). Furthermore, a poor therapeutic alliance predicts increased dropout from treatment (e.g., Johansson & Eklund, 2006; Samstag, Batchelder, Muran, Safran, & Winston, 1998). The fact that these findings cut across different therapeutic approaches with presumably different specific therapeutic techniques has led many observers to conclude that the main curative factor in virtually all types of therapy is the therapeutic relationship (e.g., Lambert, 2001; Lambert & Barley, 2001). Indeed, taking this view quite seriously, Safran and Muran (2000) have formulated a brief relational therapy model in which the primary tasks of the treatment are to track ruptures in the therapeutic alliance and to help the patient become more aware of how he or she relates to the therapist and implicitly negotiates and communicates with him or her.

It should be noted, however, that although a strong therapeutic alliance is consistently related to therapeutic outcome, its contribution to outcome has been a modest one. In a recent paper, Beutler (2009) estimates that the therapeutic relationship accounts for less than 7% of the variation among outcomes. It is important not to confuse consistency with size of contribution to outcome, for the modesty of its contribution suggests that factors other than alliance contribute to therapeutic outcome. Furthermore, I know of at least one study, dealing with drug abuse (Barber et al., 2001), in which the strength of the alliance was *not* a significant predictor of outcome and in which it was *negatively* correlated with therapy retention in cognitive therapy.

How does the therapeutic alliance influence therapeutic outcome? Through what processes and mechanisms? The ways in which psychotherapy researchers have grappled with these (and similar) questions can serve as a model for how to carefully address the role of relationship factors in treatment. Although, as noted, the quality of the therapeutic alliance is the single best predictor of psychotherapy outcome, one should not necessarily assume that it always functions as a direct causal factor. As Kazdin (2007) has observed, the patient's experience of a stronger therapeutic alliance may be the *effect* of other therapeutic processes. For example, the experience of symptom relief or reduced anxiety following, say, an empathic and accurate interpretation may strengthen the patient's sense of a collaborative relationship, an affective bond with the therapist, and the feeling that the patient and the therapist agree on the same treatment goals. The patient's experience of a strengthened therapeutic alliance may then, in turn, facilitate his or her ability to benefit from other interventions (e.g., empathic understanding, interpretations). In other words, I am suggesting what one might call a causal network or circular causal chain in which the therapeutic alliance can be understood as both an effect of other therapeutic processes and a causal agent that facilitates other therapeutic processes and is itself directly linked to therapeutic outcome.

Quite early on, Luborsky (1976) distinguished between the "facilitative" function of the therapeutic alliance and, its role as an "active ingredient" itself. The above distinction suggests that the therapeutic alliance (that is, the patient's experience of a collaborative relationship, of an affective bond with the therapist, and of agreement on treatment goals) is the product of some ongoing processes between patient and therapist. However, whatever way the therapeutic alliance comes about and whatever other factors it is an effect of, it also likely operates as a causal agent itself, both indirectly, by facilitating the positive effects of other therapeutic interventions, and directly, by influencing therapeutic outcome. The latter simply reflects the plausible assumption that a sense of collaboration, an affective bond, and a feeling of being on the same track as one's therapist are likely not only to make the patient more receptive to other interventions but also themselves to represent new healing experiences. Indeed, there is some evidence, in at least in some studies, that even when prior symptom change is accounted for, strength of therapeutic alliance still significantly predicts outcome (Barber, Connolly, Crits-Christoph, Gladis, & Siqueland, 2000).

Although therapeutic alliance may predict outcome when symptom change is accounted for, and although it is plausible that experiences associated with a strong therapeutic alliance would be healing, its role as a causal agent is still not entirely established. One possibility is that the link between therapeutic alliance and outcome is at least partly due to a third common factor. For example, Kazdin (2007) has shown that the patient's baseline functioning accounts for part of the therapeutic alliance. In other words, a pretreatment healthier patient may both have a better prognosis and also be more likely to form and experience a stronger therapeutic alliance. To complicate matters even further, one reason for the better prognosis may be the patient's greater capacity for forming and experiencing a stronger therapeutic alliance.

Rupture and repair and analysis of the transference

Earlier in this chapter, I noted the similarity between Kohut's concept of optimal failure Safran and Muran's (1996, 2000) concept of rupture and repair. I want to return to that concept in the context of discussing the therapeutic alliance. When Safran and Muran use the term *rupture and repair,* they refer specifically to the patient's experience of the therapeutic alliance. As noted, attention to and dealing with breaks in the alliance constitutes the core of their brief relational therapy model. Kohut's (1984) description of optimal failures does seem to constitute, in effect, an account of rupture and repair in the therapeutic alliance. That is, the patient's experience of not being perfectly mirrored can be thought of as a rupture in the alliance, and the therapist's attention to and empathic understanding of this experience, as well as acknowledgment of his or her failures, can be thought of as contributing to the repair of the rupture. Furthermore, repeated experiences of this sequence increase the patient's trust in the ability of the relationship to withstand ruptures and in the ability of the therapist to attend to and attempt to deal with experienced ruptures. Safran and Muran have presented some preliminary findings suggesting that resolution and nonresolution of alliance ruptures are associated with different therapeutic trajectories.

As Safran and Muran (1996) observe, the idea of rupture and repair, in certain respects, also bears a strong family resemblance to the concept of analysis of negative transference, particularly when transference is defined not solely in terms of the patient's projections onto the blank screen of the analyst but in the more contemporary terms of responding to cues emitted by the analyst (Gill, 1982, 1994). In a relational context, the very process of attending to and empathically interpreting the negative transference, particularly when the interpretation focuses on the here-and-now interaction between patient and therapist and when it includes acknowledgment of and attention to the patient's experience of the therapist's behavior, can be understood, in part at least, as attempts to understand and repair ruptures in the therapeutic relationship.

As noted earlier, there is some evidence suggesting that, contrary to what one might intuitively think, transference interpretations are more effective in patients showing less mature object relations (Hogeland et al., 2007). Safran, Muran, Winston, and Samstag (2005) have presented some preliminary data suggesting that alliance-focused interventions (which can be seen as roughly similar to transference interpretations) are especially useful with patients with whom it is difficult to establish a therapeutic alliance. In this context, one can perhaps understand the development of self psychology, particularly its central concepts of empathic understanding and optimal failures, as a response to the challenges of working with narcissistic patients who have difficulty establishing and maintaining a therapeutic alliance.

Finally, one of the findings of the Menninger project (Kernberg et al., 1972) was that patients assessed as showing ego weakness responded better to expressive therapy, which included transference interpretations, than to supportive psychotherapy. It is likely that Kernberg's formulation of transference focused psychotherapy with borderline patients was influenced by these findings. One way of understanding them is that the therapist's attention to the therapeutic relationship and sensitivity to ruptures (or negative transference), as well as to the need to repair these ruptures, is especially critical with patients who have difficulty establishing and maintaining a therapeutic alliance. In short, the above findings suggest that it is especially important with difficult patients to attend to and deal with the vicissitudes of the therapeutic relationship.

THE PERSONAL EQUATION

So long as one held to a conception of the analyst in a blank-screen role, one could minimize the role of individual differences among analysts and maintain that all well-trained analysts are essentially interchangeable. Contrastingly, an important implication of the contemporary emphasis on a two-person psychology and the enlarged role of countertransference is that the personal qualities of the analyst, as well as the match between the analyst and the personal qualities of the patient, are likely to be quite important in influencing therapeutic process and outcome.

If we have learned anything about the psychotherapy process, we have learned that there is no such thing as a disembodied or blank-screen intervention. There is only an intervention—say an interpretation—made by a particular therapist, with a particular phrasing, with a particular tone of voice, at a particular time, to a particular patient who is in a particular frame of mind. Furthermore, each intervention takes place in the context of an ongoing relationship and framework, with the impact likely to vary as a function of context and framework. It is very likely that the impact of interpretations—say, expressions of empathic understanding—with the same semantic content will vary with the various factors I have noted.

There are certain ways of putting things to someone, and ripe times in which they can be put, so as to have a greater impact than the same semantic content put in a different way or at a different time. I recall saying to a friend who had just had a disturbing fight with his wife: "Do you want to be right or do you want to be married?" According to my friend, this spontaneous comment—which seemed to me to get to at least one aspect of the heart of the matter—had more of an impact on him and his relationship with his wife than the many sessions of couples therapy he and his wife attended. I am certain that the impact of my comment was at least partly due to the tone in which it was delivered, the moment I chose to make it, and the nature of our relationship.

It seems to me that one cannot fully know what a therapist does in treatment or the way he or she does it based mainly on knowledge of his or her theoretical affiliation. I also strongly believe that the influence of personal qualities of a therapist is likely to predominate over the influence of theoretical affiliation in determining how that therapist carries out treatment. For example, as noted earlier, despite advocating the analyst's opaqueness and use of the surgeon metaphor to prescribe the proper analytic stance, Freud disclosed his personal interests to patients and fed a hungry patient.

On the other hand, although Fairbairn wrote about the importance of the analyst being a good object, according to Guntrip (1996), he was detached and austere as an analyst.

The manner in which any manual or theory-driven prescription regarding analytic or therapeutic stance is implemented or enacted is necessarily filtered through and revealing of the personal qualities of the therapist. It could not be otherwise. Furthermore, the analyst's personality will influence, often in subtle ways, the at least partly idiosyncratic way in which the prescription is understood. This means that therapist A's implementation of empathic understanding or analytic neutrality or being a good object may have quite a different flavor from therapist B's implementation of the same stance. Although these various instantiations of empathic understanding or analytic neutrality or being a good object may, in Wittgenstein's (1953/1973) term, bear a family resemblance to each other, they may also be quite different, in certain respects, from each other.

I recall an experience of a colleague who, as he became increasingly devoted to self psychology, spoke in an increasingly mellifluous tone of voice. Whereas for him, this constituted empathic understanding, for me, it was saccharine and inauthentic. I and my students in a graduate class on psychotherapy had a similar experience in viewing a segment of a DVD of a therapy session in which, presumably in an attempt to show how empathic he was being, the therapist leans forward toward the client, looks intently at him, and whispers with aching sincerity some purportedly understanding comment. The students burst out in laughter in response to this behavior, which they clearly experienced as theatrical, inauthentic, and a caricature of empathic understanding.

Although one may get some idea of what therapists do and how they do it based on publications of case studies and clinical vignettes, they provide only a general and often inadequate idea. This is partly so because of the inherently selective nature of reporting in these publications. Therapists report what they are aware of; they cannot report those aspects of the patient's and their own behavior of which they are unaware. Anyone making a videotape of his or her own behavior is struck by the sense of unfamiliarity of many aspects of his or her behavior. Also, therapists are likely to selectively report clinical data (e.g., interventions) that are congruent with their theoretical affiliation and that of the audience they intend to address and are likely to omit incongruent date (see Spence, 1990).

Finally, in reading accounts of clinical material, it is often difficult to get a good sense of such qualities as the therapist's affective presence and degree of interest and caring. It is all well and good to write about "analytic love" and to state that the love one feels for patients is not essentially different from the love one feels for one's best friend and children (Bach, 2006). However, without knowing how this love is actually and concretely expressed in the treatment of a particular patient—how it is, so to speak, embodied—it is difficult to know what to make of it all. In short, we need to keep in mind that our discussions and debates in regard to analytic stance and therapeutic interventions are constrained by our very limited knowledge of how an analytic stance and therapeutic interventions are personally implemented.

Recently, a university clinic at which I supervise implemented the policy that trainees videotape their therapy sessions. Thus, I have had the experience of supervision of the same trainees with and without videotaping. What is striking is the marked difference between the two. The videotapes reveal important aspects of the therapist's (and patient's) behavior that are simply not reported in supervision without videotapes. Given this experience with videotapes, it is difficult for me to return to supervision limited to the therapist's process notes.

THERAPEUTIC CHANGE AND RESEARCH

In coming to the end of this overly long chapter, I want to address an issue that is central to any conception or theory of psychotherapy, namely, what are the processes and mechanisms that bring about therapeutic change? As Kazdin (2007) asks, "how does one get from 'my therapist and I are bonding' to 'my marriage, anxiety, and ties are better'"? (p. 8). What are the processes and mechanisms involved in getting from A to B? I fully agree with Kazdin that this question is the most fundamental one for psychotherapy theory and research and that it is no longer sufficient, in describing different therapeutic approaches, to remain at the global conceptual level of, for example, psychodynamic or cognitive behavioral. I also agree with him (and with Kandel, 1998, 1999) that the answers to this fundamental question are likely to lie in attention to basic biological and psychological processes having to do with learning, memory, beliefs, self-concept, expectations, attitudes, wants and desires, conflicts, cognitions, affects and affect regulation, the acquisition and reduction of fear and anxiety, and so on.

One implication of this view is that in assessing therapeutic change, one should aim to adopt a common transtheoretical language that cuts across different schools and different global theoretical commitments, that is, a language that refers to basic biological and psychological processes. I am not suggesting that different therapeutic approaches all have the same goals and the same specific outcomes. This is not likely the case. What I am suggesting is that as far as possible, goals and outcomes should be stated in a common language of basic biological and psychological processes. Although this aim is not easily achieved, it is an ideal worth pursuing.

Part III

Overview and integration

Chapter 11

Divergences and convergences

This final chapter will be devoted to some of the major issues discussed throughout the book from the perspective of divergences and convergences between classical and contemporary psychoanalytic theories, as well as within contemporary theories. I begin with a reiteration of the broad cultural and philosophical contexts that form the background for the more specific differences between classical and contemporary views.

THE ENLIGHTENMENT VISION
AND PSYCHOANALYSIS

As noted in Chapter 9, classical psychoanalytic theory is a product of what Searle (1998) refers to as the Enlightenment vision. This is evident in a number of ways. As Peter Gay (1996a, 1996b) has observed, in the primacy it places on insight, awareness, and self-knowledge, classical psychoanalysis reflects many Enlightenment attitudes and values. It fits neatly into a tradition that stretches from Socrates' admonition to "know thyself" to the Enlightenment valuing of self-emancipation. Indeed, for Habermas (1971), psychoanalysis is a quintessentially self-emancipatory discipline whose aim is the liberation of consciousness through subjecting it to self-criticism and reflection (see Gedo, 1977).

Also, paralleling the Enlightenment perspective that has roots as far back as Plato, according to classical psychoanalytic theory, human nature is characterized by an ongoing conflict between the irrational passions and the voice of reason and reality. Just as, from the Enlightenment perspective, there are irrational forces in the physical and social worlds that need to be understood and controlled and from which we need to be liberated, from the perspective of classical psychoanalytic theory, similarly, are there irrational forces in the individual that need to be understood and controlled and from which one needs to be liberated. In both cases, the primary means of dealing with those irrational forces are reason and knowledge—self-knowledge, in the context of the individual.[1]

As we have seen in Chapter 1, these basic Enlightenment ideas are also reflected in the classical psychoanalytic links between, on the one hand, neurosis and repression—a form of not knowing—and on the other hand, between cure of neurosis and knowing—insight, awareness, and self-knowledge. From the classical psychoanalytic perspective, in what seemed to be a fortunate and remarkable convergence, the Enlightenment imperative to know thyself, at one and the same time, is also a necessary condition for clinical cure. Clinical cure and liberation—from ignorance and from inner tyranny—are seen as synonymous. To put it another way, not knowing—in the form of repression—constitutes an etiological factor in neurosis, and self-knowledge—in the form of lifting repression—constitutes a precondition for liberation from neurosis. Just as social, political, and scientific enlightenment entails liberation from ignorance and adherence to irrational dogma and replacing them with knowledge and reason, so similarly does individual enlightenment entail liberation from repression and irrational fear and replacing them with self-knowledge and deliberative reason. In short, in the classical view, there is no essential disjunction between pursuit of Enlightenment values and clinical cure. To be cured was to be enlightened, at least in regard to one's inner world.

As discussed in Chapter 9, skepticism toward the therapeutic sufficiency of insight, awareness, and self-knowledge began to appear in the classical psychoanalytic literature, although it was expressed largely in the context of treatment of more disturbed patients. However, a more pervasive skepticism developed based partly on the common clinical experience that at least apparent insight was often not accompanied by therapeutic cure or even therapeutic progress. Skepticism toward the therapeutic efficacy of insight, awareness and self-knowledge found perhaps its clearest expression in Alexander and French's (1946) claim that "corrective emotional experiences" rather than insight and self-knowledge constituted the main agent of therapeutic action and therapeutic change. The introduction of this idea considerably weakened the convergence between the Enlightenment vision and psychoanalysis. One could no longer as readily claim that self-knowledge was both an Enlightenment value and a clinical necessity.

As we have seen in previous chapters, skepticism toward the Enlightenment idea that the truth shall set one free is not limited to the psychoanalytic context but is also characteristic of broad cultural-philosophical trends, as expressed, for example, in the passage cited below from Rorty (1991), one

---

[1] One of the ironies of Freudian theory is that although it stresses the ubiquitousness and power of dark and irrational forces within the individual, it also locates in reason, awareness, consciousness, and reality testing the only means for at least partly overcoming and controlling these forces. In that sense, Freudian theory is a clear product and expression of the Enlightenment and the Age of Reason.

of the most influential philosophical critics of the Enlightenment vision. The philosophical positions expressed by Rorty find clear parallels in contemporary psychoanalytic formulations, particularly in Mitchell's writings but also in those of Renik, Hoffman, Schafer, and Spence. For example, paralleling Rorty's eschewal of truth value are Mitchell's (1998) views that analysts offer "interpretative constructions" rather than anything one can be right or wrong about and that analysis entails organizing and reorganizing experience rather than uncovering or discovering something.

The shift from classical to contemporary psychoanalytic theories in their underlying philosophical positions has led Hoffman (1991) to observe that the theoretical differences within psychoanalysis are no longer a matter of different psychoanalytic schools but rather entail a mini-paradigm shift. Hoffman characterizes this shift as one from positivism to constructivism. Although I believe that Hoffman is mistaken in his characterization of it, I believe that he is correct in noting the occurrence of a philosophical shift.

Perhaps the most interesting and striking convergence between Rorty's philosophical position and contemporary psychoanalysis lies in the parallel between his (1991) call for the privileging of solidarity over objectivity and the contemporary psychoanalytic privileging of the therapeutic relationship over insight, awareness, and self-knowledge. Rorty writes:

> The tradition in Western culture which centers around the notion of the search for truth, a tradition which runs from the Greek philosophers through the Enlightenment, is the clearest example of the attempt to find a sense of one's existence by turning away from solidarity to objectivity. The idea of truth as something to be pursued for its own sake, not because it will be good for oneself, or for one's real or imagined community, is the central theme of this tradition. (p. 121)[2]

In short, I would suggest that the contemporary psychoanalytic attitudes toward uncovering truths and the privileging of the therapeutic relationship—solidarity—over insight, awareness, and self-knowledge—objectivity—is not simply attributable to clinical experience but is also an expression of the cultural-philosophical zeitgeist—just as Freud's privileging of the Enlightenment value of objectivity over solidarity was also partly an expression of the zeitgeist. In any case, I believe it is useful to keep in mind the general background and contexts I have outlined in considering at least some of the specific points of divergence and convergence between classical and contemporary psychoanalytic theories that I will discuss in the remainder of this chapter.

---

[2] Note that the dictionary definition of *solidarity* is "unity and mutual support resulting from shared interests, feelings, or opinions" (*Compact Oxford English Dictionary*, 2000).

CONCEPTIONS OF MIND: DIVERGENCES

It is not easy to compare classical and contemporary psychoanalytic conceptions of mind across the board because there is nothing in the latter that is comparable to Freud's formulation of the nature and function of the mind. Indeed, contemporary psychoanalytic theories appear to show little interest in the systematic formulation of the origin or conception of mind. For example, there is virtually no discussion of the nature of mind in Kohut's writings. This is not surprising insofar as unlike contemporary psychoanalytic theories, the ambition of classical theory (including ego psychology) was to develop a comprehensive and more or less complete theory of psychological functioning.

Apart from this general divergence, as the previous chapters have made clear, there are marked specific divergences between classical and contemporary psychoanalytic conceptions of mind. According to Freudian theory, the primary function of the mental apparatus is to discharge excitation, particularly excitations generated by drive demands. Insofar as contemporary psychoanalytic theories reject Freudian drive theory, as well as the constancy principle, they also reject the conception of mind as a discharge apparatus.

As we have seen in the previous chapters, according to Freudian theory, the early and basic tendency of mind to seek immediate gratification through hallucinatory wish fulfillment is modulated by the infant's and child's growing recognition that gratification requires thinking, planning, and action that take account of means–ends relationships and requires commerce with real objects in the world. That is, the infant becomes increasingly capable of reality-testing. Thus, the development of both thinking and object relations is contingent upon the fact that hallucinatory wish fulfillment does not succeed in achieving gratification.

Although contemporary theories reject the above formulation, they do not offer any systematic alternative account of the development of reality-testing. For example, if one examines the references to reality and reality testing in Kohut's (1984) book, one finds (a) the comment that "reality ... is in essence unknowable" (pp. 222–223, fn 6); (b) a critical reference to "reality principle morality" (p. 84); (c) a criticism of the idea that psychoanalytic cure "is equated with the dominance of the reality principle over the pleasure principle" (p. 95); and (d) another criticism "of the confining influence of the moralistic framework provided by the pleasure principle" (i.e., the clinging to childish pleasures and the avoidance of anxiety) and the "reality principle" (p. 114).

Although, as noted, the origin and development of reality-testing is not explicitly and systematically addressed in contemporary psychoanalytic theories, certain contemporary conceptualizations suggest that reality-testing is an inborn capacity rather than something forced upon the individual by drive demands. Thus, Bowlby (1973) maintains that the infant's and child's internal working models (IWMs) are reasonably accurate and realistic representations of infant-caregiver interactions. Similarly, D. N. Stern (1985) suggests that the infant's Representations of Interactions Generalized (RIGs) are also reasonably accurate reflections of prototypic interactions between infant and caregiver. Thus, if indeed IWMs and RIGs do accurately reflect infant-caregiver interactions, it suggests that from early on and independently of the pressure of drive demands, the infant is capable of a surprising level of learning and reality-testing. It should be added that there is a great deal of infant research that supports this conclusion.

Unconscious processes

As we have seen in Chapter 6, perhaps the most fundamental and radical divergence between classical and relational conceptions of mind lies in their respective conceptualizations of unconscious processes, including the nature of defense. In contrast to the Freudian conception of specific and determinate unconscious wishes and desires, which are not essentially different from conscious wishes and desires, relational theory views unconscious mental contents as vague and indeterminate unformulated experiences, the determinate content of which, if they are formulated, will be determined by ongoing social interactions (D. B. Stern, 2003). Furthermore, from the latter perspective, defense is understood as motivated failure to formulate the unformulated rather than in terms of keeping determinate contents (i.e., specific and identifiable wishes and desires) from conscious experience. As discussed earlier, a conception of mind as indeterminate is also reflected in Mitchell's (1998, 2000) rejection of the idea that mind is preorganized and his suggestion that organization occurs as a function of each ongoing relationship (see Chapter 6). This view starkly contrasts with the Freudian conception of mind and of unconscious contents as relatively stable structures (characterized by, among other things, fundamental wishes and desires, a set of core conflicts, characteristic defenses, and so on).

Partly as a consequence of the above conceptualizations, the cornerstone Freudian concept of repression has virtually disappeared from the contemporary psychoanalytic literature and has been replaced by an emphasis on dissociation—often linked to a renewed interest in trauma. In general, the role of unconscious processes and contents in psychological life, certainly as understood by Freud, has been greatly deemphasized. As far as I am aware, there is also little in contemporary psychoanalytic theories that parallels the Freudian emphasis on *disavowal* of determinate unacceptable wishes as a central aspect of defense, that is, on the transformation of certain aspects of oneself ("I") into a nonpersonal "it." These reconceptualizations essentially replace the dichotomy between unconscious and conscious with an unconscious–conscious continuum in effect, replace Freud's dynamic unconscious with James's (1890) momentary and fleeting states of consciousness.

Another stark contrast between classical and contemporary psychoanalysis is the transformation of the Freudian dynamic unconscious of drive-related wishes and desires, "a cauldron full of seething excitation" (Freud, 1932/1933, p. 84), into an unconscious of representations, interactional schemas, expectations, beliefs, and working models that are unconscious not by virtue of defense but because they have been acquired nonverbally, early in life. They comprise implicit procedural rules that govern our interactions with others, as well as representations of self and other.

One needs to note here that there are two directions in the reconceptualization of mind and unconscious processes in relational psychoanalysis, and these directions are not entirely compatible with each other. As we have seen, rather than thought of as preorganized, mind is viewed as fluid and ever-shifting as a function of ongoing social interactions. From this perspective, unconscious contents are vague and unformulated, and any determinate shape they acquire will be determined by ongoing and fluid social interactions in the interpersonal field. On the other hand, according to relational psychoanalysis, mind, including unconscious contents, can be understood as "relational configurations, transactional patterns, and internal structures derived from an interactional and interpersonal field" (Mitchell, 1998, p. 17). Surely, the latter suggests a conception of mind in terms of preorganized stable structures rather than as fluid and ever-shifting.

CONCEPTIONS OF MIND: CONVERGENCES

Despite the stark contrasts discussed above, there are some areas of convergence between classical theory and, at least, those contemporary theories (i.e., object relations theory, relational psychoanalysis, neo-Kleinian theory, and control-mastery theory) that emphasize inner conflict. Although they differ with regard to the particular conflicts that each views as fundamental, there is convergence on the view of mind as inherently conflictual. This convergence in conceptions of mind has, of course, implications for convergence regarding certain aspects of approach to treatment—for example, attention to conflict in the treatment process and more adaptive resolution of conflict as a treatment goal.

Although there are differences regarding what is defended against and the specific nature of defensive processes, with the possible exception of self psychology, there is a clear convergence on the fundamental idea that a primary function of psychological defenses is to keep anxiety-laden and threatening material from being fully consciously experienced and from threatening one's sense of who one is. Whatever other differences there may be, this idea is at the core of the concept of defense from many different theoretical perspectives. It is the element that is common to such diverse concepts as repression, dissociation, "not me" experiences (Sullivan, 1953), failing to make connections and recognize the personal significance of experiences (G. S. Klein, 1976), and failing to formulate the unformulated (D. B. Stern, 1989, 2003).

It is a robust idea that has found expression in the nonpsychoanalytic literature, for example, in Greenwald's (1980) classic paper on the "totalitarian ego," a term intended to convey the basic idea that we tend to exclude from consciousness information that is sharply at variance with our preexisting beliefs and our sense of who we are. Its heuristic value is reflected in the large body of empirical research it has generated (e.g., Cramer, 2006) and its applicability to a number of different areas. For example, there is evidence not only that information at variance with one's political beliefs tends to be ignored and discounted but also that such information activates brain areas associated with feelings of distress (Westen, Blagov, Harenski, Kilts, & Hamann, 2006).

There is also convergence on the idea that the anxiety-arousing potential of certain mental contents (i.e., thoughts, feelings, connections), which leads to the need for defense, is at least partly attributable to their association with early parental negative reactions such as disapproval, punishment, failure to validate, and anxiety. Thus, there are clear points of convergence between Freud's (1925/1926) formulation of the role of the danger situations (particularly loss of the object and loss of the object's love) in influencing what mental contents can become conscious and the contemporary formulation that one's horizons of awareness (Stolorow et al., 2002) are influenced by early parental validation and invalidation, approval and disapproval. Both formulations converge on the central idea that one's range of conscious experiences—what one is permitted to consciously experience—is strongly influenced by the anxiety (and guilt) associated with early parental reactions. It should be noted that this basic idea is also enunciated in nonpsychoanalytic theories, for example, in Rogers's (1961) concept of "conditions of worth," which also refers to the range of the individual's experience being influenced by parental responses of rejection or acceptance.

NATURE AND ORIGIN OF OBJECT RELATIONS: DIVERGENCES

There is a clear divergence between the Freudian view that the development of object relations is contingent upon the failure of hallucinatory wish-fulfillment and the contemporary view that object relations develop independently of drive gratification. As we have seen in previous chapters, an assumption central to most contemporary theories is that we are *inherently* object-seeking (Fairbairn, 1952) or, in Mitchell's (1988) words, "relational by design" (p. 21) rather than contingently or secondarily object relational.

Contemporary theorists reject both the hallucinatory wish-fulfillment failure theory of the origin of object relations and the Freudian concept of primary narcissism (as well as related concepts such as "normal autism," Mahler, 1968; see M. Klein, 1981, and Peterfreund, 1978, for cogent critiques of these ideas.) The evidence makes it increasingly difficult to portray young infants as encased in a shell of primary narcissism, seeking hallucinatory wish-fulfillment, incapable of any degree of reality-testing, and forced to turn to objects and take account of reality by the demands of drive gratification.

Drive-reduction versus object relational motives

In contrast to the classic emphasis on motives that entail buildup and discharge of excitation, contemporary psychoanalytic theories emphasize the quieter motives having to do with the need for support from the object (e.g., safety, felt security). However, as I will discuss below, a concern with object relations and object relational motives is compatible with certain aspects of an excitation or tension regulation model.

Object love in classical theory and self psychology

Ironically, in important respects, object relations are far more central in Freudian theory than in self psychology. In *On Narcissism*, Freud (1914b) wrote quite poetically that "in the last resort, one must love in order not to fall ill" (p. 85)—although he follows it with the considerably less poetic metapsychological reason that if one does not direct libidinal cathexis on to the object, excessive cathexis of the ego will be damaging (a version of the constancy principle). As noted earlier, Kohut objects to Freud's insistence that healthy development is characterized by the move from narcissism to object love (cathexis of objects). He argues, instead, that narcissism is a separate line of development and that psychological health is marked not by the progression from narcissism to object love but from archaic to mature narcissism. Indeed, Kohut (1984) writes that joyful and meaningful lives can be led without object love at their center. Thus, ironically, with regard to the centrality of object relations and object love in psychic life, classical theory and object relations theory have far more in common than either has with self psychology (see Chapter 6).

NATURE AND ORIGIN OF OBJECT
RELATIONS: CONVERGENCES

The need for homeostasis and the role of the object in regulating tension and affect states

Despite differences regarding the origin and course of development of object relations, both classical and contemporary psychoanalytic theories converge on the central idea that the object serves the vital function of regulating tension and affect states and supporting intact ego functioning. In Freudian theory, this idea is expressed in two theoretical contexts: the object's role in drive gratification and the need to direct libido from the ego to objects, that is, the need to move from narcissism to object love. As discussed in previous chapters, in both cases the object is necessary in order to avoid the danger of inundating and damaging the ego with excessive excitation and thereby disrupting ego functioning. If one translates the above formulations from the metapsychological languages of drive theory and theory of narcissism into a more neutral language, one would state that the object plays a vital role in regulating physiological processes, tensions, and affect states, which serves to maintain intact ego functioning.

This conception of the role of the object is entirely compatible with a variety of contemporary conceptions, as well as empirical findings, regarding the role of the object and object relations in psychological and physiological functioning. Thus, Fairbairn's (1952) identification of the experience of living in an inner world devoid of objects and object relations as the ultimate threat to psychological functioning facing the individual is entirely compatible with—indeed, parallels—Freud's insistence that intact psychological functioning requires the progression from narcissism to object love and that the object is necessary if one is to avoid the damage to the ego resulting from the buildup of excessive excitation emanating from drives. Of course, Fairbairn does not use the language of drives and excessive excitation. However, both Freud and Fairbairn converge on the central ideas that intact ego functioning is not possible in the absence of the regulating function of the object and object relations, as well as of a cognitive-affective connection to the object (which, of course, constitutes a definition of object relations); and that the absence of object relations constitutes the ultimate psychological disaster for the individual.

One can draw a similar parallel between Freud's conception of object relations and other contemporary psychoanalytic formulations. For example, according to self psychology theory (Kohut, 1984), self-cohesiveness (which can be viewed as adequate ego functioning), one criterion of which is adequate regulation of affect and tension states, requires the availability of regulating empathic mirroring from the object—the selfobject, in Kohut's terminology. Similarly, according to attachment theory, the infant's experience of the caregiver's "sensitive responsiveness" is a critical ingredient for "felt security." Here, too, one can recognize the role of the object in regulating affect states (i.e., felt security versus anxiety) as well as ego functions involved in self-representation and regulation of self-esteem. One also needs to point to the empirical evidence cited in Chapter 7 attesting to the role of the caregiver in regulating different physiological systems in the infant.

Dichotomy between object-seeking and pleasure-seeking in infant–caregiver attachment

In light of the above evidence, the dichotomy between pleasure-seeking and object-seeking posited by Fairbairn (1952) and endorsed by relational theorists (e.g., Mitchell, 1988) is not warranted. That is, the regulating effects of the substances provided by the object are undoubtedly associated with experiences of well-being and pleasure (or at least, the avoidance of unpleasure), just as the dysregulating effects of loss of the object and of the substances the object provides are undoubtedly associated with distress. In other words, although as Fairbairn suggests, there is an inborn readiness to seek and become attached to objects, it appears that objects are sources of pleasure associated with adequate regulation of different psychological systems. Furthermore, it is likely that as Anna Freud (1960) suggests, at least one factor determining the particular object to whom the infant becomes attached is the experience of at least some degree of pleasure and well-being associated with adequate regulation and felt security.[3]

Consider the above in the light the classic Harlow (1958) study. According to Harlow, the infant monkey becomes attached to the terry cloth surrogate

---

[3] There is evidence that punishment at the hands of the caregiver strengthens rather than attenuates the infant's attachment response. For example, when the caregiver is hooked up so that when the infant monkey approaches her, she emits a noxious puff of air, the infant monkey clings to the caregiver even more intensely. This finding is paralleled by the observation that abused children become intensely attached to the abusing caregiver. This kind of evidence would appear to contradict the proposition that pleasure provided by the caregiver constitutes an important basis for determining the specific figure to whom the infant becomes attached. However, that conclusion would not be warranted for a number of reasons. First, unless the caregiver provided some degree of regulation and associated experience of well-being, the infant would not survive. Second, because there is generally one primary caregiver, the infant has no choice as to whom he or she becomes attached. There is only one game in town. Third, related to this point, we know that distress intensifies the attachment response. Normally, when the distress is not caused by the caregiver herself, turning to her will likely be comforting and serve to relieve the infant's distress. However, when the caregiver herself is the source of the distress, the infant is in an impossible situation. He or she has no choice but to cling more intensely to the attachment figure, the very source of the distress. There is evidence that in this kind of situation in which no coherent strategy is possible—for example, when the infant experiences the caregiver as frightened or frightening—is associated with disorganized attachment and is a serious risk factor for later psychopathology.

mother because of the "contact comfort" (i.e., tactile stimulation) it provides. As we have seen, tactile stimulation is one of the stimulus inputs that regulate aspects of the infants' physiological and psychological state. And, of course, the very term *contact comfort* suggests that the terry cloth mother is a source of sensual pleasure. In other words, although the infant monkey may be inherently object-seeking, the particular object it seeks and becomes attached to is the one associated with the sensual pleasure provided by tactile stimulation. It is interesting to observe, in this regard, that Freud (1905) refers to the entire surface of the skin as an erogenous zone *par excellence*, notes that being held, cuddled, touched, and fondled is a source of libidinal pleasure for the infant, and refers to Moll's instinct of "contrectation," which represents "a need for contact with the skin" (p. 169). Indeed, it is difficult not to think of Harlow's concept of contact comfort when reading Freud's description of the skin as an erogenous zone.

Recall that the motivation for Harlow's (1958) study was to refute the secondary drive theory claim that the infant becomes attached to the caregiver because of the caregiver's association with the reduction of the primary drive of hunger. It was not intended to refute, nor did it refute, the idea that the object to which the infant monkey becomes attached is associated with sensual pleasure and that an important basis for the infant monkey's attachment is the pleasure provided by the object. Indeed, as noted, the contact comfort emphasized by Harlow clearly suggests pleasure associated with tactile stimulation. One way to put this is to say that whereas Harlow's results tend to refute a drive-reduction version of a secondary reinforcement theory of infant-mother attachment, it tends to support a sensual pleasure version of that theory.

In short, not only is there no contradiction between object-seeking and pleasure-seeking but there is also no contradiction between positing an inborn readiness to become attached (i.e., to posit our inherent object-seeking propensity) and also positing that the experience of sensual pleasure and well-being associated with regulation constitutes a critical basis for determining the specific figure to whom one becomes attached. It is important to keep in mind this distinction between the inborn and autonomous nature of our object-seeking propensity—which is not a secondary product of pleasure—and the particular object to whom the infant becomes attached—which *does* appear to be influenced by pleasures associated with the object. One needs to acknowledge the failure of classical theory to recognize our inborn object relational nature while at the same time acknowledging the failure of contemporary theories to recognize the role of various forms of regulation and pleasure in influencing the object(s) to whom the infant becomes attached.

From this perspective, it is unfortunate that Freud and Anna Freud placed so much emphasis on the hunger drive. As noted in Chapter 3, from the perspective of psychoanalytic theory, what is psychologically significant about feeding is not simply that it reduces hunger tensions—hardly a psychoanalytic insight—but also that it provides oral gratification and other forms of sensual pleasures. Clearly, as elaborated in Chapter 3, Freud's and Anna Freud's secondary drive theory, which led them to overemphasize the role of hunger reduction as a basis for infant-mother attachments, constitutes an inadequate account. However, the general claim that one basis for the infant's attachment to a particular object is the pleasures provided by that object does appear to be supported by the evidence, including the evidence provided by the Harlow (1958) study, as well as the work of Hofer and his colleagues discussed earlier on the regulating functions of the object.

One also needs to note here that although hunger reduction may not serve as the primary basis for attachment to the object, it would be a mistake to conclude that it plays no role at all. As Polan and Hofer (1999) have noted, in the design of the Harlow study, feeding and tactile stimulation were radically partitioned, a situation one does not normally encounter in the natural environment. In normal circumstances, mother is the source of both milk and a wide range of sensory inputs, and the infant is not forced to choose one or the other. Of course, Harlow made the important discovery that when, through experimental manipulation, the infant is forced to choose, the sensory qualities win out over milk-provision as a basis for attachment. This was found not only for monkeys but also for dogs (Igel & Calvin, 1960). However, puppies reared with a lactating (i.e., milk-providing) terry cloth surrogate spent significantly more nonfeeding time with it than nonfeeding time spent by puppies with a nonlactating (i.e., nonmilk-providing) terry cloth surrogate. In contrast, puppies spent no more nonfeeding time with a lactating (i.e., milk-providing) wire surrogate than a nonlactating (i.e., nonmilk-providing) wire surrogate. On the one hand, these results support Harlow's conclusion that infants do not become attached by milk alone. On the other hand, they indicate that the provision of milk *does* strengthen attachment when the object "possesses other significantly potent proximity-promoting qualities" (Polan & Hofer, 1999, p. 168)—in this case, the sensory qualities associated with the texture of terry cloth.

Although I have referred to the provision of milk in the above description, the fact is that the infant receives milk through the activity of suckling. As Freud (1905) recognized, one needs to distinguish between the nutritional and the hunger-reducing factor of receiving milk and nonnutritional sucking. Brake and Hofer (as cited in Polan & Hofer, 1999) have shown that rat "pups presented with an anesthetized dam, which gives no milk, remain nipple-attached and engage in 'dry-sucking' for at least 3 hours … the longest interval tested" (p. 168). For rat pups as young as seven days, the reward of suckling a nonlactating nipple can serve as a reinforcer in learning to negotiate a maze (Kenny & Blass, 1977). Further, as mothers have long known, both the provision of milk and nonnutritive sucking (e.g., of the pacifier) serve to soothe and calm the infant.

In short, the infant's early attachment to the caregiver appears to be based on various physiological systems being regulated by a range of maternal sensory cues and stimulus inputs—tactile, oral, milk, thermal, olfactory, and vestibular. Further, as we have seen in discussing the interaction between milk provision and tactile stimulation in determining proximity-seeking behavior, these various sensory cues interact in complex ways. Because Harlow's results were so dramatic and so forcefully and decisively demolished the secondary drive theory of attachment, it has been tempting to conclude that contact comfort constitutes *the* sole basis for infant-mother attachment. However, as the work of Hofer and his colleagues, as well as other related work, has shown, that would be a mistaken conclusion. The point here is that no single input—contact comfort or hunger reduction—constitutes the sole basis for infant-mother attachment. Each sensory input, in interaction with other inputs provided by the mother, contributes to the formation of attachment. The inborn readiness to become attached finds a reception, so to speak, and is guided by various maternal sensory cues and stimulus inputs. Furthermore, these various stimulus inputs entail pleasures associated with adequate regulation. As Hofer (1995) notes, these early experiences of pleasure and physiological regulation are likely to constitute the basis for later psychological attachment.

The dichotomy between pleasure-seeking and object-seeking needs to be understood in historical-theoretical context. From the perspective of Freudian drive theory, pleasure-seeking is essentially equivalent to drive-reduction behavior. Hence, Fairbairn's statement that libido is primarily object-seeking rather than pleasure seeking can be understood as a rejection of Freud's claim that we relate to objects primarily because of their role in drive reduction (i.e., in providing pleasure) and an insistence instead on our inborn propensity to seek and relate to objects independently of their association with drive reductions (i.e., pleasure). However, what has followed a rejection of Freudian drive theory is a general neglect of the role of pleasure in object relations—as if pleasure has been preempted by drive theory and as if to recognize and acknowledge the role of pleasure in object relations is to endorse the drive theory account of object relations.

As Slade and Aber (1992) point out, there is virtually no mention of pleasure in Bowlby's account of attachment theory. The role of pleasure in object relations is also neglected by Fairbairn and contemporary relational theorists and is associated with a general reluctance to go beyond insisting that we are relational "by design" and to examine the determinants of object relations and the functions of the object in psychic life. As an example of this tendency, in contrasting drive and relational psychoanalytic theories, Mitchell (1988) characterizes the latter as maintaining that the infant seeks "*contact qua contact*, interaction in and for itself, not contact as a means of gratifying and channeling something else" (p. 24, emphasis in original). He then goes on to state that "the other is not simply a vehicle for managing internal pressures and state; interactive exchanges with and ties to the other become the fundamental psychological reality itself" (p. 24). I assume that what Mitchell means by this is that the object is not sought because of its role in drive reduction but rather that we are object-seeking by design.

That we are relational by design and inherently object-seeking is very likely the case. There is much evidence for that view. However, as we have seen, that is only the beginning of a complex story regarding the nature and function of object relations. Although perhaps understandable in the context of contrasting drive and relational theories, to say that infants seek "*contact qua contact*, interaction in and for itself" invites no further questions about the functions served by contact with the object or about how and why one becomes attached to particular objects. All we know of what an infant seeks is what we can infer from that infant's behavior. As we have seen from the work of Hofer and his colleagues, what we do know is that object-seeking (i.e., proximity-seeking) behavior of the infant, as well as his or her attachment to the object, is facilitated by certain stimulus inputs of the object and that contact with the object does, indeed, "serve as a means of gratifying ... something else," namely, the need for homeostatic regulation of physiological states and developmental processes. Furthermore, much behavioral evidence warrants the inference that such regulation is associated with the infant's pleasure and well-being, just as there is much evidence indicating that withdrawal of these regulations triggers distress. Hence, one can say that the infant is both object-seeking in the sense of an inborn readiness to seek and relate to objects and pleasure-seeking in the sense of seeking and becoming attached to particular objects who are the source of pleasures associated with regulation of various physiological and psychological states. In the debates in the literature, this distinction is often overlooked

There seems to be a tendency among relational theorists to resist any idea that the object and object relations serve functions beyond object relating itself—as if to recognize and examine these functions is to threaten the primacy, autonomy, and elevated status of object relations, and as if such recognition is the equivalent to stating that "the other *is* ... simply a vehicle for managing internal processes and states" and denying that "interactive exchange with and ties to the other become the fundamental psychological reality itself" (Mitchell, 1988, p. 24).

Although the other is certainly not *simply* a vehicle for managing internal processes and states, as we have seen, relating to the other *does* serve to manage or regulate internal processes and states. As the work I have described demonstrates, this is especially the case early in life, when the primary function of the caregiver is to manage and regulate the infant's internal processes and states. Furthermore, it is very likely that the regulation by the object of these early experiences of one's internal processes and states constitutes the building blocks necessary for ties to the other to become a fundamental psychological reality itself. The development of that fundamental reality does not occur in a vacuum but rather is built on repeated early experiences in which one's internal processes and states are regulated by the object.

To sum up, although there are differences regarding the origin and development of object relations between classical and contemporary psychoanalytic theories, there is convergence on the fundamental idea that objects and object relations serve regulatory functions and are necessary for intact ego development and intact ego functioning.

Before leaving this topic, a final comment is in order. I doubt that it is profitable to limit one's discussion to debates about such issues as whether libido is primarily object-seeking or pleasure-seeking. Rather, the challenges are to identify—in a manner exemplified by Hofer's research—the specific role of objects in regulating specific physiological and psychological systems, the processes through which regulation takes place, the relationship between variations in object relations and the specific aspects of psychological functioning (e.g., attachment patterns), and the specific processes involved in that relationship.

Object relations and object love

We know that in the course of development, the infant and child come to respond to the caregiver not only as a source of regulation and pleasure through her ministrations but also as an object that is loved. Indeed, as Benjamin (1998) points out, in the ideal development of object love, the term *object relations* becomes increasingly awkward and, at a certain point, perhaps warrants replacement by the term *subject relations* to reflect the developmental move from experiencing the other entirely as an instrumental object in relation to one's needs to experiencing the other as a subject, as a separate center of existence with his or her own needs, attitudes, and so on.

I want to pursue the question of object love by returning to Freud's (1914b) dramatic statement that "in the last resort, one must love in order not to fall ill" (p. 85) and his general view that in healthy development one moves from narcissism to object love. Recall that for Freud, failure to negotiate that move—in metapsychological terms, failure to cathect objects with libido or the marked withdrawal libido from objects (in ordinary language, the withdrawal of one's cognitive-affective investment in and connection to objects)—is associated with such severe pathological consequences as psychotic megalomania and world destruction fantasies, a formulation that is strikingly similar to Fairbairn's (1952) statement that "failure to direct libido towards the object is, of course, equivalent to loss of the object" (p. 51). Thus, Freud assigns as profound an importance to the role of object and object relations in maintaining psychic functioning as one can find in the psychoanalytic literature.

It will be noted that there has been a marked absence of reference to self psychology in the above discussion of object relations and object love. Why is that so? As we have seen, the answer to this question is quite evident. As stated earlier, self psychology is not an object relations theory but, true to its appellation, a theory of the self. One needs to recall that the theoretical starting point lies in Kohut's (1984) rejection of Freud's (1914b) insistence that in healthy development one must move from narcissism to object love. One can lead a productive and satisfying life, Kohut tells us, without object love at its center. For Kohut, it is the capacity not for object love but for self-cohesiveness and realization of the self that is the main criterion for mental health.

It is ironic that Freud, who, in the context of drive theory, begins with a conception of the object as entirely instrumental—as a "thing in regard to which and through which the instinct achieves its aim" (Freud, 1915a, p. 122) eventually formulates a theoretical position in which the capacity for loving the object is central to healthy functioning. There is little in relational and intersubjective theories that speak directly to the issue of the capacity for object love and its role in psychic functioning.[4]

Relatedness and autonomy

The position taken in relational theories is that there is an inherent conflict between relatedness to the object and autonomy and self-definition—a position reminiscent of Freud's (1914b) formulation of the conflict between object-libido and ego-libido.

As noted in Chapter 7, I would suggest that positing an inherent conflict between relatedness and self-definition is not warranted and that, indeed, to the contrary, that in healthy development, there is a mutually facilitating and reciprocal relationship between the two. I would suggest further that the assumption of an inherent conflict between the two is based on pathological and problematic relatedness. The mutually facilitating relationship between relatedness and self-definition and autonomy is made especially

---

[4] It is interesting to comment on the ethical aspects of this issue. Kant tells us that the use of the other as an instrumental object, as a means to an end, is a primary source of evil and immorality. Obviously, Kant had the adult in mind, not the infant or child who relates to the caregiver as a regulating object. That is, implicit in Kant's position is the expectation that in the course of development, the moral individual will become increasingly able to relate to the other as an end in herself or himself rather than primarily as an instrument or means to meet his or her needs. The desire to dispute an entirely instrumental view of the object may have motivated Mitchell's (1998) insistence that the infant seeks contact qua contact. However, the fact is that the infant has little choice but to relate to the object instrumentally. Also, to be able to relate to the other as a subject is, as Benjamin (1998) suggests, not a given but a developmental achievement that occurs in varying degrees.

clear in the context of attachment theory, particularly in considering the facilitating relationship between the secure base (relatedness) and exploratory activity (autonomy) (see Chapter 7).

When relatedness and autonomy are experienced as inherently and inevitably in conflict, the form of relatedness is likely to be a regressive and pathogenic one, and the form of autonomy is likely to be on the dimension of what Fairbairn (1952) describes as a schizoid fantasy of self-sufficiency. To be more specific, if one's experience of relatedness is characterized by clinging to early object ties or a stifling symbiotic enmeshment or painful rejection, then, of course, relatedness will be likely to be experienced as inimical to self-definition and autonomy. Furthermore, under these circumstances, in reaction to painful rejection or stifling enmeshment, autonomy will be defensively sought as an escape from relatedness—rather than the "mature dependence" referred to by Fairbairn (1952).

The idea that it is pathological relatedness rather than relatedness per se that conflicts with autonomy and self-definition is also implicit in Freud's (1912a) elaboration of the nature of oedipal conflicts. Freud proposes that it is the persistence of incestuous wishes—an example of clinging to early objects—that keeps the individual from finding and emotionally investing in a new object—an expression of autonomy and self-definition. Furthermore, Freud (1912a) tells us that even when in literal reality a new object is found, the early ties can persist, and the new object becomes a stand-in for that early tie, as evidenced by such symptoms as "psychical impotence" (p. 183).

Before leaving the topic of relatedness and autonomy, one must note the important work over the years on this topic from a group of feminist writers from the Stone Center at Wesleyan University (e.g., Jordan, 1997; Jordan, Kaplan, Miller, Stiver, & Surrey, 1991; Jordan, Walker, & Hastlings, 2004). These writers have consistently argued against a notion of autonomy that is inherently inimical to relatedness. Although they have focused primarily on women, as noted in the abstract of a 1997 book edited by Jordan on the writings from the Stone Center, "The authors advocate not just a more accurate understanding of women, but also a major paradigm shift in all of Western psychology, from a psychology of the separate self to a psychology of relational being."

CONCEPTIONS OF PSYCHOPATHOLOGY: DIVERGENCES

At the center of the classical conception of psychopathology is the presence of inner conflicts between anxiety-laden wishes and desires and defenses erected against them. This can be described as a drive-defense or id–ego model and is another way of saying that it is neurosis that is the main arena for the classical psychoanalytic theory of psychopathology. The divergences from this classical perspective take a number of different directions.

Virtually all contemporary psychoanalytic theories (with the exception of the contemporary Kleinians of London) share in common a rejection of Freudian drive theory and hence do not, of course, adopt a drive-defense model of psychopathology. However, beyond this common shared element, there is a good deal of diversity among contemporary psychoanalytic views of psychopathology.

Greenberg and Mitchell (1983) contrast their conflict-relational theory with a classical conflict-drive theory. The point to be noted is that *conflict* is retained as a central aspect of personality functioning, as well as of psychopathology. However, the conflicts that are stressed are not between instinctual wishes and ego defenses against them but rather between our effort "both to maintain our ties to others and to differentiate ourselves from others" (Mitchell, 1988, p. 3). As we have seen, variations and versions of this conflict have been described in various ways, including the regressive lure of identification versus the progressive urge toward separation (Fairbairn, 1952), relatedness versus autonomy (Blatt, 2008), symbiosis versus separation–individuation (Mahler, 1968), and safety versus effectance (Greenberg, 1991). As we have also seen, in contrast to the classical emphasis on conflictual infantile wishes and aims as the main triggers of anxiety, in contemporary views, it is not only the regressive lure of identification that triggers anxiety but also the progressive urge toward separation. As discussed in Chapter 8, whereas in classical theory, the danger situations of loss of the object's love is associated with infantile wishes and impulses (e.g., oedipal wishes), in the contemporary view, parental disapproval and consequent anxiety are as likely to be associated with mature wishes for autonomy.

Some contemporary psychoanalytic theories of psychopathology can be seen as partial theories that are intended to account for specific forms of psychopathology. Early on (e.g., Kohut, 1971), self psychology could be viewed as a partial theory in that its applicability was originally intended to be limited to narcissistic personality disorders, whereas classical theory was viewed as applicable to neurosis and structural conflicts. However, in the course of time, Kohut came to view self-defects as fundamental to all psychopathology.

An example of a partial theory that focuses on developmental arrest but limits its applicability to a particular form of psychopathology is seen in Kernberg's (1976) account of borderline personality disorder. According to this account, borderline patients either have regressed from or have not traversed the normal developmental pathway from the use of splitting as a primary defense to the capacity for repression. It is the latter trajectory that, of course, constitutes a developmental arrest, one characterized by primary reliance on a defense that is more aptly described as dissociation rather than repression. In Kernberg's view (as well as related views), the borderline patient's pathology is best described not in terms of conflict between instinctual impulses and repressive defenses but rather in terms of an incapacity to integrate good and bad self and object representations along with their associated affect states that are split or dissociated from each other.

A component of contemporary psychoanalytic theories of psychopathology that is difficult to place in either a drive-defense or a defect-developmental arrest model is the emphasis on maladaptive cognitive-affective schemas or templates of interactional patterns along with associated representations of self and other (e.g., RIGs, IWMs) that have been acquired early in life.

A feature shared by virtually all contemporary psychoanalytic theories is the primary role of *parental failure* in the etiology of psychopathology. The nature of the posited parental failure varies with the particular theory— for example, traumatic lack of mirroring, lack of maternal responsiveness, deprivation and rejections, seductiveness and competitiveness, failure to provide a secure base, reinforcement of helpless and dependent behavior, induction of guilt and of pathogenic beliefs, and so on. However, the assumption they all share is that some form of early parental failure is a primary causal factor in the development of psychopathology.

This contemporary emphasis on early parental failure can be contrasted with Freud's relative deemphasis (following his abandonment of the seduction hypothesis) of the role of parental behavior in the development of psychopathology. Freud attempted to identify etiological factors in the development of psychopathology (e.g., unhealthy sexual practices, sexual precocity, accidental events), but with the exception of citing parental threats such as castration threats as an etiological factor in neurosis, he did not place much direct emphasis on the role of parental failure.

Interestingly enough one of the few times that Freud (1905) comments directly on parental behavior, he warns not about the deleterious effects of rejection and deprivation but rather of the dangers of "excessive affection." He writes:

> One of the clearest indications that a child will later become neurotic is to be seen in an insatiable demand for his parents' affection. And on the other hand neuropathic parents, who are inclined as a rule to display excessive affection, are precisely these who are most likely by their caresses to arouse the child's disposition to neurotic illness. (p. 223)

Rather than an explicit emphasis, there is an implicit reference to the role of parental behavior in Freud's writings on psychopathology, mainly in his concept of fixation and in his discussion of the danger situations. With regard to the former, Freud tells us that the consequence of either excessive deprivation or excessive gratification—which are presumably a matter of parental behavior—at a particular psychosexual stage can be fixation at that stage. However, the concept of fixation does not play much of a role in Freud's clinical descriptions of neurosis. With regard to the latter, surely the nature of the infant's and child's experience of the danger situations of loss of the object, loss of the object's love, castration anxiety, and superego condemnation must have something to do with parental behavior. However, with few exceptions, Freud devotes little time to delineating individual differences in parental behaviors that would be associated with the child's degree of anxiety about, say, loss of the object or loss of the object's love. Rather, the danger situations are discussed primarily as universal vicissitudes. (As we shall see, however, the danger situations are implicitly invoked to account for the constriction of experience associated with repression.)

CONCEPTIONS OF PSYCHOPATHOLOGY: CONVERGENCES

Clinging to early object ties

As noted in Chapter 8, in addition to an emphasis on the early acquisition of maladaptive modes of relating—which is essentially a learning model of etiology—an element common to most contemporary psychoanalytic theories is an equal emphasis on the role of active, highly motivated emotional clinging to early objects in psychopathology. Examples here include Fairbairn's (1952) reference to the patient's "devotion" and "obstinate attachment" to bad objects; Mitchell's (1988) "conflictual attachments to ... early objects" (p. 278); Weiss et al.'s (1986) "unconscious pathogenic beliefs" fueled by loyalty and guilt in relation to early objects; Modell's (1965, 1971) "survivor guilt" and "separation guilt"; and Kohut's (1984) archaic self–selfobject relationships.

As noted in Chapter 8, Freud (1916–1917/1917) also identified the persistence of early object ties as a central factor in pathology, which he attributed to "adhesiveness of the libido" (p. 348). Also, quite apart from this metapsychological description, implicit in Freud's account of an unresolved or poorly resolved oedipal conflict is the persistence of early object ties. That is, insofar as a central feature of an unresolved oedipal conflict—a major constituent of psychopathology in classical theory—is the persistence of incestuous wishes toward the parental figure of the opposite sex, it is clear that, along with contemporary theories, Freudian theory also identifies the persistence of early object ties as a core aspect of psychopathology.

Of course, Freudian theory and contemporary theories differ regarding the *nature*, motives, and functions of the persistent clinging to these early ties. For Freud, these ties are characterized by the failure to relinquish incestuous wishes, whereas other motives and functions are identified in contemporary theories. However, the fact remains that both Freudian and contemporary theories converge on the idea that one's inability to relinquish early object ties—whether these ties are thought of as incestuous, matters of devotion, guilt, self-sustaining, and so on—is a central feature of psychopathology.

Furthermore, even among some Freudians, there has been a tendency to think of oedipal ties in broader terms that are more compatible with contemporary theories. For example, as noted in Chapter 8, Schafer (1968) has interpreted anxiety regarding oedipal incestuous wishes as fear of dedifferentiation. The implication is that what has been thought of as incestuous wishes in classical conceptions of the oedipal complex are not necessarily literally incestuous wishes but rather symbolically represent regressive dedifferentiation. In other words, the Oedipus complex is essentially reinterpreted as a struggle between symbiotic union and separation–individuation (Mahler, 1968)—a formulation quite similar to Fairbairn's (1952) description of the conflict between "the regressive lure of identification and the progressive urge toward separation" and to Mitchell's emphasis on "conflictual attachments to early objects" (p. 278). In short, the central role of clinging to early objects in psychopathology represents a point of convergence between classical and contemporary theories.

Difficulties in affect and tension regulation

Another point of convergence between classical and contemporary theories is the common emphasis, whether explicit or implicit, on the central role of poor affect and tension regulation in psychopathology. Indeed, a central motive for clinging to early object ties can be understood as an attempt to regulate tension and affect states. For example, according to Kohut (1984), in individuals with poor self-cohesiveness, archaic self–selfobject relationships are maintained because they regulate tension states and ward off the ever present danger of "disintegration anxiety" (p. 213). Similarly, according to Fairbairn (1952), particularly with schizoid individuals, ties to internalized bad objects are maintained by the fear of an empty inner world, a fear akin to Kohut's disintegration anxiety. Furthermore, in both cases, the warding off of disintegration anxiety is tenuous and can all too easily be disrupted.

Maladaptive regulation of affect and tension states is also critical in the classical conception of psychopathology in a number of ways. Defense, a central concept in classical theory, is essentially a means of regulating affect and tension states. Although defense, like clinging to early object ties, serves adaptive functions (e.g., the warding off of anxiety), it also has maladaptive consequences, such as requiring a "persistent expenditure of force" (Freud, 1915c, p. 151) and restricting awareness. However, the link between maladaptive affect regulation and psychopathology becomes far more evident when there is a *failure of defense* and the consequent eruption of anxiety and other symptomatology. Indeed, although different language is used, intact defense is essentially an affect regulator (limiting anxiety to only a signal of danger), and the failure of defense that precedes the outbreak of neurosis can be meaningfully understood as essentially a failure of affect regulation (a small dose of "signal anxiety" is transformed into intense anxiety). In short, in both classical and contemporary theories a central aspect of psychopathology lies in the failure of affect and tension regulating functions.

Constriction of awareness and range of experience

Another area of convergence between classical and contemporary psychoanalytic theories of psychopathology is a common emphasis on the role of anxiety and defense in restricting the individual's range of awareness and richness of experience. Certain areas of potential experience that are associated with anxiety are cut off from consciousness. Although positing processes different from the classical concept of repression (e.g., not formulating), both classical theory and many contemporary psychoanalytic theories have in common the identification of constriction of awareness and range of experience as significant features of psychopathology. Both classical and contemporary theories converge on the idea that it is mainly in response to certain invalidating, disapproving, and punitive parental behaviors that constriction of experience occurs. Thus, there is convergence between Freud's (1925/1926) discussion of the relationship between the danger situations and anxiety and defense and Stolorow et al.'s (2002) discussion of the relationship between parental invalidation and the constriction of the child's range of experience. However, it should be noted that Freud views some degree of limitation in what one can consciously experience (e.g., incestuous wishes) to be an inevitable aspect of socialization. One can also include Sullivan's (1953) account of the self systems' function of excluding from conscious awareness potential experiences that are at sharp variance with the self, which itself is the product of reflected appraisals of significant others; and Rogers's (1951) earlier noted concept of conditions of worth. In all these formulations, classical and contemporary, not only is there convergence on a common emphasis on constriction of experience but there is also the implication that inevitably accompanying this constriction is a goodly degree of ridigity and stereotypy of cognition and affect.

   Both classical and contemporary psychoanalytic theories are quite wanting with regard to the formulation of etiological theories of psychopathology. Although Freud (1905) formulated a rather sophisticated etiological model that he referred to as an "aetiological series" and later a "complemental series" (pp. 239–240) that anticipated a diathesis-stress model of the interaction between predisposing and precipitating factors, the model was never filled in with much detail.

Freud's view of psychoanalysis as a discipline that could retrodict and make sense of phenomena that had already occurred but could not predict did not encourage the development of predictive etiological hypotheses and formulations. This continues to be true in contemporary psychoanalysis. For the most part, not only are psychoanalytic accounts understandably used in the clinical situation in the service of trying to make sense of pathology that has already occurred but, most important, psychoanalytic etiological theories are almost exclusively based on "follow-back" rather than longitudinal follow-up data (Kohlberg, LaCrosse, & Ricks, 1972). This is inevitable when one's etiological theories are derived almost entirely from the treatment situation. To the extent that is so, it is equally inevitable that one's etiological theories will be incomplete and/or misleading.

To take a simple hypothetical example, let us say that 100% of the patients one sees in treatment of pathology X have been subject to parental deprivation and rejection (and that the deprivation and rejection can be independently confirmed—which, of course, is not the case in practice). However, one is far less likely to see in treatment those individuals who were subject to parental deprivation and rejection and *did not* develop pathology X. Thus, if one's etiological theory of pathology X is based entirely on the follow-back data of one's clinical experiences with patients with pathology X—which, it most often is—it will necessarily be misleading and incomplete. At best, parental rejection and deprivation could constitute only one factor that interacts with other factors in determining the incidence of pathology X.

CONCEPTIONS OF TREATMENT: DIVERGENCES

As we have seen in previous chapters, there are a great many points of divergence between classical and contemporary psychoanalytic theories, including differences regarding analytic stance, the nature of therapeutic action, and treatment goals. The blank -screen, authoritative (some would say authoritarian) classical analyst has been transformed into an egalitarian interactive participant; the objective observer has been transformed into an irreducibly subjective analyst who offers his or her own psychic reality and no longer pretends to be reading the patient's psychic reality; the erstwhile opaque analyst is now one who does not hesitate to disclose personal aspects of himself or herself; the concepts of transference and countertransference have been redefined to reflect their more interactional nature; analytic neutrality has been eschewed in favor of taking positions in regard to the patient's conflicts; and most striking, the patient's love for the analyst (Freud's "cures of love") has been transformed into the analyst's love for the patient.

As for the nature of therapeutic action, interpretation has lost its exalted status as the primary mode of therapeutic action and has largely been replaced by various forms of corrective emotional experience. Furthermore, when interpretation is used, its function is not so much to generate insights through "tally[ing] with what is real in the patient" but rather to provide coherent narratives and serviceable constructions (Freud, 1916–1917/1917, p. 452). Although all forms of treatment have among their goals the amelioration of suffering and making possible a greater opportunity for the patient to live a better life, there is much divergence regarding how these goals are understood and achieved. From a classical perspective, these goals are more likely to be achieved through avowal of one's disavowed impulses and desires ("where id was, there shall ego be"); insight into one's unconscious conflicts and defenses; awareness of one's wishes, desires, and fantasies; and greater self-understanding—all of which ideally serve to restore unity to the personality and to enhance the patient's sense of agency, capacity to make judgments (e.g., regarding pursuit of gratification versus renunciation), and capacity to deal with conflicts more adaptively (i.e., reach more adaptive and satisfying compromises).

In the classical view, in an ideally successful analysis, the observing function of the ego (i.e., capacity for self-reflection) is strengthened; self-knowledge and self-understanding are enhanced; and the patient is less at war with himself or herself, has less of a need to disavow central aspects of himself or herself, is more in touch with his or her wishes and desires, and is better able to pursue their gratification when possible without undue guilt or anxiety. When gratification of these wishes and desires is not possible or exacts too high a cost, the patient is better able to consciously relinquish them or find sublimatory substitutes.

In contrast to the above classical view, contemporary psychoanalytic theories are likely to emphasize such treatment goals as greater self-cohesiveness (self psychology); modification of unconscious pathogenic beliefs (control-mastery theory); greater security of attachment (attachment theory); the exorcism of internalized bad objects and their replacement with good objects (object relations theory); and, generally, replacement of maladaptive representations and cognitive-affective schemas with more adaptive representations and schemas.

As noted earlier, a fundamental treatment goal of classical theory is the avowal and making an integral part of oneself those mental contents that were defensively disavowed and rendered ego-alien. There would appear to be little room for this goal in contemporary theories that take a constructivist perspective, for what is there to internalize and make part of oneself when treatment goals are construed as constructing new and persuasive narratives, creating new meanings, formulating aesthetic fictions, and taking new perspectives? It is not as if these narratives, meanings, fictions, and perspectives are the sorts of things that are properly part of oneself, have been defensively disowned and made into an impersonal "it," and now need to be taken back in into an expanded and more fully integrated self. Rather, they are the sorts of things, to put it in an extreme way, that one takes from the outside and tries on—much like a new role—to see if they are suitable, that is, to see if they make sense and help one feel better and less confused. Putting it another way, unless constructed narratives, new meanings, and new perspectives are linked in an integral way to what one has learned about oneself, they have an inevitable third-person status. That is, they could just as well constitute plausible accounts of someone else as of oneself.

It may well be that constructing persuasive narratives, creating new meanings, and taking new perspectives is more therapeutically effective than uncovering and discovering, gaining self-knowledge, and owning what was disowned. That is, one must repeatedly say, an empirical question. However, if that turns out to be the case, one may have to confront the fact that the psychoanalytic project faces a crisis, and one may have to acknowledge that although psychoanalysis may be matchless in providing an opportunity for self-knowledge and for owning the disowned—for, as Stone (1997) puts it, learning about the "otherness" of oneself—it may be less effective as a treatment for various kinds of pathology. Perhaps, contrary to the guiding axiomatic assumption of psychoanalysis since its very inception, psychopathology is not primarily a matter of such factors as inner conflict, failures of awareness, and failure to own disowned aspects of oneself.

In contrasting uncovering, self-knowledge, and owning the disowned, on the one hand, with constructing narratives, creating new meanings, and taking new perspectives, on the other, I am not disputing the idea that in successful treatment coherent and plausible narratives are formulated, new meanings may be created, and new perspectives taken. However, from a classical psychoanalytic perspective, these narratives, meanings, and perspectives are not *alternatives* to discovering and owning disowned aspects of oneself. Rather, they are the modes and frames in which what is discovered, understood, and owned is put and a consequence and product of what has been discovered, understood, and owned. For example, consider Renik's (1996) interpretation to his patient that a central function of her anger at her sister is to avoid experiencing anger at her parents because the former is more acceptable to her than the latter. This is, indeed, a new perspective. However, it is not just any plausible new perspective (or narrative or meaning) but one based on the presumed discovery and awareness that the patient has been angry at her parents and defended against becoming aware of that anger and owning it as hers. Without this assumption, the new perspectives, however plausible they may be—there are probably an indefinite number of plausible perspectives and narratives—are essentially arbitrary and indistinguishable from ordinary suggestion. I do not deny the possibility that these perspectives, narratives, and meanings may help the patient feel better, but the question is what this would have to do with the psychoanalytic project?

As Freud (1937) recognized, it may be difficult to ascertain the links between "constructions in analysis," that is, between narratives, perspectives, and meanings and what is there to be discovered in the patient's mind. However, that is mainly an epistemological problem. In some contemporary views, the epistemological issue has been transformed into an ontological one. That is, as we have seen, the position taken by some contemporary theorists is that there is nothing to be uncovered and discovered, no self-knowledge to be gained, no understanding to be acquired, only narratives to be constructed, new meanings to be created, and new perspectives to be taken. Hence, the latter cannot be linked to the former. They are, so to speak, on their own and must sink or swim as a function of their persuasiveness and helpfulness (the latter being most often asserted but not systematically tested).

Having new experiences versus examining old experiences

Mitchell (1988) has remarked that whereas classical psychoanalysis focuses on the examination of old experiences, more contemporary theories emphasize the role of new experiences as the primary factor in the therapeutic action of psychoanalytic treatment. A moment's thought suggests that this remark speaks to one variation of the role of insight and awareness versus new corrective emotional experiences. That is, Mitchell is contrasting the therapeutic role of gaining insight into and understanding of old experiences with the therapeutic role of having new corrective emotional experiences in interaction with the analyst. It constitutes a form of the comment that the patient needs not an interpretation, but a new experience.

On the surface, this seems to be a meaningful distinction, and in certain respects, perhaps it is. Thus, although analysis of the transference is presumably a common ground (Wallerstein, 1991) among analysts of different theoretical orientations, whereas a classical analyst would be more likely to view the patient's reactions as expressions of old wishes and conflicts, the relational (and perhaps self psychology) analyst would be more likely to focus on the current interaction in its own right. Furthermore, for the relational and self psychology analyst, the therapeutic action would mainly reside not in the patient's insight into how his or her reactions recapitulate infantile wishes and conflicts but in a new experience with the analyst.

A number of questions and issues arise with regard to the latter position. In what way does a primary emphasis on the patient–analyst interactions in their own right—without much reference to how these interactions recapitulate early conflicts, defenses, patterns, and the like—constitute transference reactions? What is being transferred? In this view, it would make more sense to refer to the therapeutic interaction and the therapeutic relationship rather than to the concept of transference. I recall Merton Gill making this suggestion, but I do not know whether he explicitly took this position in any of his published work.

A variant of the above issue arises with regard to Mitchell's (1998, 2000) earlier noted rejection of the preorganized nature of mind and his suggestion that the patient's mind is organized as a function of each new object relation. The question is: If there is no stable structure or preorganization of wishes, conflicts, defenses, and so on with which the patient comes to treatment, what is being transferred to the analyst? Once again, one would have to distinguish between analysis of the transference and an ongoing examination of the patient–analyst interactions.

Even the latter is problematic, for if one does not believe that there are central dynamics that are preorganized in the patient's mind and maintains instead that the analyst "interpretively constructs" and organizes the patient's mind, if one believes that "to understand unconscious processes ... is to use language in a fashion that actually creates new experience, something that was not there before" (Mitchell, 1998, pp. 17–18), if every fluid and momentary interaction with the analyst organizes the patient's mind, and if the function of interpretation is not to identify a preexisting pattern, how can the analyst turn to the patient and convey the message, "How you interact with me (or how we interact with each other) tells us something about your general expectations, conflicts, defenses, and relationship patterns"? I am, of course, not suggesting this language; rather, I am pointing to the difficulty of making such interpretations if one does not believe that the patient comes into analysis with preexisting organization and relatively stable structures. In short, Wallerstein's assertion notwithstanding, an emphasis on the analysis of the transference does not constitute a common ground among different theoretical orientations.

Although Mitchell's distinction between focusing on old experiences and providing new experiences seems to have a certain plausibility, the fact is that the patient's understanding of how his or her reactions to the analyst constitute, in part at least, new wines in old bottles is no less a new experience than the analytic process described by Mitchell and other relational analysts. A situation in which the patient is free to say whatever comes to mind without criticism or judgment and in which the other person's main task is to disinterestedly concern himself or herself with attentive listening and trying to understand and communicate that understanding is, indeed, a new and rare experience. Further, a sense of being accurately represented in another's mind may indeed be a new and rare experience. One should not be misled by words like *old* and *new*. An examination of the old and its influence on current thoughts, feelings, and interactions can itself constitute a new and corrective experience. Thus, I am suggesting that the therapeutic role of new and corrective experiences is as much an aspect of classical theory as it is of contemporary theories.

It may or may not be legitimate to argue that a relatively greater focus on the current patient–therapist interaction rather than on how the patient's reactions recapitulate old patterns, fantasies, and wishes is more therapeutically effective. This is, of course, an empirical question to be answered by outcome and process data rather than authoritative assertions and theoretical trends. However, even if empirical investigation showed that to be the case, it would not be a matter of the relative value of examining old experiences versus focusing on new experiences in the patient–therapist interactions. For one thing, one need not choose between the two experiences. For another thing, as I have tried to show, examining old experiences and how they influence current feelings and thoughts can be as much a new experience as examining current interactions with the therapist. Both are new experiences. What the call for a greater focus on current patient–therapist interactions amounts to is the claim that *this kind* of new experience (i.e., focusing on current interactions) is likely to be more effective than another kind of new experience (i.e., examining the influence of the old). However, that, again, is an empirical question rather than a matter of assertion and argumentation.

One must add that awareness and insight, whether in relation to the old or the new, particularly in the context of a relationship with another, are themselves a class of new experiences rather than something to be contrasted with new experiences. It has become virtually a cliché to decry the dichotomy between interpretation-insight, on the one hand, and therapeutic relationship-corrective emotional experience, on the other. However, in one form or another, the dichotomy continues to creep into discussions of therapeutic action. I think that the actual contrast that is often intended is between the therapeutic effects of insight, awareness, and self-knowledge and the therapeutic effects of certain interactional experiences in which the acquisition of insight, awareness, and self-knowledge do not seem to be prominent. The enactment case I discussed in Chapter 9 in which despite the relative absence of interpretation and evidence of insight, the patient's symptoms disappeared following a critical patient–therapist interaction (i.e., a corrective emotional experience) would perhaps instantiate the contrast intended. Another way to put this is to say that there are different kinds of corrective emotional experiences, including those in which explicit awareness, insight, and self-knowledge are not especially prominent. The point I want to reiterate from previous chapters and am stating in different ways and undoubtedly belaboring is that the dichotomy between insight, awareness, and corrective emotional experience is a false one insofar as meaningful insight and awareness are particular kinds of corrective emotional experiences. The real challenge that an emphasis on corrective emotional experiences presents to classical theory lies in the claim that positive therapeutic outcome can occur at least somewhat independently of the acquisition of insight, awareness, and self-knowledge. To the extent that classical theory gives special and primary emphasis to these factors, the claim that positive therapeutic outcome can occur independently of the operation of these factors would appear to constitute a real challenge. Indeed, as we have seen, there a number of contemporary theories that locate therapeutic action in processes (e.g., test-passing, Weiss et al., 1986), empathic understanding (Kohut, 1984), and noninterpretive factors (D. N. Stern et al., 1998) outside the domain of awareness and insight.

According to the classical theory of treatment, when an analyst accurately interprets, say, oedipal wishes, although the patient may feel understood and although that may further the treatment (in the same way that rapport would), the therapeutically active ingredients are located in the patient's insight into his or her wishes and defenses (making the unconscious conscious), and the avowal and owning of those wishes, etc. (where id was, there shall ego be). Contrastingly, according to self psychology, when an analyst interprets the patient's need to be perfectly mirrored and relates that presumed need to early parental traumatic failures in empathic mirroring, it is the empathic understanding conveyed by the interpretation and the empathic bond generated by that understanding that constitute the active therapeutic ingredients.

It will be noted that each theory of treatment is associated with a particular theory of pathology. If the sources of pathology are believed to lie in conflict, defense, and disavowal, then although feeling understood may be a desideratum, it could not be curative insofar as it would not have an impact on the sources of pathology. Only interventions such as interpretation would get to the source of the pathology. However, when the sources of pathology are believed to lie in lack of empathic understanding, then it is the provision of that empathic understanding that gets to the source of the pathology.

In one way or another, the therapeutic relationship has replaced interpretation and self-knowledge as the central therapeutic agent. The classical view of the therapeutic relationship as a background factor that serves to facilitate the work of interpretations has been reversed so that interpretation is now viewed as a background factor the main function of which is to strengthen and facilitate the therapeutic relationship through the patient's experience of feeling understood by the therapist. In short, contemporary psychoanalytic theories and approaches to treatment are marked by a shift from, to borrow from the philosopher Rorty (1991), the Enlightenment emphasis on objectivity to the current emphasis on solidarity.

Hence, although embedded in different theoretical contexts and although different terms are used, a common theme in contemporary psychoanalytic theories of treatment—one that especially distinguishes these theories from a classical perspective—is the overriding importance of corrective emotional experiences. Although this distinctive emphasis is quite explicit in Alexander and French's (1946) original work, it is implicitly echoed in a variety of contemporary formulations, including Weiss et al.'s (1986) concept of test-passing, Kohut's (1984) empathic understanding, Fairbairn's (1952) total therapeutic relationship, Lyons-Ruth's (1999; also Lyons-Ruth et al., 1998) "implicit relational knowing," and Bowlby's (1988) conception of the therapist as a secure base. Common to all these conceptions are the core ideas that the therapist behaves differently and is experienced differently from parental figures and that these new experiences eventually succeed in altering the patient's expectations and cognitive-affective schemas. Furthermore, these changes can occur without explicit interpretations and without explicit insight.

There are different components that comprise an individual's cognitive-affective schemas, including what one wishes and wants from significant others, one's expectations and beliefs regarding how the significant others will respond (along with their associated affects), and one's representations of oneself (along with associated affects). One question that arises is which of the above components are likely to change in successful treatment. Using his core conflictual relationship theme method, Luborsky (1996) has reported that even in successful treatment the patient's wishes are not likely to change. Rather, what tends to change are the patient's experienced reactions of significant others and subsequent reactions to himself or herself. This finding tends to indirectly support the hypothesis that the patient's experience of the therapist's accepting and nonjudgmental response to his or her expression of his or her wishes and wants—a corrective emotional experience—generalizes to his or her reactions to and expectations in relation to significant others outside the treatment, and further, that these altered experiences of the reactions of significant others also then influence self-representations.

Whereas for Freud, the goal of psychoanalytic treatment is to own and repossess what had been defensively disowned ("Where id was, there shall ego be"), for many contemporary theories, the therapeutic goal is reversed, that is, to disown or, in Fairbairn's (1952) words, to exorcise what had been improperly owned, to dispossess what had been defensively possessed and to replace these structures (i.e., internalized bad objects, maladaptive cognitive-affective schemas, etc.) with new representations and schemas arising out of the therapeutic experience.

CONCEPTIONS OF TREATMENT: CONVERGENCES

Despite the above and other sharp differences between classical and contemporary theories, including the nature of appropriate analytic stance (e.g., with respect to analytic neutrality, blank screen, self-disclosure, and so on), there is convergence on the therapeutic necessity of the analyst's nonjudgmental attitude and the importance of this attitude in facilitating the therapeutic process and in modulating the harshness of the patient's superego. If, as Kohut (1984) maintains, an attitude of adult morality characterizes classical analysis, this constitutes a misapplication rather than an appropriate use of classical theory. There is nothing, I believe, inherent in classical theory that dictates a judgmental attitude of adult morality toward the patient.

As noted above, although Wallerstein (1991) refers to an analysis of the transference as a core element of the psychoanalytic process—what Wallerstein refers to as a common ground—this is not really the case. Rather, one can say that an examination of the patient–therapist relationship and interactions constitutes a common ground.

With the exception of self psychology, a treatment goal common to classical and contemporary theories is expansion of the patient's range of experience, whether this is expressed as making the unconscious conscious in classical theory or enlarging the patient's horizons of awareness in contemporary theory (Stolorow, Atwood, & Orange, 2002, p. 47).

As noted in Chapter 5, from a classical perspective, the analysis of the transference, particularly of the transference neurosis, is important because the patient's transference projections on to the analyst lay bare, in vivo, the patient's neurosis. Although there is no talk of transference neurosis in contemporary theories, a similar assumption is made to the effect that the patient's reactions to the analyst reveal, indeed enact, his or her "habitual relationship patterns" (Schachter, 2002). Hence, in analyzing these reactions, one is shedding light on these patterns. If one is not making the (repressed) unconscious conscious, one is certainly making the implicit (i.e., expectations, automatic assumptions, etc.) explicit, and one is also certainly making use of interpretation for the purpose of generating insight into and awareness of the patient's hidden expectations, assumptions, anxieties, desires and wishes, defenses, and so forth underlying his or her habitual relationship patterns (or if one prefers, internal working model, representations of interactions generalized, or interactional patterns).

Thus, even if contemporary psychoanalysis is characterized by skepticism toward the therapeutic value of insight and awareness, to the extent that one continues to view identification and analysis of relationship patterns and representations as central features of the analytic process, to that extent, one continues to give an equally central role to insight and awareness. After all, why would one want to pursue the task of making habitual relationship patterns explicit in treatment unless one believed that doing so was important in effecting therapeutic change?

Let me take a concrete example: As noted, Kohut (1984) does not believe that insight and expansion of cognitive are necessary for therapeutic change. Rather, in his view, empathic understanding and optimal failure are the effective ingredients of therapeutic change, which consists mainly in enhancing self-cohesiveness. However, consider Kohut's elucidation of the role of optimal failures in therapeutic change. He writes that when the analyst fails to meet the patient's need for perfect mirroring (which is, of course, inevitable), the patient may react with rage and despair. Kohut then goes on to suggest that the analyst acknowledge his or her failure and link that failure to the patient's experience of rage and despair. The point here is that Kohut's eschewal of insight notwithstanding, this *interpretive* linking of the patient's rage and despair to the analyst's behavior is a straightforward example of analysis of the transference—or, if one prefers, of the therapeutic relationship—designed to enhance the patient's insight into and awareness of how he or she reacts in the face of experienced failures of less than perfect mirroring. Indeed, in his discussion of the role of explaining in treatment, Kohut includes linking of the patient's transference reactions to his or her past, despite viewing the goal of such interventions as the strengthening of the empathic bond between patient and analyst rather than the achievement of insight. It is difficult to believe that the interpretation linking the patient's rage and despair to his or her experience of the analyst's empathic failure does not entail some degree of insight and enhanced self-knowledge.

With perhaps some exceptions, there is convergence between classical and contemporary theories on a central goal of psychoanalytic treatment as the enhanced capacity of the patient to relate increasingly to the other in terms of who that other actually is rather than as a stand-in for early figures. Indeed, an implicit assumption in analytic work is that one important purpose of the analysis of the transference is not only for the patient to come to experience the analyst more realistically (i.e., less as a stand-in for early parental figures) but also to generalize this experience to significant others outside the treatment. One can think of one purpose of analysis of the transference as strengthening the patient's reality-testing in the sphere of representations of and relationships with significant others. This is perhaps less evident in the classical context. Surely, though, in that context, one expected outcome of successful treatment is that the patient will come to experience not only the analyst but significant others outside the treatment less and less as, say, oedipal figures from the past. This area of convergence can be obscured by differences in theoretical language. For example, although Kohut uses the language of replacement of archaic with more mature self–selfobject relationships and Freud the language of relinquishment of infantile wishes and an increasing capacity for mutuality, both are pointing to new ways of relating as a central goal of psychoanalytic treatment.

As noted, one central line of tension between classical and contemporary theories revolves around the question of whether insight-generating interpretations or the therapeutic relationship is the primary carrier of therapeutic action and the main agent of therapeutic change. That this remains very much an active issue that can generate a great deal of heated debate within psychoanalysis is indicated by recent reactions to a 2006 article by Hanna Segal in which she states:

> After those discussions, the British Society had a curriculum in which both trends were taught. Some parts of the curriculum were joint and some, mainly technical, were taught separately. The balance was called the Middle Group. In further developments, the Middle Group, which changed its name to the Independents, also established a new model of the mind, deriving from Ferenczi and developed by Balint, Winnicott, and, later in the United States, by Kohut. The fundamental difference between this model and those of Freud, Klein, and their followers lay not in the fact that it took into account new clinical evidence, but rather in the kinds of uses that it made of clinical evidence. A new concern emerged that focused on various notions of cure and change that did not rest on attaining truth and that considered the personal influences of the analyst—e.g., his support, advice, and comfort—to be integral to the analytic process. Here the changes in technique were of a kind that made them essentially nonanalytic. They went against the psychoanalytic effort to bring about change through the search for truth. For when the analyst actively takes upon himself the parental role, he invites the patient to live in a lie. This in turn promotes concrete functioning rather than symbolization and psychic growth. (p. 288)

Fifty members and honorary members of the British Psychoanalytic Society wrote to the Editor of *American Imago* disputing the accuracy of Segal's description of the clinical work of the British Independent Group, decrying her repetition of "disparagements of the past," her eschewal of "a fresh commitment to [a] tradition of philosophical pluralism," the absence of any scientific basis for her comments, and ending with a call on Segal to apologize (Letter to Editor of *American Imago*, February 2, 2007).

In an August 16, 2009, e-mail to the New York University Postdoctoral mailing list, while applauding "indignation over Hanna Segal's ad hominem attack on psychoanalytic pluralism," Bromberg wrote:

> I believe that what Segal, in these capitalized lines, attributes to these towering figures is accurate, and that she was quite brilliant in her

perceptiveness despite her failure to comprehend the scope of what she was perceiving. In my view, if Ferenczi, Balint, Winnicott and Kohut were alive today they should wear this "accusation" as a badge of honor, though I suspect that one or two of them might be ambivalent about it.

One can see from the foregoing material that despite repeated pronouncements that it represents a false dichotomy, the debate between therapeutic relationship versus interpretation and insight is alive and well. My own view is that the debate largely rests on a false dichotomy and that it is possible to formulate a position that succeeds in integrating the two factors. Let me elaborate.

One can outline two broad positions. One position is that it is primarily the corrective emotional experience implicit in the therapeutic relationship that is mutative and, further, that interpretation and insight are not a necessary component of this process. This position is exemplified by Alexander and French's (1946) writings and by such statements as "the patient needs a new experience, not an interpretation." It is also appears to be exemplified by the finding that the therapist's test-passing alone, without interpretation, can lead to positive therapeutic change (Silberschatz, Fretter, & Curtis, 1986; Weiss et al., 1986). The other position is that it is primarily is insight, self-understanding, and self-knowledge generated by interpretations that are mutative and that to the extent that the therapeutic relationship plays an important role, it does so through facilitating the effectiveness of interpretation.

Consider again the first position. What is it about the therapeutic relationship that makes it therapeutic and that serves to provide corrective emotional experiences? After all, *therapeutic relationship* is an abstract term and consists of many activities. From the patient's perspective, it can include interventions, interactions, and experiences, such as being listened to, feeling supported and comforted, experiencing the therapist's attitude and behavior as different from one's expectations and fears, feeling understood, and so on. The therapeutic relationship is not anything one does or experiences but comprises things one feels and does (and also that one does not do, for example, be judgmental). Among other things one does or can do, as an analyst, is offer interpretations. Of course, along with listening, trying to understand, and the like, interpreting is, or can be, one activity that makes up the therapeutic relationship. The point here is that rather than being in opposition to the therapeutic relationship, interpreting is as much part of that relationship as listening, supporting, and the like. At this level, there is no dichotomy between interpretation-insight and the therapeutic relationship—unless one believes either that interpretation as an activity has no place in a therapeutic relationship or, conversely, that the nature of the relationship has no influence on how interpretations are experienced.

What, then, is the nature of the dichotomy? It lies mainly, I believe, in competing claims regarding the nature of the therapeutic action and of what is mutative: corrective emotional experiences that implicitly alter the patient's maladaptive beliefs, expectations, and representations versus experiences that consist mainly in gaining insights and learning truths about oneself. Of course, an obvious response to this kind of either/or perspective is that both sets of factors may be mutative and may be important ingredients of therapeutic action. However, I believe that one needs to go further than that in unpacking the dichotomy.

Once one focuses on the issue of the nature of therapeutic action rather than on the broad categories of the therapeutic relationship versus interpretation-insight, the dichotomy breaks down. A number of mutative factors and experiences in the treatment may belong to and instantiate both categories at one and the same time. For example, feeling empathically understood is often viewed as a noninterpretive product of the therapeutic relationship. Assuming that one can, in practice, distinguish clearly between interpretations intended to make the unconscious conscious or make the implicit explicit and interventions intended to convey empathic understanding—a questionable assumption itself—it is possible, perhaps likely, that an insightful interpretation intended to uncover unconscious material that is presented in a well-timed and tactful way and in a particular manner may contribute as much if not more to the patient's experience of feeling understood than an intervention explicitly intended to convey empathic understanding. In the former case, the patient's feeling of being understood is, so to speak, a byproduct of interpretation. Furthermore, such an interpretation may not only generate insight and self-understanding but also constitute a corrective emotional experience and, as such, serve to modify maladaptive expectations, beliefs, and representations. Conversely, interventions that are made by an analyst who believes that only empathic understanding is mutative may (again, the analyst's theory notwithstanding) be largely helpful through generating insight and self-understanding.

Just as interpretation may constitute a new experience and, as such, may strengthen the therapeutic relationship—as Mitchell (1988, p. 295) notes, an interpretation is "a complex relationship event"—starting from the other end, one can say that the relational context in which the interpretation, or any other intervention is made, influences the meaning and impact of the interpretation or any other intervention (Spence, 1987). In other words, it is likely that there is a circular causal relationship in which specific interventions influence the patient's experience of the therapist and the therapeutic relationship (e.g., degree of trust, feeling safe, feeling understood, feeling cared for and valued, etc.) and, conversely, in which the nature of the existing relationship influences the meaning and impact of the specific interventions. One should also add that just as an interpretation may constitute a new corrective emotional experience, so similarly may a corrective emotional experience of the therapist behaving differently from parental figures constitute a silent or implicit interpretation, the implicit content of which is: "I am different from your parent(s) and am not the figure your engrained expectations suggest I am." Were such an interpretation made explicitly, it would likely, it seems to me, fall flat. It is not very useful, I believe, to tell a patient explicitly that he or she is reacting to you as if you were a parental figure and that, in fact, you are not. It is far more emotionally convincing to demonstrate through one's demeanor and attitudes, as well as interventions, that one is different from parental figures in specific ways (see Eagle, 1993). Although the therapist's demeanor and attitudes may or may not elicit explicit verbalizable insight and self-knowledge, they may have an impact on some form of knowing, what Lyons-Ruth (1999; Lyons-Ruth et al., 1998) refers to as implicit relational knowing.

Indeed, the impact of the therapist's test-passing behavior on disconfirmation of the patient's unconscious pathogenic beliefs highlighted by the control-mastery theory of Weiss et al. (1986) can be understood from the perspective of silent interpretations influencing the patient's implicit relational knowing. Similarly, it can be understood in relation to the influence of the analyst's nonjudgmental attitude in modulating the harshness of the patient's superego emphasized by Strachey (1934). Here the silent interpretation in effect is: "Your feelings, thoughts and fantasies do not merit the kind of guilt and self-condemnation that you have internalized based on your early experiences."

It should be noted that from the perspective I am proposing, corrective emotional experiences are understood not simply as some general feel-good experiences that serve to enhance the patient's self-esteem but rather are linked to specific contents—that is, to specific pathogenic beliefs or to specific expectations and schemas. I emphasize this distinction in order to reinforce my point that insofar as they are linked to specific contents, corrective emotional experiences can be understood as entailing silent transference interpretations of the patient's implicit beliefs, expectations, and schemes. In short, we have still another reason to resist a sharp dichotomy between therapeutic relationship factors, including corrective emotional experiences, and interpretation, insight, and self-knowledge.

We know from child development that much of what a child learns about himself or herself and about the interpersonal world is through the solidarity of the child-parent relationship. Indeed, as Fonagy et al. (1995) suggest, this may be one of the vital functions of the attachment bond. In other words, much of what we learn during our period of prolonged dependency and attachment is indispensable for functioning in a social world. However, some of what we acquire during that period and take for granted is maladaptive. It appears that just as the early maladaptive representations were acquired in the context of human relationships, they can only be deeply understood and altered in the context of a human relationship. Thus, from a psychoanalytic perspective, the appropriate model for the pursuit of objectivity in regard to oneself is not the Cartesian one of retreat into oneself but the Socratic one of interpersonal dialogue. It is not only the child who acquires a sense of self and gains a self-knowledge through cognitive and affective interaction with another but also the adult. Although self-understanding and self knowledge—the presumed products of interpretation—have been distinguished from feeling understood—the presumed product of the therapeutic relationship—it is likely that the two are indistinguishable in the therapeutic situation. It is difficult to imagine how the patient can feel understood by the therapist without some contribution to his or her self-understanding; and conversely, it is equally difficult to imagine, in an interactional context, how the patient can gain self-understanding and self-knowledge without feeling understood by the therapist.

Here we come full circle to the link between psychoanalysis and the Enlightenment vision. The maladaptive schemes we acquire early in life are analogous to the engrained and unquestioned assumptions handed down by dogmatic authority. Just as in the view of the Enlightenment vision, one needs to emancipate oneself from, for example, dogmatic religious authority, similarly, in the psychoanalytic version of the Enlightenment vision, one needs to emancipate oneself from the unquestioned dogmatic assumptions, fantasies, rules, expectations, and representations that have governed important aspects of one's cognitive, affective, and interpersonal life. In some important sense, the struggle to emancipate oneself from the tyranny of dogma, whether in a social-political or personal developmental context, entails the replacement of dogma by the pursuit of objectivity. However, and this is the main point, it appears that the pursuit of greater objectivity is likely to be mutative and transformative when it takes place in and through the solidarity of a human relationship.

Therapeutic alliance

The general finding that across a wide range of different therapeutic approaches, the quality and strength of the therapeutic alliance makes a consistent (even if modest) contribution to therapeutic outcome has been taken to indicate that it is the therapeutic relationship that is the main ingredient of therapeutic change and is the common factor of effective treatment. Of course, even if this were the case, it would not mean that other factors do not contribute to positive outcome. However, that aside, it is a hasty conclusion for a number of reasons.

First, it would be a mistake to equate therapeutic alliance with therapeutic relationship insofar as there are other components of the latter. Second, as Kazdin (2007) has pointed out, the patient's experience of a stronger therapeutic alliance may not play a direct causal role in therapeutic outcome but may be an *effect* of other therapeutic factors or may play a mediating role in outcome. Also, the link between therapeutic alliance and outcome may be at least partly due to a third common factor. For example, as noted in Chapter 9, there is evidence that pretreatment healthier patients are more likely both to form a stronger therapeutic alliance and to have a better prognosis. As another example, one that is essentially a reiteration of an argument made above, it is possible that accurate and empathic interpretations not only generate insight but also, through the experience both of insight and of feeling understood, strengthen the therapeutic alliance—which, in turn, serves to make the patient more receptive to other interpretations and other interventions. Third, although the strength of the therapeutic alliance is the single best predictor of treatment outcome in psychotherapy research, its contribution to outcome is a modest one.

SOME FURTHER INTEGRATIVE CONSIDERATIONS

First-person versus third-person self-knowledge

Let me turn now to some general integrative considerations that are not directly linked to a comparison between classical and contemporary views. In the above discussion I have referred to self-knowledge as if it were a simple, unitary concept. However, as some philosophers have pointed out, one needs to distinguish between first-person and third-person self knowledge, a distinction that is especially relevant in the psychoanalytic context. As Moran (2001) observes, first-person self-knowledge is characterized by immediacy and by the fact that it does not require observational evidence and inference. Although it may occur, normally one does not observe one's behavior and then infer one's desires, intentions, and wants. For example, I do not normally observe my behavior and then infer that I am thirsty. I just *feel* thirsty. Knowing that I want or intend, say, to go to the library to obtain a particular book does not normally rest on my observation of some aspect of myself. I just know that I want to go to the library. In contrast to first-person self-knowledge, third-person self-knowledge *is* based on observation and inference and, as such, is not essentially different from the way one acquires knowledge about another person.

In some respects, the distinction between intellectual and emotional insight discussed earlier parallels the distinction between third-person and first-person self-knowledge. Although intellectual insight, as well as third-person self-knowledge, may be useful—for example, in bringing some order and meaning to what is experienced as chaotic and meaningless—they do not seem to bring about the kind of transformation or structural change that is associated with emotional insight as well as first-person self-knowledge. During what one might call the period of innocence of classical psychoanalytic theory, the assumption seemed to be that once repression was lifted, the patient would consciously experience the hitherto unconscious wishes or desires that had been repressed with an immediacy and transparency that is characteristic of first-person knowledge of any conscious desire rather than something inferred on the basis of observation. Using an analogy employed by Mitchell (1998), after lifting a rock and finding insects underneath (analogous to repressed wishes), one now perceives them directly and immediately, rather than inferring their existence.

Once the experience was fully conscious, one could then attempt to pursue the gratification of desire X in reality or repudiate it through conscious decision and judgment. However, even if one ultimately renounced or repudiated desire X, one could only meaningfully, or perhaps one should say authentically, do so if one *avowed* desire X as one's own personal desire. That is, to endorse or fail to endorse (i.e., repudiate) desire X is only meaningful if one has owned or acknowledged desire X in the first place.

The assumption that lifting repression and making the unconscious conscious would automatically result in the avowal and first-person experience of hitherto repressed contents seemed to be based on the model of hypnosis in which unavailable mental contents (e.g., memories) presumably became directly available (i.e., not inferred) under hypnosis. We know that Freud turned away from the use of hypnosis for a number of reasons, including the experience that simply bringing unconscious mental contents to consciousness did not bring about lasting therapeutic change. One of the main reasons that that was so, he maintained, was that the material brought to consciousness via hypnosis was not necessarily thereby *integrated* into the patient's personality—in Freud's (Breuer & Freud, 1893–1895) words, into the "great complex of associations" (p. 9) that constitutes the ego.

The early realization that making unconscious material conscious did not necessarily lead to the integration of that material was fully articulated many years later when making the unconscious conscious was replaced, or at least supplemented, by "where id was, there shall ego be" (Freud, 1932/1933, p. 80) as the primary goal of psychoanalytic treatment. When one unlinks id and ego from drive theory and translates id as the ego-alien and impersonal "it" and ego as the personal "I," "where id was, there shall ego be" is best understood as "where ego-alien impersonal 'it' was, there shall personal and avowed 'I' be." This way of understanding Freud's dictum is essentially equivalent to stating that the goal of psychoanalysis is *integration* of the hitherto impersonal "it" into the personal "I." That is, the aim of psychoanalysis is to bring about the unity of the personality.

Significant structural change, including greater integration and unity of the personality, it appears, is more difficult to bring about through third-person self-knowledge (or its parallel intellectual insight). For example, although it may be helpful to know that one has an avoidant attachment pattern and that this pattern developed in response to repeated experiences of rejection, that knowledge is unlikely to alter the avoidant pattern itself. This kind of self-knowledge is not essentially different from the knowledge one could have about another person. Just as one could observe another person's behavior (e.g., he or she tends to avoid intimacy and close relationships), obtain information about his or her early life (e.g., repeated rejections on the part of the attachment figure), and then infer an avoidant pattern, one could carry out the same process in relation to oneself. In contrast, experiencing anxiety at the prospect of being close to or dependent on someone or expecting to be rejected and, as a consequence, avoiding intimacy—and knowing that one is anxious, that one expects to be rejected, and that one has made a decision to avoid further intimacy—would constitute first-person self-knowledge and, as such, is assumed to play a more significant role—or at least, a different role in therapeutic change than third-person knowledge.

If this is so, and let us assume that it is, it raises a number of interesting questions, including the question of why this should be the case. Just why should first-person self-knowledge—or emotional insight—be more facilitative of therapeutic change than third-person self-knowledge? The answer seems so obvious and self-evident and yet difficult to pin down. One likely reason that this is so is that, as Moran (2001) points out, first-person self-knowledge is not simply an epistemological matter, that is, not only a question of knowing but also a matter of avowal of a mental state as one's own, standing behind it. To that extent, first-person self-knowledge already entails some degree of integration of that mental state into one's "dominant mass of ideas." Also, any meaningful further action one takes with regard to that mental state (e.g., pursuing or repudiating certain aims) presupposes that one has avowed it as one's own.

Self-knowledge and conscious versus unconscious mental states

The distinction between on the one hand, the direct I desire X (I want to go to the library) and therefore I know I desire X (I know I want to go to the library) as instances of first-person self-knowledge and, on the other hand, I know I desire X (I know that I want to go to the library) based on observation and inference from my behavior as instances of third-person self-knowledge is quite evident and straightforward with regard to conscious desires and intentions. However, the distinction becomes more problematic when one is dealing with unconscious desires and intentions. So long as one assumes that once the unconscious becomes conscious, hitherto unconscious desires and intentions automatically emerge in consciousness as ordinary conscious desires and intentions, one can maintain that once repression is lifted, the individual will have first-person knowledge of his or her desires and intentions, rather than third-person self-knowledge based on inferences made from observations (e.g., of his or her dreams, free associations, or interpretations).

However, once it becomes clear that this assumption turns out to be a simplistic one, the question arises as to what kind of self-knowledge obtains when repression is lifted and the unconscious becomes conscious. If, following the lifting of repression of desire X, the patient does not directly and consciously experience desire X but rather knows about it, indirectly and inferentially via the analyst's interpretation, then we are clearly talking about third-person, not first-person self-knowledge. It is not surprising that this kind of knowledge about oneself would have limited success in bringing about basic changes in personality structure. Indeed, as Moran (2001) points out, viewing oneself primarily in terms of third-person theoretical knowledge may contribute to and itself constitute a form of self-estrangement. Without using the language of first-person and third-person self-knowledge, both classical and contemporary psychoanalytic theories of therapeutic action and therapeutic change have grappled with this issue, as expressed, for example, in the distinction between intellectual and emotional insight or in the identification of implicit relational knowing (Lyons-Ruth, 1999; Lyons-Ruth et al., 1998).

Self-reflection

I turn now to enhancement of the capacity for self-reflection in psychoanalytic treatment as an area of partial convergence between classical and contemporary theories. There is a great deal of emphasis these days, both within and outside the psychoanalytic context, on enhancing the individual's capacity for reflection as a therapeutic goal. Although there may be differences between them, there seems to be a good deal of overlap between the concepts of reflective capacity and mentalization and mindfulness. Furthermore, these concepts bear a family resemblance to the classical psychoanalytic goal of strengthening the observing function of the ego.

I also bring up the issue of self-reflection at this point to examine its relationship to the question of third-person versus first-person self-knowledge. The essential idea I want to convey is that in self-reflection, *the object* on which one is reflecting is different in third-person and first-person self-knowledge. In other words, although self-reflection entails taking a perspective on oneself as object, it would be mistaken to equate self reflection with third-person self-knowledge. The main reason that is so is that the object on which one is reflecting varies with third-person versus first-person self-knowledge.

It is one thing to reflect on, say, a particular desire that one experiences and knows about in a direct, unmediated way. Here, the object of one's reflection is first-person experience. It is another thing to reflect on knowledge of a particular desire that has come about through observation and inference. Here, the object of one's reflection is third-person self-knowledge. To be noted here is that third-person self-knowledge itself entails a form of self-reflection, one in which one reflects on one's behavior as a basis for inferring one's mental state. Here the reflection is not essentially different from reflecting on another's behavior—the object of reflection is one's behavior as observed from an external perspective.

To say that a goal of psychoanalytic treatment is to strengthen the observing function of the ego or to enhance the patient's self-reflection is to suggest that what is important in treatment is the enhancement of *a capacity* rather than the uncovering of specific unconscious mental contents or conflicts. It is almost as if the work of uncovering—of making the unconscious conscious—that goes on in treatment is useful not only, or perhaps not mainly, because it identifies and reveals specific unconscious wishes, conflicts, and defenses but because it entails a prolonged opportunity to practice and strengthen the skill of self-reflection.

As Sugarman (2006) puts it in a recent paper, the function of interpretation (which in his view generally consists in analysis of defense) is not to uncover repressed wishes but to enable the patient to better learn and understand how his or her mind works. So, from this perspective, insight and self-knowledge do not necessarily take the form of either a direct and immediate "I desire X" or the inference "I desire X," but rather of something like "this is what I do when I am anxious or conflicted or worried that I will offend you." Of course, implicit in this form of self-knowledge is non-inferential access to such feelings and experiences as being anxious or conflicted or worried about offending. This kind of insight and self-knowledge is one of making meaningful connections among different aspects of one's thoughts, feelings, and behaviors, the kinds of connections that, according to G. S. Klein (1976) are blocked by repression.

Although I have referred repeatedly to self-reflection, one should speak more broadly of reflective capacity to highlight the fact that reflective capacity refers to reflection not only on one's own mental states and processes but also the mental states and processes of others.

It is difficult to imagine enhanced self-reflection without enhancement of one's ability to reflect on others' mental states. There is little said in classical theory on the link between these two expressions of reflective capacity. The observing function of the ego seems to refer mainly to self-reflection. However, both from developmental and adult functioning perspectives, the capacity to reflect on one's own mental state is closely linked to the capacity to reflect on the mental state of others. Also, in interactional situations, reflection on one's own mental state often implicitly entails reflecting on another's mental state. Reflecting on, say, feeling hurt by or angry at another often entails reflecting on the other's intentions: Did he or she really reject me or intend to dismiss me? For example, in a recent paper, Gabbard and Horowitz (2009) provide a brief description of working with a borderline patient who goes into a rage in response to feeling humiliated by a sales clerk. Helping the patient reflect on her own feelings of humiliation and rage necessarily entails reflecting on whether the sales clerk intended to humiliate her or was concerned with following the store policy.

In my own clinical experience, I have been struck by the role of strengthening the patient's ability to reflect on the other's mental state as a critical element in treatment and, in particular, as an affect regulator with patients who are prone to feelings of humiliation and rage. Let me provide a brief clinical example. A patient takes the train to spend the weekend at her father's vacation home. When she arrives, she calls and asks her father to pick her up at the train station. He replies that he and his wife (who is not my patient's biological mother) are in the middle of dinner and suggests that she take a taxi, for which he will pay. She recounts this exchange to me in great rage as an obvious and egregious rejection and as further evidence of her father's utter lack of caring for her. In the past, this would have been followed by her determination to have nothing to do with him, declarations of not needing him, and so on—a familiar sequence that usually ended with my patient feeling impotent (because she does need him and cannot carry out her angry determination to have nothing to do with him) and depressed. However, on this occasion, she was able to reflect on her enraged reaction and construal of her father's state and intentions. The simple idea that he just might not want to interrupt his dinner had an enormous impact on her rage and on short-circuiting the above pattern. She would refer to her increased ability to reflect on another's mental state as a new tool, one that she found very useful in many situations in which she was prone to feel defensive, humiliated, and enraged.

There is, of course, much more that can be said about the above vignette. However, the points I want to illustrate with it are (a) the affective regulating function of an enhanced reflective capacity, and (b) the importance of expanding the concept of the observing function of the ego to include the capacity for reflection on the other's mental states, as well as self-reflection. Indeed, to reiterate a point made earlier, in many situations, a core aspect of self-reflection is reflection on how one understands and construes the feelings and intentions, that is, the mental states, of others.

Reductionism in psychoanalytic theorizing

Although as we have seen, there are sharp differences in the *content* of their formulations, there is a goodly degree of convergence in the *form or structure* of theorizing between classical and contemporary psychoanalytic theories. I refer here to the strong tendency common to both classical and contemporary theories to posit one or two superordinate motive systems as primary and fundamental and then viewing a wide range of disparate behaviors as derivatives and direct or indirect (sometimes transformed) expressions of these or two motive systems. This type of theorizing is quite apparent in the tendency of classical theory to view a wide range of behaviors as derivatives, symbolic expressions of, and in the service of gratifying the purported primary and fundamental sexual and aggressive drives. For example, as we have seen, according to classical theory, early in life, object relations are secondary to and in the service of the gratification of the more supposedly fundamental hunger drive and the component instincts of infantile sexuality.

In direct contrast to this view, Fairbairn (1952) maintains that "libido is primarily object-seeking *rather than* pleasure-seeking as in classic theory" (p. 82, emphasis added) and that "the function of libidinal pleasure is essentially to provide a sign-post to the object" (p. 33). Thus, whereas for Freud, object relations are secondary to supposedly more fundamental sexual drives, for Fairbairn, sexual drives are secondary to supposedly more fundamental object relational tendencies and proclivities. What remains the same is the structure of the theorizing. As another example of the reductionistic tendency in psychoanalytic theorizing, one can point to Kohut's (1984) claim that driven sexuality is a "disintegration product" of self-defects. One wonders whether this tendency is partly a product of the unwitting attempt to model psychoanalytic theorizing after the successful attempt in physics to reduce the great variety of material phenomena to variations of the basic units of the physical world.

It seems to me that it would be far more useful (and valid) to resist the reductionistic impulse, recognize the multiplicity of motivational systems, and devote one's efforts to understanding how these different systems interact and become integrated (or fail to become integrated) with each other. A step in the direction of the former has been taken by Pine's (1990) insistence that motives relevant to drive, ego, object, and self are all relevant in clinical work. The second step has yet to be taken (although see Eagle, 2007, for an example of a first effort to understand the relationship between the attachment and sexual instinctual systems).

FINAL COMMENTS

This chapter began with a consideration of the role of self-knowledge in psychoanalysis, its connection to the Enlightenment vision, and the tension between objectivity and solidarity. It is fitting to end the chapter with a consideration of the inextricable links between self-reflection and reflection on the mental states of others, for the conclusion that we come to is that meaningful self-knowledge, at least self-knowledge that leads to therapeutic change, emerges in the context not only of interacting with the other but also of reflecting on and trying to understand how one construes the other and the relationship between these construals and who the other actually is. Thus, the Enlightenment vision is expanded from "know thyself" to include "know the other." The tension between "objectivity" and "solidarity" is dissolved in the recognition not only that objectivity about oneself cannot be separated from objectivity about the other but also that objectivity about both self and other can be achieved only in the context of solidarity with the other.

References

Ach, N. (1905/1951). Determining tendencies; awareness. In D. Rapaport (Ed. & Trans.), *Organization and pathology of thought: Selected sources* (pp. 15–38). New York, NY: Columbia University Press.

Adler, G., & Buie, D. H. (1979). Aloneness and borderline psychopathology: The possible relevance of child development and issues. *International Journal of Psychoanalysis, 60*, 83–96.

Ainsworth, M. D. S., Blehar, M. C., Waters, E., & Wall, S. (1978). *Patterns of attachment: A psychological study of the strange situation*. Hillsdale, NJ: Erlbaum.

Alexander, F. (1950). Analysis of the therapeutic factors in psychoanalytic treatment. *Psychoanalytic Quarterly, 19*, 482–500.

Alexander, F., & French, T. M. (1946). *Psychoanalytic therapy: Principles and application*. New York, NY: The Ronald Press.

Andre, J. (2002). Separation. In D. Widlöcher (Ed.), *Infantile sexuality and attachment* (pp. 123–131). New York, NY: Other Press.

Arlow, J. A., & Brenner, C. (1964). *Psychoanalytic concepts and the structural theory*. New York, NY: International Universities Press.

Apfelbaum, B. (1966). Ego psychology: A critique of the structural approach to psychoanalytic theory. *International Journal of Psychoanalysis, 47*, 451–475.

Atwood G. E., & Stolorow, R. D. (1984). *Structures of subjectivity: Explorations in pschoanalytic phenomenology*. Hillsdale, NJ: Analytic Press.

Bacal, H. A. (1985). Optimal responsiveness and the therapeutic process. In A. Goldberg (Ed.), *Progress in self psychology* (Vol. 1, pp. 202–227). New York, NY: Guilford Press.

Bacal, H. A., & Newman, R. M. (1990). *Theories of object relations: Bridges to self psychology*. New York, NY: Columbia University Press.

Bach, S. (1961). Symbolic associations to stimulus words in subliminal, supraliminal, and incidental presentation. *Dissertation Abstracts International, 21*(11), 3519–3520.

Bach, S. (2006). *Getting from here to there: Analytic love, analytic process*. Hillsdale, NJ: The Analytic Press.

Bakan, D. (1971). *The duality of human existence: Isolation and communion in Western man*. Boston: Beacon Press.

Baldwin, S. A., Wampold, B. E., & Imel, Z. E. (2007). Untangling the alliance-outcome correlation: Exploring the relative importance of therapist and patient variability in the alliance. *Journal of Consulting and Clinical Psychology, 75*(6), 842–852.

Balint, A. (1949). Love for the mother and mother-love. *International Journal of Psychoanalysis, 30*, 251–259.

Balint, A. (1959/1965). *Primary love and psychoanalytic technique.* London, United Kingdom: Tavistock Publications.

Balint, M. (1937/1965). Early developmental states of the ego: Primary object love. In M. Balint (Ed.), *Primary love and psychoanalytic technique.* New York, NY: Liveright.

Balint, M. (1956). Pleasure object and libido: Some reflexions on Fairbairn's modifications of psychoanalytic theory. *British Journal of Medical Psychology, 29*, 162–173.

Banaj, M. R., & Greenwald, A. G. (1994). Implicit stereotyping and prejudice. In M. P. Olson (Ed.), *TW Psychology of prejudice: The Ontario symposium* (Vol. 7, pp. 55–76). Hillsdale, NJ: Lawrence Erlbaum.

Barber, J., Connolly, M., Crits-Christoph, P., Gladis, L., & Siqueland, L. (2000). Alliance predicts patients' outcome beyond in-treatment change in symptoms. *Journal of Consulting and Clinical Psychology, 68*(6), 1027–1032.

Barber, J., Luborsky, L., Crits-Christoph, P., Thase, M., Weiss, R., Frank, A., ... Gallop, R. (1999). Therapeutic alliance as a predictor of outcome in treatment of cocaine dependence. *Psychotherapy Research, 9*(1), 54–73.

Barber, J. P., Luborsky, L., Gallop, R., Crits-Christoph, P., Frank, A., Weiss, R. D., ... Siqueland, L. (2001). Therapeutic alliance as a predictor of outcome and retention in the National Institute on Drug Abuse Collaborative Cocaine Treatment Study. *Journal of Consulting and Clinical Psychology, 69*(11), 119–124.

Basch, M. (1986). How does analysis cure? An appreciation. *Psychoanalytic Inquiry, 6*(3), 403–428.

Beck, A. T., Rush, A. J., Shaw, B. F., & Emery, G. (1979). *Cognitive therapy of depression.* New York, NY: Guilford Press.

Beebe, B., Lachmann, F., & Jaffe, J. (1997). Mother-infant interaction structures and presymbolic self- and abject representatives. *Psychoanalytic Dialogues, 7*(2), 133–182.

Bellak, L. (1958). *Schizophrenia: A review of the syndrome.* New York, NY: Cogos Press.

Benjamin, J. (1988). *The Bonds of love: Psychoanalysis, feminism and the problems of domination.* New York, NY: Pantheon.

Beutler, L. E. (2009). Making science matter in clinical practice: Redefining psychotherapy. *Clinical Psychology: Science & Practice, 16*(3), 301–317.

Black, M. (1967). Review of A. R. Couch's *Explanation and human action. American Journal of Psychology, 80*, 655–656.

Blatt, S. J. (2008). *Polarities of experience: Relatedness and self-definition in personality development, psychopathology, and the therapeutic process.* Washington, D C: American Psychological Association Press.

Blatt, S., & Blass, R. (1996). Relatedness and self-definition: A dialectic model of personality development. In G. Noam & K. Fischer (Eds.), *Development and vulnerability in close relationships* (pp. 309–338). New York, NY: Psychology Press.

Blatt, S., & Zuroff, D. (1992). Interpersonal relatedness and self-definition: Two prototypes for depression. *Clinical Psychology Review, 12*(5), 527–562.

Bonanno, G. (2005). Resilience in the face of potential trauma. *Current Directions in Psychological Science, 14*(3), 135.

Bonanno, G., Field, N., Kovacevic, A., & Kaltman, S. (2002). Self-enhancement as a buffer against extreme adversity: Civil war in Bosnia and traumatic loss in the United States. *Personality and Social Psychology Bulletin, 28*(2), 184.

Bonanno, G., Keltner, D., Holen, A., & Horowitz, M. (1995). When avoiding unpleasant emotions might not be such a bad thing: Verbal-autonomic response dissociation and midlife conjugal bereavement. *Journal of Personality and Social Psychology, 69,* 975–989.

Bonanno, G., Rennicke, C., & Dekel, S. (2005). Self-enhancement among high-exposure survivors of the September 11th terrorist attack: Resilience or social maladjustment? *Journal of Personality and Social Psychology, 88*(6), 984.

Bordin, E. S. (1976). The generalizability of the psychoanalytic concept of the working alliance. *Psychotherapy, Theory, Research & Practice, 16*(3), 252–260.

Bower, G. (1981). Mood & memory. *American Psychologist, 36*(2), 129–148.

Bowlby, J. (1958). The nature of the child's ties to his mother. *International Journal of Psychoanalysis, 30,* 350–373.

Bowlby, J. (1969/1982). *Attachment and loss: Vol. 1. Attachment.* New York, NY: Basic Books.

Bowlby, J. (1973). *Attachment and loss: Vol. 2. Separation.* New York, NY: Basic Books.

Bowlby, J. (1980). *Attachment and loss: Vol. 3. Loss.* New York, NY: Basic Books.

Bowlby, J. (1984). Psychoanalysis as a natural science. *Psychoanalytic Psychology, 1*(1), 7–21.

Bowlby, J. (1988). *A secure base.* New York, NY: Basic Books.

Brandchaft, B. (2007). Systems of pathological accommodation and change in psychoanalysis. *Psychoanalytic Psychology, 24*(4), 667–687.

Brandt, L. W. (1966). Process or structure? *Psychoanalytic Review, 53,* 50–54.

Brenner, C. (1955). *An elementary textbook of psychoanalysis.* New York, NY: International Universities Press.

Brenner, C. (1979). Working alliance, therapeutic alliance and transference. *Journal of the American Psychoanalytic Association, 27*(Suppl.), 137–157.

Brenner, C. (1982). *The mind in conflict.* New York, NY: International Universities Press.

Brenner, C. (1994). The mind as conflict and compromise. *Journal of Clinical Psychoanalysis, 3,* 473–488.

Brenner, C. (1998). Beyond the ego and the id revisited. *Journal of Clinical Psychoanalysis, 7*(1), 165–180.

Breuer, J., & Freud, S. (1893–1895). *Studies on hysteria.* In J. Strachey (Ed. & Trans.), *The standard edition of the complete psychological works of Sigmund Freud* (Vol. 2). London, United Kingdom: Hogarth Press.

Bromberg, P. (1996). Standing in the spaces: The multiplicity of self and the psychoanalytic relationship. *Contemporary Psychoanalysis, 32,* 509–535.

Bromberg, P. (2009, August 16). E-mail to New York University postdoctoral listserv.

Bucci, W. (1997). *Psychoanalysis & cognitive science: A multiple code theory.* New York, NY: Guilford Press.

Buie, D. H., & Adler, G. (1982–1983). Definitive treatment of the borderline personality. *International Journal of Psychoanalytic Psychotherapy, 9,* 51–87.

Burlingham, D., & Freud, A. (1944). *Infants without families.* New York, NY: International Universities Press.

Burston, D. (1986). The cognitive and dynamic unconscious: A critical and historical perspective. *Contemporary Psychoanalysis, 22,* 133–157.

Busch, F. (2001). Are we losing our mind? *Journal of the American Psychoanalytic Association, 49,* 739–751.

Caligor, E., Diamond, D., Yeomans, F. E., & Kernberg, O. (2009). The interpretive process in the psychoanalytic psychotherapy of borderline personality pathology. *Journal of the American Psychoanalytic Association, 57,* 271–301.

Cassidy, J. (1999). The nature of the child's ties. In J. Cassidy & P. R. Shaver (Eds.), *Handbook of attachment theory, research & clinical applications* (pp. 20–30). New York, NY: Guildford Press.

Chodorow, N. J. (2007). Uncertainty and loss: Two inevitable concomitants of psychoanalysis: Sclarf lecture given to New York University Psychoanalytic Institute, April 28, 2007.

Christensen, P. R., Guilford, J. P., Merrifield, P. R., & Wilson, R. C. (1960). *Alternate uses.* Beverly Hills, CA: Sheridan Psychological Services.

Clarkin, J. F., Levy, K. N., Lenzenweger, M. F., & Kernberg, O. F. (2007). Evaluating three treatments for borderline personality disorder: A multivariate study. *American Journal of Psychiatry, 164*(6), 1–7.

Compact Oxford English Dictionary. (2000). New York, NY: Oxford University Press.

Compton, A. (1986). Freud: Objects and structure. *Journal of the American Psychoanalytic Association, 34*(3), 561–590.

Compton, A. (1987). Objects and Attitudes. *Journal of the American Psychoanalytic Association, 35*(3), 609–628.

Connolly, M. B., Crits-Christoph, P., Shappell, S., Barber, J. P., Luborsky, L., & Shaffer, C. (1999). Relation of transference interpretations to outcome in the early sessions of brief supportive-expressive psychotherapy. *Psychotherapy Research, 9,* 485–495.

Cooley, C. H. (1902). *Human nature and the social order.* New York, NY: Charles Scribener's Sons.

Craik, F. M., & Lockhart, R. S. (1972). Levels of processing: A framework for memory research. *Journal of Verbal Learning and Verbal Behavior, 11*(6), 671–684.

Cramer, P. (2006). *Protecting the self: Defense mechanisms in action.* New York, NY: Guilford Press.

Damasio, A. R. (1994). *Descartes' error: Emotion, reason, and the human brain.* New York, NY: G. P. Putnam's Sons.

Davies, J. M. (1998). Between the disclosure and foreclosure of erotic transference-countertransference: Can psychoanalysis find a place for adult sexuality? *Psychoanalytic Dialogues, 8*(6), 747–766.

Dawkins, R. (1976/2006). *The selfish gene.* New York, NY: Oxford University Press.

Deutsch, H. (1929). The genesis of agoraphobia. *International Journal of Psychoanalysis, 10,* 51–69.

Dollard, J., & Miller, N. E. (1950). *Personality and psychotherapy.* New York, NY: McGraw-Hill.

Duhem, P. (1954). *The aim and structure of physical theory* (P. P. Wiener, Trans.). Princeton, NJ: Princeton University Press, 1991.

Eagle, M. (1959). The effects of subliminal stimuli of aggressive content upon conscious cognition. *Journal of Personality, 27,* 578–600.

Eagle, M. (1980a). Psychoanalytic interpretations: Veridicality and therapeutic effectiveness. *Nous, 14,* 405–425.

Eagle, M. (1980b). A critical examination of motivational explanation in psychoanalysis. *Psychoanalysis and Contemporary Thought, 3,* 329–380.

Eagle, M. (1982). Privileged access and the status of self-knowledge in Cartesian and Freudian conceptions of the mental. *Philosophy of the Social Sciences, 12,* 349–373.

Eagle, M. (1984a). Psychoanalysis and "narrative truth": A reply to Spence. *Psychoanalysis & Contemporary Thought, 7,* 629–640.

Eagle, M. (1984b). Geha's vision of psychoanalysis as fiction. *International Forum for Psychoanalysis, 1,* 141–162.

Eagle, M. (1984c). *Recent developments in psychoanalysis: A critical evaluation.* New York, NY: McGraw-Hill. (Published as paperback, 1987. Cambridge, MA: Harvard University Press.)

Eagle, M. (1987a). The psychoanalytic and the cognitive unconscious. In R. Stern (Ed.), *Theories of the unconscious and theories of the self* (pp. 155–189). Hillsdale, NJ: The Analytic Press.

Eagle, M. (1987b). Theoretical and clinical shifts in psychoanalysis. *American Journal of Orthopsychiatry, 57*(2), 175–185.

Eagle, M. (1990). The concepts of need and wish in self psychology. *Psychoanalytic Psychology, 7*(Suppl.), 71–88.

Eagle, M. (1993). Enactment, transference, and symptomatic cure: A case history. *Psychoanalytic Dialogues, 3*(1), 93–110.

Eagle, M. (1995). The developmental perspectives of attachment and psychoanalytical theories. In S. Goldberg, R. Muir, & J. Kerr (Eds.), *Attachment theory: Social, developmental and clinical perspectives* (pp. 123–150). Hillsdale, NJ: The Analytic Press.

Eagle, M. (2000a). A critical evaluation of current conceptions of transference and countertransference. *Psychoanalytic Psychology, 17*(1), 24–37.

Eagle, M. (2000b). Repression: Part I. *Psychoanalytic Review, 87*(1), 1–38.

Eagle, M. (2001, December). *Unconscious fantasy.* Paper presented at the Midwinter Meetings of the American Psychoanalytic Association, New York, NY.

Eagle, M. (2003). The postmodern turn in psychoanalysis: A critique. *Psychoanalytic Psychology, 20*(3), 411–424.

Eagle, M. (2007). Attachment and sexuality. In D. Diamond, S. J. Blatt, & J. D. Lichtenberg (Eds.), *Attachment and sexuality* (pp. 27–50). Hillsdale, NJ: Analytic Press.

Eagle, M. (2009, March). Agoraphobia: A case study. Franz Alexander lecture presented at the New Center for Psychoanalysis, Los Angeles, CA.

Eagle, M., & Ortof, E. (1967). The effects of level of attention upon "phonetic" recognition errors. *Journal of Verbal Learning and Verbal Behaviour, 6,* 226–231.

Eagle, M., Wakefield, J., & Wolitzky, D. (2003). Interpreting Mitchell's constructivism: Reply to Altman and Davies. *Journal of the American Psychoanalytic Association, 51*(Suppl.), 163–178.

Eagle, M., & Wolitzky, D. L. (2009). Adult psychotherapy from the perspectives of attachment theory and psychoanalysis. In J. H. Obegi & E. Berant (Eds.),

Attachment theory and research in clinical work with adults (pp. 351–378). New York, NY: Guilford.

Eagle, M., Wolitzky, D. L., & Wakefield, J. (2001). The analyst's knowledge and authority: A critique of the "New view" In psychoanalysis. *Journal of the American Psychoanalytic Association, 49,* 457–489.

Ehrenberg, D. B. (1995). Self-disclosure: Therapeutic tool or indulgence? Countertransference disclosure. *Contemporary Psychoanalysis, 31,* 213.

Eissler, K. R. (1953). The effect of the structure of the ego on psychoanalytic technique. *Journal of the American Psychoanalytic Association, 1,* 10.

Ellenberger, H. (1970). *The discovery of the unconscious.* New York, NY: Basic Books.

Ellman, C. S., Grand, S., Silvan, M., & Ellman, S. J. (Eds.) (1998). *The modern Freudians: Contemporary psychoanalytic technique.* Northvale, NJ: Jason Aronson.

Ellman, S. J. (1991). *Freud's technique papers: A contemporary perspective.* New York, NY: Jason Aronson.

Erdelyi, M. (1990). Repression, reconstruction and defense: History and integration of the psychoanalytic and experimental framework. In J. L. Singer (Ed.), *Repression and dissociation: Implications for personality theory* (pp. 1–32). Chicago, IL: University of Chicago Press.

Fairbairn, W. R. D. (1952). *Psychoanalytic studies of the personality.* London, United Kingdom: Tavistock.

Fairbairn, W. R. D. (1958). On the nature and aims of psycho-analytical treatment. *International Journal of Psychoanalysis, 39,* 374–385.

Fenichel, O. (1945). *The psychoanalytic theory of neurosis.* New York, NY: W. W. Norton.

Ferenczi, S., & Rank, O. (1924/1956). *The development of psychoanalysis.* New York, NY: Dover.

Field, G. C., Averling, F., & Laird, J. (1922). Is the conception of the unconscious of value in psychology? A symposium. *Mind, 31,* 413–442.

Fingarette, H. (1963). *The self in transformation.* New York, NY: Harper & Row.

Fingarette, H. (1969). *Self-deception.* New York, NY: Humanities Press.

Fonagy, P. (1999). Memory and therapeutic action. *International Journal of Psychoanalysis, 80,* 215–223.

Fonagy, P. (2006). The mentalization-focused approach to social development. In J. G. Allen, P. Fonagy, & P. Chichester (Eds.), *Handbook of mentalization-based treatment* (pp. 53–99). New York, NY: Wiley.

Fonagy, P., & Bateman, A. W. (2006). Mechanisms of change in mentalization-based therapy of borderline personality disorder. *Journal of Clinical Psychology, 62,* 411–430.

Fonagy, P., Steele, M., Steele, H., Leigh, T., Kennedy, R., Mattoo, N. G., & Target, M. (1995). Attachment, the reflective self and borderline states: The predictive specificity of the Adult Attachment Interview and Pathological Emotional Development. In S. Goldberg, R. Muir, & J. Kerr, (Eds.), *Attachment theory: social, developmental and clinical perspectives* (pp. 233–278). Hillsdale, NJ: The Analytic Press.

Fraiberg, S., Adelson, E., & Shapiro, V. (1975). Ghosts in the nursery: A psychoanalytic approach to the problem of impaired infant-mother relationships. *Journal of the American Academy of Child Psychiatry, 14,* 387–422.

Francis, D. D., Caldi, C., Champagne, F., Plotsky, P. M., & Meany, M. J. (1999). The role of corticotropin-releasing-factor-noredinephrine systems in mediating the effects of early experience on the development of behavioral and endocrine responses to stress. *Biological Psychiatry, 46*(9), 1153–1166.

Francis, D. D., & Meaney, M. J. (1999). Maternal care and the development of stress responses. *Current Opinion in Neurobiology, 9*(1), 128–134.

Freud, A. (1954). The widening scope of indications for psychoanalysis. *Journal of the American Psychoanalytic Association, 2,* 607–620.

Freud, A. (1954/1968). *The writings of Ann Freud, Vol. IV.* New York, NY: International Universities Press.

Freud, A. (1960). Discussion of Dr. John Bowlby's paper. *Psychoanalytic Study of the Child, 15,* 53–62.

Freud, A. (1966). *The ego and the mechanisms of defense* (Rev. Ed.). New York, NY: International Universities Press.

Freud, A. (1971). *The writings of Anna Freud: Vol. VII, 1966–1970.* New York, NY: International Universities Press.

Freud, S. (1893a). Some points for a comparative study of organic and hysterical motor paralyses. In J. Strachey (Ed. & Trans.), *The standard edition of the complete psychological works of Sigmund Freud* (Vol. 1, pp. 157–172). London, United Kingdom: Hogarth Press.

Freud, S. (1893b). On the psychical mechanisms of hysterical phenomena. In J. Strachey (Ed. & Trans.), *The standard edition of the complete psychological works of Sigmund Freud* (Vol. 3, pp. 25–39). London, United Kingdom: Hogarth Press.

Freud, S. (1894). The neuro-psychoses of defense. In J. Strachey (Ed. & Trans.), *The standard edition of the complete psychological works of Sigmund Freud* (Vol. 3, pp. 41–68). London, United Kingdom: Hogarth Press.

Freud, S. (1895). *Project for a scientific psychology.* In J. Strachey (Ed. & Trans.), *The standard edition of the complete psychological works of Sigmund Freud* (Vol. 1, pp. 295–397). London, United Kingdom: Hogarth Press.

Freud, S. (1896). Further remarks on the neuropsychoses of defense. In J. Strachey (Ed. & Trans.), *The standard edition of the complete psychological works of Sigmund Freud* (Vol. 3, pp. 157–185). London, United Kingdom: Hogarth Press.

Freud, S. (1900). *The interpretation of dreams.* In J. Strachey (Ed. & Trans.), *The standard edition of the complete psychological works of Sigmund Freud* (Vols. 4 and 5, pp. 1–625). London, United Kingdom: Hogarth Press.

Freud, S. (1901). *The psychopathology of everyday life.* In J. Strachey (Ed. & Trans.), *The standard edition of the complete psychological works of Sigmund Freud* (Vol. 6, pp. 1–279). London, United Kingdom: Hogarth Press.

Freud, S. (1901/1905). Fragment of an analysis of a case of hysteria. In J. Strachey (Ed. & Trans.), *The standard edition of the complete psychological works of Sigmund Freud* (Vol. 7, pp. 1–122). London, United Kingdom: Hogarth Press.

Freud, S. (1905). Three essays on the theory of sexuality. In J. Strachey (Ed. & Trans.), *The standard edition of the complete psychological works of Sigmund Freud* (Vol. 7, pp. 130–243). London, United Kingdom: Hogarth Press.

Freud, S. (1910a). The psycho-analytic view of psychogenic disturbance of vision. In J. Strachey (Ed. & Trans.), *The standard edition of the complete psychological works of Sigmund Freud* (Vol. 11, pp. 211–280). London, United Kingdom: Hogarth Press.

Freud, S. (1910b). Future prospects of psychoanalysis. In J. Strachey (Ed. & Trans.), *The standard edition of the complete psychological works of Sigmund Freud* (Vol. 11, pp. 139–151). London, United Kingdom: Hogarth Press.

Freud, S. (1911). Psychoanalytic notes on an autobiographical account of a case of paranoia (dementia paranoids). In J. Strachey (Ed. & Trans.), *The standard edition of the complete psychological works of Sigmund Freud* (Vol. 12, pp. 3–82). London, United Kingdom: Hogarth Press.

Freud, S. (1912a). On the universal tendency to debasement in the sphere of love (Contributions to the psychology of love II). In J. Strachey (Ed. & Trans.), *The standard edition of the complete psychological works of Sigmund Freud* (Vol. 11, pp. 177–190). London, United Kingdom: Hogarth Press.

Freud, S. (1912b). The dynamics of transference. In J. Strachey (Ed. & Trans.), *The standard edition of the complete psychological works of Sigmund Freud* (Vol. 12, pp. 97–108). London, United Kingdom: Hogarth Press.

Freud, S. (1912c). Recommendations to physicians practicing psychoanalysis. In J. Strachey (Ed. & Trans.), *The standard edition of the complete psychological works of Sigmund Freud* (Vol. 12, pp. 109–120). London, United Kingdom: Hogarth Press.

Freud, S. (1912d). Types of onset of neurosis. In J. Strachey (Ed. & Trans.), *The standard edition of the complete psychological works of Sigmund Freud* (Vol. 12, pp. 227–238). London, United Kingdom: Hogarth Press.

Freud, S. (1914a). On the history of the psychoanalytic movement. In J. Strachey (Ed. & Trans.), *The standard edition of the complete psychological works of Sigmund Freud* (Vol. 14, pp. 1–66). London, United Kingdom: Hogarth Press.

Freud, S. (1914b). On narcissism: An introduction. In J. Strachey (Ed. & Trans.), *The standard edition of the complete psychological works of Sigmund Freud* (Vol. 14, pp. 67–102). London, United Kingdom: Hogarth Press.

Freud, S. (1914c). Remembering, repeating and working-through. In J. Strachey (Ed. & Trans.), *The standard edition of the complete psychological works of Sigmund Freud* (Vol. 12, pp. 145–156). London, United Kingdom: Hogarth Press.

Freud, S. (1914/1915). Observations on transference love. In J. Strachey (Ed. & Trans.), *The standard edition of the complete psychological works of Sigmund Freud* (Vol. 12, pp. 157–171). London, United Kingdom: Hogarth Press.

Freud, S. (1915a). Instincts and their vicissitudes. In J. Strachey (Ed. & Trans.), *The standard edition of the complete psychological works of Sigmund Freud* (Vol. 14, pp. 117–140). London, United Kingdom: Hogarth Press.

Freud, S. (1915b). The unconscious. In J. Strachey (Ed. & Trans.), *The standard edition of the complete psychological works of Sigmund Freud* (Vol. 14, pp. 159–225). London, United Kingdom: Hogarth Press.

Freud, S. (1915c). Repression. In J. Strachey (Ed. & Trans.), *The standard edition of the complete psychological works of Sigmund Freud* (Vol. 14, pp. 141–158). London, United Kingdom: Hogarth Press.

Freud, S. (1915–1917/1916–1917). Introductory lectures on psychoanalysis. In J. Strachey (Ed. & Trans.), *The standard edition of the complete psychological works of Sigmund Freud* (Vol. 15, pp. 243–263). London, United Kingdom: Hogarth Press.

Freud, S. (1916–1917/1917). General theory of the neuroses. In J. Strachey (Ed. & Trans.), *The standard edition of the complete psychological works of Sigmund Freud* (Vol. 16, pp. 243–463). London, United Kingdom: Hogarth Press.

Freud, S. (1918/1919). Lines of advance in psychoanalytic therapy. In J. Strachey (Ed. & Trans.), *The standard edition of the complete psychological works of Sigmund Freud* (Vol. 17, pp. 157–168). London, United Kingdom: Hogarth Press.

Freud, S. (1920). Beyond the pleasure principle. In J. Strachey (Ed. & Trans.), *The standard edition of the complete psychological works of Sigmund Freud* (Vol. 18, pp. 7–64). London, United Kingdom: Hogarth Press.

Freud, S. (1923). The ego and the id. In J. Strachey (Ed. & Trans.), *The standard edition of the complete psychological works of Sigmund Freud* (Vol. 19, pp. 12–66). London, United Kingdom: Hogarth Press.

Freud, S. (1924). The economic problem of masochism. In J. Strachey (Ed. & Trans.), *The standard edition of the complete psychological works of Sigmund Freud* (Vol. 19, pp. 159–170). London, United Kingdom: Hogarth Press.

Freud, S. (1924/1925). An autobiographical study. In J. Strachey (Ed. & Trans.), *The standard edition of the complete psychological works of Sigmund Freud* (Vol. 20, pp. 3–74). London, United Kingdom: Hogarth Press.

Freud, S. (1925/1926). Inhibitions, symptoms and anxiety. In J. Strachey (Ed. & Trans.), *The standard edition of the complete psychological works of Sigmund Freud* (Vol. 20, pp. 77–175). London, United Kingdom: Hogarth Press.

Freud, S. (1926). The question of lay analysis. In J. Strachey (Ed. & Trans.), *The standard edition of the complete psychological works of Sigmund Freud* (Vol. 20, pp. 179–258). London, United Kingdom: Hogarth Press.

Freud, S. (1927). The future of an illusion. In J. Strachey (Ed. & Trans.), *The standard edition of the complete psychological works of Sigmund Freud* (Vol. 21, pp. 3–56). London, United Kingdom: Hogarth Press.

Freud, S. (1929/1930). Civilization and its discontents. In J. Strachey (Ed. & Trans.), *The standard edition of the complete psychological works of Sigmund Freud* (Vol. 21, pp. 57–146). London, United Kingdom: Hogarth Press.

Freud, S. (1932/1933). New introductory lectures on psychoanalysis. In J. Strachey (Ed. & Trans.), *The standard edition of the complete psychological works of Sigmund Freud* (Vol. 22, pp. 3–182). London, United Kingdom: Hogarth Press.

Freud, S. (1937a). Analysis terminable and interminable. In J. Strachey (Ed. & Trans.), *The standard edition of the complete psychological works of Sigmund Freud* (Vol. 23, pp. 209–253). London, United Kingdom: Hogarth Press.

Freud, S. (1937b). Constructions in analysis. In J. Strachey (Ed. & Trans.), *The standard edition of the complete psychological works of Sigmund Freud* (Vol. 23, pp. 255–270). London, United Kingdom: Hogarth Press.

Freud, S. (1938/1940). An outline of psychoanalysis. In J. Strachey (Ed. & Trans.), *The standard edition of the complete psychological works of Sigmund Freud* (Vol. 23, pp. 144–207). London, United Kingdom: Hogarth Press.

Friedman, L. (1986). Kohut's testament. *Psychoanalytic Inquiry, 6*, 321–347.

Friedman, L. (1998). Overview. In O. Renik (Ed.), *Knowledge and authority in the psychoanalytic relationship* (pp. viii–xxii). Northvale, NJ: Jason Aronson.

Friedman, L. (2008a). A renaissance for Freud's papers on technique. *The Psychoanalytic Quarterly, 77*, 1031–1044.

Friedman, L. (2008b). Loewald. *Journal of the American Psychoanalytic Association*, *56*, 1105–1115.

Friedman, M. (1985a). Survivor guilt in the pathogenesis of anorexia nervosa. *Psychiatry, 48*(1), 25–39.

Friedman, M. (1985b). Toward a reconceptualization of guilt. *Contemporary Psychoanalysis, 21*, 501–547.

Fromm, E. (1955/1990). *The Sane Society*. New York, NY: Henry Holt & Co.

Fromm, E. (1973/1992). *The anatomy of human destructiveness*. New York, NY: Henry Holt & Co.

Gabbard, G. (1995). Countertransference: The emerging common ground. *International Journal of Psychoanalysis, 76*, 475–485.

Gabbard, G., & Horowitz, M. J. (2009). Insight, transference interpretation, and therapeutic change in the dynamic psychotherapy of borderline personality disorder. *American Journal of Psychiatry, 166*(5), 517–521.

Gallese, V., Eagle, M. N., & Migone, P. (2007). Intentional attunement: Mirror neurons and the neural underpinnings of interpersonal relations. *Journal of the American Psychoanalytic Association, 55*(1), 131–175.

Gaston, L. (1990). The concept of the alliance and its role in psychotherapy: Theoretical and empirical considerations. *Psychotherapy: Theory, Research, Practice, Training, 27*(2), 143–153.

Gay, P. (1996a, October). The living enlightenment. The Tanner lectures on human values delivered at the University of Toronto, Toronto, Ontario, Canada.

Gay, P. (1996b). *The enlightenment: The science of freedom*. New York, NY: W. W. Norton.

Gedo, J. (1977). Sigmund Freud and the Socratic tradition. *Psychoanalytic Dialogues, 1*, 2–15.

Geha, R. (1984). On psychoanalytic history and the "real" story of fictitious lives. *International Forum for Psychoanalysis, 1*, 221–291.

Gendlin, E. T. (1962). *Experiencing and the creation of meaning*. Glencoe, NY: The Free Press.

George, C., Kaplan, N., & Main, M. (1996). *The Adult Attachment Interview Protocol* (3rd ed.). Unpublished manuscript, Department of Psychology, University of California at Berkeley, Berkeley, CA.

Gill, M. M. (1982). *Analysis of transference, Vol. 1: Theory and technique*. Madison, NJ: International Universities Press.

Gill, M. M. (1994). *Psychoanalysis in transition*. Hillsdale, NJ: The Analytic Press.

Gill, M. M., & Hoffman, I. Z. (1982). A method for studying the analysis of aspects of the patient's experience of the relationship in psychoanalysis and psychotherapy. *Journal of the American Psychoanalytic Association, 30*, 137–167.

Gitelson, M. (1963). On the problem of character neurosis. *Journal of the Hillside Hospital, 12*, 3–17.

Glover, E. (1931). The therapeutic effect of inexact interpretation: A contribution to the theory of suggestion. *International Journal of Psychoanalysis, 12*, 397–411.

Goldberg, F. H., & Fiss, H. (1959). Partial cues and the phenomenon of "discrimination without awareness." *Perceptual Motor Skills, 9*, 243–251.

Goldberger, L., & Holt, R. (1961). *Experimental interference with reality contact: Individual differences*. Cambridge, MA: Harvard University Press.

Gray, P. (1994). *The ego and analysis of defense*. Lanham, MD: Jason Aronson.

Green, A. (1992). A propos de l'observation des bébés: Interview par P. Geissmann. *Journal de Psychanalyse de l'Enfant, 12*, 133–153.

Greenberg, J. (1991). *Oedipus and beyond*. Cambridge, MA: Harvard University Press.

Greenberg, J., & Mitchell, S. A. (1983). *Object relations in psychoanalytic theory*. Cambridge, MA: Harvard University Press.

Greenson, R. R. (1965). The working alliance and the transference neurosis. *Psychoanalytic Quarterly, 34*, 155–181.

Greenson, R. (1967). *The technique and practice of psychoanalysis*. New York, NY: International Universities Press.

Grunbaum, A. (1984). *The foundations of psychoanalysis: A philosophical critique*. Berkeley, CA: University of California Press.

Guntrip, H. (1969). *Schizoid phenomenon, object-relations and the self*. New York, NY: International Universities Press.

Guntrip, H. (1996). My experience of analysis with Fairbairn and Winnicott. *International Journal of Psychoanalysis, 77*, 739–754.

Guthrie, G., & Wiener, M. (1966). Subliminal perception or perception of partial cue with pictorial stimuli. *Journal of Personality and Social Psychology, 3*, 619–628.

Habermas, J. (1971). *Knowledge of human interests* (J. J. Shapiro, Trans.). Boston, MA: Beacon Press.

Hamilton, V. (1996). *The analyst's preconscious*. Hillsdale, NJ: The Analytic Press.

Harlow, H. (1950). Learning and satiation of response in intrinsically motivated complex puzzle performance by monkeys. *Journal of Comparative and Physiological Psychology, 43*(4), 289–294.

Harlow, H. (1958). The nature of love. *American Psychologist, 13*(12), 673–685.

Harlow, H. (1974). *Learning to love*. New York, NY: Jason Aronson.

Harlow, H., Harlow, M., & Meyer, D. (1950). Learning motivated by a manipulation drive. *Journal of Experimental Psychology, 40*(2), 228–234.

Hartmann, H. (1958). *Ego psychology and the problem of adaptation* (D. Rapaport, Trans.). New York, NY: International Universities Press.

Hartshorne, H., & May, M. A. (1928). *Studies in deceit*. New York, NY: Macmillan.

Heim, C., Newport, D. J., Wagner, D., Wilcox, M. M., Miller, A. H., & Nemeroff, C. D. (2002). The role of early adverse experience and adulthood stress in the prediction of neuroendocrine stress reactivity in women: A multiple repression analysis. *Depression and Anxiety, 15*, 117–125.

Heimann, P. (1950). On counter-transference. *International Journal of Psychoanalysis, 31*, 81–84.

Hendrick, I. (1943). The discussion of the "Instinct to master." *Psychoanalytic Quarterly, 12*, 561–565.

Hermann, I. (1933). Zum triebleben der primaten. *Imago, 19*, 113.

Hofer, M. (1995). Hidden regulators: Implications for a new understanding of attachment, separation, and loss. In S. Goldberg, R. Muir & J. Kerr (Eds.), *Attachment theory: Social, developmental, and clinical perspectives* (pp. 203–230). Hillsdale, NJ: The Analytic Press.

Hofer, M. A. (2008). Early relationships as regulators of infant physiology and behaviour. *Acta Paediatrica, 83*(397), 9–18.

Hoffman, I. (1991). Discussion: Toward a social-constructivist view of the psychoanalytic situation. *Psychoanalytic Dialogues, 1*(1), 74–105.

Hoffman, I. (1994). Dialectical thinking and therapeutic action in the psychoanalytic process. *Psychoanalytic Quarterly, 63*, 187–218.

Hoffman, I. (1998). *Ritual and spontaneity in the psychoanalytic process: A dialectical constructivist point of view.* Hillsdale, NJ: The Analytic Press.

Hogeland, P. (2004). Analysis of transference in psychodynamic psychotherapy: A review of empirical research. *Canadian Journal of Psychoanalysis, 12,* 279–300.

Hogeland, P., Bogwald, K. P., Amlo, S., Marble, A., Ulberg, R., Sjaastad, M. C., ... Johansson, P. (2008). Transference interpretations in dynamic psychotherapy: Do they really yield sustained effects? *American Journal of Psychiatry, 665*(6), 763–771.

Hogeland, P., Johansson, P., Marble, A., Bogwald, K-P., & Amlo, S. (2007). Mediators of the effects of transference interpretations in brief dynamic psychotherapy. *Psychotherapy Research, 17*(2), 162–174.

Holt, E. B. (1915). *The Freudian wish and its place in ethics.* New York, NY: H. Holt & Company.

Holt, R. R. (2009). *Primary process thinking: Theory measurement, and research.* New York, NY: Rowman and Littlefield.

Holzman, P. S. (1976). The future of psychoanalysis and its institutes. *Psychoanalytic Quarterly, 65*, 250–273.

Horney, K. (1945). *Our inner conflicts.* New York, NY: W. W. Norton.

Horvath, A. O., & Symonds, B. D. (1991). Relation between working alliance and outcome in psychotherapy: A meta-analysis. *Journal of Counseling and Clinical Psychology, 61*, 561–573.

Hull, C. (1939). Modern behaviorism and psychoanalysis. *New York Academy of Science, 1*(11), 78–82.

Hull, C. (1943). *Principles of behavior: An introduction to behavior theory.* New York, NY: Appleton-Century.

Hull, C. (1951). *Essentials of behavior.* New Haven, CT: Yale University Press.

Hunt, J. (1965). Intrinsic motivation and its role in psychological development. In D. Levine (Ed.), *Nebraska symposium on motivation* (Vol. 13, pp. 189–282). Lincoln, NE: University of Nebraska Press.

Igel, G. J., & Calvin, A. D. (1960). The development of affectional responses in infant dogs. *Journal of Comparative and Physiological Psychology, 53*(3), 302–305.

James, W. (1890). *The principles of psychology* (Vols. 1 & 2). New York, NY: Holt.

Janet, P. (1889). *L'Automatisme psycologique.* Paris: Alcan.

Janet, P. (1907). *The major symptoms of hysteria.* New York, NY: Macmillan Publishing.

Janov, A. (1970). *The primal scream: Primal therapy, the cure for neurosis.* New York, NY: G. P. Putnam's Sons.

Johansson, H., & Eklund, M. (2006). Helping alliance and early dropout from psychiatric outpatient care: The influence of patient factors. *Social Psychiatry and Psychiatric Epidemiology, 41*, 140–147.

Jordan, J. (Ed.) (1997). *Women's growth in diversity: More writings from the Stone Center.* New York, NY: Guilford.

Jordan, J. V., Kaplan, A. G., Miller, I. B., Stiver, I. P., & Surrey, J. L. (1991). *Women's growth in connection: Writings from the Stone Center.* New York, NY: Guilford.

Jordan, J. V., Walker, M., & Hastling, L. M. (Eds.). (2004). *The complexity of connection: Writings from the Stone Center's Jean Bauer Miller Training Institute.* New York, NY: Guilford.

Jung, C. G. (1920). Studies in word association. *Journal of Nervous & Mental Disease, 54*(6), 593–611.

Kandel, E. R. (1998). A new intellectual framework for psychiatry. *American Journal of Psychiatry, 155*, 457–469.

Kandel, E. R. (1999). Biology and the future of psychoanalysis: A new intellectual framework for psychiatry revisited. *American Journal of Psychiatry, 156*, 505–524.

Kazdin, A. (2007). Mediators and mechanisms of change in psychotherapy research. *Annual Review of Clinical Psychology, 3*, 1–27.

Kenny, J. T., & Blass, E. M. (1977). Suckling as incentive to instrumental learning in preweaning rats. *Science, 196*, 898–899.

Kernberg, O. (1975). *Borderline conditions and pathological narcissism.* New York, NY: Jason Aronson.

Kernberg, O. (1976). *Object relations theory and clinical psychoanalysis.* New York, NY: Jason Aronson.

Kernberg, O. (1993). The current status of psychoanalysis. *Journal of the American Psychoanalytic Association, 41*, 45–62.

Kernberg, O., Burnstein, E., Coyne, L., Applebaum, A., Horowitz, L., & Votk, H. (1972). Psychotherapy and psychoanalysis: Final report of the Menningen Foundation's psychotherapy research project. *Bulletin of the Menningen Clinic, 36*, 1–275.

Kernberg, O., Yeomans, F. E., Clarkin, J. F., & Levy, K. N. (2008). Transference focused psychotherapy: Overview and update. *International Journal of Psychoanalysis, 89*(3), 601–620.

Kierkegaard, S. (1886/1948). *Purity of heart is to will one thing* (D. V. Steere, Trans.). New York, NY: Harper.

Kihlstrom, J. F. (1987). The cognitive unconscious. *Science, 237*(4821), 1445–1452.

Klein, G. S. (1973). Two theories or one? *Bulletin of the Menninger Clinic, 37*, 102–132.

Klein, M. (1946–1963/1975). *Envy and gratitude and other works.* New York, NY: Delacorte Press.

Klein, M. (1981a). Freud's seduction theory: Its implications for fantasy and memory in psychoanalytic theory. *Bulletin of the Menninger Clinic, 45*(3), 185–208.

Klein, M. (1981b). On Mahler's autistic and symbiotic phases: An exposition and evaluation. *Contemporary Thought, 4*, 69–105.

Klein, M., Heimann, P., Isaac, S. & Riviere, J. (1952). *Developments in psychoanalysis.* London, United Kingdom: Hogarth.

Knafo, D. (2002). Revisiting Ernst Kris' concept of "Regression in the service of the ego" in art. *Psychoanalytic Psychology, 19*(1), 24–49.

Knight, R. P. (1953a). Borderline states. *Bulletin of the Menninger Clinic, 17*, 1–12.

Knight, R. P. (1953b). Management and psychotherapy of the borderline schizophrenic patient. *Bulletin of the Menninger Clinic, 17*, 139–150.

Kohlberg, L., LaCrosse, J., & Ricks, D. (1972). The predictability of adult mental health from childhood behavior. In B. B. Wolman (Ed.), *Manual of child psychopathology* (pp. 1217–1284). New York, NY: McGraw Hill.

Kohut, H. (1971). *The analysis of the self*. New York, NY: International Universities Press.

Kohut, H. (1977). *The restoration of the self*. New York, NY: International Universities Press.

Kohut, H. (1984). *How does analysis cure?* (A. Goldberg & P. Stepansky, Eds.). Chicago, IL: University of Chicago Press.

Kris, E. (1952). *Psychoanalytic explorations in art*. New York, NY: International Universities Press.

Lambert, M., & Barley, D. (2001). Research summary on the therapeutic relationship and psychotherapy outcome. *Psychotherapy, 38*(4), 357–361.

Laplanche, J. (1970/1998). Life and death in psychoanalysis (J. Mehlman, Trans.). Baltimore, MD: Johns Hopkins University Press.

Laplanche, J., & Pontalis, J. B. (2003). Fantasy and the origins of sexuality. In R. Steiner (Ed.), *Unconscious phantasy* (pp. 107–145). London, United Kingdom: Karnac.

Letter to the Editor. (2007). Truth and tradition. *American Imago, 64*(1), 121–125.

Levine, W. B. (1997). The capacity for countertransference. *Psychoanalytic Inquiry, 17*(1), 44–68.

Levy, K. N., Meehan, K. B., Kelly, M. M., Reynoso, J. S., Weber, M., Clarkin, J. F., & Kernberg, O. F. (2006). Change in attachment patterns and reflective function in a randomized control trial of transference-focused psychotherapy for borderline personality disorder. *Journal of Consulting and Clinical Psychotherapy, 74*, 1027–1040.

Lieberman, A. (1999). Negative maternal attributions: Effects on toddlers' sense of self. *Psychoanalytic Inquiry, 19*, 737–756.

Loewald, H. (1960). On the therapeutic action of psycho-analysis. *International Journal of Psychoanalysis, 41*, 16–33.

Loewald, H. (1979). The waning of the Oedipus complex. *Journal of the American Psychoanalytic Association, 27*, 751–775.

Lohser, B., & Newton, P. M. (1996). *Unorthodox Freud: The view from the couch*. New York, NY: Guilford.

Lorenz, K. (1981). *The foundations of ethnology* (R. W. Kickert, Trans.). New York, NY: Springer.

Luborsky, L. (1976). Helping alliances in psychotherapy. In J. L. Cleghorn (Ed.), *Successful psychotherapy*. New York, NY: Brunner/Mazel.

Luborsky, L. (1996). Theories of cure in psychoanalytic psychotherapies and evidence for them. *Psychoanalytic Inquiry, 16*(2), 257–264.

Lyons-Ruth, K. (1999). The two-person unconscious. Intersubjective dialogue, implicit relational knowing, and the articulation of weaning. *Psychoanalytic Inquiry, 19*, 567–617.

Lyons-Ruth, K., Bruschweiler-Stern, N., Harrison, A., Morgan, A., Nahum, J., Sander, L., ... Tronick, E. Z. (1998). Implicit relational knowing: Its role in development and psychoanalytic treatment. *Infant Mental Health Journal, 19*(3), 282–289.

Macmillan, M. (1991). *Freud evaluated: The completed arc*. New York, NY: Elsevier Science Publishing Co.

Mahler, M. (1968). *On human symbiosis and the vicissitudes of individuation* (vol. 1): *Infantile psychosis*. New York, NY: International Universities Press.

Maslow, A. H. (1952). *Motivation and personality*. New York, NY: Harper.

Maslow, A. H. (1968). *Toward a psychology of being* (2nd ed.). Princeton, NJ: Van Nostrand.

Masterson, J. F. (1976). *Psychotherapy of the borderline adult: A developmental approach.* New York, NY: Brunner/Mazel.

Mead, G. (1934). *Mind, self and society from the standpoint of a social behaviorist.* Chicago, IL: University of Chicago Press.

Meehl, P. E. (1994). Subjectivity in psychoanalytic inference: The persistence of Wilhelms Achensee question. *17,* 3–82.

Meier, P. S., Barrowclough, C., & Donmall, M. C. (2005). The role of the therapeutic alliance in the treatment of substance misuse. *Addiction, 100*(3), 304–316.

Meissner, W. W. (1998). Review of S. A. Mitchell's *Influence and Autonomy in Psychoanalysis. Psychoanalytic Books, 9,* 419–423.

Miller, A. (1997/2007). *The drama of the gifted child: The search for the true self* (R. Ward, Trans.). New York, NY: Basic Books.

Mitchell, S. A. (1988). *Relational concepts in psychoanalysis.* Cambrige, MA: Harvard University Press.

Mitchell, S. A. (1995). *Hope and dread in psychoanalysis.* New York, NY: Basic Books.

Mitchell, S. A. (1998). The analyst's knowledge and authority. *Psychoanalytic Quarterly, 67*(1), 1–31.

Mitchell, S. A. (2000). Reply to Silverman. *Psychoanalytic Psychology, 17,* 153–159.

Modell, A. H. (1965). On having the right to a life: An aspect of the superego's development. *International Journal of Psychoanalysis, 46,* 323–331.

Modell, A. H. (1971). The origins of certain forms of pre-oedipal guilt and the implications for a psychoanalytic theory of affects. *International Journal of Psychoanalysis, 52,* 337–346.

Modell, A., Weiss, J., & Sampson, H. (1983). Narcissism, masochism and the sense of guilt in relation to the therapeutic process. *Bulletin of the Menninger Clinic, 6,* 22.

Moran, R. (2001). *Authority and estrangement: An essay on self knowledge.* Princeton, NJ: Princeton University Press.

Motley, M. (1980). Verification of "Freudian slips" and semantic prearticulatory editing via laboratory-induced spoonerisms. In V. A. Fromkin (Ed.), *Errors in linguistic performance: Slips of the tongue, ear, pen, and hand* (pp. 133–147).

Nagel, T. (1986). *The view from nowhere.* New York, NY: Oxford University Press.

Nelson, K., & Gruendel, J. (1986). *Event knowledge: Structure and function in development.* Hillsdale, NJ: Lawrence Erlbaum.

Ogden, T. (1982). *Projective identification and psychotherapeutic technique.* New York, NY: Jason Aronson.

Ogrodnicuk, J. S., Piper, W. E., Joyce, A. S., & McCallum, M. (1999). Transference interpretations in short-term dynamic psychotherapy. *Journal of Nervous and Mental Disease, 187*(9), 571–578.

Orenstein, P., & Orenstein, A. (2003). The function of theory in psychoanalysis: A self psychological perspective. *Psychoanalysis Quarterly, 72,* 157–183.

Orwell, G. (1949). *1984.* London, United Kingdom: Secker and Warburg.

Peterfreund, E. (1978). Some critical comments on psychoanalytic conceptions of infancy. *International Journal of Psychoanalysis, 59,* 427–437.

Piaget, J. (1954). *The construction of reality in the child.* New York, NY: Basic Books.

Pine, F. (1960). Incidental stimulation: A study of preconscious transformations. *Journal of Abnormal and Social Psychology, 60*(1), 68–75.

Pine, F. (1961). Incidental versus focal presentation of drive related stimuli. *Journal of Abnormal and Social Psychology, 62*(3), 482–490.

Pine, F. (1990). *Drive, ego, object, and self: A synthesis for clinical work.* New York, NY: Basic Books.

Pinker, S. (2003). *The language instinct: How the mind creates language.* New York, NY: Perennial Classics.

Pinker, S., & Bloom, P. (1992). Natural language and natural selection. In J. H. Barkow, L. Cosmides, & J. Tooby (Eds.), *The adapted mind: Evolutionary psychology and the generation of culture* (pp. 451–494). New York, NY: Oxford University Press.

Piper, W. E., Hassan, F. A., Joyce, A. S., & McCallum, M. (1991). Transference interpretations: Therapeutic alliance and outcome in short-term individual psychotherapy. *Archives of General Psychiatry, 48*(10), 946–953.

Polan, H., & Hofer, M. (1999). Psychobiological origins of separation and attachment responses. In J. Cassidy & P. R. Shaver (Eds.), *Handbook of attachment: Current theory and research* (pp. 162–180). New York, NY: Guilford Press.

Poland, W. S. (1984). On the analyst's neutrality. *Journal of the American Psychoanalytic Association, 32*(2), 283–299.

Poland, W. (2000). The analyst's witnessing of otherness. *Journal of the American Psychoanalytic Association, 48*(1), 17–35.

Putnam, F. W. (2003). Ten-year research update review: Child sexual abuse. *Journal of the American Academy of Child & Adolescent Psychiatry, 3,* 17–26.

Racker, H. (1968). *Transference and countertransference.* Madison, CT: International Universities Press.

Rapaport, D. (1951). Toward a theory of thinking. In D. Rapaport (Ed.), *Organization and pathology of thought* (pp. 689–730). New York, NY: Columbia University Press.

Rapaport, D. (1957/1967). The theory of ego autonomy: A generalization. In M. M. Gill (Ed.), *The collected papers of David Rapaport* (pp. 722–744). New York, NY: Basic Books.

Rapaport, D. (1967). *Collected papers.* New York, NY: Basic Books.

Renik, O. (1996). The perils of neutrality. *Psychoanalytic Quarterly, 65,* 495–517.

Renik, O. (1998). The analyst's subjectivity and the analyst's objectivity. *International Journal of Psychoanalysis, 79,* 487–498.

Ribble, M. (1943). *The rights of infants.* New York, NY: Columbia University Press.

Ricoeur, P. (1970). *Freud and philosophy: An essay on interpretation.* New Haven, CT: Yale University Press.

Rock, I. (1983). *The logic of perception.* Cambridge, MA: MIT Press.

Rogers, C. R. (1951). *Client-centered therapy.* London, United Kingdom: Constable.

Rogers, C. R. (1961). *On becoming a person: A therapist's view of psychotherapy.* Chicago, IL: University of Chicago Press.

Rorty, R. (1991). *Objectivity, relativism, and truth: Philosophical papers* (Vol. 1). New York, NY: Cambridge University Press.

Rubinstein, B. B. (1974). On the role of classificatory processes in mental functioning. Aspects of a psychoanalytic theoretical model. In L. Goldberger & V. H. Rosen (Eds.), *Psychoanalysis and contemporary science* (Vol. 3, p. 1). New York, NY: International Universities Press.

Rubinstein, B. (Ed.) (1976). *On the possibility of a strictly clinical psychoanalytic theory: An essay in the philosophy of psychoanalysis.* New York, NY: International Universities Press.

Ryle, G. (1949/2002). *The concept of mind.* Chicago, IL: University of Chicago Press.

Safran, J., & Muran, J. (1996). The resolution of ruptures in the therapeutic alliance. *Journal of Consulting and Clinical Psychology, 64*(3), 447–458.

Safran, J. D., & Muran, J. C. (2000). *Negotiating the therapeutic alliance: A relational treatment guide.* New York, NY: Guilford Press.

Safran, J., Muran, J., Samstag, L. W., & Stevens, C. (2001). Repairing alliance ruptures. *Psychotherapy: Theory, Research, Practice and Training, 38*(4), 406–412.

Safran, J., Muran, J., Winston, A., & Samstag, L. W. (2005). Evaluating alliance-focused intervention for potential treatment failures: A feasibility study and descriptive analysis. *Psychotherapy: Research, Practice and Training, 42*(4), 512–531.

Samstag, L. W., Batchelder, S. T., Muran, J., Safran, J., & Winston, A. (1998). Early identification of treatment failures in short-term psychotherapy: An assessment of therapeutic alliance and interpersonal behavior. *Journal of Psychotherapy Practice and Research, 7,* 126–143.

Sandler, J. (1976). Countertransference and role-responsiveness. *International Review of Psychoanalysis, 3,* 43–47.

Sandler, J., & Sandler, A. M. (1978). On the development of object relationships and affects. *International Journal of Psychoanalysis, 59,* 285–296.

Sartre, J. (1956). *Being and nothingness* (H. Barnes, Trans.). New York, NY: Washington Square Press Philosophical Library.

Schachter, J. (2002). *Transference: Shibboleth or albatross?* Hillsdale, NJ: The Analytic Press.

Schafer, R. (1968). *Aspects of internalization.* New York, NY: International Universities Press.

Schafer, R. (1978). *Language and insight.* New Haven, CT: Yale University Press.

Schafer, R. (1983). *The analytic attitude.* New York, NY: Basic Books.

Schafer, R. (1992). *Retelling a life: Narrative and dialogue in psychoanalysis.* New York, NY: Basic Books.

Schanberg, S. M., & Kuhn, C. M. (1980). Maternal deprivation: An animal model of psychosocial dwarfism. In E. Usdin, T. L. Sourkes, & M. B. Youdin (Eds.), *Enzymes and neurotransmitters* (pp. 374–393). New York, NY: Wiley.

Scarfone, D. (2002). Sexual and actual. In D. Widlöcher (Ed.), *Infantile sexuality and attachment* (pp. 97–110). New York, NY: Other Press.

Schimek, J., & Goldberger, L. (1995). Psychoanalytic theory of thinking. In B. E. Moore & B. D. Fines (Eds.), *Psychoanalysis: The major concepts* (pp. 209–220). New Haven, CT: Yale University Press.

Searle, J. (1992). *The rediscovery of the mind.* Cambridge, MA: MIT Press.

Searle, J. R. (1998). *Mind, language and society: Philosophy in the real world.* New York, NY: Basic Books.

Segal, H. (2006). Reflections on truth, tradition, and the psychoanalytic tradition of truth. *American Imago, 63*(3), 283–292.

Sellars, W. (1963). *Science, perception and reality.* London, United Kingdom: Routledge & Kegan Paul.

Shaffer, J. (1968). *Philosophy of mind.* Englewood Cliffs, NJ: Prentice Hall.

Silberschatz, G., Fretter, P. B., & Curtis, J. T. (1986). How do interpretations influence the process of psychotherapy? *Journal of Consulting and Clinical Psychology*, 54, 646–652.

Skolnick, N. (2006). What is a good object to do? *Psychoanalytic Dialogues*, 64, 269–276.

Slade, A., & Aber, J. L. (1992). Attachments, drives and development: Conflicts and consequences in theory. In J. W. Barron, M. N. Eagle, & D. L. Wolitzky (Eds.), *Interface of psychoanalysis and psychology* (pp. 154–185). Washington, DC: American Psychological Association.

Socarides, D. D., & Stolorow, R. D. (1984). Affects and self objects. *Annual of Psychoanalysis*, 12, 105–119.

Spence, D. (1984). *Narrative truth and historical truth: Meaning and interpretation in psychoanalysis*. New York, NY: W. W. Norton.

Spence, D. (1987). *The Freudian metaphor: Toward paradigm change in psychoanalysis*. New York, NY: W. W. Norton.

Spence, D. (1990). The rhetorical voice of psychoanalysis. *Journal of the American Psychoanalytic Association*, 38(3), 579–603.

Spitz, R. A. (1945). Hospitalism: An inquiry into the genesis of psychiatric conditions in early childhood. *The Psychoanalytic Study of the Child*, 1, 53–74.

Spitz, R. (1960). Discussion of Dr. John Bowlby's paper. *Psychoanalytic Study of the Child*, 15, 85–94.

Spitz, R. A. (1965). *The first year of life*. New York, NY: International Universities Press.

Spitz, R. A., & Wolf, K. M. (1946). Anaclitic depression: An inquiry into the genesis of psychiatric conditions in early childhood. *The Psychoanalytic Study of the Child*, 2, 313–342.

Stechler, G. (2003). Affect: The heart of the matter. *Psychoanalytic Dialogues*, 13(5), 711–726.

Steingart, I. (1995). *A thing apart: Love and reality in the therapeutic relationship*. Northvale, NJ: Jason Aronson.

Stepansky, P. (1999). *Freud, surgery and the surgeons*. Hillsdale, NJ: The Analytic Press.

Stern, D. B. (1989). The analyst's unformulated experience of the patient. *Contemporary Psychoanalysis*, 25(1), 1–33.

Stern, D. B. (2003). *Unformulated experience: From dissociation to imagination in psychoanalysis*. Hillsdale, NJ: The Analytic Press.

Stern, D. N. (1985). *The interpersonal world of the infant*. New York, NY: Basic Books.

Stern, D. N. (1990). *Joy and satisfaction in infancy*. In R. A. Glick & S. Bone (Eds.), (pp. 13–23). New Haven, CT: Yale University Press.

Stern, D. N. (1998). The process of therapeutic change involving implicit knowledge: Some implications of developmental observations for adult psychotherapy. *Journal of Infant Mental Health*, 19(3), 300–308.

Stern, D. N., Sander, L. W., Nahum, J. P., Harrison, A. M., Lyons-Ruth, K., Morgan, A. C., Bruschweilerstern, N., & Tranick, E. Z. (1998). Non-interpretive mechanisms in psychoanalytic therapy: The "something more" than interpretation. *International Journal of Psychoanalysis*, 79, 903–921.

Sternberg, R. J., & Lubart, T. I. (1996). Investing in creativity. *American Psychologist*, 51, 677–688.

Stich, S. (1983). *From folk psychology to cognitive science: The case against belief.* Cambridge, MA: MIT Press.

Stolorow, R. D., & Atwood, G. E. (1992). *Contexts of being: The intersubjective foundations of psychological life.* Hillsdale, NJ: Analytic Press.

Stolorow, R. D., Atwood, G. E., & Orange, D. (2002). *Worlds of experience.* New York, NY: Basic Books.

Stolorow, R. D., & Lachmann, F. M. (1980). *Psychoanalysis of developmental arrests: Theory and treatment.* New York, NY: International Universities Press.

Stone, A. (1997). Where will psychoanalysis survive? *Harvard Magazine,* 35–39.

Stone, L. (1954). The widening scope of indications for psychoanalysis. *Journal of the American Psychoanalytic Association, 2*(4), 567–594.

Strachey, J. (1934). The nature of the therapeutic action of psychoanalysis. *International Journal of Psychoanalysis, 15,* 127–159.

Strupp, H. H., & Binder, J. J. (1984). *Psychotherapy in a new key: A guide to time-limited dynamic psychotherapy.* New York, NY: Basic Books.

Sugarman, A. (2006). Mentalization, insightfulness, and therapeutic action: The importance of mental organization. *International Journal of Psychoanalysis, 87*(4), 965–987.

Sullivan, H. S. (1940). *Conceptions of modern psychiatry.* New York, NY: W. W. Norton.

Sullivan, H. S. (1953). *The interpersonal theory of psychiatry* (H. S. Perry & M. L. Gawel, Eds.). New York, NY: Norton.

Sullivan, H. S. (1956). *Clinical studies in psychiatry.* New York, NY: W. W. Norton.

Suttie, I. D. (1935). *The origins of love and hate.* London, United Kingdom: Kegan Paul.

Talvitie, V., & Tiitinen, H. (2006). From the repression of contents to the rules of the (narrative) self: A present-day cognitive view of the Freudian phenomenon of repressed contents. *Psychology and Psychotherapy: Theory, Research and Practice, 79*(2), 165–181.

Tansley, M. J. & Burke, W. F. (1995). *Understanding countertransference: From projective identification to empathy.* Hillsdale, NJ: Analytic Press.

Taylor, S. E., & Brown, J. D. (1994). Positive illusions and well-being revisited: Separating fact from fiction. *Psychological Bulletin, 116,* 21–27.

Taylor, S., Kemeny, M., Reed, G., Bower, J., & Gruenewald, T. (2000). Psychological resources, positive illusions, and health. *American Psychologist, 55*(1), 99–109.

Von Eckardt, B. (1981). On evaluating the scientific status of psychoanalysis. *Journal of Philosophy, 78,* 570–572.

Waelder, R. (1936). The principle of multiple function: Observations on overdetermination (1930). *Psychoanalytic Quarterly, 5,* 45–62.

Waelder, R. (1960). *Basic theory of psychoanalysis.* New York, NY: International Universities Press.

Wakefield, J. C. (1992). Freud and cognitive psychology: The conceptual interface. In J. W. Barron, M. N. Eagle, & D. L. Wolitzky (Eds.), *Interface of psychoanalysis and psychology* (pp. 77–98). Washington, DC: American Psychological Association.

Wallerstein, R. S. (1988). Assessment of structural change in psychoanalytic theory and research. *Journal of the American Psychoanalytic Association, 36S,* 241–261.

Wallerstein, R. S. (1990). Psychoanalysis: The common ground. *International Journal of Psychoanalysis, 71,* 3–20.

Wallerstein, R. S. (1991). *The common ground of psychoanalysis.* Northvale, NJ: Jason Aronson.

Webster's New American Dictionary. (1995). New York: Merriam-Webster, Inc.

Weiss, J., Sampson, H., and the Mount Zion Psychotherapy Research Group (1986). *The psychoanalytic process: Theory, clinical observation, and empirical research.* New York, NY: Guilford Press.

Westen, D., Blagov, P. S., Harenski, K., Kilts, C. & Hamann, S. (2006). Neural bases of motivated reasoning: An MRI study of emotional constraints on partisan political judgment in the 2004 U.S. presidential election. *Journal of Cognitive Neuroscience, 18*(11), 1941–1958.

White, R. W. (1959). Motivation reconsidered: The concept of competence. *Psychological Review, 66,* 297–333.

Widlöcher, D. (2002). Primary love and infantile sexuality: An eternal debate. In D. Widlöcher (Ed.), *Infantile sexuality and attachment* (pp. 1–35). New York, NY: Other Press.

Wiesel, T. (1982). The postnatal development of the visual cortex and the influence of environment. *Bioscience Reports, 2*(6), 351–377.

Winnicott, D. (1958). *Collected papers: Through paediatrics to psycho-analysis.* London, United Kingdom: Tavistock.

Winnicott, D. W. (1965). *The maturational process and the facilitating environment: The theory of emotional development.* New York, NY: International Universities Press.

Wittgenstein, L. (1953/1973). *Philosophical investigations.* New York, NY: Macmillan.

Wzontek, N., Geller, J. D., & Farber, B. A. (1995). Patients' posttermination representations of their therapists. *Journal of the American Academy of Psychoanalysis and Dynamic Psychiatry, 23,* 395–410.

Young, J. E., Klosko, J. S., & Weishaar, M. E. (2006). *Schema therapy: A practitioner's guide.* New York, NY: Guilford.

Zetzel, E. (1956). Current concepts of transference. *International Journal of Psychoanalysis, 37,* 369–378.

Index